Women's Suffrage in the Americas

WOMEN'S
SUFFRAGE
in the AMERICAS

Edited by Stephanie Mitchell

University of New Mexico Press | Albuquerque

First paperback edition, 2025

ISBN 978-0-8263-6895-9 (paper)
ISBN 978-0-8263-6614-6 (cloth)
ISBN 978-0-8263-6615-3 (ePub)

Library of Congress Control Number: 2024934717

Founded in 1889, the University of New Mexico sits on the traditional homelands of the Pueblo of Sandia. The original peoples of New Mexico—Pueblo, Navajo, and Apache—since time immemorial have deep connections to the land and have made significant contributions to the broader community statewide. We honor the land itself and those who remain stewards of this land throughout the generations and also acknowledge our committed relationship to Indigenous peoples. We gratefully recognize our history.

Cover illustration by José Montoto.
Designed by Felicia Cedillos
Composed in Alegreya

Contents

Acknowledgments

This book is the work of many hands. It was Patricia Harms's idea to begin with, and her leadership saw us through the first five of the ten years we have been working on this project. She was the one who realized that Donna Guy and Asunción Lavrin were far more than just intellectual mentors and started calling them our *madrinas*, our suffrage godmothers. Nothing good in either of our academic careers would ever have happened without their guidance and support. The Rocky Mountain Council for Latin American Studies gave us a place to meet with both of them as well as innumerable other wonderful colleagues in related disciplines every year. Every idea in this book has benefited from conversations facilitated by RMCLAS. Special credit also goes to the National Endowment for the Humanities (NEH) grantees who in the summer of 2018 came to Wisconsin to take seriously the ideas that ended up in this book. They are Alison Graham-Bertolini, Anya Jabour, Augusto Espíritu, Bonnie Lucero, Caroline Merrithew, Carrie Bremen, Courtney Thompson, Daniela Traldi, Ellie Walsh, Francesca Vassallo, Gregory Hammond, Heather Sinclair, Jennifer Helton, Kathleen McIntyre, Kelly Bauer, Kim Maslin, Lucy Grinnell, María Aguilar Dornelles, Mary Antoinette Smith, Mercedes Fernández Asenjo, Neici Zeller, Rachel Nolan, Roxanna Domenech, Sara Sundberg, Sarah Ball, Sarah Piña, Stephanie Opperman, Susan Goodier, Susan Stanfield, Tabitha Bonilla, and Victor Macías. All these brilliant scholars joined the remaining authors of these chapters, as well as Katharine Marino, Corrine McConnaughy, Dawn Teele, Ana Lau Jaiven, both madrinas, Patti Harms, and me for two weeks on the shores of Lake Michigan at Carthage College to ask how women in the Americas obtained the suffrage. The NEH made all this possible, and I am as grateful to that organization as I am to all the people who came and did the work together. Lau, Guy, and Lavrin graced us not only with extraordinary reflections on suffrage history at the opening and closing of the institute but also with personal meditations on the development of women's history as a field of study, which each of them shaped in powerful ways. Speaking of grace, I am ever mindful of the long hours my children have spent amusing themselves on campus and elsewhere while I work. You are my laughter and my joy, my sure and certain hope that beauty is saving the world.

Prologue

This book is not about pan-American feminism; it is about women gaining the right to vote within their own national contexts. Nevertheless, national struggles took place within the context of a well-published and rapidly developing international movement. What follows is a brief overview of the origins of that movement, with an emphasis on pan-Americanism.

American women's movements began with the rise of elite ladies' clubs during the last two or three decades of the nineteenth century. This was a period of enormous change. Railroads, telegraph lines, and public education expanded to support export-based economies that traded with new international partners. The United States and Britain grew in importance in relation to Latin America as Spain and Portugal declined. These same changes laid the foundation for the growth of mass culture, which, especially for urbanites, was increasingly aware of internationalism. In many countries, the normative gender of the category "citizen" came under scrutiny.

During this same period, women's access to education expanded. Countries began seeing their first women doctors and lawyers, and swelling public education systems meant more normal schools, many of which filled with young women. By 1900 there were women's organizations in every country discussed in this book; they fell into predictable categories: beneficence, temperance, religious, and literary societies. We see the first ladies' magazines flourish among the same, relatively small circle of educated, affluent women. As the twentieth century began, some women's societies focused more on gender, and women's suffrage became a frequent topic of conversation. Other social movements that were dominated by men but included women, such as the abolition movements in Brazil and the United States, or labor movements in Peru, Argentina, Uruguay, Puerto Rico, and Mexico, produced more radical proposals for social change.

The turn of the twentieth century saw the birth of the international women's movement, although that label is something of a misnomer. There were really four international women's movements that influenced and interacted with each other. The first of these movements, the World Women's Christian Temperance Union, was important in Canada, the United States, Europe, Asia, and Africa, and less so in Latin America. The second international movement did not begin as a women's movement at all but rather as women's participation in international scientific congresses in Latin America, principally the Southern Cone. The third movement, the one usually referred to as *the* international women's movement, began simultaneously with the second but among elite women in Europe, Canada, and the United States. The fourth movement had an entirely different character from the other three: it was a semi-intentional offshoot of the Socialist International. Its creation and interaction with members of the other three movements initiated another long-lived trend: the sometimes creative and sometimes destructive tension between socialist and bourgeois feminists that characterized nearly all national cases.[1]

All four international women's movements were meaningfully interconnected: temperance advocates, peace activists, and labor organizers all occasionally advanced suffrage; individuals held memberships in multiple organizations; and transnational friendships propelled collaboration on manifold fronts. There was, however, very little agreement over even the most fundamental concepts, such as defining "feminism."[2] Race, class, and colonialism further divided participants in the international movements.

The first women's histories created origin stories for contemporary feminism by lifting up what they sometimes called "proto-feminists" as "antecedents" to social movements that occurred later. Scholars sometimes pointed to female independence heroes or even the seventeenth-century savant Sor Juana Inés de la Cruz as antecedents. The connections between "proto-feminists" and later activists is not always easy to establish however. In the 1990s, Leila Rupp more believably traced the origins of international feminism to the late eighteenth-century publication of Mary Wollstonecraft's *Vindication of the Rights of Women*, which was translated into French and German in 1792. Informal international travelers, correspondents, and shared texts like Wollstonecraft's laid the foundation for a web of friend-ships that predated the reformist movements of the mid-nineteenth cen-tury, in which individuals reached across international borders in mixed-gender organizations.[3]

In 1878 relatively well-heeled, literate, and politically connected women from North America and Europe came together for the first time in Paris for a world exposition. After the Paris exposition, US suffragists Elizabeth Cady Stanton and Susan B. Anthony traveled to England and France with the explicit purpose of forming an enduring international organization that would connect existing national ones, such as the US National Women's Suffrage Association (NWSA). The NWSA sponsored a meeting in Washing-ton, DC, in 1888. The International Council of Women (ICW) emerged from this meeting.[4]

According to Susan Zimmerman, both the ICW and the International Women's Suffrage Alliance (IWSA) "conceptualized the international as a multiplication of the national."[5] Within each country, a process of consoli-dation was therefore necessary, producing a national umbrella (called a national council for the ICW and an auxiliary for the IWSA) that affiliated with the international organ. Both aimed to expand beyond Europe and the United States by promoting chapters in new, unrepresented national con-texts. Correspondence from the International Alliance of Women (IAW) repeatedly affirmed its "sincere wish to be as international as possible."[6]

However, "sincere wishes" were fraught with racist and colonialist assumptions about what the relationship between women's leaders in dif-ferent parts of the world should look like. Leading international crusader Carrie Chapman Catt, for example, was hardly shy when articulating her bigotry. Eugenics, which most educated people still considered to be a legit-imate science, informed Catt's understanding of racial difference. Her con-fused evolutionary thinking justified white supremacy, but it also permitted different races to, "like the sexes, also participate together in the same nar-rative of progress."[7] She argued, "There are doubtless many reasons for the dominance of the Anglo-Saxon race, but none more important than the fact that the Anglo-Saxons have permitted to their women a larger individuality and independence than any other people."[8] Eugenics explained and validated US and European international dominance, but it also led her to advocate for women's liberation as widely as possible.[9]

Leila Rupp's version of history from Wollstonecraft to the creation of the ICW is an important and valuable work, but it can also mislead. A focus on Wollstonecraft can give the impression that transnational women's organizing was primarily about women's rights, for example, but that was not always true.[10] The largest women's organization in the United States and the first to establish an international network was the Women's Christian Temperance Union (WCTU). Although its leadership came to embrace women's suffrage, its members did not always (or even usually) see their activities through the lens of advancing women's rights. The WCTU spawned one of the first transnational women's organizations: the World WCTU. Temperance evangelists traveled to India, China, Japan, Australia, and New Zealand, not only to preach the abstinence gospel but also to found affiliated groups in each national setting.[11] The IWSA was following in the footsteps of earlier activists when Carrie Chapman Catt embarked, in 1911–1912, on an Asian tour, where she was surprised to find thriving women's organizations already in place.[12]

A second problem occurs simply from telling the story from the perspective of events in the North Atlantic. Doing so can inadvertently end up duplicating and extending imperialist assumptions about US and European leadership. Francesca Miller, Asunción Lavrin, and Katherine Marino have shown that pan-American women's organizing came from Latin America to the United States, not the other way around.[13] It began at a series of scientific congresses, the first of which took place in Buenos Aires in 1898; there women participated as equals alongside men.[14] The fourth such meeting, held in Santiago in 1908–1909, became the First Pan American Scientific Congress. Columbia University's W. R. Shepherd was in attendance. He noted in surprise, "Women school teachers constituted a large part of the audience. . . . And it must be said that they express their opinions as well as their difference in opinion from those held by the other sex, with a freedom and frankness quite surprising to anyone who might fancy that no phase of the feminist movement has yet reached Latin America."[15]

In Buenos Aires in 1916, at the first Pan-American Child Congress, Uruguayan physician Paulina Luisi first suggested that women's rights should become a pan-American goal. According to Katherine Marino, Luisi believed that women's suffrage "would perfect the two critical objectives of the Western Hemisphere: political sovereignty and cultural advancement of the Western Hemisphere."[16] The Americas were where self-governing republics had taken root, and Europe's descent into war only enhanced Americans' sense of themselves as beacons for peace and democracy. For Luisi, women's suffrage would help fulfill American destiny.[17]

The second Pan American Scientific Conference took place in Washington, DC, in 1915–1916. Unlike either of the conferences in Buenos Aires, at the Washington, DC, conference, the men in charge excluded women from participating. In one of the many ironies associated with this history, the move to reject women inadvertently led to increased women's transnational communication and cooperation. Those women who had planned to attend the Washington, DC, conference but were now excluded created a parallel all-women's "Auxiliary Conference." That meeting resulted in the decision to begin a pan-American women's union, which eventually became the Pan American International Women's Committee.[18]

That committee coordinated with Carrie Chapman Catt's US League of Women Voters to convene the first Pan American Congress of Women in Baltimore in 1922. In Baltimore, for the first time and following on the heels of the passage of the Nineteenth Amendment in the United States, suffrage superseded social issues. Following the conference, Catt and fellow IAW member Rosa Manus set out on what Francisca de Haan termed a "nine month international propaganda tour for women's suffrage through Latin America."[19] Catt's efforts contributed to ongoing internationalization of women's movements in Latin America, yet her racist and imperialist mentality offended people everywhere she went. She undertook her Latin American tour because she thought the IAW "really ought to go hot and fast after those Spanish countries and wake the women up to demand their rights."[20] She assumed, incorrectly, that Latin Americans were not already doing so. That assumption was certainly connected to her sense of racial superiority. As she remarked in a private letter home during her tour, "The South American mind is slow."[21] Racist, colonialist attitudes endured and worked at cross purposes to hemispheric unity, as Katherine Marino's careful development of Doris Stevens's relationship to her Latin American counterparts makes clear.

The Pan American International Women's Committee prepared for and sent unofficial delegates to the 1923 meeting of the International Conferences of American States, held in Santiago, Chile. There, delegate Máximo Soto Hall introduced a motion to direct member states to dismantle legal inequalities between the sexes and also to designate women delegates for the next inter-American meeting.[22] The motion passed unanimously, but five years later there were no women delegates in Havana. Women representing organizations from countries throughout the Americas showed up again anyway and were granted a hearing.[23] They were successful in persuading the delegates to create the Inter-American Commission of Women. Permanent institutionalization of pan-American feminism had been accomplished.[24]

Notes

1. Dubois, "Woman Suffrage around the World," 256–65.
2. Karen Offen traces common usage of the term *feminism* to France in the 1890s; Offen, "Defining Feminism," 126.
3. Rupp, *Worlds of Women*, 14–15.
4. Rupp, 14–15. The ICW maintained the position that anti-suffragists deserved inclusion, a posture that led to the creation of a separate organization, the International Women's Suffrage Alliance, in 1904. While not exactly a schism, the creation of the new organization (which later became the International Alliance of Women for Suffrage and Equal Citizenship and finally the International Alliance of Women after 1946) was clearly the result of frustration on the part of suffragists within the ICW.
5. Susan Zimmerman, "The Challenge of Multinational Empire for the International Women's Movement: The Habsburg Monarchy and the Development of Feminist Inter/National Politics," *Journal of Women's History* 17, no. 2 (2005): 89.
6. Quoted in Francisca de Haan, "A 'Truly International' Archive for the Women's Movement (IAV, now IIAV): From Its Foundation in Amsterdam in 1935 to the Return of Its Looted Archives in 2003," *Journal of Women's History* 16, no. 4 (2004), 155.
7. Kevin S. Amidon, "Carrie Chapman Catt and the Evolutionary Politics of Sex and Race, 1885–1940," *Journal of the History of Ideas* 68, no. 2 (April 2007): 321.
8. Quoted in Amidon, 318.
9. Megan Threlkeld's *Pan American Women* is especially helpful in explaining the tensions these racialized colonialist assumptions on the part of North American feminists created in relations between the United States and Mexico in

particular. Christine Peralta covers Catt's visit to the Philippines in chapter 13 of this volume.

10. To be clear, Rupp acknowledges that nineteenth-century mixed-gender internationalism advocated a variety of reforms, such as "abolitionism, socialism, peace, temperance, and moral reform." Rupp, *Worlds of Women*, 14–15.

11. "WWCTU Beginnings," World Woman's Christian Temperance Union, February 28, 2021, http://www.wwctu.org/pages/history.html. As in the United States, some of these chapters became critical to the suffragist effort. Most notably, New Zealand and Australia vie for the honor of being the first country in the world to enact women's suffrage. For further discussion, see Caroline Daley and Melanie Nolan, *Suffrage and Beyond: International Feminist Perspectives* (New York: NYU Press, 1994).

12. June Hannam, Mitzi Aucheterlonie, and Katherine Holden, *International Encyclopedia of Women's Suffrage* (Santa Barbara, CA: ABC-CLIO, 2000), xiii. See Christine Peralta's chapter in this volume regarding Catt's visit to the Philippines.

13. Lavrin, *Women, Feminism, and Social Change*; Francesca Miller, "The International Relations of Women of the Americas 1890–1928," *Americas* 43, no. 2 (October 1986); Marino, *Feminism for the Americas*.

14. Miller, 173–74.

15. Quoted in Miller, "International Relations," 174.

16. Marino, *Feminism for the Americas*, 14.

17. In this book, the word *American* refers to the Americas rather than just the United States.

18. Miller, "International Relations," 176.

19. De Haan, "A 'Truly International' Archive," 150.

20. Quoted in Corinne A. Pernet, "Chilean Feminists, the International Women's Movement, and Suffrage, 1915–1950, *Pacific Historical Review* 69, no. 4 (November 2000), 673.

21. Quoted in Pernet, 673, n37.

22. Francesca Miller (180–81) records Soto Hall's nationality as Argentine. The ICW says he was Guatemalan. "Comisión Interamericana de Mujeres (CIM)," Organization of American States, 2023. https://www.oas.org/es/cim/historia. asp.

23. Miller, "International Relations," 182.

24. The ICW later worked as the vehicle for allowing especially Latin American feminists to shape what Marino calls the "constitution of the world," the UN Charter.

Introduction

STEPHANIE MITCHELL

GOVERNMENT OF, BY, AND FOR the people, the grand experiment to determine if people can successfully govern themselves, is perhaps the Western Hemisphere's finest contribution to humanity. At the heart of this great, unfinished project is the franchise. When the project was conceived, small minorities in every new American nation understood self-government to mean oligarchy. Many were eager to dispense with the trappings of monarchy and aristocracy, but in practice they tended to replace old systems built on exclusivity with new ones that excluded different groups of people. Scholars of citizenship note that any system of inclusion is necessarily also, fundamentally, about exclusion. Despite de Tocqueville's rosy assessment that democratic expansion was inevitable, groups holding power generally resisted sharing it with others whenever they could. One partial expansion of the franchise did not inexorably lead to others. Suffragists waged battle with power over generations to achieve what rights women now enjoy.

Women's Suffrage in the Americas is a collaborative project working to understand how women in the Americas obtained the suffrage. We are a group of scholars from across the hemisphere, each with knowledge about a particular piece of this vast geography but none capable of answering the question on her own. We know that suffragists throughout the hemisphere worked together, that they formed collegial networks that supported each other's work, and that victories in one country encouraged advances in others. It is nevertheless unusual to view suffrage history through a hemispheric lens. This is the first project to place this many American suffrage stories side by side in an explicit, methodical way. In 2013 collaborators began meeting in small groups at conferences in the United States, Colombia, and Canada, where we presented our research to one another and began to discuss the big questions to do with understanding this history. Finally, in 2018, a grant from the National Endowment for the Humanities from the US government made possible a large gathering that included all the original participants plus thirty additional scholars. Subsequent meetings, which can now be held more frequently and less expensively thanks to Zoom, have allowed us to continue to advance our understanding. This book therefore has emerged from a process not unlike that which gave us women's suffrage—transnational, collaborative, labored, and fruitful.

Our goal of understanding suffrage in a hemispheric perspective has numerous challenges. For example, emphasizing suffrage over other markers of equality feeds into an already problematic history. Because many western European nations, the United States, and Canada enfranchised some groups of women early, suffragists from those countries (together with the vast majority of political researchers and commentators) espoused a counterfactual narrative that asserted that Latin Americans lagged behind northerners, necessitating paternalistic encouragement from their more advanced, whiter, English-speaking sisters. Latin American activists, who were often browner and more Catholic, resented and resisted this replication of the imperialist relationship that already existed between the regions, but the story was nevertheless perpetuated in the historiography and endures to this day.

Then there is the question of dates. If the United States changed its constitution to remove restrictions on sex in 1920 but waited until 1965 to pass the Voting Rights Act, which made it harder to disenfranchise African American citizens, which date should we use?[1] Clearly, either date on its own would be misleading. Indeed, most countries enfranchised some groups of women before others and frequently opened participation on unequal terms long before enacting anything like universal suffrage. Many, like the United States, allowed decades to pass between a partial or unequal extension and full legal parity with European-descended men.

Finally, any attempt to tell a macro-level story necessarily flattens out important differences among cases while somewhat artificially highlighting similarities. Looking at a landscape from a higher vantage point will always obscure details that are more visible on the ground. The same distance, however, can illuminate patterns that can only be observed with distance. This volume aims to construct the first meta-narrative of women's suffrage in the Americas. To do that, we have to place national histories into categories by identifying and underscoring certain transnational similarities. We recognize that any attempt like this will tend to simplify stories that were, in reality, more complex. Nevertheless, the exercise of proposing and debating categories for thinking about how women obtained the suffrage has already pushed the scholars involved in this project to think more deeply about important questions we hope future scholars will help us answer.

One of the thorniest of those questions involves the way we, as women's historians, have struggled to balance our desire to focus on the activities of women with our recognition that male-dominated states were the only entities capable of enacting suffrage extensions. The first generations of scholars to write about women's suffrage focused almost exclusively on the movements themselves. A reliance on veterans of the struggles, subsequent archival bias, and a desire to resist casual neglect in the academy led historians, most of whom could be described as feminists, to favor the perspectives of suffragist activists. The advantage to this kind of historiography was that we heard women's voices directly and paid attention to the arguments and strategies they used to advocate for the vote.[2]

More recent scholars, however, have recognized limitations to this approach. Corrine McConnaughy helpfully distinguishes between suffrage "supply and demand"—that is, those who agitate to gain the vote versus those with the power to extend it. Some statistical analyses suggest there may be little connection between the vigor or even longevity of a national movement for suffrage and its eventual extension to women.[3] In fact, a number of factors that intuitively seem linked may not be. For example, the timing of the extension of universal male suffrage fails to predict women's suffrage.[4] There also does not seem to be a correlation with economic development.[5] De Tocqueville's "invariable rule," which argued that "the further electoral rights are extended, the greater is the need of extending them," was simply wrong.[6] Suffrage extensions are far from inevitable. As Adam Przeworski put it, "Why would people who monopolize political power ever decide to put their interests or values at risk by sharing it with others? Specifically, why would those who hold political rights in the form of suffrage decide to extend these rights to anyone else?"[7] It is helpful to recall Karen Offen's observation: "The history of feminism is inextricable from the time-honored concerns of historiography: politics and power."[8]

Focusing more attention on the "people who monopolize political power" may get us closer to understanding why suffrage extensions occurred when and where they did, but it also diverts the narrative away from the people women's historians wanted to study in the first place. For example, "office seeking" theories, which "imply that parties will only endorse reforms that favor their ability to obtain or retain control of public offices," offer a promising perspective from which to view suffrage extensions.[9] Przeworski undertook a statistical analysis of 185 suffrage extensions by class, 70 by gender, and 93 by both class and gender. His calculations support the idea that political parties behaved strategically, acting in response to assumptions about the way enfranchised women would be likely to vote. "Many women," he noted, "were active and some important protagonists in these parties before they had voting rights, but the calculus was electoral."[10] Looking at suffrage through this lens, however, can problematically cast women back into the role of passive objects. A balancing act is required to recall both truths at once: states would likely never have extended suffrage to women without women's activism, but women never extended the suffrage to themselves.

Another challenge, one that begs for further investigation, involves the interplay between national and international women's movements. The impact of the international women's movement over time is hard to overstate. There is wide agreement on the impact of international norms: "overwhelming."[11] Women's transnational organizing helped shape a general cultural endorsement of "liberal" values and democracy that included women as political subjects. Katherine Marino's pathbreaking *Feminism in the Americas* shows how feminists from the Americas worked successfully to formulate an international framework around human rights. Following their signature success, the UN Charter in 1945, it became increasingly difficult for national leaders anywhere to lay claim to democracy or modernity while also excluding women from the suffrage on the basis of sex.[12]

Many nations continued to exclude women as well as men from participation using proxies for race, ethnicity, or class, such as literacy, but explicit exclusion on the basis of sex dwindled.

For all these reasons, this volume and the version of history it presents should be viewed as the beginning of a conversation, not the end of one. That conversation starts with understanding that this book organizes countries according to five "scenarios" based on intersections between three "commonalities" (characteristics shared broadly across the hemisphere) and three sets of "differences" (characteristics that differ sharply from one country to another).

Commonalities

1. SHARED HISTORICAL TRAJECTORY

All American suffrage movements trace their origins to nineteenth-century elite and middle-class women's organizations, usually dedicated to reforms in education, health care, child welfare, family and property law, and/or equal citizenship. These organizations were sometimes religious and sometimes secular and liberal. August Bebel's *Die Frau und der Sozialismus* was first published in 1879. By the start of the First World War, it had been translated and disseminated throughout the Americas, which gave rise to another genealogical branch based on class.

Those early efforts placed the normative masculine quality of citizenship, which had been assumed during the independence era, into question. This is why María Eugenia Bordagaray argues that the Ecuadorian National Assembly was making progress when it added the word *varón* (male) to the definition of citizenship in 1883–1884: the implication was that the addition "denaturalized [the] masculine character" of citizenship.[13] That critical shift took place within a cultural context where women increasingly occupied roles that had heretofore been assigned as male. This included but was not restricted to education and the professions. (Women athletes may have been as important as women doctors.) Most people felt that gender norms were changing fast. Every country we have looked at had categories like "modern woman," "new women," and "modern girl" in the early twentieth century.

2. SHARED ASSUMPTIONS

American suffrage movements took place within an international context that universally associated women's rights with modernity, transnationalism, social welfare, and usually peace. Consider the first example of women's international cooperation on what Francesca Miller describes as a "professedly woman theme": the 1892 Colombian Exposition in Chicago. The world expos were sites in which nations competed to display qualities associated with modernity, and American women's internationalism began here. Whether politicians thought women voters would help them politically or not, leaders of all political persuasions were concerned with appearing to keep up with the times.

Most of the shared assumptions have to do with a largely unquestioned belief in the existence and relevance of sexual dimorphism. In Roman Catholic areas, there was wide agreement among political actors of all ideological persuasions that women were likely to be more conservative, more religious, and more vulnerable to clerical influence than men. In Protestant areas, there were often associations between femininity and temperance and other social welfare issues. Maternalism frequently entered into these arguments. There was broad agreement everywhere that women tended to be more moral than men but more easily manipulated, whether by priests, populists, or patriarchs.[14]

3. DIVISIONS

In every country, women were divided by power structures where gender intersected with sexuality, class, and race/ethnicity. Intersectionality often determined who would be included in and who would be excluded from the franchise.[15] Few elite women's organizations included women from marginalized ethnicities or class groups, and most were content to trade the exclusion of other women in exchange for their own inclusion.

Every country also contained multiple, competing, ideologically inconsistent articulations of feminism, including compensatory feminism (women's rights were necessary to compensate for women's special vulnerability); Catholic feminism (women needed the suffrage to protect the traditional Catholic household); maternalist feminism (women needed the suffrage to be better mothers and better educators of future generations); rights-based or individualist feminism (women were equal to men in terms of their intellectual and labor capacities and obligations and therefore deserved equal rights); socialist feminism (women's subordination stemmed from class injustices, so feminists needed to be primarily concerned with the rights of working women); and New Liberal feminism (the state should save capitalism by introducing regulatory regimes).

Proponents of any one of these strands sometimes argued that their own ideas constituted "true" feminism, discrediting ideological opponents. That tendency did not stop suffragists from shifting among arguments, responding to their own prejudices/preferences and those of their audiences. Ideological inconsistency and divergences of opinion were the norm everywhere.

Differences

1. TRANSNATIONAL AND INTERNATIONAL CONTEXT

Suffragists' experiences within their own countries were shaped by the global historical moment in which they took place. Here the "transnational" context refers to connections domestic suffragists had with leaders from other countries, participation in international congresses and organizations, and interactions among suffragists in different national contexts. The "international" context refers to the broader historical moment. Both mattered.

"Participation in international conferences," writes Asunción Lavrin, "gave personal and political strength to those returning home as well as to those who stayed behind."[16] Women returning from an international conference could make headlines, creating an impression that was often out of step with the actual numbers of suffragists in a given country and resulting in an outsized political influence. Leila Rupp and Verta Taylor have argued that, despite tensions and inevitable schisms, participants in the international women's movement(s) "forged . . . interacting layers of collective identity."[17] Their most immediate loyalties lay with their particular organizations, but they also expressed a sense of belonging to something bigger. Canadian historian Joan Sangster reminds us that we ignore these affective considerations at our peril.[18] Ellen Carol DuBois explains that "women's international co-operation gave them resources to combat their marginalization in the politics of their own nations."[19] Megan Threlkeld describes attendance at international conferences as the "best method" for Jane Addams–style "human internationalism," even though these conferences were the "most expensive and time-consuming."[20]

The international context forcefully shaped the contours of the political world in which suffragists worked. For example, suffrage movements everywhere received a boost after 1945 with the founding of the UN Charter, and especially after the 1948 adoption of the Universal Declaration of Human Rights, itself a triumph of the international women's movement. The declaration asserted that the "authority of government" must stem from the "will of the people," expressed through "universal and equal suffrage." Any number of international factors like this one impacted suffragists' labors. Suffragists tended to follow the news of victories elsewhere carefully. Early extensions in the UK, New Zealand, and Australia were crucial. As more countries extended the franchise to women, political leaders ran the risk of appearing backward when they wanted to be modern. In this way, women's suffrage acquired both a global and a regional snowball effect. Ramírez et al. report that "with every percentage point increase in the regional percentage of countries, the rate of franchise acquisition increases by almost one percentage point."[21]

We also know that political leaders closely followed international news on the consequences of votes for women. Mexico's Lázaro Cárdenas, for example, could not have failed to notice the impact of the women's vote in Spain after the Republican Congress nervously extended the franchise to women over the objections of feminist activist Victoria Kent. The 1933 election swung conservative, and many Spaniards blamed or credited women, depending on their political persuasion. Observers in Spain and across the ocean linked the subsequent rise of Spanish fascism with the republic's extension of the vote to conservative women. Similarly, we know that Perón in Argentina considered both Mussolini's treatment of women in Italy and

Getulio Vargas's in Brazil. In other words, suffragists worked within political contexts shaped by recent events near and far.

Other political currents not directly related to women's politics mattered as well. For example, during the 1930s and 1940s, socialists and communists formed a potent political force, which tended to ally with liberals against conservatives and Catholics, especially in Latin America. Catholics often saw women's suffrage as a necessary evil to combat radicalism, which they associated with moral degeneracy and atheism. During the cold war, Catholics allied with liberals against socialists. That had the effect of diminishing the political threat to liberals of enlarging the franchise to include Catholic, conservative women.

2. POLITICAL ENVIRONMENT

Suffragists everywhere had to work within regional and national political environments that could determine their success or failure. Their work was especially challenging because women lacked, by definition, full citizenship.[22] Instead they exercised what Mexicanist historian Jocelyn Olcott calls "contingent" citizenship. Aspects of that political environment to consider include the relative power of various political parties; the quality, charisma, and relative force of individual leaders (for example, both Perón's role in Argentina and Cárdenas's in Mexico were decisive, but with opposite outcomes); the extent to which liberal, progressive, and socialist-leaning leaders stressed anticlericalism in their agendas or, conversely, managed to distance themselves from this nineteenth-century legacy; the relative stability of liberal caudillos or the single-party alternative to caudillismo (Mexico's PNR-PRM-PRI; Nicaragua's Somocistas) vis-à-vis the efficacy of the suffrage in determining political outcomes; the strength of imperialist influence on domestic political actors who may not have been sovereign in their own countries; the type of government (parliamentary versus presidential democracy, for example); and the presence or absence of revolutionary movements.

3. THE EFFECTIVENESS OF SUFFRAGIST MOVEMENTS

Any reading of suffrage history from any of the countries under study is likely to result in a renewed appreciation of the persistence, creativity, and genius that suffragists employed to obtain their rights. Their task—to persuade the powerful to share power—demanded endless ingenuity over generations of struggle. Strategies that bore fruit in one political environment failed elsewhere. For example, it was common to employ what might be called the grammatical argument, in which suffragists would argue that the language of existing laws did not technically prevent women from voting. They would proceed to demand their rights by attempting to register to vote. In 1924 this strategy worked when Matilde Hidalgo de Procel went before the electoral board in Machala, Ecuador. This resulted in one of the earliest partial extensions in the hemisphere. The same grammatical strategy went nowhere in Mexico, Brazil, and Argentina, however. In Chile, some women registered successfully using this ploy, only to provoke an explicit prohibition later. In the US state of New Jersey, property owners of any race or gender actually voted from 1776 to 1807, when legislators decided that electors also needed to be free, white, and male.

Broadly speaking, strategies fell into two camps, which we might label liberal bourgeois and socialist.[23] The first group had access to more powerful connections, which they used to lobby legislators, advance their causes through the courts, and engage in the politics of persuasion through the press. They often preferred to organize autonomously. They used a mix of rights-based and difference-based arguments, but their primary concerns were advancing women's positions in society vis-à-vis men. The second group was less concerned about autonomous organizing and often lacked access to the spheres of legislative, judicial, or cultural power. These strategies merged gender-based organizing with labor and agrarian movements, resulting in a broader set of demands.[24]

A disappointingly successful strategy for the first group involved sacrificing the interests of the second. Marginalizing subaltern women was a two-edged sword, however. On the one hand, it could work as an expedient to overcoming concerns about enfranchising a large number of new voters at once. Would Bertha Lutz, in Brazil, have been successful if she had not embraced literacy restrictions? Would Puerto Rican legislators have accepted the inclusion of lower-class women if elite suffragists had demanded it? Maybe not. On the other hand, exclusion deepened the divide between women who exercised privilege and power on the basis of their race, ethnicity, or class position and those who struggled against multiple, intersecting structures of dominance and oppression.[25] It negated any possibility of unity. It also narrowed the efficacy of the suffrage itself in effecting meaningful change. As bourgeois suffragists leaned into gender and away from racial or class equity, they missed the opportunity to make women's suffrage about far more than the vote itself. Proletarian suffragists were clearer than their more comfortable counterparts in understanding that the struggle for the vote needed to be embedded in other demands—for labor rights, land reform, Indigenous rights, and racial equity—for the suffrage to be meaningful.

Scenarios

This book categorizes suffrage histories in the Americas into five scenarios: the Liberal Democratic Scenario; the Crisis of Representation; the Liberal Delay; the Perceived Conservative Strategic Advantage; and the Imperialist Scenario. A brief introduction to each scenario precedes two or three national histories that have been grouped together to highlight certain similarities between them. These short introductions serve to define the criteria for inclusion in the category and to identify the similarities readers should look for. Each scenario calls attention to factors from the above list of differences. With countries grouped according to similarities and differences instead of according to geography or chronology, readers can understand that while Costa Rica might be geographically close to Nicaragua, its suffrage history has more in common with Canada than with its neighbor. In the same way, Ecuador, one of the first countries in Latin America where any women voted, has more in common with Peru, one of the last, than it does with other countries with early suffrage extensions.

The selection of the word *scenario* was deliberate. Generous funding provided by the National Endowment for the Humanities in 2018 allowed fifty women's and gender scholars to hash out together how best to describe the categories into which we wanted to place national histories. (The categories changed in response to those conversations as well.) We settled on *scenarios* for two reasons. The first is a recognition that the criteria for categorization refer more to the political realities in which suffragists acted than to the arguments or strategies suffragists employed, their ideological persuasions, geography, chronology, or another organizing principle. In the chapters, our scholars try to balance the vital work of suffragists with considerations about power in political context to make sense of why some groups of women voted earlier or later than others.

The second reason is to distinguish what this book offers from what political scientists call models, which, among other differences, are often expected to be useful for predicting behavior. Scenarios are historical categories, not abstract representations. In a related way, it is important to remember that historical categories are not organic. We might draw a useful parallel to periodization. Historians use periodization to help visualize change over time. We err, however, when we fall into the habit of seeing historical periods as anything more than imaginative devices with important limitations. Contributors to this project have frequently observed that many of the countries we included could logically fit into more than one category, depending on which historical moment or political reality the author chooses to highlight. Please remember that the five scenarios in this book are cognitive maps designed to help us see and grasp dynamics of the history; they are not objective realities unto themselves.

Conclusion

Most American suffrage historiography asks how women got the vote within a given national context, and we have national histories on nearly every country in the Americas. A few multinational histories exist, and there is some work on pan-American, transnational organizing. What we lack, however, is a comprehensive approach that joins together knowledge production from across the hemisphere to tell a larger story. When we do look at the national histories together, we begin to notice trends, articulated in the "Commonalities" section above. All national histories took place within a shared international context, informed by world events, such as the world wars, the Great Depression in between, industrialization, urbanization, the rise of a mass, consumer culture, and international feminist cooperation. The fact that in some countries groups of women began voting early in the twentieth century while others waited decades longer seems mystifying unless we apply some sort of theoretical framework to the whole.

Still, it is important to remember that the scholars whose work is presented here do not always agree with one another or with me. Some emphasize ideology; others the geography of power. Some stress long-fought legislative triumphs; others the long road still ahead. We do not shrink from disagreement because it is fertile ground. When we have opportunities for conversations together, we usually find ourselves laughing, because every question we answer seems to raise two more. We trust that over time, collaborative inquiry will lead to better and more understanding. You are invited to join us in that pursuit.

Notes

1. Other racialized groups voted somewhat earlier: Chinese in 1943, most Native women in 1948, Japanese women in 1952.
2. The first-generation historiography often had the advantage of interviewing/ knowing veterans.
3. Ramirez et al., "Changing Logic of Political Citizenship," 736; Przeworski, "Conquered or Granted?," 318.
4. Trineke Palm, "Embedded in Social Cleavages," 2.
5. Przeworski, "Conquered or Granted?," 307.
6. Quoted in McConnaughy, *Woman Suffrage Movement*, 23.
7. Przeworski, "Conquered or Granted?," 291.
8. Karen Offen, "Defining Feminism," 142.
9. Lehoucq and Molina, "Stuffing the Ballot Box Fraud," 8.
10. Przeworski, "Conquered or Granted?," 318.
11. Przeworski, 305. Ramirez et al., "Changing Logic of Political Citizenship," 742.
12. Marques, "Women's Rights and Regional Politics under Cold War."
13. Prieto and Goetschel, "El sufragio femenino," 227–30.
14. Sadly, subsequent historiography often reinforced this particular trope. To make sense of the impact of this thinking, it is vital to distinguish between the assumptions about women and the way real women actually acted. There is of course no reason to imagine that women were really any more susceptible to political manipulation then men. Only the prejudice was real.
15. Kimberlé Crenshaw coined the term *intersectionality* in 1989 in

"Demarginalizing the Intersection of Race and Sex: A Black Feminist Critique of Antidiscrimination Doctrine, Feminist Theory and Antiracist Politics," *University of Chicago Legal Forum* 1989, no. 1. Since that time, the term has gained widespread usage among historians of all parts of the Americas.

16. Asunción Lavrin, "International Feminisms: Latin American Alternatives," *Gender and History* 10, no. 3 (1998): 521.

17. Leila J. Rupp and Verta Taylor, "Forging Feminist Identity in an International Movement: A Collective Identity Approach to Twentieth-Century Feminism," *Signs* 24, no. 2 (1999): 381.

18. Sangster, *One Hundred Years of Struggle*, 139.

19. DuBois, "Woman Suffrage around the World," 254.

20. Threlkeld, *Pan American Women*, 36.

21. Ramirez et al., "Changing Logic of Political Citizenship," 742.

22. There were, of course, male suffragists, some of whom possessed not only citizenship but also significant power and influence.

23. Susie Porter cautions against making too much of this distinction. She argues, "To distinguish between middle-class women who mobilized for political rights and working women who made practical demands contributes to a false dichotomy that obfuscates the extent to which the Mexico City women's movement was a labor movement." She also problematizes the notion that "working class" and "middle class" were distinct, non-overlapping categories. The office workers who are the subjects of her study could fit into either classification and described themselves as either working class or middle class, depending on the context. Porter, *From Angel to Office Worker*, 237.

24. August Bebel's 1879 *Women and Socialism* argued that femininity should be disassociated from domesticity. The implication was that gendered inequities existed irrespective of class oppression. Clara Zetkin's reinterpretation of Bebel instead reaffirmed women's presumed innate domestic role and probably contributed to the way socialists subsequently tended to collapse gender into class.

25. Crenshaw, "Mapping the Margins."

(IL?)LIBERAL DEMOCRATIC SCENARIO

Examples: Costa Rica, Canada, United States

Understanding this scenario requires a knack for grasping paradox because the scholars writing about these three countries need us to hold competing, seemingly incompatible truths in mind at once. They need us to view the political systems under question as both "liberal" and "illiberal" at the same time. The key to understanding this is context. Let us begin with the "illiberal" side of the scenario. Costa Rica, Canada, and the United States shared a history of excluding poor and racialized groups from power. All three crafted national mythologies that emphasized egalitarian, liberal democracy, while in practice those in power marginalized, dispossessed, and enslaved members of other groups, especially Indigenous people and those of African descent. Various immigrant ethnicities also faced exploitation and disenfranchisement. If we diminish these truths and reproduce uncritically the mythologies that gave cover to chattel slavery and outright genocide, we are complicit in the ongoing oppression of the descendants of the survivors. It would also make for very bad history.

Nevertheless, if we look only at the "illiberal" nature of these "democracies with adjectives," we miss crucial ways in which these three political systems differed from others in the hemisphere. Costa Rican scholars, especially, stress the ways in which their political system, like those of Canada and the United States, has functioned in the way it was designed. Indeed, their history of oppressing non-elite groups is hardly distinctive. It is shared by every country in the Americas. What these three countries shared, however, which many others did not, was a history relatively free from dictatorship, coups, and significant electoral fraud. The "liberal" side of this scenario looks at these countries in a context where they are compared, for example, with Nicaragua under the Somoza dynasty, Argentina during the Infamous Decade, or Colombia during the War of a Thousand Days. In Costa Rica, Canada, and the United States, elections generally determined political outcomes, and those who were able to vote had reasonable confidence that their votes would be counted.

The "liberal" side of this scenario meant that suffragists in these three countries had different strategic opportunities than those in many other political environments. While suffragists in other countries almost always lobbied their legislatures, they often did so with the full knowledge that the overweening power of the executive branch would ultimately determine their success or failure. Similarly, efforts to persuade ordinary members of the public were much more efficacious in an environment where fraud was relatively low. As everywhere, politics in these three countries was mostly about power, and suffragists were only successful when they understood and worked within the power dynamics of their political systems. They could trust, however, that if they convinced enough voters and legislators to support their agenda, they would win.

CHAPTER ONE

"Affronting Electoral Law"

Struggle, Conquest, and Approval of Women's Suffrage in Costa Rica (1890–1949)

EUGENIA RODRÍGUEZ SÁENZ

THE COSTA RICAN CONSTITUTION OF 1848 established in its Article 9 that only men had electoral rights. Subsequent constitutions failed to mention gender until the beginning of the twentieth century. The Costa Rican electoral law of 1913 established for the first time in explicit terms that mentally incapacitated people, criminals, and women were not allowed to vote. Such a discriminatory and sexist law was in force until June 20, 1949, when women's suffrage was enacted. Within the context of increasing feminist and suffragist debates and with the first proposals for women's suffrage sent to Congress in the 1920s, Sara Casal's article "Feminism and Costa Rican Woman," published in 1924, stands out. She writes, "Those women who do not want to vote are unaware that there is an affronting list in our electoral law [of 1913], in which women are placed last, among those who cannot vote, equating them with the insane, mentally incapacitated, petty and serious convicted criminals, deaf mutes, debtors, and finally women."[1]

Within this framework, the main objective of this article is to analyze the fight for, conquest of, and approval of universal women's suffrage and women's conversion into legal citizens with the right to be elected to government posts in Costa Rica. This was a result of a long and hard struggle, which included advances, setbacks, and contradictions, from 1890 to 1949.

This chapter tries to answer Adam Przeworski's main questions: "Why would people who monopolize political power ever decide to put their interests or values at risk by sharing it with others? Specifically, why would those who hold political rights in the form of suffrage decide to extend these rights to women in 1949?"[2] In particular, what were the roles played by feminists and international treaties in such a process?[3] In contrast to the dichotomist perspective of Przeworski, I argue that the feminine vote in Costa Rica was both conquered and granted.

As in other Latin American countries, and in Europe, Canada, and the United States,[4] the struggle for women's suffrage in Costa Rica was led by the feminist movement, which was always supported by a minority of men. However, compared to the feminist movement in the United States and England, the one in Costa Rica—and those of most Latin American countries— was much more embryonic. It came later and lacked an important base of support from women.[5] In fact, even though the suffragist movement took its first steps in Brazil as early as the second half of the nineteenth century, it was mainly during the first half of the twentieth century that it took strong hold and succeeded in getting women's suffrage approved, mainly in the 1940s and 1950s but first in Ecuador in 1929.[6]

Central to this chapter is demonstrating that to better understand why women's suffrage was not approved until thirty years after the period of struggle, one must go beyond an analysis of the changes in legislative arguments, perceptions for or against the participation of women in politics and their right to vote, and exaltation of the important work carried out by feminists throughout this struggle.[7] One must also include an analysis of the key role played by the dynamics of the political and electoral context.

According to Molina and Lehoucq's theses, the development of democratic institutions in Costa Rica resulted from efforts among politicians to control power in a context where none of the contending political forces could monopolize it. Therefore they had to compromise, make arrangements with other sectors, and run the risk of fostering temporary or uncertain political reforms and alliances. This explains why it took such a long time to reform electoral practices to stop fraudulent activities (first half of the twentieth century) and to get women's suffrage approved. After the failure of approval in the 1920s, it was necessary to wait until 1949 for legislation to pass.[8]

In synthesis, a crucial element to answer the question about why women's suffrage had to wait until 1949 is found in the need for at least two strategic conditions to be present in the political-electoral dispute. The first condition was that a party had to seriously take into consideration that promoting the new legislation would bring electoral benefit. In the second place, there had to be a set of well-organized social movements—suffragists—to pressure conservatives and moderates in power to accept that by passing the bill they would in fact attract a considerable number of votes. The existence of both conditions would create a large coalition able to promote far-reaching reforms, and this situation was only possible in the context of the political polarization of the 1940s.[9]

The main sources for this work are newspaper and magazine articles, as well as legislative debates about women's participation in politics and women's access to the vote during the period between 1900 and 1949.[10] Even though these sources are limited, I agree with Asunción Lavrin that "they are adequate for intellectually approaching historical subjects and their experiences."[11]

The first section of this essay deals with the context of political and electoral disputes in Costa Rica in order to frame the origins of the feminist and suffragist movement. The second section outlines the main history of the Costa Rican suffragist movement and its main stages in comparative perspective. The third section analyzes the changing dynamics in the political-electoral context, as it was within this context that several strategies were disputed and negotiated among the political sectors in order to control power. This section explains why women's suffrage was not approved until 1949. Finally, the conclusion addresses the process by which women organized and participated in building and strengthening Costa Rican democracy.

Costa Rican Political and Electoral Context

In this section I establish some key elements in the evolution of the Costa Rican political and electoral context in order to contextualize the subject of study. Feminist and suffrage struggles take place in a context in which Costa Rica, unlike the other Central American countries, was characterized by great stability with brief conflicts. After 1902 the country consolidated electoral democracy, a stable system of political parties, civil governments, legitimate institutional spaces, and strategic channels between popular demands and public policies. In addition, Costa Rica was part of what can be considered the first world democratic wave, which was socially reformist from early on.[12]

To better understand the process of winning women's suffrage, it is necessary to consider the prior evolution of citizenship and universal male suffrage. The evolution of male citizenship was rapid after independence in 1821, helped along by the development of state institutions with national coverage and periodic elections. Between 1848 and 1859, male citizenship was limited by economic (income) and educational (literacy) criteria. These requirements disappeared in the 1859 constitution, which extended citizenship to all adult men and established universal masculine suffrage, which was consolidated in the constitution of 1871.[13]

Consequently, we find a trend of increasing political inclusion of the popular sectors in electoral registrations, reflected early in the electoral census of 1885. In this context, "class and ethnicity did not become sources of electoral exclusion. . . . [Available information suggests that] in the first half of the 20th century, indigenous people were systematically included in the elections."[14] This inclusive tendency is important considering that other countries in the hemisphere continued to exclude men as well as women from the suffrage on the basis of class or ethnicity until much later. Costa Rica preceded even Argentina[15] and Great Britain, where universal male suffrage was approved in 1918. Additionally, in the 1897 elections, electoral participation of men in Costa Rica was well above the average in other parts of Latin America and closer to the British trend. And unlike Great Britain, where the census included 59 percent of eligible voters in 1911, in Costa Rica the proportion increased from 63 percent in the 1885 census to nearly 100 percent in 1913, when direct voting was approved. That trend was maintained when the secret ballot was approved in 1925. Between 1936 and 1948, Costa Rica had compulsory voting to counteract electoral abstentionism, increase turnout at the polls, and reduce the number of provincial parties.[16]

The constitution of 1949 (which is still in force today) introduced three important reforms: the female vote, banning the Communist Party of Costa Rica (CPCR), and the Supreme Electoral Tribunal (SET). The SET was created as an independent power—pioneering in Latin America—in charge of providing voting identity cards, ensuring the national application of electoral legislation, and guaranteeing the development of fair, transparent, and free electoral processes, becoming a "Latin American record."[17] In addition, Article 95 of the 1949 constitution includes another important advance, mandating that the state automatically register citizens for voting. Thus it is not necessary to register before voting, as is the case in many countries in the Americas, such as the United States. Incarcerated citizens also have the right to vote—except those declared in a state of interdiction and those specifically sentenced to the suspension of the exercise of political rights.[18]

Historical Antecedents of the Costa Rican Feminist and Suffragist Movement

The conquest of the female vote is strongly connected to women's access to education, which expanded in the cities between the 1920s and 1950s, along with access to primary education in general. Only in Costa Rica, however, did rural literacy rates increase significantly. Educational gaps according to gender also decreased in urban areas (mostly Ladino) but not in rural areas, where peasant and Indigenous women predominated.[19] (In 1950 urban literacy in Guatemala stood at 69 percent for Ladinas but just 11 percent for Indigenous women.[20]) Similarly, women's access to secondary education increased, especially for young middle- and upper-class women in the cities, while the majority of young Indigenous and Afro-descendant women remained excluded.[21] This expansion of female secondary education was associated with growing access to normal schools and technical training, which made it possible for women to enter the teaching and service labor market.[22]

An important change in this period was that the middle classes had greater access to public higher education. Although they entered school in a limited and unequal way with respect to men, women began to pursue university degrees. The first female professional graduates were pharmacists in

Costa Rica (1914) and Guatemala (1919), followed by lawyers in Panama (1922), Costa Rica (1925), and Guatemala (1927).[23] Greater access to education favored the growing participation of women in political party campaigns (although they could not vote); in philanthropic, cultural, and intellectual organizations; in unions and teachers' associations; and in various social movements.

This female role, reinforced by the emergence of the first generations of women artists, writers, intellectuals, and professionals, was helped by reactivation of the unionist movement (which sought to reconstitute the Federal Republic of Central America) during the 1920s. Salvadoran, Guatemalan, and Honduran women played a decisive role in unionism, in which they saw the best option to fight for peace and stability in their countries and to confront the imperialism of the United States, which had a military presence in the Panama Canal Zone (1903–1979) and in Nicaragua (1912–1933).[24] Trade unions and left-wing political parties encouraged women's participation through committees, clubs, and women's wings.[25]

During the 1920s, debates on women's rights intensified, a process linked to the founding of women's organizations, the emergence of feminist and suffrage movements, and the formulation of new proposals in favor of women's suffrage. Women's support for unionism influenced the ephemeral constitution of the Federal Republic of Central America, enacted by Guatemala, El Salvador, and Honduras in 1921, to introduce the female vote for the first time. This constitution made women's suffrage personal, secret, and nondelegable—but also restricted, since it could only be exercised by married or widowed women over twenty-one years of age who knew how to read and write, and by single women over twenty-five with primary education who had income or their own capital.[26] Thus Salvadoran women became the first to vote in Latin America, electing Salvadoran representatives of the Federal Republic in 1921, eight years before the suffrage reform in Ecuador in 1929.[27]

In addition, it can be argued that Central American feminist and suffragist struggles, as in other American countries, gained strength between the end of the nineteenth century and the beginning of the twentieth century. The late nineteenth century saw the beginning of suffrage campaigns and thriving women's movement in Europe and some American countries, and the beginning of the twentieth century saw the strengthening of links with feminist organizations worldwide.[28] These processes of struggle were characterized by the fact that the construction of women as citizens and political subjects preceded the conquest of the vote, which legitimized and legalized their status as citizens.

Despite great political repression, the opening of temporary democratization spaces in the 1940s belatedly led to a greater development of these organizations and movements in Guatemala, El Salvador, Honduras, and Nicaragua. Some sectors of the Honduran, Nicaraguan, and Panamanian feminist organizations did not identify with suffrage struggles. Starting in the 1940s, Guatemalan, Salvadoran, and Honduran women became actively involved in the processes of overthrowing authoritarian governments and in trying to build, albeit temporarily, more democratically open regimes.[29]

Three patterns can be distinguished in the development of these movements according to the characteristics of the political regimes. A first pattern is the dictatorial regimes of El Salvador and Honduras, in which the feminist and suffragist struggles developed late in the 1940s. A second pattern is the Somocista regime (1936–1979), which had a strategy to support the development of the Nicaraguan feminist and suffragist movements but at the same time delayed the approval of women's suffrage until 1955 and its effective exercise until the 1957 elections.[30] The third pattern encompasses regimes with broader democratic conditions, such as those of Costa Rica and Panama, which had favored the early development of women's, feminist, and suffrage movements since the 1920s. Finally, two patterns can be distinguished in the process of struggle to win women's suffrage. A first pattern was characterized by the evolution of the female vote from restricted to universal in Guatemala (restricted in 1945 and 1950 and universal in 1965), El Salvador (restricted in 1939 and universal in 1950), and Panama (restricted in 1941 and universal in 1945–1946). The second pattern was characterized by the conquest of universal female suffrage directly in Costa Rica (1949), Nicaragua (1955), and Honduras (1957).[31]

In Costa Rica, throughout this process of suffragist struggle we also find the specific and decisive influence of several junctures, among them: (1) electoral reforms for men: 1913 (direct vote) and 1925 and 1927 (secret vote); (2) the political crisis that began with the coup d'état of 1917, an event that stimulated women's active participation to overthrow the Tinoco dictatorship—the last and a brief dictatorship in Costa Rica—in 1919 and brought the issue of women's suffrage before a constitutional congress; (3) the workers' movement in the early twentieth century and the Reformist Party in 1923, which stimulated wider participation of women in political struggles; (4) the key role played by the founding of the Feminist League in 1923 and its constant suffragist campaigns; and (5) the decisive impact of anticommunist women's movements in favor of civil and electoral rights in 1943 and 1947 and social reforms during the Civil War of 1948.[32]

Between 1917 and 1949, and as far as it has been established, fourteen proposals for feminine suffrage in Costa Rica were set before Congress: in 1917, 1920, 1923, 1925, 1929, 1931, 1932, 1934, 1939, 1940, 1943, 1945, 1947 and 1949. Only four of them came to a vote: in 1917, 1925, 1945, and 1949.

FIRST STAGE: 1890–1910

This stage was characterized by the fact that women's equality and political rights were opened to debate in the newspapers and were discussed in Congress. Apparently, President José Joaquín Rodríguez was the first public figure to raise the issue of enfranchising women, in the course of a speech on electoral reforms he delivered before Congress on June 4, 1890.[33]

SECOND STAGE: 1910–1923

During the period between 1910 and 1923, the struggle for women's suffrage took on strength in the context of sociopolitical effervescence, electoral reforms, and the boom of the international feminist movement. Since the 1910s, the working-class movement had increased its participation in debates about the woman question and was willing to support women's political mobilization through the endorsement of social reforms, the development of organizations, and the dignifying of working-class conditions. It also emphasized giving working women access to education so they could better pursue their roles as mothers and wives.[34]

In discussing this 1910–1923 period, we must mention individual efforts made by women who, inspired by the international feminist movement, laid the foundations for the feminist movement. Ángela Acuña stands out among them as the first female Costa Rican lawyer (bachelor's degree in 1915; lawyer in 1925) and one of the founders of the Feminist League in 1923. Acuña first tried to promote women's suffrage in newspaper articles published as early as 1912, and in 1916 she succeeded in forcing the amendment of Article 12 of the Statute of the Higher Court, which banned women from serving as public notaries.[35]

Although the electoral reform of 1913 allowed for universal male suffrage, giving all men the right to vote regardless of their socioeconomic conditions, at the same time it became the first to explicitly deny the right to vote to women. This discriminatory bias is established in Article 3, in which women are ranked last among people who cannot exercise the vote. They are equated with criminals, those under prosecution, the insane or mentally deficient, deaf mutes, and debtors:

Article 3°. Cannot exercise the right to vote:

1° Those who, by final judgment of a competent court, have been sentenced to perpetual, absolute or special disqualification from political rights, unless they have been pardoned or rehabilitated in the exercise of citizenship, in the manner prescribed by law;

2° Those who, in compliance with a sentence of equal legal force, find themselves discounting a sentence that carries with it temporary, absolute or special disqualification for political rights;

3° Those who are prosecuted for a crime or simple offense that deserves permanent or temporary, absolute or special disqualification, for political rights;

4° The crazy, imbecile or insane, even if they have lucid intervals, and the deaf-mute who do not know how to read and write;

5° Those who are in a state of bankruptcy or insolvency; and

6° THE WOMEN[36]

It can be argued that electoral reform that prohibited women from voting was in part a preventive measure to face the increasing influence of feminist and suffragist debates. This in part explains why the 1913 exclusion stayed in force until June 20, 1949, when women's suffrage was approved.

During Federico Tinoco's brief dictatorship (1917–1919), the congressman and lawyer Alejandro Alvarado Quirós submitted a bill to approve restricted women's suffrage to the constitutional congress in 1917; however, it did not pass.[37] In 1920, after the political crisis of 1917–1919 that stimulated women's active participation in overthrowing the dictatorship, another bill to approve restricted women's suffrage was submitted to the congress, but it also failed to pass. Such proposals of reform would have allowed literate Costa Rican women over twenty years old to vote and to be elected in municipal elections. In this stage the Reformist Party (founded in January 1923), led by Jorge Volio, became the first political party to promote women's participation in politics and equal rights for women. Members dressed in white as public speakers, signed a women's manifesto, and sang a party hymn in the electoral campaign of 1923–1924.[38]

On June 20, 1923, and prior to the founding of the Feminist League, sixty-four women brought forth before Congress the first petition for feminine suffrage led by women. They based their proposal on one from a group of students at the Colegio Superior de Señoritas, who were motivated by the prevailing atmosphere. Their proposal was also ignored.[39]

THIRD STAGE: 1923–1949

The 1923–1949 period was characterized by a more systematic organization of Costa Rican feminism, stimulated by the international boom of the movement. This entailed the founding of the Liga Feminista, the Feminist League, on October 12, 1923, led by Ángela Acuña Braun. From its very beginning, it had close links with other organizations and was the representative chapter in Costa Rica of the International League of Iberian and Hispano American Women, the League for Peace and Liberty, and the Pan American Round Table. Even though the league did not have important support from a broad base of women, it was supported by some presidents, intellectuals, and progressive liberal congressmen.[40]

The Feminist League, like feminist organizations in Europe, the United States, and elsewhere in Latin America, was made up mainly of intellectual women from the middle and upper classes,[41] including teachers, students, and graduates of the Colegio Superior de Señoritas.[42] The Feminist League

Figure 1. Cartoon, *Diario de Costa Rica*, July 15, 1924.

played a key role in the struggle for women's rights and put forth six proposals before Congress—in 1931, 1932, 1934, 1939, 1940, and 1943. The league also
led several campaigns in favor of women's suffrage in the press and in Congress, in 1925, 1929, 1945, and 1947. The debate over women's equality and
political rights intensified, including a great deal of opposition, as reflected
in a cartoon from 1924 that shows inverted gender roles (Figure 1).

As mentioned at the beginning of this chapter, in 1924 Sara Casal
denounced that women were lumped together with criminals and the mentally incapacitated. Due to the pressure generated by this denunciation by
Casal and other feminists, women were eliminated from the list of prohibi-
tions in the electoral laws of 1925 and 1927. At the same time, however, those
laws established that only men had the right to vote. According to Article 1,
"The right to vote is essentially political and can only be exercised by (male)

Sara C. v. de Quirós   *Figure 2.* Cover of *El voto femenino*,
1925 book by Sara Casal.

El Voto Femenino

Imprenta Nacional

San José, Costa Rica

1925

citizens."[43] The secret vote for men passed, while women's suffrage failed (February 1925).

Casal pushed Congress to pass women's suffrage in 1925 by founding two groups: Consejo Nacional de Mujeres de Costa Rica and the Feminista de Puntarenas.[44] She led a petition campaign that collected more than twenty-five hundred signatures, but it was unsuccessful. Casal's *El voto femenino* (1925), published during this campaign, can be considered Costa Rica's first political treatise written by a woman.[45]

During the 1930s, the CPCR (founded in 1931) was the first political party to include in its programs proposals in favor of women's political rights—the vote in particular—and civil and labor rights.[46] In addition, the CPCR was the second organization of its type that understood clearly the important political potential associated with women's organizing, a key aspect in its strategies of consolidation, struggle, and political and electoral expansion from 1931 to 1948. It can be argued that the CPCR was the first party to contribute in a systematic way to constituting the first block of organized women in politics, in urban areas in particular. Nevertheless, within its political agenda, the CPCR sustained ambiguous postures about women's rights, especially the vote.[47]

Later, in the polarized sociopolitical atmosphere of the 1940s, the league joined with other women to demand compliance with laws on men's civil and electoral rights that were already established but not enforced in practice. Recent research has shown that the league actively participated in demonstrations by students and women during the Civic Movement of May 15, 1943, and the Movement of Women on August 2, 1947. Those movements became the basis to constitute a decisive oppositional and anticommunist sector of women, who also took part actively in the Civil War of 1948.[48]

In this way, the efforts for women's suffrage initially led by the league were completely absorbed by women who joined the struggles of the main political forces. The parties fought for civil rights for all citizens, and for "the moral improvement of our Fatherland and the dignity of republican institutions."[49]

Figure 3. "Movilización de las mujeres por las garantías electorales, 2 de agosto de 1947," photograph, August 2, 1947. Museo Nacional de Costa Rica, San José.

The Context of Political-Electoral Struggle
and the Approval of Women's Suffrage

After the Civil War of 1948, which cannot be considered the revolution that followers of the National Liberation Party designate it to be, José Figueres Ferrer took power during eighteen months through the Government Board. He abolished the army in 1948. During this period the board convoked a constitutional assembly that approved the constitution of 1949, created the Supreme Electoral Tribunal as an independent power, criminalized the Communist Party (or Popular Vanguard Party), and culminated in the Act of June 20, 1949, which constitutionally decreed women's suffrage after a thirty-year struggle.[50]

It took a long time to reform electoral practices to stop fraud (first half of the twentieth century), and a long time passed between the unsuccessful attempts to approve women's suffrage in the 1920s and its final approval in 1949. We must remember that prior to the electoral reforms undertaken between 1890 and 1949, the vote was not cast directly or secretly. Besides, there were no institutions to effectively regulate voting, such as the Civil Registry or the Electoral Committee, so electoral fraud was rampant.[51] It is against this backdrop that we must place most proposals congressmen and presidents submitted between 1890 and 1949 to get women's suffrage approved.

In general terms, legislative debate on women's suffrage evolved from great opposition to great approval in 1949. This is shown, for instance, in the congressional votes of 1925 and 1949. In 1925 the count was twenty-four votes (61.5 percent) against women's suffrage and fifteen (38.5 percent) in favor, but in 1949 the count changed to thirty-three votes (80.5 percent) in favor and eight votes (19.5 percent) against.[52] In other words, congressmen who favored reform increased from one-third to three-fourths. Nevertheless, support did not imply the disappearance of conservative attitudes regarding the participation of women in politics and their right to vote.

Why was there such significant variation? Obviously, the first thing we notice is the weight of congressmen's sexist and conservative attitudes as an element that delayed reform. However, we hold the thesis that the dynamics of the struggle for power and electoral reforms also played a decisive role in this process. In fact, as pointed out at the beginning of this chapter, at least two strategic conditions were apparently required in this stage of political-electoral struggle for women's suffrage to be approved. The first was that a party had to consider it advantageous in electoral terms to promote the reform; in the second place, there had to exist a set of well-organized social movements—suffragists—capable of pressuring conservative and moderate politicians to recognize that approving the reform would indeed attract many voters. The existence of both conditions would create a coalition able to promote far-reaching reforms, a situation that was only possible in the context of the political polarization of the 1940s.[53]

On the other hand, we must take into account that it was complicated for political parties to control voters. Therefore any electoral reform would necessarily result from a long process of conflict and negotiation. The approval of women's suffrage, which would double the size of the electorate, meant increasing the range of uncertainty for subsequent elections once the reform took effect. These contradictions and strategies were already clearly evident, for example, in political junctures before 1925, when initiatives to reform legislation to approve women's suffrage were put forth, as in the case of the proposals made by President José Joaquín Rodríguez in 1890 and by President Julio Acosta in 1920.

Both presidents argued that women deserved the right to vote on the basis of egalitarian ideals, their participation in the defense of democracy, and because they were the bearers of the highest moral and democratic values. This was exemplified during the overthrow of Tinoco's dictatorship in 1919, an event in which women played an active role. For that reason, Acosta made an appeal to allow for women's suffrage in municipal elections, as stated in his congressional address of May 8, 1920. Acosta based his arguments on the need for women to become more actively involved in politics and on the need to increase participation of the electorate at large, as male absenteeism had increased.[54]

In summary, we may state that some electoral strategies to increase control of power and broaden the electoral base lay beneath the arguments stated by political parties. This sometimes meant risking a possible reform to allow women to vote, particularly in political and electoral junctures where certain reforms were opened to negotiation, as was the case in 1890, 1913, 1917, 1920, 1925, 1927, and 1946.

In the context of this power struggle, we must also place the systematic political strategy of the Reformist Party (1923) and the workers' movement, which supported actively incorporating women in political activities to broaden its influence and political force from its very roots. As already pointed out, in the case of the Reformist Party, children and especially women became the key elements to bring dignity and inspiration to politics. They were now the emblems of morality and the highest values of social justice, as well as a group to legitimize, organize, and expand the movement. The workers' movement turned to women so that, once educated, they could improve life for workers, improve the upbringing of children, better support their spouses' struggle, and help consolidate a united front for workers.

The year 1925 is a particularly interesting historical moment, since it marked the beginning of a systematic campaign by politicians and the league to support legislation in favor of women's suffrage. Most congressional debate focused on approving electoral reforms to make men's vote secret and direct, which was ratified in March.[55] Consequently, the proposal in favor of women's suffrage remained a weak position. Politicians resisted making their electoral clientele even more vulnerable. This is shown partly in the conciliatory reasoning of the resolution by the congressional committee on electoral reform to include women's suffrage. The document recognized women's intellectual equality and used that same argument to hesitantly support women's suffrage but restricted it to "a select group of women . . . because we do not think they should all be granted such rights, since a large number of them have not received a broad enough education. . . . We do not consider ourselves enemies of women's suffrage, as we would admit their electing certain officials and with some restrictions."[56]

An analysis of these arguments supports the hypothesis that beyond the arguments put forth in favor of progress, civilization, democracy, and equality of capacities and rights, the demands in favor of women's suffrage were eventually used by political parties as a strategy to favor reforms tending to make the electoral system based on men's votes a more democratic one. As Lehoucq and Molina point out, "The absence of a broad-based woman's movement also allowed politicians to torpedo this measure without angering any of their constituents. Political calculations, not social interests, determined when women would get the right to vote."[57]

What, then, were the options for the league in this context so adverse to women's suffrage? From the previous analysis of the arguments held by politicians and league leaders, it follows that by 1930, women's suffrage had already become a topic of public debate[58] but that the league had not advanced enough and was therefore forced to modify its original stance in favor of unrestricted votes for women.

League leaders, like other contemporary suffragists,[59] chose the strategy of restricted votes for women because they were aware of political resistance, the lack of enough broad-based support by women—at least women workers—to put pressure on politicians, and the threat politicians perceived in duplicating the electoral base once women massively became part of the voting numbers. The latter was clearly seen in the proposal the league submitted to Congress in 1931, which stated that the right to vote would be restricted to women with formal instruction and technical or professional training.[60]

The 1940s are a special landmark in the struggle to strengthen social institutions, as well as civil and democratic rights. This emphasis resulted in the approval of women's suffrage in 1949. The process took place in the context of a highly polarized sociopolitical juncture, massive mobilization of women in favor of civil and electoral rights, and the outbreak of the Civil War of 1948.

The 1940s were dominated by the rise to power of a group led by Rafael Ángel Calderón Guardia and his successor, Teodoro Picado, a group that made an alliance with the Communist Party (then Partido Vanguardia Popular) in 1943. In fact, Calderón Guardia rose to power in 1940 due to significant support from the oligarchy and from the group that followed León Cortés within the National Republican Party. However, once the party became a majority group, "competition among the parties was replaced by political struggle within the National Republican."[61] This resulted in the confrontation and later breakup between Cortés and Calderón and the ensuing formation of a new party by the former.

Communists began to approach Calderón in May 1942 and finally sealed an alliance in June of that year. What political benefits did this alliance bring communists and Calderón's followers? For the latter, their alliance with the left, "from strictly electoral matters . . . allowed them to compensate for the loss of support resulting from the split of the National Republican Party after the conflict with Cortés; and in political terms, it won them support by an organized and disciplined party which was very active in urban areas and capable of providing ideological support to the government."[62] In the case of communists, if we rule out Mora's thesis, the most convincing hypothesis is that their alliance with Calderon's government was based on political calculation: it was made to avoid electoral erosion or maybe to maintain and strengthen the electoral base they already had. The reason might also have been that this alliance "allowed them to look as promoters of a social policy that, otherwise, was seriously threatening to surpass them."[63]

In summary, the alliance between Calderon's followers and the communists became, after 1942, "the basis for Costa Rican politics to turn into ideological struggle and polarization."[64] Systematic campaigns questioned the political system, electoral practices, and electoral fraud in 1942, 1944, 1946, and 1948. Massive participation of women in confrontations in 1943 and 1947 and the outbreak of the Civil War of 1948 contributed to the process and made it far more complex.

In the midst of this polarized sociopolitical context, what was the path of the proposals in favor of electoral reform to allow women to vote? The Feminist League tried to take advantage of the 1940s debate on civil and democratic rights, which questioned the unfair nature of the electoral and democratic system, but it once again failed to get Congress to approve its two proposals in favor of women's suffrage in 1943 and 1947. The league took advantage of the situation and put forth its proposal amid the protest of May 15, 1943, which opposed electoral reform to reduce the rights of polling committees in the process of counting ballots.[65] However, the debate turned sexist and violent, with a strong rejection of the statements of Teodoro Picado—deputy president of Congress and next president in 1944—who stated that "the country is for [the electoral] reform, that little groups of students and hysterical women prove nothing against the reform."[66]

The reason for repeated failure lies in the analysis above, which suggests that in this political context, women's suffrage was not a priority for either of the two majority groups in power (Calderon's followers and the communists). What really mattered was establishing a political alliance that would help them consolidate and expand their power, not risk it by doubling the electorate.[67] Additionally, the political sense of the risk implicit in approving women's suffrage can be inferred from the underlying thesis in the declarations given by Manuel Mora, who stated that Republicans had always opposed women's suffrage because "they believed that supporting the reform to allow women to vote was going to damage them because women themselves, the large masses of ignorant women, were against it and said: 'that is women trying to act like men; voting is for men'; they had all those prejudices then and still have them now, so these allies of ours we talked to thought that agreeing on women's right to vote was losing support from the large masses of women."[68] Mora added that they had to make a series of modifications to the electoral platform shared with the Republicans and give priority to social reforms over women's suffrage. In contrast to the Calderón–communist faction, once Cortes's followers left the Republican Party, women's suffrage became one of their main campaign arguments in 1943, even though they had always duly opposed it, possibly as a tool to overcome the decrease in the electorate.[69] Later, Teodoro Picado sent the second proposal for women's suffrage to Congress on June 4, 1947, relying on the need to fulfill the commitment made to the United Nations. This proposal was discussed, but it also did not have the necessary support in Congress, since some were in favor of a constitutional reform and others in favor of reforming the election law. The first option was adopted.[70]

An additional contribution to this struggle in favor of justice in the exercise of civil and democratic rights was pressure put by an important group of women led by teachers. These women organized themselves in the movement of August 2, 1947, in which the league's participation was not as belligerent as in 1943. Even though the secrecy of the ballot was vindicated, they did not explicitly object to the absence of women's suffrage. This was probably because, at the time, the general objective of purifying a democratic political system was more important than channeling the struggle for women's suffrage.[71] Thus emerged a situation where the suffrage struggle initially led by the league was completely absorbed by integration of its members in the fight between the main political forces in favor of the exercise of democratic and civil rights by all citizens.

Once the Civil War of 1948 was over, which meant a serious readjustment of political forces that made Calderón, Picado, and the communists losers while the followers of Ulate and Figueres became winners, there opened the possibility for a new constitutional congress. Precisely in the context of this constitutional congress, women's suffrage was approved on June 20, 1949, along with a series of other profound electoral reforms, including creation of the Supreme Electoral Court, issuing citizen identity cards with photographs, and secret and direct voting for all adult men and women.[72]

The legislative debate of 1949, unlike that of 1925, was overwhelmingly in favor of women's suffrage. Like the political junctures of 1890 and 1920, the arguments brought forth by congressmen centered on women's central role and civic spirit in the political events of the previous years, women's intellectual capacity, women's increasing access to formal education, their key role raising children for the Fatherland, and in their potential for exerting a moralizing influence on political practices. The congressman who submitted the motion for reform in favor of women's suffrage was Gonzalo Ortiz Martín, whose arguments included, among others, that "the events lately experienced in the country, in which women had active participation, are enough to grant them the right to vote." He noted that women "in college classrooms have developed their intellectual personality, the basis for their economic independence," and said that their "involvement in political and patriotic struggles during recent years has simply won them the right to vote . . . and [their] accomplishments should not be argued."[73] Congressman Everardo Gómez seconded Ortiz and added that women's suffrage was justified by the moralizing role women played in their families and in society. He noted "a woman's behavior and the role she is to play in marriage, as spiritual guide and molder of her children's character."[74] Finally, Congressman Fernando Baudrit Solera added that approving women's suffrage could purify politics: "It is hoped that the moral sense of politics will be set straight, as long as passion is not stronger than the amount of respect due to women and which they owe themselves."[75]

Beyond these arguments that emphasized the right to vote as a result of women's participation in the political life of the nation and their nature as moral standard bearers, a series of hidden underlying factors explain why women's suffrage was approved at that time. It might be that even though politicians argued in favor of or against women's suffrage, their position did not depend on their ideology but on political strategy. As already pointed out, approving women's suffrage would have meant doubling the size of the electorate and increasing the range of uncertainty in the following elections.

In light of the polarization of the 1940s, approving women's suffrage was secondary; massive participation by women in favor of electoral rights was not linked to obtaining the right to vote. Consequently, what happened during the 1940s was similar to what had happened in the 1920s: women's mobilization in favor of suffrage during the 1920s and their mobilization in favor of electoral rights in the 1940s contributed to reform electoral legislation to guarantee men's suffrage. So who stood to benefit?

Approving women's suffrage in 1949 can only be understood if we take into account that the two political parties at the time (National Republican and Popular Vanguard) had been persecuted and dismembered. In this context, the winners of the civil war (*ulatistas* and *figueristas*) supported the approval of the women's vote in 1949 because it did not significantly increase uncertainty for them in the 1953 national elections and they calculated that enlarging the electorate would benefit them. This is in part suggested in the sweeping support for women's suffrage (80.5 percent in favor and 19.5 percent against it) by congressmen of the National Union Party and the Social Democratic Party, who were the winning groups in 1948.[76]

Some years after, Ángela Acuña sustained that "President Figueres won [the elections of 1953 with] a lot of women's votes, because he supported [the reform] in the Constitution of 1949 that gave women the vote."[77]

Conclusion

The main conclusion of this chapter is that women's suffrage was the result of a hard and long struggle by feminists and of the negotiation of a series of strategies to control political power. The process of gaining political and civil spaces and rights for all citizens and approving the right to vote for Costa Rican women did not result from mere concession by politicians. On the contrary, it was the outcome of a long and difficult struggle to gain those rights. The Feminist League played a key role in that struggle, which included advances, setbacks, and contradictions.

On the other hand, it is clear that if we are to understand why approving women's suffrage was delayed until 1949, we must look beyond the changes in arguments in favor or against suffrage and beyond the struggle undertaken by the Feminist League. Women's suffrage also resulted from political struggle in an electoral-political context full of immense contradictions and severe confrontations, where political parties fought over control and expansion of political power by means of a series of uncertain, changing, and temporary strategies and alliances. This explains why it took so long to reform electoral practices to stop fraudulent activities (the first half of the twentieth century) as well as to approve women's suffrage. It was necessary to wait until 1949 after attempts failed in the 1920s.

In addition, for women's suffrage to be approved, at least two strategic conditions had to be met in this context of political-electoral dispute. The first condition was that a party had to believe that promoting reform would be advantageous from an electoral perspective. In the second place, there had to be a series of well-organized social movements to put enough pressure on politicians. Meeting both conditions would create a great coalition capable of promoting far-reaching reforms, a situation that was only possible in the context of the political polarization of the 1940s.

With the approval of suffrage in 1949, women legally acquired the right to elect and be elected. However, nearly seventy-five years later, the struggle to give women access to power democratically continues, and we keep asking ourselves if perceptions on women's participation in politics have really changed. The struggle now focuses more on making viable parity reform, approved in 2009; on broadening political participation; and on negotiating, maintaining, and improving a series of reforms that tend to promote gender equality.[78]

Notes

1. Casal, "El feminismo y la mujer costarricense," 7.
2. Przeworski, "Conquered or Granted?," 291.
3. Przeworski, 291.
4. Purvis and Stanley Holton, *Votes for Women*; Rowbotham, *A Century of Women*; Lavrin, *Women, Feminism, and Social Change*, 257–352; Lavrin, "Recordando la Génesis del Sufragio Femenino en América Latina; Marino, "Latin America and the Caribbean."

5. Rodríguez, "La lucha por el sufragio femenino"; Rodríguez, "Movimientos Feministas y Sufragistas en América Central (1890–1965)."

6. Lavrin, *Women, Feminism, and Social Change*, 15–52, 257–352; Barrancos, *Historia mínima de los feminismos en América Latina*; Barrancos, *Mujeres en la Sociedad Argentina*; Valobra, *Del Hogar a las Urnas*; Barry, *Sufragio Femenino*; Miller, "The Suffrage Movement in Latin America," 168.

7. Acuña, *La Mujer Costarricense a través de Cuatro Siglos*, Tomo II; Rodríguez, "La lucha por el sufragio femenino"; Sharrat, "The Suffragist Movement in Costa Rica, 1889–1949."

8. Molina and Lehoucq, *Urnas de lo Inesperado*, 77–81; Lehoucq and Molina, *Stuffing the Ballot Box*, 118–55. For further analysis reassessing the women's suffrage movement, see McConnaughy, *Woman Suffrage*; Banaszak, *Why Movements Succeed or Fail?*; Aidt and Dallal, "Female Voting Power"; Caraway, "Inclusion and Democratization."

9. Molina and Lehouq, *Urnas de lo Inesperado*, 77–81, 193–200; Lehoucq and Molina, *Stuffing the Ballot Box*, 118–55.

10. For further analysis of topics, sources, and methodologies in women's and gender history in Costa Rica, see Rodriguez, "Historia de las Mujeres y de Género."

11. Lavrin, "Género e Historia," 72.

12. Molina, "Costa Rica," 599, 607; Molina and Palmer, *History of Costa Rica*.

13. Molina, "Reforma educativa y resistencia ciudadana en la Costa Rica de finales del siglo XIX," 60; Molina, *Demoperfectocracia*, 35–37.

14. Molina, *Demoperfectocracia*, 51–52.

15. Universal male suffrage was established in the city and province of Buenos Aires in 1821 and at the national level in 1853. Sabato, "Elecciones y prácticas electorales en Buenos Aires, 1860–1880," 108–13; Alonso, "Politics and Election in Buenos Aires," 474; Molina, *Demoperfectocracia*, 50.

16. Molina, *Demoperfectocracia*, 50, 56, 48, 132, 262–65.

17. Sobrado, "El régimen electoral en la Constitución de 1949," 8–9, 12–14, 25.

18. Sobrado, "La inscripción automática de electores en el ordenamiento electoral costarricense," 6; Sobrado, "Experiencia costarricense del voto de personas privadas de libertad," 2–3.

19. In Central America, *Ladino* refers to someone who speaks Spanish, who dresses in Western clothing, and whose cultural and religious practices are mostly derived from Europe. This category is contrasted against Indigenous people and people of African descent. Ladinos may have Indigenous ancestry, but their cultural practices distinguish them from those still living in Indigenous communities. Molina and Palmer, "Popular Literacy in a Tropical Democracy"; Molina, *La estela de la pluma*, 68–69.

20. Harms, *Ladina Social Activism in Guatemala City 1871–1954*, 165.

21. Rodríguez, "Women in Central America," 434–35; Rodríguez, "Del hogar al colegio y del colegio al hogar y a la calle."

22. Rodríguez, "Women in Central America," 434–35; Molina, "Desertores e inva-
     soras," 156; Eugenia Rodríguez, "Disciplinar para la maternidad y la acción
     social en el Colegio Superior de Señoritas (Costa Rica, 1888–1940)," *Descentrada*
     4, no. 1 (2020): 1–16; Palmer and Rojas, "Educando a las señoritas"; Palmer and
     Rojas, "Educating Señorita."
23. Rodríguez, "Women in Central America," 435; Marco, *Clara González de Beh-
     ringer*, 72; Acuña, *La Mujer Costarricense a través de Cuatro Siglos*, Tomo I, 367;
     Harms, *Ladina Social Activism*, 133; Borrayo, *Por la equidad de género en la edu-
     cación superior*, 19.
24. Rodríguez, "Women in Central America," 435; Rodríguez, "Desde Hoy el Voto";
     Villars, *Para la casa*, 186–87, 242–45, 248–49; Sonia Ticas, "Avances y retrocesos
     en el movimiento sufragista femenino salvadoreño en la década de 1920";
     Pérez, *Brief History of Central America*, 66–97.
25. Rodríguez, "Women in Central America," 435; Villars, *Para la casa*, 210, 222–50,
     256–80; Carrillo, *Las luchas de las guatemaltecas del siglo XX*, 47.
26. Rodríguez, "Women in Central America," 435; Rodríguez, "Desde Hoy el Voto,"
     397–98, 403–4; Mérida, "Mujer y ciudadanía," 38.
27. Lindo, "Las salvadoreñas fueron las verdaderas pioneras del voto femenino en
     Latinoamérica"; Miller, "Suffrage Movement," 168.
28. Miller, *Latin American Women*, 68–109; Lavrin, *Women, Feminism, and Social
     Change*, 1–14.
29. Rodríguez, "Women in Central America," 434–38; Rodríguez, "Movimientos
     Feministas y Sufragistas," 290–91; González, *Before the Revolution*, 49–51; Marco,
     "El Movimiento Sufragista en Panamá y la Construcción de la Mujer Moderna."
30. See Victoria González's chapter in this volume.
31. Rodríguez, "Movimientos Feministas y Sufragistas," 290–91; Rodríguez,
     "Women in Central America," 434–38.
32. Mora, *Rompiendo Mitos y Forjando Historia*, 245–81; Mora, "Redefiniendo la
     política"; Rodríguez, "Mujeres, Elecciones, Democracia y Guerra Fría en Costa
     Rica (1948–1953)"; Rodríguez, "Madres, Reformas Sociales y Sufragismo."
33. Barahona, *Las Sufragistas de Costa Rica*, 43.
34. Mora, "La mujer obrera en la educación y en el discurso periodístico en Costa
     Rica (1900–1930)."
35. Acuña, *La Mujer Costarricense*, 1:343–58.
36. *La Gaceta*, August 21, 1913 (44), 229.
37. Obregón, *Las Constituciones de Costa Rica*, 12–15.
38. Mora, *Rompiendo Mitos*, 245–61.
39. Acuña, *La Mujer Costarricense*, 315; Palmer and Rojas, "Educando a las señori-
     tas," 121–22; Palmer and Rojas, "Educating Señorita," 78–80.
40. Rodríguez, "La lucha por el sufragio femenino," 87–110.
41. Miller, *Latin American Women*, 68–109; Lavrin, *Women, Feminism, and Social
     Change*, 15–52.

42. Palmer and Rojas, "Educando a las señoritas"; Palmer and Rojas, "Educating Señorita."

43. *La Gaceta*, July 26, 1925 (170); *Gaceta*, August 31, 1927 (200), 1338.

44. Solano, "La Liga Feminista Costarricense," 42–43.

45. Casal, *El voto femenino*.

46. Molina, *Moradas y Discursos*, 37–38; Molina, *Anticomunismo Reformista*.

47. Rodríguez, "Madres, Reformas Sociales," 49–84; Rodríguez, "Las mujeres y el Partido Comunista de Costa Rica."

48. Rodríguez, "Mujeres, Elecciones, Democracia," 39–75; Rodríguez, "Anticomunismo, Género y Guerra Fría," 144–46.

49. Chacón,"Las Mujeres del 2 de Agosto de 1947 en la Vida Política del País," 172.

50. Bowman, "¿Fue el Compromiso y Consenso de las Elites lo que Llevó a la Consolidación Democrática en Costa Rica?"

51. Lehoucq and Molina, *Stuffing the Ballot Box*; Lehoucq, "Political Competition and Electoral Fraud."

52. "La mayoría se pronuncia contra el voto femenino. Se hacen objeciones al trámite especial adoptado en este caso," *Diario de Costa Rica*, February 25, 1925, 4; "Por 33 votos contra 8 quedó establecido el voto femenino," *Diario de Costa Rica*, June 21, 1949, 1, 8; "Otorgado el voto femenino," *La Nación*, June 21, 1949, 1, 7.

53. Lehoucq and Molina, *Stuffing the Ballot Box*, 118–55; Molina and Lehoucq, *Urnas de lo inesperado*, 77–81, 193–200.

54. *La Gaceta*, November 5, 1920.

55. "El discurso del diputado Quirós al discutirse el voto femenino en el Congreso," *Diario de Costa Rica*, March 15, 1925, 6.

56. "La Comisión Especial del Congreso y la Ley de Elecciones. No podrán votar las mujeres," *Diario de Costa Rica*, February 20, 1925, 1.

57. Lehoucq and Molina, *Stuffing the Ballot Box*, 252.

58. Acuña, *La Mujer Costarricense*, 2:362.

59. Lavrin, *Women, Feminism, and Social Change* 312–13, 355.

60. *La Gaceta*, May 3, 1931, 723.

61. Molina and Lehoucq, *Urnas de lo inesperado*, 155.

62. Molina and Lehoucq, *Urnas de lo inesperado*, 158.

63. Molina and Lehoucq, *Urnas de lo inesperado*, 160.

64. Molina and Lehoucq, *Urnas de lo inesperado*, 161.

65. Rodríguez, "Mujeres, Elecciones, Democracia," 39–75; Rodríguez, "Anticomunismo, Género y Guerra Fría," 144–46.

66. Flores, "'Ni Histéricas, Ni Reinas . . . Ciudadanas,'" 147–48.

67. For further analysis on changing CRCP positions about the women's vote, see Rodríguez, "Las mujeres y el Partido Comunista," 1–16.

68. Barahona, *Las sufragistas*, 175.

69. "La nación debe dar prueba mayor y más tangible de su confianza en la mujer

costarricense," *Diario de Costa Rica*, May 16, 1943, 1, 3; Rodríguez, "Madres, Reformas Sociales y Sufragismo."

70. "Comentario en torno al voto femenino," *Mujer y Hogar*, May 29, 1947, 2; "Mujeres de Costa Rica: Ha llegado el momento de que se reconozcan vuestra personalidad y vuestros derechos," *Mujer y Hogar*, June 12, 1947, 1, 2, 5.

71. Rodríguez, "Mujeres, Elecciones, Democracia," 39–75; Rodríguez, "Anticomunismo, Género y Guerra Fría," 144–46; Chacón, "Las Mujeres del 2 de Agosto de 1947," 134–45.

72. Molina and Lehouq, *Urnas de lo inesperado*, 181–91.

73. Fernández, *El voto femenino en Costa Rica*," 49–50. These statements by the deputies were transcribed from the constituent debate of June 20, 1949.

74. Fernández, *El voto femenino en Costa Rica*, 52.

75. Lawrence, "Desde la barra. 8 contra el voto femenino," *La Prensa Libre*, June 21, 1949, 3.

76. "La mayoría se pronuncia," *Diario de Costa Rica*, February 25, 1925, 4; "Por 33 votos contra 8," *Diario de Costa Rica*, June 21, 1949, 1, 8; "Otorgado el voto femenino," *La Nación*, June 21, 1949, 1, 7; Lawrence, "Desde la barra," *La Prensa Libre*, June 21, 1949, 3; "Mayoría abrumadora en la constituyente obtuvo el Partido Unión Nacional," *La Prensa Libre*, January 4, 1949, 2.

77. Acuña, "'Nuestros derechos' nos interesan a las feministas," 6.

78. Rodríguez, "Mujeres, Elecciones, Democracia," 39–75; Rodríguez, "Women in Central America"; Zamora, *Mujeres y derechos políticos electorales*; Isabel Torres, "Paridad para el fortalecimiento de la democracia incluyente: el caso de Costa Rica."

CHAPTER TWO

Fractured Landscapes

Women and the Long Struggle for Suffrage and Political Equality in Canada

VERONICA STRONG-BOAG

UNTIL RECENTLY, SCHOLARSHIP AND POPULAR opinion largely took for granted Canadians' achievement of the electoral franchise for all women. As the account commonly went, women easily won the federal vote during World War I (with the Wartime Elections Act in 1917 and the Act to Confer the Federal Franchise upon Women in 1918) and in the provinces and territories beginning in 1916 with Manitoba, Saskatchewan, and Alberta and in 1917 with British Columbia and Ontario, followed in 1918 by Nova Scotia, in 1919 by New Brunswick and the Yukon, in 1922 by Prince Edward Island, in 1925 by Newfoundland and Labrador (not part of Canada until 1949), in 1940 in Quebec, and in 1951 in the Northwest Territories. Very tardily admitted was the exclusion of many Asian and Indigenous women and men until after World War II. The imposition of European patriarchy on Indigenous communities and the persistence of colonialism in Canada's constitutional monarchy and parliamentary governments were similarly largely ignored, as was women's ongoing disadvantage in many urban governments and in post-suffrage elections. Democracy remains an unfinished project in the northernmost state of the Americas.

Fortunately, at the end of the twentieth century, Canadian feminists—both scholars and activists—emerged to challenge inadequate memory and representation. They did so in the context of growing recognition of the nation's history as a colonial state founded on the dispossession of Indigenous peoples and the oppression of non-British settler peoples, and a lesser appreciation that class remained a key determinant of political as well as other rewards. Canada was increasingly understood as far from the "just society" it often claims to be. The recent six-volume series *Women Suffrage and the Struggle for Democracy in Canada*, published by UBC Press, targets long-standing assumptions about women's struggle for political equality.[1] Critically expanding on earlier studies on the Canadian movement,[2] its feminist authors present suffrage stories as expressions of a politics of colonialism, race, and class, as well as gender. For the first time, Indigenous, Asian, Black, and working-class women are integrated into Canada's struggle for female enfranchisement. This chapter benefits from my general editorship of the series and my authorship of *The Last Suffragist Standing: The Life and Times of Laura Marshall Jamieson* (2018) and *A Liberal-Labour Lady: The Times and Life of Mary Ellen Spear Smith* (2021), which spotlight, respectively, the last suffragist elected to a Canadian legislature and the first female cabinet minister in the British Empire and Commonwealth.

Arguments here emphasize three themes in women's struggle for greater democracy in the northern half of North America, and none are unique to Canada. They begin with the commonly overlooked difficulties for reformers presented by Canada's structure of multilevel governance. Whether you examine the political institutions of Indigenous or settler communities, Canada has produced diverse, evolving, and confusing forms of rule. These challenge women's (and other) movements seeking to expand political rights. The second theme emphasizes the continuing masculinism, colonialism, and partiality of all governments. With rare exceptions, such as the Six Nations of the Iroquois Confederacy in Ontario, the public realm everywhere (like much of the private) favored and subsidized male leadership. Race, ethnicity, status, and property further largely determined who got to exercise political power. Those constraints did not end with suffrage victories. The third theme stresses the diversity of women's movements for recognition and redress.[3] Feminism never provided a unifying standard for the suffragists or their successors. Identities associated with class and status, race/ethnicity, religion, and region regularly generated distinctive and sometimes conflicting agendas. The middle-class European and Christian settler women who dominated the suffrage campaigns did not readily share power with Indigenous, Asian, African, or working-class Canadians, and women in those communities often had their own agendas for improving their lives. In other words, fractured governance; masculinist, colonialist, and otherwise prejudiced authorities; and diverse women's movements offer plentiful reminders that Canada's struggle for democracy has been difficult, contested, and incomplete.

The Challenge of Fractured Governance

The governance of the territory now known as Canada has never been simple. Imperial governments' occupation of Indigenous territories, beginning with New France and continuing into British North America and the Dominion of Canada, kept duties and rights in flux and generally far from clear to residents, who originated in many different Indigenous and settler communities and often had little trust in or experience with formal electoral politics as it evolved in a parliamentary system headed by a constitutional monarch after the 1760 British conquest. Suspicion of authorities and ignorance of the details of rule, not to mention the demands of survival and communication, in the largest nation in the Americas, which eventually claimed almost 10 million square kilometers, always undermined attention to formal politics and collaboration in its reform.[4]

Officially established in 1867, the Dominion of Canada has not been set in stone: experimentation with Indigenous–settler relations, political boundaries, legislative representation, financial arrangements, areas of jurisdiction, and franchises continued into the twenty-first century. Canadians brought diverse histories to their encounter with an evolving political landscape. There was never a single response to Indigenous–settler, national–imperial, federal–provincial/territorial, or urban–senior government relations. Shifting arrangements proved a recurring minefield that few women or men fully understood or felt capable of mastering. Scholars have often been of little help in explaining fundamental "political architecture" or "how functions are shared or divided between different levels of government."[5] Another recurring failing has been general indifference to Indigenous governance before and after contact. Many Indigenous women and men, although not all or at all times, have felt "neither part of settler society nor the settler state."[6]

The dispossession and continuing oppression of Indigenous nations has been fundamental to imperial governance and largely taken for granted by settler society, including the suffragists. After confederation, the federal Indian Act installed a system of subordinated local rule on reserves somewhat akin to but ultimately far more oppressive than the lower levels of government established in Canadian cities and towns.[7] Like European conventions regarding nationality, the act confirmed male authority in public life. Unfortunately, little has been published about Indigenous women's involvement in the politics of their communities, and next to nothing about their attitudes toward the suffrage campaigns. Most Indigenous women, like those interviewed by Audra Simpson in *Mohawk Interruptus*, have reason to consider Canadian citizenship at best a matter of convenience, especially when crossing state borders, rather than a primary identification.[8]

In fact, only a minority of women anywhere have ever been active in rights campaigns. While federal systems can offer the advantage of "competing" governments with possibilities for "policy innovation and policy experimentation" or, less positively, "exit" from hostile environments,[9] pervasive misogyny and domestic and caring responsibilities have everywhere handicapped women's political choices in a nation long coined a liberal democracy. Most Indigenous people and Canadians have focused on local issues commonly far from the attention of scholars. Ultimately, suffrage supplied the "great cause," as it was known in the English-speaking world, for only a relatively small number of determined activists. Whatever their prioritization of the vote, however, suffragists and other women's rights activists navigated a political landscape that offered little encouragement or access, although admittedly sometimes more, even a great deal more, than that in many other nations of the Americas.

In (re)settling the northern half of the continent,[10] newcomers, like Indigenous peoples, were far from homogenous. Scattered across the continent, few shared histories of political engagement and much prejudice divided them, even as emerging federal, provincial, and territorial administrations deliberately shored up colonial elites. While the British asserted dominance everywhere, French Canadians (France and Britain were routinely considered Canada's two "charter" nations) similarly insisted upon the superiority of their own traditions, and both groups readily discriminated against others. French Canadian activists faced the special challenge of having to assert their right to "survivance" as Catholic and French in a continent dominated by English-speaking Protestants. As Denyse Baillargeon has confirmed in *To Be Equals in Our Own Country*, the Quebecois, of whom only a handful were anticlerical, fought to develop an activism marked by social Catholicism and nationalism in groups such as the Fédération nationale Saint-Jean-Baptiste (founded in 1907). Their Eurocentrism had counterparts in groups such as the Imperial Order Daughters of the Empire (founded in 1900) with its celebration of a Britannic sisterhood. Such perspectives readily viewed woman suffrage and other ethnic or racial groups with suspicion and associated them with American lawlessness.

Politics was additionally shaped by strong regional identities rooted in geography and history. The expansion of imperial Canada from dispersed colonies to ten provinces and three territories by 1949 challenged activists and the electorate to learn what services would be delivered by what level of government, to whom, and what citizens owed in return. As the UBC suffrage series confirms, activists were often isolated in Atlantic, central, prairie, Pacific, and northern Canada. Many reform-minded Canadians sought inspiration from the United Kingdom (the British suffragists/suffragettes were especially influential), from adjacent US states, and from New Zealand (a suffrage pioneer) and Australia. Indigenous activists have similarly been in contact with counterparts elsewhere. Global linkages could sometimes be more significant than what was happening in other Canadian regions, but few Canadians paid close attention to nations south of the United States.

Although the 1885 Franchise Act introduced by the government of Prime Minister John A. Macdonald asserted federal control of voting regulation, including the exclusion of all women, Canadians, except for activists in the Woman's Christian Temperance Union (WCTU) who provided the early suffrage muscle in most provinces and a handful in Ontario who aspired to national leadership, largely ignored the central government before World War I. After 1898, when the administration of Prime Minister Wilfrid Laurier surrendered the right to determine the federal franchise, campaigns concentrated on the provinces, with the expectation that victories there would confer federal rights. Suffrage and political equality groups emerged, especially in the West and Ontario, to target provincial exclusions. When in 1910 the cautious National Council of Women of Canada (founded in 1893 by Ishbel, Lady Aberdeen [1857–1939], a British suffragist and the wife of the governor-general, the monarch's representative) endorsed enfranchisement, victory seemed close at hand. The demands and conflicts of World War I initially curtailed momentum, but when a national wartime government reasserted federal control over voters' lists in 1917, attention returned to Ottawa battles. The highly controversial Wartime Elections Act enfranchised military nurses and some female relatives of Canadian servicemen in the government's desperate effort to secure reelection in a nation divided by war. A year later, amid much talk of gratitude for war service and suggestion that women had now proved their merits, the House of Commons federally enfranchised most white women, including those still denied the provincial ballot in the Maritimes and Quebec, even as it continued to exclude Indigenous women everywhere and Asian women already disenfranchised, along with Asian men, by provinces. After World War I, the vast majority of suffrage agitation focused on provincial holdouts and ignored racial exclusions.

Canada's political landscape for rights-seekers was further complicated by deepening urban development. Organized farmers, such the Women's Section of the Saskatchewan Grain Growers (founded in 1913), could be powerful suffragists and were especially influential on the Canadian prairies, but agriculturalists were increasingly on the defensive. By 1921 the majority of Canadians resided in towns and cities. While many suffragists professed to revere rural life, most targeted urban governments to improve lives. Such was the choice of the Vancouver suffragist—later social democratic member of the BC legislature and city councilor—Laura Jamieson (1882–1964), who championed a broad municipal franchise, since "civic government is the beginning of socialism," alongside inclusive provincial and federal franchises.[11] Although her social democratic hopes were unusual, many activists prioritized municipal franchises, and Canadian victories in cities and towns began in the 1870s, even as women remained a force in agricultural organizations.

Multiple levels of rule mounted enormous challenges for democratic reformers. Canadians have often been ill-informed about entitlements and exclusions, and suffragists confronted ignorance and isolation. On the other hand, competing sites of governance sometimes presented what political scientists term "new political opportunity structures."[12] Band, civic, and school and library board campaigns could prove consciousness-raising and help foster broader political networks. Some suffragist and other veterans of local causes gained the experience and the self-confidence to demand a hearing as well from other levels of government.

Partial Authorities

Advocates of greater democracy in Canada faced more than a complicated, intimidating, and obscure landscape of governance. Everywhere the right to rule involved exclusion and prejudice. Reflecting the spirit of earlier northern Loyalists (as refugees from the American Revolution were termed) who had equated the United States with lawlessness,[13] the 1867 confederation of the British colonies was not intended to unleash democracy.[14] Indeed, earlier colonial governments had eliminated franchises that included a few propertied women. Although African, Asian, and Indigenous men never faced wholesale formal exclusion, no woman of any origin entered the new nation as a politically enfranchised subject.

While Indigenous societies ranged from the relatively egalitarian to the highly ranked, from the matrilineal to the patrilineal, and differed in expectations for women, whose status ranged from leadership to slavery, the 1876 federal Indian Act imposed a homogenous Euro-patriarchal band government that enfranchised only men and counted descent solely through the male line.[15] In 1885 Canada's first nationwide franchise act confirmed discrimination. It explicitly excluded all Indians west of Ontario (who were reckoned less assimilated or civilized than their eastern counterparts) and most elsewhere, all Chinese, and all women. One parliamentary speaker summed up the preferred crew for northern North America's new "ship of state":

> As that beautiful craft came sailing in, we saw a fair spinster and a charming widow standing on the deck; the "heathen Chinee" was in the cabin, and the banded Indian was concealed in the hold. Sir, we have quickly disposed of the ladies; we have kicked them on shore; the "heathen Chinee" we have strangled; the banded Indian we have dragged from his concealment, and those of them that were of no immediate use, we have put on shore, but we will retain them in the old Provinces.[16]

Whiteness and masculinity formed the original linchpins of full citizenship.

The emergence of the modern party system in the late nineteenth and early twentieth centuries confirmed women's political exclusion. Parties disproportionately organized middle-class men of British (and occasionally French) descent for the spoils of office. Before World War I, none paid much attention to women. Only female enfranchisement changed their calculation. Canada's two mainstream parties, the Liberal Party and the Conservative Party, followed by later parties on the left, such as the Cooperative Commonwealth Federation (CCF), and on the right, such as Social Credit, largely enlisted female recruits for organizational chores, fundraising, and the pretense of democracy. Women were expected to supply loyal subordinates and promote male rule without asking troublesome questions.[17] That strategy would not have surprised suffragists, whose earliest campaigns identified "partyism" and male cronyism as central to inequality.[18]

Male partisanship was accompanied by racial and class prejudice. Chinese, East Asians, and Japanese in British Columbia and all Inuits, Doukhobors (with their conscientious objections to war), and status Indians waited for federal enfranchisement until after World War II.[19] Similarly, many working-class Canadians were rarely credited with qualities suitable for intelligent citizenship. Urban franchises routinely rewarded propertied residents, and some jurisdictions allowed corporations multiple votes, effectively reinforcing gender and racial advantage. Not until the 1960s and beyond did major cities like Toronto, Vancouver, and Halifax slowly broaden the electorate. In Halifax, married women lacked full municipal voting rights until 1963.[20] The survival of nonresident property franchises into the twenty-first century in some cities maintained the old equation of "the franchise with property and wealth" and thus the practical favoring of white men.[21] The emergence of what has been termed the "liberal order" in the course of the nineteenth and early twentieth centuries, with the introduction of the secret ballot and voter registration rules,[22] did little to challenge the systemic power of long-standing settler elites. Not surprisingly, voter apathy, notably among disadvantaged populations, has undermined the legitimacy of Canadian elections.[23]

The situation within modern First Nations communities has been little better. Until 1951 the federal Indian Act denied women the vote in band elections and the right to hold band office.[24] Many "male Indigenous leaders resisted women's mandates, arguing that their claims to membership and gender equality undermined the overall Indigenous rights movement."[25] Prejudice showed in women's access to official positions. Only in 1954 was the first woman (Elsie Knott [1922–1995] of Ontario's Curve Lake Band) elected chief of a First Nations band.[26] Only in 2021, despite earlier well-qualified candidates, was a woman, RoseAnne Archibald (b. 1966) of Ontario's Taykwa Tagamou Nation, elected grand chief of the Assembly of First Nations, Canada's leading official champion for Indigenous peoples. In short, Indigenous governments, overwhelmingly dominated by men, were often uncertain allies in challenging the patriarchal order imposed and enforced by Ottawa.[27] The Native Women's Association of Canada (founded in 1974) and Pauktuutit Inuit Women of Canada (founded in 1984) emerged to channel claims for justice and political rights.

Other levels of government also proved reluctant when it came to post-suffrage equality. Not until 1929 did women, effectively those who were white, gain recognition as "persons" under the 1867 British North America Act from the judicial committee of the British Privy Council and become eligible for appointment to the Canadian Senate.[28] Not until 1947 did the nationality of settler women become independent of marriage. Not until 1985 did the Canadian Charter of Rights and Freedoms guarantee women equality with men. It took until that year as well to see the federal government start to equalize women's status under the Indian Act. While Canada produced its first female premier in 1991 (Social Credit's Rita Johnston [b. 1935] for six months in British Columbia) and its first female prime minister (the Conservative Party's Kim Campbell for four months in 1993), both of whom inherited toppling regimes,[29] gender equality in cabinets waited until 2000 in the Yukon Territory and until 2007 in the province of Quebec. Alberta and the federal government followed in 2015. While there were notable exceptions, such as Ottawa's Charlotte Whitton (1896–1975), who became the first mayor of a major city in 1951 (supplying a commonplace instance of a politician denying feminist sympathies), municipal victories were similarly glacial. Not until 1989 did Edmonton elect a female mayor (Jan Reimer [b. 1952]), while Toronto waited until 1991 (June Rowlands [1924–2017]) and Halifax a year longer (Moira Ducharme). Montreal's first came in 2017 (Valérie Plante [b. 1974]). In Vancouver the glass ceiling survived in 2021.

At the beginning of the 2020s, a bedrock of prejudice persists in the anti-women politics of some administrations. Although a self-professed male feminist deposed a reactionary administration federally in 2015, an anti-feminist provincial government was elected in Ontario in 2018 and in Alberta in 2019.[30] Yet, although male elites continue to dominate both Indigenous and settler communities, "tradition itself is contested terrain."[31] Some Indigenous and settler men have always questioned patriarchy and sought to share power. Male suffragists have successors in male allies of subsequent feminist movements.[32] The history of the struggle for democracy and decolonization includes conflict among men, as well as women, about what exactly constitutes the proper gendering of political life.

Diverse women's movements

Women developed no single response to Canada's multiple sites of patriarchal and colonial rule. The size of the country, the diversity of the population, the imposition of colonialism, the effective obscurity of many rights and obligations, and the rivalries and prejudices of different communities fostered isolation and fragmentation. Women regularly disagreed about the most meaningful field of action, specific strategies, and preferred outcomes.

That fact that the "personal is political" often encouraged a focus on individual groups and disinterest in the plight of others.

Indigenous communities are the place to begin in acknowledging women's ongoing diversity. Different economies, kinship systems, and relations with colonial authorities have fostered diverse responses. While frequently handicapped by disproportionate responsibility for maintaining households and families, some Indigenous women publicly challenged colonial rule. The Ojibwa Catherine Sutton, or Nahnebahwequay (1824–1865), took demands for land rights to Queen Victoria in 1860, and the Mohawk-English poet-performer Emily Pauline Johnson (1861–1913) appealed to the general public in declaring that "might did not make right" in Ottawa's suppression and starvation of western tribes.[33] In the later twentieth century, Indigenous activists organized in groups such as Ontario's Women's Institutes, the Indian Homemakers of British Columbia, Indian Rights for Indian Women, and the Native Women's Association of Canada.[34] Until the 1980s, links with settler women activists were rare. Although a few voted in pre-confederation elections,[35] Indigenous women were largely invisible in suffrage campaigns; their exclusion from band government was similarly ignored. The commonplace prejudice of settler activists only hardened during the intensified dispossession of Indigenous peoples that occurred alongside the emergence of Canada's first feminist movement.

Indigenous women were not the only group absent from mainstream suffragist campaigns. The French–English divide stretching from the British conquest to the present almost always fractured mainstream Canadian women's politics. Francophones often concentrated on cultural survival in a continent dominated by English speakers. The hostility of the Catholic Church to feminism and recurring Anglophone prejudice made alliances between the Quebecois and the heavily Protestant English-speaking suffrage movement, with its frequent sense of Britannic superiority, all the more difficult. Nevertheless, activists such as Idola Saint-Jean (1880–1945)[36] and Thérèse Casgrain (1896–1981) led groups such as the Alliance canadienne pour le vote des femmes au Québec, which were essential in securing the last provincial franchise for white women. The double meaning of *To Be Equals in Our Own Country*, the title of Denyse Baillargeon's contribution to the series

Women's Suffrage and the Struggle for Democracy, provides an apt reminder of both gender and ethnic oppression.

Although they were often suspicious of non-British communities, mainstream suffragists found allies in preferred immigrants such as the Icelanders who settled in Manitoba, where they proved a match for activists anywhere. Women with origins in southern and eastern Europe were far more unusual as suffrage advocates. A Black American abolitionist, Mary Ann Shadd Cary (1823–1893), pioneered Ontario's suffrage politics, but she remained an isolated figure.[37] Asian women, such as the pathbreaking journalist Edith Maude Eaton (1865–1914; known better by her pen name, Sui Sin Far), found no warmer welcome and have been hard to find among suffragists.[38] Not surprisingly, women in disadvantaged groups largely concentrated on their own communities rather than seeking uncertain suffragist allies.

Canada's franchise crusade was frequently equally inadequate when it came to courting working-class women, who faced assessment as in need of guidance and remaking in the national interest. Not surprisingly, female workers did not readily rally to the cause. Activists generally preferred to concentrate their hopes for equality in the nation's early Social Democratic and socialist groups, whose support proved far from certain, as they prioritized class. A few such as British Columbia's Helena Gutteridge (1879–1960), an activist with the Vancouver Trades and Labour Council and a veteran of Britain's Women's Social and Political Union, strengthened suffrage campaigns while maintaining working-class loyalties.[39] Lara Campbell's contribution to the UBC Press suffrage series, *A Great Revolutionary Wave,* highlights the uniqueness of Canada's Pacific province in possessing a significant group of working-class suffragists.

As difficult as relations were with women beyond the British and French middle class, Canada's suffragists could not rely on full support even from their own communities. Relatively privileged settler women might resent gender unfairness in families, schools, churches, employment, and law, but many accepted ubiquitous traditions insisting that they defer to men in public life. Many also cherished the privileges of class and race. And just as with other women, domestic and caring responsibilities, increasingly combined with waged labor, left few with the time, energy, or inclination to organize for political rights.[40] Nellie L. McClung (1873–1951), Canada's best-known suffragist and later a member of Alberta's provincial legislature, condemned such bystanders to politics in her polemical *In Times Like These* (1915) as "gentle ladies" who cared for no one but themselves.[41]

In the final analysis, only a relatively small cadre of largely middle-class and British women maintained Canada's suffrage crusade. Their mobilization depended heavily on the feminist consciousness developed by pioneers in nineteenth- and early twentieth-century schools and universities and in employment and professions, a coterie highlighted in the monumental volume *Women of Canada: Their Life and Work* (1900), produced by the National Council of Women for the Great Paris Exposition of that year. Such Canadian "new women" formed part of a courageous international brigade in highlighting the limits of so-called chivalry and in demanding justice for those like themselves. Suffragists' investigation of violence against women and children, notably by the ubiquitous WCTU, was equally important in consciousness-raising. Its activists were early advocates of the vote to combat the male drinking, violence, and waste of family resources familiar to many communities. Such reformers easily linked their sex's vulnerability to political exclusion. By the beginning of the twentieth century, women's press clubs, business and professional women's clubs, the National Council of Women, university women's clubs, and the WCTU had joined a host of political equality clubs and equal franchise clubs to demand the vote. Their members found regular pulpits in the popular press, which in Canada, as elsewhere, was central to the expansion of democracy.

Suffragists achieved pioneering (and often deeply resisted) improvements in maternity care, schools, education, child welfare, rights to property, and guardianship of children. Their efforts underpinned the slow emergence of Canada's modern welfare state and were often associated with what was known as the New Liberalism, which sought to counter socialist and communist challenges to capitalism. A handful of female politicians, such as Agnes Macphail (1890–1954) in the federal arena, Mary Ellen Smith (1863–1933) in British Columbia, and McClung in Alberta fought to transfer progressive, liberal, and occasionally socialist hopes for equality into electoral politics. Despite significant advances, they could only temper men's control of government and confidence in their own superiority. Not until the

1970s, with the reappearance of organized feminism, would women appear in any numbers in Canada's provincial or federal legislatures.

Only slowly did lessons learned by groups in antifascist, civil rights, and peace movements, such as the Women's International League for Peace and Freedom after World War I and the Voice of Women/la Voix des femmes after World War II, enlarge mainstream consciousness of prejudice and disadvantage. In 1970, the report of the landmark federal Royal Commission on the Status of Women/la Commission royale d'enquête sur la situation de la femme highlighted both sexism and the wrongs done to Indigenous women. In subsequent decades, mainstream feminism's growing recognition of Canada as a state founded in the dispossession of Indigenous peoples, racial prejudice, and class division slowly produced dreams of a new politics. The Fédération des femmes du Québec, the National Action Committee on the Status of Women (NAC), and the Canadian Feminist Alliance for International Action/l'Alliance féministe pour l'action internationale adopted an intersectional analysis of oppression that linked them to antiracist and civil rights campaigners.[42]

While solidarity remained uncertain, the demand of Indigenous women for equal status under the Indian Act "fostered unity with non-Indigenous feminists" against both colonial governments and Indigenous opponents. The Native Women's Association of Canada became the first nationwide group to question male leaders' use of tradition as a defense of gender inequality and men's monopoly of political life.[43] In the 1980s it found major feminist mainstream allies in insisting on women's representation in national discussions about constitutional reform.[44] Such alliances prompted unprecedented conclusions from Indigenous women that feminism "does not belong to any particular group, and those who understand and practice the social idea of ending gender inequality and injustice are feminist."[45] One expression of new links was the 2019 election of the Inuk Mumilaaq Qaqqaq (b. 1993) as the New Democratic Party's member of Parliament for Nunavut. The twenty-five-year-old was a veteran of the Daughters of the Vote, a feminist program run by Equal Voice/À Voix égales, which focused on increasing the number of women in political office even as it cited the suffragist legacy. However, her choice not to contest the 2021 federal election confirmed the obstacles facing Indigenous women in particular, and even the selection of an Inuit woman, Mary Simon (b. 1947), as governor-general in the same year does not supersede that harsh fact.

By the end of the twentieth century, Asian women, Black women, and other women of color, such as Rosemary Brown (1930–2003) of the New Democratic Party and Sunera Thobani (b. 1957) of the National Action Committee, became outspoken in feminist campaigns for equality, but they continued to face prejudice. Protests such as Idle No More and Black Lives Matter, which included many feminists, testify to Canada's battle with systemic racism in the twenty-first century. Lesbians similarly challenged intolerance even as women such as Judy Rebick (b. 1945) of NAC supplied some of Canadian feminism's most effective representatives.

Yet ultimately, for all their differences, Canada's female and feminist champions have shared powerful clusters of mutual interest, many dating from the nineteenth-century suffrage campaigns. First of all, advocates for women in all communities paid special attention to caring labor, notably with regard to children, and regularly espoused maternalist ideals of their sex's duties to the world.[46] Second, they condemned violence against women and children and more generally in society. Third, they readily denounced discrimination against wives and mothers in family law (notably equality in marriage, divorce, and child custody) and demanded legal reforms. Fourth, they demanded equality in education and employment and recognition of women's responsibilities as mothers. And fifth, female activists were everywhere linked to transnational movements of protest. Such shared concerns foster alliances across many divides even as differences have to be acknowledged and negotiated.

Conclusion

By the end of the twentieth century, Canada had produced two prime ministers (Kim Campbell [b. 1947] and Justin Trudeau [b. 1971]) and several premiers (for example, Alberta's Rachel Notley [b. 1974] and British Columbia's John Horgan [1959]) who publicly identified as feminists. In 1999 a Chinese Canadian, Adrienne Clarkson (b. 1939), was appointed governor-general. Six years later the post went to a feminist of Haitian origin, Michaëlle Jean (b.

1957). In 2015 it went to Canada's second female astronaut, Julie Payette (b. 1963), and in 2021 it went to Mary Simon, a long-standing champion of Inuit rights. In 2017 "nearly 23 percent of women" in Parliament were "visible minorities, while the same is true of only 16 percent of men," and in 2015 an Indigenous woman activist from British Columbia, Jody Wilson-Raybould (b. 1971), became the federal minister of justice. While shifts were far from secure, as was evident in Notley's loss in 2019 to a reactionary regime and Wilson-Raybould's resignation that same year, advances depended on suffragist and subsequent feminist activism.[47]

The Canadian situation is best characterized as "stalled," the title of a 2013 volume on women's representation in government.[48] As Indigenous scholar Joyce Green concluded, "Incremental successes occasionally obtained by using a legal and political system designed by and for settler, race, class and male privilege will not secure profound institutional and cultural changes any time soon." It is estimated that "at the current pace, it will be more than 90 years" before women match men's numbers in the federal Parliament.[49] Provinces, territories, cities, and First Nations are often only little better. Canada has a long way to go to get beyond "the anemic equality values of the settler state."[50]

In sum, the original Canadian suffragists and subsequent equality seekers sought justice in a landscape of complex, conflicting, and often obscure governance. The patriarchal and colonial contamination of all sites of rule divided and exhausted activists. Settler suffragists fought hard and courageously for political rights for themselves, but only late in the twentieth century, under pressure from Indigenous and women activists of color, did mainstream Canadian feminists question class and race hierarchies. Long after the battles for the vote, northern North America continues to struggle for democracy.

Notes

1.   See Sangster, *One Hundred Years of Struggle*; Brookfield, *Our Voices Must Be Heard*; Baillargeon, *To Be Equals in Our Own Country*; Campbell, *A Great Revolutionary Wave*; Carter, *Ours by Every Law of Right and Justice*; and MacDonald, *We Shall Persist*.

2. The most important of these include Cleverdon, *The Woman Suffrage Movement in Canada*, and Bacchi, *Liberation Deferred?*

3. These politics, associated with theorists Charles Taylor and Nancy Fraser, are effectively summed up in Paddy McQueen, "Social and Political Recognition," *Internet Encyclopedia of Philosophy*, https://www.iep.utm.edu/recog_sp, accessed August 24, 2023.

4. In the twenty-first century, much is said about the distrust of politicians and politics. Often it is offered as an explanation of the rise of right-wing populism. Women's distrust was often mentioned during suffrage campaigns, but this is for the most part unstudied. Rare scholarly discussion of distrust often concentrates on class, race, and indigeneity. See, for example, Monica Hwang, "Ethnicity and Political Trust in Canada: Is There a Deepening Divide?" *Canadian Journal of Sociology/Cahiers Canadiens de sociologie* 42, no. 1 (2017): 22–54. Her otherwise interesting analysis ignores gender.

5. Marian Sawer and Jill Vickers, "Introduction: Political Architecture and Its Gender Impact" in *Federalism, Feminism and Multilevel Governance*, ed. Melissa Haussman, Marian Sawer, and Jill Vickers (London: Routledge, 2016), 3.

6. I add the reservation here, but Kiera L. Ladner does not in her invaluable reminder "Indigenous Peoples and Multilevel Governance in Canada" in Haussman et al., *Federalism, Feminism and Multilevel Governance*, 68. I also question her assertion that "Indigenous women's movements are grounded in completely different cultural realities and historical circumstances" (68) as failing to acknowledge the diversity of both Indigenous and non-Indigenous women's lives. Despite these reservations, Ladner's insistence on the ongoing significance of Indigenous governance remains very true and is too often overlooked.

7. For the similarity to municipalities, see J. Anthony Long and Menno Boldt, "Leadership Selection in Canadian Indian Communities: Reforming the Present and Incorporating the Past," *Great Plains Quarterly* (Spring 1987): 103–15. Long and Boldt also confirm the earlier findings of H. B. Hawthorn, ed., *A Survey of the Contemporary Indians of Canada: Economic, Political, Educational Needs and Policy* (Ottawa: Indian Affairs Branch, 1967), which emphasized the significance of kinship in determining candidates and election outcomes, almost all of which favored men. Unfortunately, neither the Hawthorn nor the Long and Boldt studies pay attention to male privilege. Cora Voyageur regularly documents the significance of kin in her study of Canada's female chiefs but fails to question its implications for democracy. See her *Firekeepers of the Twenty-First Century: First Nations Women Chiefs* (Montreal: McGill-Queen's University Press, 2008).

8. Audra Simpson, *Mohawk Interruptus: Political Life across the Borders of Settler States* (Durham, NC: Duke University Press 2014), especially 172–75.

9. Sawer and Vickers, "Introduction," 7.

10. On the merits of "resettling" as opposed to "settling" in describing European entry into North America, see Emma LaRoque, "Métis and Feminist: Contemplations on Feminism, Human Rights, Culture and Decolonization," in Green, *Making Space for Indigenous Feminism*, 6n, 142. On the colonial landscape of dispossession and delegitimization, see Renisa Mawani, *Colonial Proximities: Crossracial Encounters and Juridical Truths in British Columbia, 1871–1921* (Vancouver: UBC Press, 2009).

11. Laura Jamieson, "At the City Hall," *CCF News*, November 23, 1949. See too Strong-Boag, *Last Suffragist Standing*. Studies of urban electors remain rare in Canada. See Sandra Breux, Jérôme Courture, and Royce Koop, "Turnout in Local Elections: Evidence from Canadian Cities, 2004–2014," *Canadian Journal of Political Science* 50, no. 3 (September 2017), especially 703–4. See also Caroline Andrew, "Federalism and Feminism: The Canadian Challenge for Women's Urban Safety," in Haussman et al., *Federalism, Feminism and Multilevel Governance*, 83–96.

12. Sawer and Vickers, "Introduction," 3.

13. See Jane Errington, *The Lion, the Eagle, and Upper Canada: A Developing Colonial Ideology* (Montreal: McGill-Queen's University Press, 1987).

14. For a succinct assessment of the efforts at recuperation and the antidemocratic reality, see Dennis Pilon, "The Contested Origins of Canadian Democracy," *Studies in Political Economy*, 98, no. 2 (2017), especially 107–10.

15. See Green, "Canaries in the Mines of Citizenship"; Green, "Constitutionalizing the Patriarchy"; Green, "Sexual Equality and Indian Government."

16. J. H. Fairbank (Liberal Party MP, East Lambton, Ontario), *House of Commons Debates*, May 12, 1885, 1783.

17. For recognition of this expectation, see feminist journalist Anne Anderson Perry, first on a Conservative Party and then on a Liberal Party convention: Perry, "Is Women's Suffrage a Fizzle?" *MacLean's*, February 1, 1928; Perry "Women Begin to Speak Their Minds," *Chatelaine*, June 1928. For a fuller treatment of this in the case of Canada's first female cabinet minister (1921), see Strong-Boag, *Liberal-Labour Lady*.

18. Lisa Young, *Feminists and Party Politics* (Vancouver: UBC Press, 2000), 57.

19. See "Elections Canada's 100th Anniversary," Elections Canada, 2023, https://www.elections.ca/content.aspx?section=abo&dir=100&document=index&lang=e.

20. Shirley Tillotson, "Relations of Extraction: Taxation and Women's Citizenship in the Maritimes, 1914–1955," *Acadiensis* 39, no. 1 (Winter/Spring 2010), paragraphs 24 and 36 https://journals.lib.unb.ca/index.php/acadiensis/article/view/15383/16521.

21. Myer Siemiatycki, *The Municipal Franchise and Social Inclusion in Toronto: Policy and Practice* (Toronto: Community Social Planning Council of Toronto and Inclusive Cities Canada, 2006), 6. See also Jamie Bradburn, "Voting Rights in

Toronto: Who Has (and Hasn't) Been Allowed to Cast a Ballot in Our Elections," *Torontoist*, September 15, 2014, https://torontoist.com/2014/09/voting-rights-in-toronto-who-has-and-hasnt-been-allowed-to-cast-a-ballot-in-our-elections.

22. See Pilon, "Contested Origins of Canadian Democracy."

23. See Heather Bastedo, Wayne Chu, and Jane Hilderman, "Outsiders: Agency and the Non-Engaged," in *Canadian Democracy from the Ground Up: Perceptions and Performance*, eds. Elisaeth Gidengil and Heather Bastedo (Vancouver: UBC Press, 2014). Unfortunately, there is a lack of intersectional research on "gender turnout and civic engagement across ethnocultural groups in Canada." See Allison Harell, "Intersectionality and Gendered Political Behaviour in a Multicultural Canada," *Canadian Journal of Political Science/Revue canadienne de science politique* 50, Special Issue 2, *Finding Feminism* (June 2017): 495–514.

24. For a discussion that illuminates some of the shifting complications of women's status, see Wendy Moss, "Indigenous Self-Government in Canada and Sexual Equality under the Indian Act: Resolving Conflicts between Collective and Individual Rights," *Queen's Law Journal*, 15, no. 2 (1990): 279–305, and Kiera L. Ladner and Michael McCrossan, *The Electoral Participation of Aboriginal People* (Ottawa: Elections Canada, 2007).

25. S. A. Nickel, "'I am not a women's libber although sometimes I sound like one': Indigenous Feminism and Politicized Motherhood," *American Indian Quarterly* 41, no. 4 (Fall 2017), 302. See also Joyce Green, "Taking Account of Indigenous Feminism" and Gina Starblanket, "Being Indigenous Feminists: Resurgences against Contemporary Patriarchy," in Green, *Making Space for Indigenous Feminism*, 21–41.

26. See Voyageur, *Firekeepers of the Twenty-First Century*, chapter 3.

27. The Canadian Indian Act imposed one definition of membership from 1869, but Indigenous communities always maintained, and debated, criteria for membership. See Martin J. Cannon, "Revisiting Histories of Gender-Based Exclusion and the New Politics of Indian Identity," National Centre for First Nations Governance, May 2008, http://fngovernance.org/ncfng_research/martin_cannon.pdf, and "Reclaiming Our Identity: Band Membership, Citizenship and the Inherent Right," National Centre for First Nations Governance, 2023, http://fngovernance.org/resources_docs/ReclaimingOurIdentity_Paper.pdf. See also Martin J. Cannon, "A History of Politics and Women's Status at Six Nations of Grand River Territory" (PhD diss., York University, 2004).

28. On the importance of this decision, see Hughes, "Women in Public Life."

29. On that recurring experience, see Bashevkin, *Doing Politics Differently?*

30. See Veronica Strong-Boag, "Rejecting Evidence for Justice: The Anti-Women Politics of Canadian Conservatism," *Journal of Law and Equality* 12 (Fall 2016): 39–62; Ira Wells, "The Unpopularity of Female Politicians Has Everything to

Do with Sexism," *Walrus*, June 5, 2018, https://thewalrus.ca/the-unpopularity-of-female-politicians-has-everything-to-do-with-sexism; Trevor Harrison, "A Jason Kenney Alberta," *Canadian Dimension*, July 29, 2019.

31. Green, "Taking Account of Indigenous Feminism," 14.

32. See Angela V. John and Claire Eustance, *Men's Share? Masculinities, Male Support and Women's Suffrage in Britain, 1890–1920* (London: Routledge, 2013) and Michael Messner, "Forks in the Road of Men's Gender Politics: Men's Rights vs Feminist Allies," *International Journal for Crime, Justice and Social Democracy* 5, no 2 (2016): 6–20.

33. Donald B. Smith, "Nahnebahwequay," *Dictionary of Canadian Biography*, vol. 9, University of Toronto/Université Laval, 2003, http://www.biographi.ca/en/bio/nahnebahwequay_9E.html.

34. See "Indian Homemakers' Association of British Columbia," First Nations & Indigenous Studies, University of British Columbia, 2009, http://indigenous-foundations.arts.ubc.ca/indian_homemakers_association; Mary Jane Logan McCallum, *Indigenous Women, Work and History, 1940–1980* (Winnipeg: University of Manitoba Press, 2014), chapter 4.

35. See Baillargeon, *To Be Equals in Our Own Country*, 9.

36. For an overdue study of this remarkable woman, see Lavigne and Stanton, *Idola Saint-Jean*. See also *Joséphine Marchand et Raoul Dandurand*, an important study of a suffragist couple by the same authors.

37. See Jane Rhodes, *Mary Ann Shadd Cary: The Black Press and Protest in the Nineteenth Century* (Bloomington: Indiana University Press, 1998) and Jason H. Silverman, "Shadd, Mary Ann Camberton," *Dictionary of Canadian Biography*, vol. 12, University of Toronto/Université Laval, 2003, http://www.biographi.ca/en/bio/shadd_mary_ann_camberton_12E.html.

38. See Mary Chapman, ed., *Becoming Sui Sin Far: Early Fiction, Journalism, and Travel Writing by Edith Maude Eaton* (Montreal: McGill-Queen's University Press, 2016) and Lorraine McMullen, "Eaton, Edith Maud," *Dictionary of Canadian Biography*, vol. 14, University of Toronto/Université Laval, 2003, http://www.biographi.ca/en/bio/eaton_edith_maud_14E.html.

39. Howard, *Struggle for Social Justice in British Columbia*.

40. On women's greater disinterest than men's in politics, see Elisabeth Gidengil, Brenda O'Neill, and Lisa Young, "Her Mother's Daughter? The Influence of Childhood Socialization on Women's Political Engagement," *Journal of Women, Politics & Policy* 31, no. 4 (2010), 334–55.

41. On McClung, see Strong-Boag and Rosa, *Nellie McClung*.

42. See Micheline de Sève, "Women's National and Gendered Identity: The Case of Canada," *Journal of Canadian Studies/Revue d'études canadiennes* 35, no 2 (Summer 2000), 61–79; Judy Rebick, "Social Movements on the Path to Economic and Social Equality" in *Inequalities and Social Justice in Canada*, ed. Janine Brodie (Toronto: University of Toronto Press, 2018); Vijay Agnew, *Resisting*

Discrimination: Women from Asia, Africa, and the Caribbean and the Women's Movement in Canada (Toronto: University of Toronto Press, 1996); Green, *Making Space for Indigenous Feminism*; Micheline Labelle, *Racisme et antiracism au Québec* (Montreal: Les Presses de l'Université du Québec, 2010); Michele Landsberg, *Writing the Revolution* (Toronto: Second Story Press, 2011); Ruth R. Pierson, and Marjorie Griffin Cohen, eds. *Canadian Women's Issues*, Vol. 2 (Toronto: J. Lorimer, 1995); Sherene Razack, *Race, Space, and the Law* (Toronto: Between the Lines, 2002); Veronica Strong-Boag, Sherrill Grace, Avigail Eisenberg, and Joan Anderson, eds., *Painting the Maple: Essays on Race, Gender and the Construction of Canada* (Vancouver: UBC Press, 1998); Sunera Thobani, *Exalted Subjects: Studies in the Making of Race and Nation in Canada* (Toronto: University of Toronto Press, 2007); Jill Vickers, Pauline Rankin, and Christine Appelle, *Politics as If Women Mattered: A Political Analysis of the National Action Committee on the Status of Women* (Toronto: University of Toronto Press, 1993).

43. Nickel, "'I am not a women's libber," 316. See also Green, "Constitutionalising the Patriarchy"; Shelagh Day and Joyce Green, "Sharon McIvor's Fight for Equality," *Herizons* (June 2010): 6–7; Shelagh Day and Joyce Green, "Bill C-3 Is Fatally Flawed," Women's Court of Canada, May 2010, http://womenscourt. ca/2010/04/bill-c-3-is-sexist-racist-and-fatally-flawed/#more-851.

44. Mary Eberts, Sharon McIvor, and Teressa Nahanee, "The Native Women's Association of Canada v. Canada," *Canadian Journal of Women and the Law* 18, no. 1 (2006): 67–119.

45. Emma LaRoque, "Métis and Feminist: Contemplations on Feminism, Human Rights, Culture and Decolonization," in Green, *Making Space for Indigenous Feminism*, 127. See also her *When the Other Is Me: Native Resistance Discourse, 1850–1990* (Winnipeg: University of Manitoba Press, 2010).

46. For a recent important consideration of the complications of the defense of motherhood, see Marks et al., "'A Job That Should Be Respected.'"

47. Grace Lore, "One Hundred Years and Counting: The State of Women in Politics in Canada," *Canadian Parliamentary Review* 40, no. 3 (Autumn 2017), 15. See also the devastating portrait of federal politics provided in Jody Wilson-Raybould, *Indian in the Cabinet: Speaking Truth to Power* (Toronto: HarperCollins, 2021).

48. Trimble et al., *Stalled*.

49. Joyce Green, "ReBalancing Strategies: Aboriginal Women and Constitutional Rights in Canada," in Green, *Making Space for Indigenous Feminism*, 170.

50. Green "ReBalancing Strategies," 187.

CHAPTER THREE

The Suffrage Movement in the United States

Demanding the Right to Vote across Gender and Racial Lines in an (Il?)Liberal Democracy

SUSAN GOODIER

FROM THE FOUNDING OF THE United States, fears of majority rule prompted the creation of systems to limit access to democratic participation—that is, to limit access to the vote. All the founders agreed with Thomas Jefferson's statement about "men" being "created equal," but disagreements raged about the meaning of equality. At first, only white, property-holding men had access to voting rights. Eventually, property ownership became less important to voting rights. Few people thought that equality and citizenship meant that women had access to the same rights as men. And virtually no one at the time would have included Indigenous or African people as eligible to access equality, citizenship, or any of the rights white men had. Yet, over time and through the work of activists from these various unenfranchised groups and their allies, demands for greater inclusiveness have been met. It took decades of change through constitutional amendments and subsequent laws to create a democracy that reflects greater inclusiveness of all diverse peoples who inhabit the United States. Nevertheless, the democracy of today has also become more creatively illiberal in its exclusionary practices.

The term *creatively illiberal* suggests, as does Carol Anderson, that access to voting rights is blocked by a "series of voter suppression tactics," including "racially neutral justifications" such as "administrative efficiency" or "fiscal responsibility." These tactics have been used for more than a century and a half, and they can be very effective.[1] The US Constitution does not guarantee its citizens the right to vote. It only guarantees that the right to vote cannot be denied on the basis of race (the Fifteenth Amendment) or sex (the Nineteenth Amendment).[2] The term *illiberal democracy*, first used by Fareed Zakaria in reference to European democracies, is defined as "democratically elected regimes often re-elected or reinforced by referendums that ignore the constitutional limits of their power and deprive their citizens of basic rights and liberties." Some of those countries "are strengthening illiberal democracy by creating forms of government that mix substantial degrees of populist democracy with strong-man leadership."[3] The history of the United States shows tension between both liberal and illiberal tendencies. While the national mythology emphasizes pride in a liberal narrative, a deeper consideration tells a more complicated story of institutional resistance to full inclusion in the democracy, especially by women and people of color. Women in the United States achieved suffrage by increasingly appealing to the conservative mainstream, white, elite men in power, but the protection of their right to vote requires constant diligence.

From demands for voting rights as early as the 1840s, the women's suffrage movement, deeply contentious and multilayered, shifted from radical to conservative punctuated by radical ideas. It remained divided over property ownership, class, religion, culture, ethnicity, and, most prominently, race.[4] Each group of women struggled with different issues, based on their historical relationships to the government, shaping the strategies they adopted over the decades to win suffrage.[5] The movement's uneven progress also resulted in significant differences across the states: some states allowed women to vote in presidential elections but not in local elections. Other states allowed women to decide local issues relating to schools, water resources, or other municipal concerns. Twenty states allowed women to vote before ratification of the Nineteenth Amendment in 1920, but many women and men of color—Native American, African American, Latinx, and Asian American—found themselves barred from voting even after its enactment. The experiences of people of color highlight some of the most illiberal aspects of the ongoing quest for democratic voting rights.

The founders of the United States of America established a government modeled in important ways on the Haudenosaunee Six Nations participatory democracy, the oldest in the world. The Haudenosaunee, or People of the Long House, had formed a confederacy in New York State by about 1142.[6] It included the Mohawk, Oneida, Onondaga, Cayuga, and Seneca peoples; the sixth nation, the Tuscarora, joined in the early eighteenth century.[7] Each nation has separate and unique powers and responsibilities within the confederacy.[8] Hundreds of Native American nations continue their struggles to share the land dominated by the United States, and each of them has a story that respects women's political participation. This chapter cannot tell them all, but it will highlight some Native women as part of the story of how women gained political rights within the settler society.

Haudenosaunee women, like Cherokee women and those in many other Indigenous groups, were responsible for childbearing, producing food, and choosing—and deposing when necessary—political leaders.[9] Women could speak in a council meeting on behalf of a young or inexperienced (male) leader.[10] George Washington and other officials of the United States knew that women held positions of authority in tribal governance, as they observed during Treaty of Canandaigua negotiations in November 1794. Seneca women spoke during the negotiations, as they did during other treaty discussions. Although the founders modeled the United States on the Haudenosaunee Confederacy, they rejected political roles for women.[11] Additionally, because the federal government had no clear way to "institute a national conception of voting rights," it left much of the details to the individual states.[12]

New Jersey, for example, allowed women to vote beginning in 1776, accepting the idea that the apparently gender-neutral language of the US Constitution implied that property-owning women and African Americans could vote. The legislators had neither erred nor overlooked this; in 1790 lawmakers affirmed this right with a statement in the state constitution: "no Person shall be entitled to vote in any other Township or Precinct than that in which he or she doth actually reside at the time of the Election."[13] The clauses seem to have caused little controversy until women's votes came to be seen as powerful enough to affect elections. In 1807 legislators changed "he or she" to "free, white, male citizens," and in a single decisive action disfranchised all women and men of color in the state.[14]

Some states allowed taxpaying, landowning Black men to vote. In New York State, for example, Black men who paid taxes on property worth at least $250 could vote after 1821, while white men had no property requirements to meet. No women could vote, regardless of their race, class status, how much property they owned, or how much they paid in taxes. Meanwhile, northern states had either abolished slavery or legislated its gradual demise in their state constitutions by 1840, although hundreds of once enslaved people had to work out terms of indenture. Organizations such as the American Anti-Slavery Society, founded in 1833 and led by William Lloyd Garrison, sought to end slavery nationwide.[15] Often Black and white women who tried to join any of the more than two thousand auxiliary societies across the nation found themselves rejected outright or consigned to silence during meetings. Men often devoted tedious hours to arguing about the "woman question," the term alluding to women's place in the polity or their meetings, as they did at the World Anti-Slavery Convention in June 1840 in London.[16] Women responded to the rejection of their contributions by founding their own antislavery organizations, thereby laying the groundwork to demand more political, economic, and civil rights for themselves.[17]

Only rarely did women establish interracial antislavery organizations.[18] Those often remained segregated, even assigning Black women separate seating.[19] When in October 1836 the Ladies' Anti-Slavery Society of New York hosted a series of lectures in conjunction with a visit by sisters Sarah and Angelina Grimke at the Beriah Baptist Church, Angelina condemned white members who refused to welcome women of color to their ranks.[20] Anne Warren Weston, one of the leading figures of abolition in Massachusetts, also criticized them.[21] Encouraged by Weston's sister Maria Weston Chapman, antislavery women held three important antislavery conventions between 1837 and 1839. The first, held in May 1837 and hosted by the Ladies' Society, was the four-day Anti-Slavery Convention of American Women. Black women, including Maria W. Stewart and at least four (unnamed) others, represented the Colored Ladies' Literary Society of New York City and the Rising Daughters of Abyssinia. These women listened as Angelina

Grimke submitted a resolution that women needed to demand greater rights for themselves. The clamor that ensued serves as a reminder that not all women wanted the right to vote, no matter how strong their activist leanings. The Philadelphia Anti-Slavery Society welcomed Black women members as well as white women. In 1838, when male building owners refused to rent meeting spaces to the women, members raised funds to build their own convention hall. Rioters burned the hall to the ground during its maiden meeting; Black women linked arms with white women to protect themselves from direct violence from the crowd.[22]

In the summer of 1848, Lucretia Coffin Mott, who ministered in the Quaker (Religious Society of Friends) meetinghouse, stopped at the Cattaraugus community in western New York on her way to visit family in Seneca Falls. While Mott struggled to understand and accept the profound differences in the role of women in the Seneca Nation as compared to settler women, she certainly saw Indigenous women exercising equal authority in discussion and decision-making.[23] Soon after, Mott and several other white Quaker women, including her sister, Martha Coffin Wright, Mary Ann M'Clintock, Jane Hunt, and the non-Quaker Elizabeth Cady Stanton, decided to call a women's rights convention to be held July 19 and 20. No scholar has yet shown that women of color attended the convention. Of the fifteen Blacks living in Seneca Falls and sixty-three in nearby Waterloo, many probably at least discussed the event, or at least read about it in Frederick Douglass's *North Star*.[24]

Black women usually found themselves silenced at all kinds of meetings—those dominated by African American men as well as those dominated by white women. Douglass, who attended the Seneca Falls convention together with about three hundred white female and male social justice activists, spoke out in his support for women's rights. He remained steadfast in his advocacy, later calling for "woman's right to freedom and equality on the same grounds he based his own" at the Eighth National Women's Rights Convention, held at Mozart Hall in New York City on May 13–14, 1858.[25] He continued that support until his death, having attended a meeting of the National Council of Women in Washington, DC, earlier that day.

Among the demands put forth by the Declaration of Sentiments, the one demanding the right to vote caused the most heated discussion before it, like all the others, finally passed. In the following years, women organized women's rights conventions, held meetings, gave speeches, wrote articles and books, and gathered signatures on petitions throughout the United States. During the Civil War (1861–1865), white and Black women set aside their activism and raised money, nursed the sick and wounded at battlefronts, and maintained their homes and farms. On May 14, 1863, northern white women's rights leaders founded the Women's National Loyal League, demanding an end to war and a constitutional amendment abolishing slavery.[26]

In 1865, following the Confederate surrender at Appomattox, legislators from the North sought to reconstruct the war-devastated country through three amendments to the US Constitution. The Thirteenth Amendment (ratified in 1865) officially abolished slavery in the United States and its environs, the Fourteenth Amendment (ratified in 1868) made former enslaved people citizens—and for the first time defined a citizen as male—and the Fifteenth Amendment (ratified in 1870) enfranchised citizens, now legislatively defined as male.[27] Former abolitionists and women's rights activists, female and male, argued about the consequences of these amendments.

The ability to vote had become fused with ideas about masculinity, manliness, and militarism. The thousands of Black men who served in the Union army during the war reinforced the idea that the right to vote necessitated military prowess. This view displaced the argument that "political rights should reflect natural rights," which had once made women's right to participate in politics seem logical and possible.[28] At odds with former collaborators, white women's rights activists increasingly expressed their fury and frustration in notably racist and exclusionary terms. The Fourteenth Amendment passed into law over the objections of Stanton and Susan B. Anthony, who submitted protest petitions with ten thousand signatures.[29]

Members of the American Equal Rights Association, founded May 10, 1866, at the Eleventh National Woman's Rights Convention, sought universal suffrage and challenged the male descriptor of citizenship. While dominated by white women, the organization did cross race and gender boundaries and drew supporters from Garrisonian abolitionists, who had long supported the equal rights principle.[30] Republicans Charles Sumner, Wendell Phillips, and Thaddeus Stevens, who all argued for Black male enfranchisement as a step in the direction of full equality for women, put into motion a process that "began what has become an incremental (and very slow) process for the achievement of egalitarian civil rights." At the time, however, efforts making men equal rested upon "making women unequal."[31] This phenomenon, in which the powerful group constructs a binary choice between enfranchising men from a subaltern racial, ethnic, or class group or enfranchising women from a dominant group, can be seen in Ecuador and other countries of the hemisphere, where literacy is used as a proxy for race or class.[32] Here is the essence of an illiberal democracy: forcing competition for political power between groups that suffer from the same lack of access to that power.

Recognizing the illiberal binary amendment discussions, Sojourner Truth articulated her pleasure in seeing Black men earn rights, but she argued for women's rights: "I want women to get theirs, and while the water is stirring, I will step into the pool."[33] Frances Ellen Watkins Harper, the author of poetry and popular novels such as *Iola Leroy or, Shadows Uplifted* spoke vehemently for African American enfranchisement at this meeting, although she would show herself willing to wait for women's voting rights. Soon after the meeting, Anthony organized a speaking tour across upstate New York during the winter of 1867 to influence delegates to an upcoming New York State constitutional convention to remove the word *male* from the descriptor of a voter. Although the tour met with some success among voters, it did not persuade state legislators.[34]

The American Equal Rights Association self-destructed three years later when states ratified the Fifteenth Amendment in 1870.[35] The demise of the organization marks a significant split in the women's rights movement, as it intensified the concentration on the right to vote to the detriment of a broader focus on women's rights.[36] Suffragists came to understand that when "men agreed as *men* about what issues belonged on the government agenda, women could not stop them." Unfortunately, women had to have male support to change the laws of the United States; they had to "eschew principle for expediency's sake."[37] Suffragists used the "New Departure," a strategy employed from 1868 to 1873, to claim that the Fourteenth Amendment already assured women the right to vote. Hundreds of Black and white women, including Sojourner Truth, Mary Ann Shadd Cary, Lucy Stone, Angelina Grimke Weld, Matilda Joslyn Gage, and Susan B. Anthony, tested its premise at the polls and in the courts.[38] Although some poll officials allowed women to register and vote, most turned women away. In extreme cases, most notoriously that of Anthony in 1872, women voters faced arrest and fines.

After the demise of the American Equal Rights Association, women who advocated for the right to vote through a federal amendment to the US Constitution worked through the New York–based National Woman Suffrage Association, led by Stanton and Anthony.[39] Those who supported a state-by-state process of enfranchisement founded the American Woman Suffrage Association, headquartered in Massachusetts. Its leaders included Stone and her husband, Henry Blackwell.[40] Some Black women joined one or the other of the two organizations, depending on where they lived and their relationships with white women supporters. Mary Ann Shadd Cary, Harriet and Hattie Purvis, and Charlotte E. Ray joined the National Association, while Frances Ellen Watkins Harper, Charlotte Forten, and Josephine St. Pierre Ruffin affiliated with the American Association. Sojourner Truth attended National Association conventions, but she worked with both organizations.[41]

Other African American women found it more expedient to establish their own organizations. Newspaper editor Cary (1823–1893) may have been frustrated by the lack of response to her 1876 request, on behalf of herself and ninety-four other Black women in the District of Columbia, to have their names added to the list of signers to the Declaration of the Rights of the Woman. The document, presented by Matilda Joslyn Gage and Susan B. Anthony during the bicentennial celebration of the birth of the nation in Philadelphia, demanded greater attention to the issue of women's rights. Later, a few Black women, including Truth, affixed their signatures in the leather-bound volume that preserved the declaration.[42] Cary founded the Colored Women's Progressive Franchise Association in Washington, DC, in 1880, while Sarah Smith Tompkins Garnet founded the Colored Women's Suffrage League of Brooklyn later that same decade.[43] Cross-race work persisted throughout the suffrage movement, but Black women constantly struggled to be heard by white women.

Virtually all Black women's organizations, regardless of the name or the ostensible purpose of their founding, supported women's right to vote. Members did not separate voting rights from racial uplift, improved working conditions, expanding education for African American children, ending lynching, or any of their other activist issues. However, women like Harper opposed unrestricted suffrage for men or women. She argued in an 1893 speech that moral and educational tests would help to prevent damage to the state from the ignorant and brutal voter.[44] The intersectionality of Black women's lived experience complicated the issue further. Many Black men wanted their wives to follow the mandates of the white women's ideology of "true womanhood," which restricted their activities to the domestic sphere.

Meanwhile, at the legislative level, Congress first debated a suffrage amendment in 1878 and reiterated many of the same arguments over four decades.[45] The suffrage movement ebbed and flowed, changing in sometimes dramatic ways depending on its leadership and the broader political situation in the United States. For example, when France gave the United States the Statue of Liberty in recognition of the centennial in 1886, suffragists complained that a woman represented liberty and freedom from oppression in a country where no woman had freedom from oppression. The ceremony took place in New York Harbor on a dreary, rainy day, and suffragists were not invited. A group of activists rented a cattle barge and protested the erection of the statue.[46] Although most newspaper journalists misinterpreted the event, these women directly challenged the illiberalness of their democracy.

At the same time, women at the local and state levels established suffrage clubs in villages, towns, and cities everywhere. Several of these groups met with success, especially in the territories of the western United States.[47] Sometimes influenced by women's organizations, but often by the need to count even women as citizens to meet population requirements for statehood, several territories and western states supported women's right to vote. Women voted in Wyoming in 1869 and kept the franchise when the territory became a state in 1890. Colorado won statehood in 1876, but until the advocacy of African American leader Elizabeth Piper Ensley and white suffragists in the Non-Partisan Equal Suffrage League in 1893, women could not vote. Women voted in Idaho six years after the territory became a state in 1890. Women in Utah had suffrage from its statehood in 1896.[48] African American women do not seem to have been targeted for disenfranchisement in these western states. Women in twenty-four states had the right to vote in school elections in certain municipalities by 1890.[49] In several states, especially in the Southeast, elite white women sought to convince legislators of the need for some women (themselves) to be enfranchised. Some suffragists in other states advocated for limits based on education or skin color to control the votes of non-English-speaking immigrants and people of color. We can observe this tendency toward exclusivity across the hemisphere for decades.

The National and American Associations merged as the National American Woman Suffrage Association in 1890. This merger marked a period of increasing conservatism among white women's suffrage leaders, predicated not on radical ideas of women's place in a democracy but on the idea that women would improve the country with their supposed greater sense of morality. Native and Black women's groups also trended in the conservative direction, with the hope that women of color would be included in the rights of citizenship. The merger also welcomed the affiliation of one of the most conservative elements of women's organized activism, the Woman's Christian Temperance Union, which had officially supported women's suffrage since 1881.

Some vocal members of the union hoped to limit religious freedom in the United States, a reaction to the increase of Jewish and other non-Christian immigration at the end of the nineteenth century. Upset by the merger, Matilda Joslyn Gage, immersed in writing *Woman, Church, and State*, where she articulates the connection between women's oppression and the church, left the mainstream suffrage movement.[50] She founded the Woman's National Liberal Union to advocate for the strict separation of church and state as well as women's right to vote.[51] As the nineteenth century waned, suffragists increased their efforts to appeal to the mainstream. Female opponents of suffrage in New York and Massachusetts reacted by founding anti-suffrage organizations in 1895; women in many states followed their lead.

Because suffragists refined their arguments in response to those presented by the anti-suffragists, the suffrage movement revitalized and further broadened its appeal. Many activists remained divided over strategy and questions related to equality and difference. Some suffrage leaders believed that women should vote because women and men were essentially the same. Other advocates claimed that women, because they were so different from men—and purportedly better than men because they were more moral and ethical—would add a crucial element to the structure of the polity. Some disagreements related to the changing of the suffrage movement leadership. The ideas Anthony, who contended that the vote represented the most important aspect of women's rights and that all other rights would come once women had the right to vote, dominated the official rhetoric.

Although women from every age group participated in the suffrage movement, those who came of age during this time could look at the movement as the defining period of their lives.[52] The second generation of women suffragists, many of them independent and seeking radical societal changes as "new women," increased interest in the movement with their enthusiasm.[53] This cohort, often recipients of higher education and greater social and economic freedoms, appropriated a vast array of new technologies and developing forms of media to reach women, (male) voters, and legislators. The excitement of the movement drew a lot of attention and made the radical idea that women and men just might be equal increasingly palatable to a widening public. Suffragists showed remarkable innovation in their appropriation of the newest technologies and media forms.

Many women found journalism to be compatible with marriage and motherhood, informing their readership of the progress the women's suffrage movement made across the country. After 1885, elite Black suffragist Gertrude Bustill Mossell encouraged her readers to vote for a candidate regardless of political party as long as the candidate would "give African Americans a fair chance." Discussions of political party adherence must have been a topic in her household, for her husband, Dr. Nathan F. Mossell, the first African American to graduate from the University of Pennsylvania Medical School, had led the retreat from membership in the Republican Party in Philadelphia. She endorsed Black candidates and filled her "Our Woman's Department" columns in the *New York Freeman* (which became the *New York Age* in 1887), the *Indianapolis World*, and Bostonian Josephine St. Pierre Ruffin's *Woman's Era* with highlights of political races across the nation. She also wrote for several magazines.[54] Many suffrage advocates provided copy to newspaper and magazine editors and published broadsides and articles.

Changes resulting from maturing industrialization, increased access to higher education for women, and cheaper forms of media broadly disseminated the ideas of the women's suffrage movement. Activists used stamps, postcards, and letter paper, wore suffrage colors and jewelry, and displayed symbolic accessories. They called friends on the telephone, drove and repaired the new automobiles they used as speaking platforms, and designed and sold fashionable clothing, playing cards, games, china, jewelry, ribbons, buttons, toys, and all kinds of items to promote their views.[55] Suffragists linked anything that happened to their cause. For example, in the weeks and months following the *Titanic* disaster in the North Atlantic on April 14, 1912, they argued that the event demonstrated that women were capable of the "discipline" and "self-control" required of voters. Anti-suffragists responded that the disaster proved the "permanence of gender roles"—men could be counted on to be chivalrous and would sacrifice themselves to save women and children.[56] Arguments between the suffragists and the anti-suffragists fascinated the public.

As we see elsewhere in the hemisphere, suffragists read about themselves as being manlike or "unsexed" for advocating for their right "to step out of their appropriate sphere." By the turn of the twentieth century, physicians and sexologists like Havelock Ellis specifically noted suffragists as representing "sexual inversion," code for lesbians. In reality, some suffrage leaders found that traditional marriages "distracted a woman's energy from the cause," while their close relationships with other women enhanced their activism.[57] Anti-suffragists argued that "real women" did not need political power. Women and men everywhere accused suffragists of being unfeminine, and suffragists often responded to these accusations by holding contests for beautiful babies and showing off their cooking abilities. While suffragists may have gained adherents by celebrating traditional gender roles, they inevitably reinforced heteronormative assumptions and made it harder to relate femininity with anything other than cookie baking and baby making.

African American Hester Jeffrey (1842–1934), a suffragist who fought racism and promoted racial uplift, joined temperance and woman suffrage organizations in Boston, and after 1891 in Rochester, New York. She traveled the country to attend meetings of the National Association of Colored Woman's Clubs, suffrage meetings, and those of groups predating the National

Association for the Advancement of Colored People. Noted for her ability to cross racial lines, she gain national attention with her activism.[58] She, like many of her colleagues, worked for greater access to the benefits of democracy.

Suffragists sought diverse support in other ways. In New York City, acknowledging the diversity inherent to a period of intense immigration, especially after 1910, suffragists published suffrage propaganda in Greek, German, Russian, Italian, Irish, and other languages. Suffrage parades featured sections focused on various immigrant groups or Black women.[59] The biggest suffrage parade ever, elaborately choreographed by Stanton's daughter Harriot Stanton Blatch, drew more than seventeen thousand participants and pushed news of the May 4, 1912, funeral of John Jacob Astor off the front page of the *New York Times*.[60]

White suffragists, acknowledging the power of Native women in their own communities, often drew on them for publicity and support for their movement.[61] In 1893 the Mohawk Nation adopted leading white women's rights activist Matilda Joslyn Gage into the Wolf Clan, giving her the right to vote for the chief.[62] Meanwhile, some Indigenous women, despite not having US citizenship, saw advantages in working for women's citizenship rights. The period near the turn of the twentieth century saw a terrible rise in corrupt governmental policies aimed at "civilizing" or taking the "savage" out of the Indian. The government broke treaties with Native people and swindled them out of their land with the Dawes Act, which claimed that millions of acres of "unused" land—land belonging to Indigenous people—could be sold or distributed to whites. Religious organizations, with government sanction, took Native children from their families and attempted to brainwash them in boarding schools.[63] Many Indigenous women who had chosen to assimilate nevertheless remained proud of their ancestry and chose to support the women's suffrage movement.

Marie L. Bottineau Baldwin (1863–1952; Chippewa from the Turtle Mountain Band in North Dakota) created a stir in the press when she participated in the 1913 parade in Washington, DC. Baldwin, a member of the American Indian Association, had worked for the Indian Office helping to settle claims brought by Native people against the federal government at least since 1908 and had attended a council of Indians in Columbus, Ohio, to call for full citizenship for Native people.[64] She advocated for a recognition of Native women as "at least the equal of white women," not the "slave and drudge of the men" of her nation.[65] Newspapers celebrated her beauty and intelligence. Her contemporary Zitkala Ŝa (or Gertrude Bonnin, 1876–1938; Yankton Sioux), who worked tirelessly for rights for Indigenous people and was the first Indigenous person to write an opera, supported women's suffrage as a path to full citizenship rights for Native people.

Chinese American Mabel Ping-Hau Lee's presence in the 1913 parade, foretold for weeks in newspaper articles, belied pervasive Chinese stereotypes. Her participation sparked widespread interest; a photograph of her astride a horse ridden in formation with fifty equestrian women leading the parade that evening appeared in newspapers across the country. Her appearance served to remind observers of the promise of the recent revolution in China and the high hopes women had for enfranchisement there. Although the United States barred Chinese Americans from naturalized citizenship, events unfolding in China pushed their cause for women's suffrage and full citizenship to the forefront of many suffrage events. Just a few months before the parade, rumors that Chinese women had the right to vote had thrilled suffragists. Other Chinese suffragists, such as Pearl Mark Loo (Mai Zhouyi) and Lee Lia Beck, had joined Anna Howard Shaw and Harriet Laidlaw at a suffrage rally in April, shaming the United States for neglecting to enfranchise women before China did.[66]

Diverse groups of women saw in the women's suffrage movement a possible pathway to citizenship for their ethnic group. Latinx women in New Mexico, California, and elsewhere also demanded the right to vote, often using Spanish to persuade women and men of the need to vote and protect their language.[67] Latinx women in California, including Maria Guadalupe Evangelina de López (1881–1977), advocated for suffrage and translated suffrage documents into Spanish during the successful 1911 state campaign. In New Mexico, Adelina (Nina) Otero-Warren, state chair of the National Woman's Party, translated much of the suffrage literature into Spanish.[68] She and her cousin Aurora Lucero advocated both for the protection of the Spanish language and for women's suffrage in the debates leading to New Mexican statehood in 1912. Some women in the state had the right to vote in school elections, but Native Americans living in the nineteen pueblos and those living on reservations did not.[69] As each state enfranchised women, the number of voters who supported suffrage increased. Concerns that women would somehow disrupt the natural order of membership in a democracy dissipated as suffragists sent observers to states where women voted to report on the success of their social activism.

By 1913 women in nine states—Wyoming (1890), Colorado (1893), Utah (1896), Idaho (1896), Washington (1910), California (1911), Oregon (1912), Kansas (1912), and Arizona (1912)—had the power of the franchise, and many of those women found ways to support activism in states that had yet to enfranchise them. On March 3, 1913, thousands of women and their male supporters marched in a huge parade, organized by Alice Paul and Lucy Burns of the National American Woman Suffrage Association's congressional committee (it would become the National Woman's Party in 1916), in Washington, DC, on the eve of Woodrow Wilson's inauguration. "General" Rosalie Jones led a hike from New York City to Washington, DC, to join the parade. At first participants refused to let Black women join the march along the way. Suffragists who joined Paul's organization "claimed the same rights and spaces as men," but they could not accept equality between the races.[70] Paul, a Quaker from a family "which has always taken a stand for the rights of the negro," was warned by several colleagues that a significant number of white women would oppose the inclusion of Black women in the parade. In the end, she opted to avoid a public about-face but "quietly" accepted Black women as marchers.[71]

This practice of ignoring race, or refusing to make public statements about race, followed the official policy of the National American Woman Suffrage Association. The association took no action when state-level affiliates refused membership to Black women. Black women's groups embraced women's suffrage, but leadership in white-dominated organizations feared that Black women's involvement would cost them membership and financial support from other whites and hurt their public image.[72] Despite Paul's lackluster support for their participation, twenty-two members of the Delta Sigma Theta Sorority from Howard University, Ida B. Wells-Barnett, Mary Church Terrell, and other Black women from New York, Illinois, and Michigan defied instructions to stay at the back of the parade and instead marched with their state delegations. Native American women, including Marie

Baldwin, marched, as did Asian American women. Newspapers almost exclusively published the photographs of white participants. However, some artists drew cartoons that illustrated the ways Black women defied white supremacy by joining the marchers.[73] Police looked the other way when parade watchers became violent, and more than one hundred people required hospitalization for treatment of injuries. Washington officials finally had to call in the cavalry to control the parade route.[74]

Paul and her supporters began picketing the White House in January 1917. The idea came from Harriot Stanton Blatch, who back in 1912 had posted "silent sentinels" at the New York State Legislature. Women in Holland and England had used a similar strategy, and Paul had used the tactic in Chicago in October 1916.[75] Holding the Democratic Party, with US president Woodrow Wilson, at its head, responsible for keeping votes from women, picketers held banners quoting phrases from the president's own speeches. Over the eighteen months of picketing, women from all over the country traveled to Washington to take up the cause.[76] The president and public generally ignored them. After the declaration of war against Germany and its allies in April 1917, however, the public and the press, which had once been sympathetic, became increasingly hostile to the picketers. By June 1917, police began arresting women for obstructing the sidewalk or other minor charges. When the women refused to pay the fines, claiming their right to engage in political demonstrations, many were imprisoned in Occoquan Workhouse in Virginia. Over the period of the picketing, more than five hundred women faced arrest. One hundred and sixty-eight women went to prison; many of them engaged in hunger strikes and endured forcible feedings.[77]

Certainly, due in part to the White House picketers, the year 1917 can be considered a tipping point in the US suffrage movement. After decades of being at the center of agitation, the women of New York State finally won full suffrage by a November 6 referendum. Women also won full suffrage in Oklahoma and South Dakota. Nebraska, Michigan, Vermont, Arkansas, and Rhode Island approved partial suffrage for women that year. Other states that held referenda in 1917—Massachusetts, Maine, and Pennsylvania— failed to enfranchise women. That same November, women who had been incarcerated at Occoquan suffered beatings and were chained to the bars of their prison in the Night of Terror, as the event is known. By the end of the month, public outrage over the treatment of the "silent sentinels" forced their release from the workhouse. Many of the picketers resumed their vigil in front of the White House gates. A highly experienced and determined cohort of dynamic, experienced women turned their formidable attention to winning a federal amendment, fearing that while states could grant the right to vote, they could also take away that hard-won right, as had happened in New Jersey in 1807.

In 1917 Woodrow Wilson finally came out in support of woman suffrage, calling it a "war measure." He allowed the suffrage organizations, nationally and in New York State, to publish his official statement to that effect. Nevertheless, and not surprisingly, members of Congress dragged their feet. The House of Representatives passed the constitutional amendment, but the Senate voted it down more than once until 1919, after the Great War had ended. Then the measure began the process of ratification in the states. Across the country, state legislatures called special sessions to vote on the amendment; suffragists and anti-suffragists eagerly observed the process. Tennessee holds the distinction of being the thirty-sixth state to ratify, and it did so in a most dramatic fashion, with the casting of just one deciding vote. Harry Burn had intended to oppose the measure but ultimately decided to follow the wishes of his mother, who supported women's suffrage. Secretary of State Bainbridge Colby certified the Nineteenth Amendment, making it officially part of the US Constitution on August 26, 1920. No one invited a single woman to observe the event, however.[78]

In 1920 Carrie Chapman Catt, president of the National American Woman Suffrage Association, established the League of Women Voters to educate and encourage newly minted voters. At first, members of the National Association of Colored Women saw the potential of league membership. Patterns of exclusion continued in the nascent organization, however, although some individual Black women joined the league or established separate branches. Evelyn Higginbotham judges that the league had lost the "potential for being an important mobilizing force among Black women" by the end of the 1920s.[79] The increasing racism and racial violence in the United States, marked by a revitalization of organizations like the Ku Klux Klan, may have frightened many women into retreat. Many of these conservative, right-wing groups formed in response to the

Nineteenth Amendment, fearing that non-white, non-Protestant women would change voting patterns.[80]

Meanwhile, many white suffrage leaders turned their attention to transnational suffrage movements. The League of Women Voters worked with governmental officials to organize a pan-American conference in Baltimore, Maryland, in 1922.[81] Delegates attended from Argentina, Bolivia, Brazil, Canada, Chili, Cuba, Costa Rica, Dominican Republic, Ecuador, Guatemala, Haiti, Honduras, Mexico, Nicaragua, Panama, Paraguay, Peru, Philippines, Puerto Rico, the United States, Uruguay, and Venezuela, some with the support of their respective governments. Many of the relationships that formed at that meeting endured for years, despite friction stemming from US imperialist and racist attitudes. Women of color engaged transnationally through a pan-African movement. Some women attended the International Council of Women of the Darker Races in 1922; the organization had been founded with Margaret Murray Washington as president in Richmond, Virginia, by members of the National Association of Colored Women. Other Black women, such as Irene Moorman Blackstone, joined Black nationalist and separatist Marcus Garvey. Blackstone probably met Garvey when he established a chapter of the Universal Negro Improvement Association in 1917 in Harlem, New York. Garvey authored the "Declaration of Rights of the Negro Peoples of the World," in 1920. His message, including the observation that the United States could not call itself a democracy as long as people of color lived with oppression, resonated with its four million members.

Even after the signing of the Nineteenth Amendment, illiberal political leaders found insidious ways to prevent people from voting. Most Indigenous women and women of color (as well as men), especially in the western states, found themselves excluded from the franchise. Native Americans did not gain citizenship rights until 1924, but many states kept Indigenous people disenfranchised until the 1965 Voting Rights Act. Previous legislation had addressed aspects of voting rights, but the 1965 act, instead of requiring formal complaints of voting violations, "put the responsibility for adhering to the Constitution onto state and local governments."[82] Black women and men faced Jim Crow restrictions such as poll taxes, formal voter identification documents, and grandfather laws (if a voter's grandfather had been able to vote, that person could vote; of course, enslaved people had not been allowed to vote, which kept many African Americans from voting). Southern Blacks who tried to vote put their lives at risk, facing Ku Klux Klan and other racial violence and lynching. Asian exclusion legislation, Supreme Court decisions, and federal policies prohibited most Chinese, Japanese, Indian, and other Asian immigrants from citizenship and voting, until the McCarran-Walter Nationality Act of 1952 gave them citizenship. Literacy tests also kept some Hispanics, Indigenous people, and other women and men of color from voting until an extension to the Immigration and Nationality Act in 1975 protected people who spoke Spanish as well as Indigenous, Asian, and other languages. The Nineteenth Amendment did not enfranchise women if they faced subjugation on grounds other than sex.

Illiberal leaders continue to find vindictive yet cunning ways to bar people from voting, jeopardizing the meaning of democracy. Based on widespread—but blatantly unfounded—fears of voter fraud, several states have recently engaged in legislative redistricting, requiring very specific government-issued photographic identification, closing polling places or relocating them away from communities of color, limiting voting hours and days, and using other, more direct strategies, including intimidation and the distribution of misinformation. The Supreme Court decision in *Shelby County v. Holder* claimed that some aspects of the 1965 Voting Rights Act were unconstitutional, opening the way for states to revise their voting requirements. Those with illiberal leanings continue to prevent people from exercising their right to cast a ballot in the United States. The need to protect the right to vote remains imperative for all democracies.

Notes

1. Anderson, One Person, No Vote, 2.
2. See Lisa Tetrault, "Lessons from the Constitution: Thinking through the Fifteenth and Nineteenth Amendments," *Social Education* 83, no. 6 (November–December 2019): 361–68.
3. Zakaria, *The Future of Freedom*, 17.
4. Keyssar, *The Right to Vote*, 80.
5. Cahill, *Recasting the Vote*, 5.
6. Barbara A. Mann and Jerry L. Fields, "A Sign in the Sky: Dating the League of the Haudenosaunee," *American Indian Culture and Research Journal* 21, no. 2 (1997): 105.

7. Haudenosaunee Confederacy, https://www.haudenosauneeconfederacy.com. The people called themselves Haudenosaunee rather than Iroquois, a name imposed by colonizers. Wagner, *Sisters in Spirit*, 23–24.

8. Sally Roesch Wagner, a scholar and executive director of the Matilda Joslyn Gage Center in Fayetteville, New York, argues that the Haudenosaunee women of the northeastern United States influenced the development of the ideas of the first feminists in settler societies who demanded equal rights, including the right to vote. Early women's rights activists could more easily envision equality between women and men because they observed it in Native American relationships. Wagner, *Sisters in Spirit*, 29–31, 41. See also Cahill, *Recasting the Vote*, 245.

9. "The Six Nations: Oldest Living Participatory Democracy on Earth," Ratical. org, https://ratical.org/many_worlds/6Nations/, accessed March 20, 2021.

10. Wagner, *Sisters in Spirit*, 28–31; Oren Lyons (faith keeper of the Turtle Clan and member of the Onondaga Council of Chiefs) made the points about peace, equity, and justice. Dunbar-Ortiz, *An Indigenous Peoples' History of the United States*, 26–27.

11. Joan M. Jensen, "Native American Women and Agriculture: A Seneca Case Study," *Sex Roles* 3, no. 5 (October 1977): 427.

12. Keyssar, *Right to Vote*, 24.

13. An Act to Regulate the Election of Members of the Legislative-Council and General Assembly, Sheriffs and Coroners, in the Counties of Bergen, Monmouth, Burlington, Gloucester, Salem, Hunterdon and Sussex, chapter CCCXXII §11, 1790 NJ Laws 669, 673.

14. Campbell Curry-Ledbetter, "Women's Suffrage in New Jersey 1776–1807: A Political Weapon," *Georgetown Journal of Gender and the Law* 21 (2020): 713.

15. States that abolished slavery, immediately or gradually, included Pennsylvania (1780), New Hampshire (1783), Massachusetts (1783), Connecticut (1784), Rhode Island (1784), New York (1799), and New Jersey (1804).

16. Kathryn Kish Sklar, "'Women Who Speak for an Entire Nation': American and British Women Compared at the World Anti-Slavery Convention, London, 1840," *Pacific Historical Review* 59, no. 4 (1990): 453–99.

17. Faulkner, *Lucretia Mott's Heresy*, 110; Tetrault, *The Myth of Seneca Falls*, 16, 21.

18. Sinha, *The Slave's Cause*, 1.

19. Yee, *Black Women Abolitionists*, 6, 75.

20. Lerner, *Grimke Sisters*, 110–11; Swerdlow, "Abolition's Conservative Sisters," 40.

21. Yellin, *Harriet Jacobs*, 69. See Swerdlow, "Abolition's Conservative Sisters"; Boylan, "Benevolence and Anti-Slavery Activity"; Boylan, *Origins of Women's Activism*.

22. Salerno, *Sister Societies*, 87–88.

23. Faulkner, *Lucretia Mott's Heresy*, 130–37; Wagner, *Sisters in Spirit*, 44.

24. Wellman, *Road to Seneca Falls*, 68.

25. Stanton et al., *History of Woman Suffrage*, 672.

26. Venet, *Neither Ballots nor Bullets*, 102–7.

27. The former Confederate states ratified the Thirteenth Amendment on December 6, 1865. McPherson, *The Struggle for Equality*, 127, 305n.

28. Marilley, *Woman Suffrage*, 69; Keyssar, *Right to Vote*, 81.

29. DuBois, *Feminism and Suffrage*, 61.

30. DuBois, 53–78; Marilley, *Woman Suffrage*, 72.

31. Marilley 73.

32. See the chapter by Erin O'Connor in this volume.

33. Stanton et al., *History of Woman Suffrage*, 2, 222.

34. See Susan Goodier, "Doublespeak: Louisa Jacobs, the American Equal Rights Association, and Complicating Racism in the Early US Women's Suffrage Movement, *New York History* 101, no. 2 (Winter–Spring 2021).

35. Galloway, *American Equal Rights Association*, 19.

36. While some members of the American Equal Rights Association sought to keep the organization alive, members voted to fold it into the National Woman Suffrage Association. Galloway, *American Equal Rights Association*, 138; Marilley, *Woman Suffrage*, 66.

37. Marilley, *Woman Suffrage*, 66.

38. Gordon, *Selected Papers of Elizabeth Cady Stanton and Susan B. Anthony*, 645–54; Lange, *Picturing Political Power*, 82, 86.

39. DuBois, *Feminism and Suffrage*, 189–95.

40. DuBois, 195–200.

41. Terborg-Penn, *African American Women in the Struggle for the Vote*, 42; Lange, *Picturing Political Power*, 71.

42. This volume is in the Onondaga Historical Society, Syracuse, New York.

43. Cary took over the editing of the *Provincial Freemen*. Chapman and Mills, *Treacherous Texts*, xii.

44. Frances Ellen Watkins Harper, "Woman's Political Future" (speech given May 20, 1893, before the World's Congress of Representative Women at the Chicago Columbian Exposition), Archives of Women's Political Communication, Iowa State University, https://awpc.cattcenter.iastate.edu/2019/05/21/womans-political-future-may-20–1893/, accessed February 24, 2021.

45. "The 19th Amendment," National Archives, https://www.archives.gov/exhibits/featured-documents/amendment-19, accessed April 15, 2021; "Woman Suffrage Centennial," United States Senate, https://www.senate.gov/artandhistory/history/People/Women/Nineteenth_Amendment_Vertical_Timeline.htm, accessed April 23, 2021.

46. Wagner, *Time of Protest*, 111–23.

47. Mead, *How the Vote Was Won*.

48. Tiffany Lewis, "Mapping Social Movements and Leveraging the US West: The Rhetoric of the Woman Suffrage Map," *Women's Studies in Communication* 42, no. 4 (2019), 490–510.

49. Lange, *Picturing Political Power*, 106. Gaylynn Welch, "Suffrage at the

Schoolhouse Door: The 1880 New York State School Suffrage Campaign," *New York History* 98, no. 3–4 (2017), 329–42.

50. Gage, *Woman Church and State*, x; Wagner, *Sisters in Spirit*, 49, 63.

51. Sally Roesch Wagner has devoted her career to the recovery of Matilda Joslyn Gage, the third member of the triumvirate leadership of the nineteenth-century women's rights movement. Visit https://matildajoslyngage.org/ for more information about this important activist.

52. Alexander Street Press has undertaken a project to collect the biographies of thousands of women who participated in the movement.

53. "The New Woman," Digital Public Library of America, https://dp.la/primary-source-sets/the-new-woman, accessed June 29, 2022.

54. Streitmatter, *Raising Her Voice*, 37–48.

55. Kenneth Florey has written two books about the ephemera of the women's suffrage movement: *Women's Suffrage Memorabilia: An Illustrated Historical Study* (Jefferson, NC: McFarland, 2013) and *American Woman Suffrage Postcards: A Study and Catalog* (Jefferson, NC: McFarland, 2015). See also his website, "Woman Suffrage Memorabilia: A Site Devoted to Such Artifacts as Buttons, Post Cards, Ribbons, Sheet Music, and Ceramics," http://womansuffrage memorabilia.com.

56. Steven Biel, *Down with the Old Canoe: A Cultural History of the Titanic Disaster* (New York: W. W. Norton, 2003), 10, 29–30.

57. Faderman, *To Believe in Women*, 17, 32, 39. Faderman is the first scholar to look closely at the relationships between suffrage activists. In recent years, more historians are focusing attention on the topic.

58. Susan Goodier, "Seeking and Seeing Black Women: Hester C. Jeffrey and Woman Suffrage Activism," *New York History* 98, no. 3–4 (Fall–Winter 2017), 475–88.

59. Appropriation accompanied inclusion, and for every instance of inclusiveness, it is probable that there were several of exclusion. Santangelo, *Suffrage and the City*, 109.

60. Biel, *Down with the Old Canoe*, 102.

61. Cathleen D. Cahill and Sarah Deer, "In 1920, Native Women Sought the Vote. Here's What's Next," July 31, 2020, https://www.nytimes.com/2020/07/31/style/19th-amendment-native-womens-suffrage.html; Wagner, *Sisters in Spirit*, 41.

62. Gage wrote extensively on the Haudenosaunee and was working on a book at the time of her death in 1898. Wagner, *Sisters in Spirit*, 28, 37.

63. Native people responded by founding nationalist organizations such as the American Indian Movement.

64. They held the event on October 12, 1911, in Columbus, Ohio. "Indian Woman Works for Uncle Sam," *Pittsburgh Post-Gazette*, March 21, 1911, 16; "From Indian Tepee to Washington Flat," *Neenah Daily Times*, January 21, 1913, 3.

65. "At the First National Conference," *Nebraska State Capital*, November 17, 1911, 2.

66. Cahill, *Recasting the Vote*, 25, 34. "Chinese Talk Suffrage," *New-York Tribune*, April 11, 1912, 3.

67. "Maria Guadalupe Evangelina de Lopez," American Women's History Museum, https://www.womenshistory.org/education-resources/biographies/maria-guadalupe-evangelina-de-lopez, accessed August 26, 2023; "Angeleno Beauties Proposed for Place in Suffrage Parade," *Los Angeles Herald*, April 12, 1913; "Former LA Teacher to Drive French Ambulance," *Los Angeles Herald*, May 26, 1917; "LA Girl Cited for Bravery," *Los Angeles Herald*, October 26, 1918; John William Leonard, ed., *Woman's Who's Who of America: A Biographical Dictionary of Contemporary Women of the United States and Canada* (New York: American Commonwealth Co., 1914), 492; Maria de E. G. Lopez, "Equal Suffrage of Most Vital Moment," *Los Angeles Herald*, August 20, 1911; R. H. Martínez, *Latinos in Pasadena* (Mount Pleasant, SC: Arcadia Publishing, 2009; Sabrina Reichert, "Latinx Women in the US Women's Suffrage Movement," Women's Museum of California, https://womensmuseum.wordpress.com/2020/05/22/latinx-women-in-the-u-s-womens-suffrage-movement, accessed November 25, 2020.

68. Cahill, *Recasting the Vote*, 51.

69. Cahill, 53, 55, 142.

70. Lange, *Picturing Political Power*, 161, 173.

71. Zahniser, *Alice Paul*, 137–39.

72. Graham posits that suffragists purged their records of correspondence with Black activists to erase their lack of support. Erasing or ignoring the contributions of Black women to the movement has compounded the racism Black suffragists faced at the time. Graham, *Woman Suffrage and the New Democracy*, 22–24, 171, 58n.

73. Lange, *Picturing Political Power*, 173.

74. Rebecca Boggs Roberts," The Great Suffrage Parage of 1913," National Park Service, https://www.nps.gov/articles/000/the-great-suffrage-parade-of-1913.htm#:~:text=Inevitably%2C%20they%20even%20injured%20some,to%20the%20local%20emergency%20hospital, accessed April 23, 2021.

75. Zahniser, *Alice Paul*, 255.

76. "Online Biographical Dictionary of the Woman Suffrage Movement in the United States," Alexander Street, https://documents.alexanderstreet.com/VOTESforWOMEN, accessed July 14, 2021.

77. For more about the picketing, see Stevens, *Jailed for Freedom*.

78. National American Woman Suffrage Association, *Victory*, 123–54; Van Voris, *Carrie Chapman Catt*, 153–55; "Colby Proclaims Woman Suffrage," *New York Times*, August 27, 1920, 1.

79. Higginbotham, "Clubwomen and Electoral Politics in the 1920s," 147–50.

80. Blee, *Women of the Klan*, 2–3.

81. "Pan-American Conference of Women," Wikipedia, https://en.wikipedia.org/wiki/Pan-American_Conference_of_Women, accessed August 26, 2023.

82. Anderson, *One Person, No Vote*, 22.

CRISIS OF REPRESENTATION

Examples: Brazil, Argentina, Colombia

Liberalism suffered a crisis of legitimacy in the period between the two world wars. In Latin America, republicanism and liberal economics had failed to produce the prosperous, egalitarian nations that the criollo leaders of the independence movements foretold. Neocolonialism had, for much of the continent, replaced colonialism. Laws abolishing slavery and caste did not usher in an era of equality. If anything, the loss of protections for Indigenous groups increased opportunities for exploitation, especially around the crucial issue of land rights. Despite shared enthusiasm for expensive projects like the expansion of public education, political elites were somewhat less zealous about taxing themselves sufficiently to fund them. By the turn of the twentieth century, many people throughout the Americas led lives of poverty and insecurity. Liberal economics had everywhere generated a great deal of wealth, but maldistribution concentrated prosperity in the hands of the few, who also dominated political systems. Nowhere in the Americas did elected representatives act for or represent the interests of the majority.

At the same time, investments in transportation and communication infrastructure, combined with incipient industrialization and urbanization, created the conditions from which a new kind of politics could emerge.

Nineteenth-century caudillismo had relied on personal relationships between a leader and groups of (typically armed) followers. Twentieth-century charismatic leadership could achieve a similar affective relationship with many more individuals at once. Messages promising changes in favor of ordinary people could be transmitted via radio or carried on trains to remote areas. Unsurprisingly, they found broad appeal. Many of those putting forward reforms included women's political rights among their proposals.

There are two pitfalls here we would like to avoid falling into. Both have to do with the problematic category "populism." The leaders whose suffrage extensions this section addresses—Getulio Vargas in Brazil, Juan Perón in Argentina, and Gustavo Rojas Pinilla in Colombia—are often classified as populist. Populism, however, is a label that has been so broadly applied as to render it almost useless. Here we prefer to focus on conditions that gave rise to a period of political experimentation, which often included suffrage extensions to new groups of people. Vargas, Perón, and Rojas Pinilla shared three characteristics associated with populism: a reformist platform intended to appeal to masses of common people, a tendency toward authoritarianism, and a willingness to try new things. Beyond this, however, national contexts varied enormously. Scholars of Argentina and Brazil, especially, have long struggled to overcome the perception that their histories were mirrors of each other. They were not.

The second pitfall has to do with those who supported so-called populist leaders. The term *populist* has been used pejoratively to ascribe certain characteristics to supporters of charismatic leaders: namely that followers are drawn, irrationally, to politicians who do not represent their interests. In the context of women's suffrage especially there has been a tendency to imagine that women may have been even more vulnerable to disingenuous manipulation than poor, uneducated men. There has been a tendency to blame women voters for extending the rule of authoritarian leaders, especially in Brazil and Argentina. But as Marques and Valobra show, in neither case were women's votes decisive. In other words, Vargas's and Perón's political fortunes did not turn on women's enfranchisement. Arguments to the contrary, abundant in the historiography, are counterfactual. In the Argentine case, reelection was not even constitutionally possible when Perón decreed women's suffrage. When the constitution was changed and he ran again for president, male voters supported his candidacy just as enthusiastically as women. Brazil's Vargas was not yet considered a populist when he extended the franchise to a much more limited group of women, and his extension was so limited that women voters could not have substantively affected its outcome anyway.

Thus we must thread the needle. We need to reject again, as emphatically as possible, the notion that women were somehow more vulnerable to any kind of manipulation than men. At the same time, we should acknowledge that multiple motivations led charismatic leaders to extend women the suffrage, including pressure from suffragists, a willingness to experiment, a desire to avoid appearing backward to audiences at home and abroad, the potential to expand their base of support to gain legitimacy, and even a genuine desire to do what they believed was right.

CHAPTER FOUR

Ideological and Political Obstacles to Enfranchising Women in Brazil

TERESA CRISTINA DE NOVAES MARQUES

GETÚLIO VARGAS'S GOVERNMENT EXTENDED THE right to vote to literate women in Brazil by decree in February 1932. For the first time since the promulgation of the 1891 republican constitution, women could vote and run for elected office.[1] As of May 3, 1933, women over age twenty-one could vote for representatives to the National Constituent Assembly, regardless of their marital status.[2] The only requirement was to demonstrate literacy, and the same was requested of men. Voting was not mandatory for women as it was for male electors, except for public employees, few of whom were women. Women's suffrage was confirmed by the 1934 constitution only to be suppressed by Vargas's dictatorship in November 1937.

The 1932 decision ended a forty-year-old controversy, which played out through making and interpreting laws as well as through the press and other means society had to express ideas. This chapter explores the long road to women's enfranchisement in Brazil, which benefited a limited number of women yet allowed some from the middle class entry into the political system; many of them ran for office in the 1933 and 1934 elections.[3]

It is still not clear why President Vargas yielded to feminists' demands. Our best information comes from the memoirs of one member of the commission responsible for writing the new electoral code.[4] Once Vargas capitulated to pressure to restore the representative system, his government acted to ensure majority in the forthcoming constitutional assembly by promoting three measures. First, Vargas selected state governors to organize parties to take part in the election. Second, Catholic Church members recovered their political rights, a prerogative lost in 1891. The code enfranchising educated women was a third measure, in the hope they would vote for candidates aligned with the government. The international atmosphere may also have influenced Vargas; women's suffrage would enhance Brazil's image abroad in the same year Uruguay and Argentina considered bills to enfranchise women.[5]

A meditated approach is required to understand a history so full of layers of meaning and interests. This chapter uses two theoretical standpoints: intellectual history is the key to approaching nineteenth-century debates on reforming the representative system. Political and legal history give us tools to understand the growing women's activism observed in the first three decades of the twentieth century.

Why choose to combine two different historical methods to explore the history of the women's vote in Brazil? From about 1850 to 1891, the defense of women's political rights took the form of an intellectual debate nourished by ideas appropriated from foreign thinkers and adapted to the Brazilian reality. The major goal was to confer legitimacy on discourses to persuade allies or dissuade opponents.

Although some rhetorical practices, such as mentioning foreign authors to justify an argument, did not disappear after the installation of the republic, the struggle to oppose them was no longer a matter of disputing which author offered a more legitimate set of ideas. The political groups of women that emerged showed new forms of action, such as writing in the press, making public demonstrations, writing petitions to the legislature, and requesting hearings before men in power.

In both periods examined here, before and after the 1890s, there are robust historiographical contributions in English. June E. Hahner is a pioneer in the subject.[6] Starting in the 1970s, she published articles and books about the long path to enfranchising women in Brazil, opening eyes to the role played by the women's press. In her work, Hahner explored the National Library's collection in Rio de Janeiro, which shows women's demand for better education in the nineteenth century. We now know that women all over the country attempted to make a living editing newspapers and that many women collaborated with the local press too. Recent research has shown that newspapers edited by women outnumber the National Library's collection. Hahner was the first to give a historiographical treatment to the republican constitutional assembly of 1890–1891, which debated enfranchising educated women. By exploring reading practices of the elite as well as the appropriation of political ideas, I offer an angle Hahner did not consider.

Susan Besse offers another remarkable historiographical exercise about gender relations in Brazil. Besse's work, together with Heleieth Saffioti's, explore the many layers of reiterated gender inequalities that marked women's lives in the first decades of the twentieth century. Being a woman in Brazil meant earning a low salary, having fewer educational and professional opportunities, and being subject to abuse in private life. These forms of oppression affected Black and Indigenous women even more severely. Besse and Saffioti acknowledge intersectionality and explore feminist groups and their strategies to conquer the vote. My aim in this chapter is to bring new archival findings and new research questions to existing knowledge of the subject.[7]

The narrative unfolds in three sections. First it develops a reprisal of the major historical trends that characterized the emerging independent nation in early nineteenth century and the formation of Brazilian society. Second it approaches the struggles to win the franchise with an emphasis on the ideological obstacles feminists encountered. This section takes the intellectual debate in Parliament and in the press as keys to understanding the limits on and possibilities for modernizing the political system in the long nineteenth century.

The third section examines the political activities developed by women's groups from the 1890s through the 1930s. By examining the trajectories of three notable women, it offers a broad canvas of the strategies activists adopted to have their voices heard in public spaces.

Freedom for the Nation; Slavery for the People

Brazil obtained its independence from Portugal in 1822 under peculiar circumstances. To avoid the fate that met the Spanish king when Napoleon's troops first invaded the peninsula, the Portuguese court decamped to its American kingdom in 1807. Thus, when Brazilian elites sent representatives to Portugal in 1820 to write a constitution, they did not expect to suffer harassment by Portuguese politicians, who found themselves in the uncomfortable position of being a colony of Brazil. Without room to negotiate a continuity of the status quo, the majority of the Brazilian provincial representatives chose independence, though most of them feared the consequences of the decision.[8] As they came back home, politicians diverged.

European political debate arrived in Brazil through books, newspapers, and materials discussed in Masonic lodges. Few historians dare to state anything conclusive about the role of Masonry, given its secretive nature. However, an important historian of the independence period affirms that two currents influenced Brazil in the 1820s.[9] Left-wing French Masonry influenced lodges in northeastern provinces, emphasizing the priority of local over centralized government. This line of thinking resulted in three attempts to seize power in Pernambuco (in 1817, 1824, and 1848). Southeastern elites, on the other hand, were under the influence of British and French lodges, for whom governability was considered the major goal. The unavoidable clash of political projects resulted in the dominance of the southeastern elites over their counterparts in the provinces. The primacy of preserving slavery directed their actions; they feared that a general political disarray could make room for a popular revolt.[10]

Brazil also differed from other countries in South America in that it emerged from the process of independence both as a monarchy and as a large and contiguous territory, whereas neighbors to the north and south saw colonial administrative units splinter into multiple republics after independence. Brazilian political stability came in the 1840s after a continuous and uniquely successful effort to subjugate provincial resistance.

Consolidating independence and building state institutions happened at the same time the Atlantic system deepened its effects. Until 1850, the Atlantic slave trade fueled Brazilian slave society on an unprecedented scale. Demographers argue that the large supply of people provided by the trade shaped the peculiar distribution of slavery in Brazil, where thousands of people were enslaved by many free Brazilians and employed in all sectors of the economy in every region.[11] The widespread feature of Brazilian slavery impacted politics because such a large portion of the free population supported slavery. This changed only after 1850, when slave ownership became more concentrated, leading fewer people to support it.

It is reasonable to question why widespread enslavement did not expose the contradiction of defending liberty as a political principle. Some interpreters argue that liberal ideas had a shallow impact on the worldview of elites. This line of thought is considered obsolete today because liberty, like equality, is a concept that requires qualification. In the 1830s, Brazilian elites were keen to defend the liberty of political expression, trade, and property ownership. The reconfiguration of the public order, largely inspired by Benjamin Constant's ideas, responded to these demands. The centrality of the state and the law aligned Brazilian liberalism with the dominant liberalism in France. All the subtle aspects of Constant's thoughts concerning political participation were subsumed by the priority of organizing public order under rules defined by a constitution.

The society that emerged in post-independence Brazil combined a public sphere ruled by updated institutions with a private sphere of power, where enslavers prevailed over enslaved and other members of the *domus* (wife and children) who were not included in the category of "citizen." A great deal of violence pervaded these relationships.

1831: Widows That May Vote

The revolutionary movement that took place in France and reverberated in Europe and the Americas overcame the privilege of birth as a criterion for the exercise of power. After dismissing the legitimacy of noble privilege, public men began a debate that continued throughout the entire nineteenth century on new criteria to define who should have a voice in politics. The French political system discussed formulas for establishing a decision-making system based on representation, capable of responding to the interests of voters and also able to ward off the specter of radicalism.

In France, political debates about the electoral system reached great intensity in the first half of 1831 culminating in the approval of a new electoral law in April of that year. The French majority were in favor of the census system, meaning that voters were qualified by income. Few preferred the capacity system, in which voters were qualified by schooling and reputation.[12] The fear of political passions aroused by elections lay in the background of the French debates. This sentiment led conservatives to imagine ways of restricting political participation. Members of the French political system debated these questions throughout the nineteenth century, just as was done in Brazil, which nourished cultural and political ties to France.

While the Americas were facing political turmoil in the first decades of the century, France itself was under transformation. The restoration of the monarchy in 1830 brought new challenges to the public debate, where different currents of thought reclaimed political space under the umbrella of liberalism. Scholars agree that there is no conclusive definition of liberalism because it consists more of a bundle of philosophical principles shared by those who oppose the absolutist state than a cohesive system of thought.[13] The keystones of liberalism are the belief in the sovereign individual and in liberty as an inalienable good. Numerous political currents offered different approaches to two central problems: how to form the virtuous individual, the cornerstone of the political community; and how to preserve that person's rights.

Experts prefer to use the term *liberalisms* instead of a singular form. In the nineteenth century, the French political debate produced two major schools of liberalism, and both had repercussions in Latin America. The first school is liberalism of the subject, and it centers on the individual who acts as a judge of those in power. For the most radical, Rousseau is the key intellectual reference, but Stael, Condorcet, and Benjamin Constant were also popular writers among readers in Latin America. The second school of French liberalism is elitist liberalism, whose paramount reference is Guizot. Elites in the Americas admired his emphasis on governability as they struggled to moderate political passions and build functional political systems after independence.

Political ideas inspired by the authors were available in the form of books or specialized publications. Those ideas supported the construction of a dual political system composed of active (men) and passive (women) citizens. The latter enjoyed some rights but did not participate in political deliberations.

This is an idea that roamed the public debate from the eighteenth century and found numerous adherents over time, including in Brazil.

To keep track of the channels of transmission of political innovations, I examined bills concerning who was eligible to vote as well as the debates congressmen had about them. I then cross-referenced the intellectual sources mentioned in the debates with the legislature's book collection, particularly the House of Representatives library, which is now in Brasília.[14]

Methodological procedures from the field of the history of reading answer fundamental questions, such as those suggested by Darnton.[15] What did nineteenth-century parliamentarians read and how did they read it? How did politicians interpret the ideas of the authors of their time? Examining the pronouncements made at the meetings and transcribed in the Parliament annals gives only a partial answer. Reading their books helps fill in the texture between the broadest strokes on the canvas.

This line of research has been successfully developed already, particularly in the United States, resulting in a vigorous academic production from which useful questions are drawn to understand other political formations, if adjustments are made. The first adjustment is related to the universe of intellectual influences that surrounded public men in Brazil, distinct from the reading patterns and circulation of ideas in the Anglo-Saxon world. Recognizing the intellectual bond that Brazilians maintained with the ongoing political and philosophical debate in France is the first necessary adjustment. Books were circulated in French, even if originally written in other languages. Another aspect that emerges from the research is the diffusion of authors who are now forgotten, such as Louis de Bonald, read in Brazil at the beginning of the nineteenth century, or Édouard Laboulaye, well-known to Brazilian parliamentarians at the end of that century.[16] It is useless to search for such authors in the historical compendiums of prominent figures in Western political philosophical thinking, even though they often figured in private collections of educated men.

With these parameters in mind, I examined the first, limited attempt to confer political rights to women, in 1831. José Bonifácio de Andrada e Silva and Manoel Alves Branco presented a bill to the Lower Chamber that proposed to change the entire election system in the country.[17] On July 28, Alves Branco took the floor at the House to present the first bill that included women as political subjects in Brazil.[18] The project combined the census system already in place under the constitution of 1824, which qualified as a voter anyone with a stipulated income, with the capacity system, which defined voters as educated and holding positions of responsibility with respect to the community and family.[19] In France, this last formula was called the family vote: a conservative political maneuver to prevent suffrage from being extended to radical sectors.[20] The Brazilian deputies followed the spirit of the French project, which permitted the vote for widows who controlled family assets. However, the Andrada-Alves Branco bill was not even discussed. Political agitation in the legislature in the second half of 1831 prevents us from examining the reception of the proposal.[21]

The Andrada-Alves Branco proposal attributed a bold interpretation to Article 90 of the 1824 constitution, which characterized the "active" citizen as one who votes at the parish level, selecting electors who would then choose representatives in the provincial and national legislatures. By enabling widows to be active citizens for certain subjects, as long as they were responsible for the family's interests, the bill recognized that sex was not an impediment for women to participate in public affairs. Rousseau, Kant, and many others argued that women lacked rationality and a sense of justice.[22] This thinking associated women with nature, praising their inherent affectivity yet recognizing a supposed inability to constrain passionate impulses. For these thinkers, women did not qualify as moral beings capable of rational deliberation over public affairs. Jose Pimenta Bueno, a politician and legal adviser of the monarch, interpreted the same constitutional article more strictly. His influential 1857 book on the principles of the imperial constitution argued that only active citizens should enjoy political rights. He said that women, especially if they were married, did not have legal autonomy for full citizenship or the moral requisites to take part in civic affairs.

Pimenta Bueno was inspired by Kant's representation of the ideal citizen, which excluded women. Commentators on the republican constitution reiterated Pimenta Bueno's work, which connects both constitutions to the same tradition regarding women's political rights. Pimenta Bueno introduced the argument that the word *citizen* in the 1824 constitution, a male word in Portuguese, referred only to men. Twenty-six years before, Andrada-Alves Branco did not seem to agree. However, when we look at the big picture, Andrada-Alves Branco's bill is an exceptional episode in a much more consistent tradition of not considering women as potential active citizens.[23] This long-lasting dispute illustrates the enduring vigor of the debate on the question of women's political status on both sides of the Atlantic.

Biological determinism updated the misogynist arguments from the mid-nineteenth century onward. Women's inferiority gained the status of scientific truth as biology emerged as a scientific discipline.[24] Following this new trend, Auguste Comte sustained that the peculiar female biology reinforced women's patriarchal duty to obey and submit. Comte occupied no place of authority in the French political system, but his work found an enormous audience in the Americas. In France, Comte aligned with those who advocated limiting power to sensible, right-minded, passion-averse individuals.[25]

Ever since the first edition of his work *Cours de Philosophie Positive*, whose first volume was published in 1829, Comte figured among the defenders of enlightened despotism. The repercussions in Brazil, however, were not immediate. His 1852 book *Système de Politique Positive* reached a much larger audience.[26] Between the 1829 work, a prolific philosophical treatise in six volumes, and the *Système*, a work that unites Comte's political ideas in a single portable volume, Brazil saw a surge of new social sectors. Engineers and members of the military, for example, were not included in the existing Brazilian representative system and were therefore excluded from well-paid public jobs. Members of these groups fed the list of positivist adherents.[27]

As I mentioned before, intellectual history offers us tools to understand the fundamentals of political debate in the 1870s. Politicians and journalists frequently discussed the electoral system, and advocates of broad reform proposed enfranchising educated women, quoting John Stuart Mill's works. On the other hand, those in favor of profound changes in the direction of a more centralized form of government found shelter in Comte's ideas. The clash of political projects resounded in parliamentary debates and in the press. To better understand the appropriation of these innovative ideas, I now explore both authors, using the collection available at the Lower Chamber library.

Like liberalism, positivism was not a monolithic philosophical school. Comte had his first contact with ideas of centralized political power from

Claude-Henri de Saint-Simon, his mentor. Years later, Comte broke with Saint-Simon and developed his own ideas, publishing the first volume of his best-known work in 1829. By the 1850s, Comte's proposals moved toward integral control of social life, including his first considerations on the religion of humanity, a cult that gained few followers in French but attracted members in Brazil and other parts of Latin America.

Both Comte and Saint-Simon agreed that governing should be reserved for the most capable, but Saint-Simon also emphasized the importance of industrial development to human progress. In Brazil there were two regional centers where positivism spread, made numerous followers, and formed worldviews: in the south and in Rio de Janeiro (southeast).[28] Elsewhere, positivism spread as a general ideology as Comte's ideas circulated. However, the religious aspect of the late phase of Comte's ideas did not raise enthusiasm outside Rio de Janeiro.

We see increased emphasis on women's political roles between Comte's 1829 and 1852 publications. John Stuart Mill, who was familiar with Comte's work since the first edition and exchanged correspondence with him between 1841 and 1847, noticed.[29] The letters they exchanged, collected in a publication acquired by the House of Representatives, reveal Mill's resistance to the notion of women's biological subordination. Comte believed women's inferiority justified their unfitness for public affairs and sole vocation for domestic life.[30] For the English philosopher, women's unwillingness to think about political issues was the result of education and was therefore reversible. Mill failed to persuade Comte, who dedicated an entire chapter in his 1852 book to keeping women in the domestic sphere. The French philosopher argued that education should be used to reinforce isolation and instill in girls the spirit of obedience to the active sex—men. Women's propensity for emotion destined them exclusively to care for offspring, he said.[31]

If Brazilian congressmen read Mill and Comte's correspondence, they would have realized that the philosophers diverged irreconcilably around two of Mill's assertions: first, the importance of universal suffrage; second, the recognition of women's rights to equal treatment. In subsequent years, Mill energetically criticized Comte's political and philosophical positions. He defended the need to reform the representative system, including enfranchising women. In the English Parliament, Mill championed egalitarianism in the House of Commons, defending measures in favor of poor workers, land reform, and women's suffrage.

Mill's commitment to these causes began with the publication of *On Liberty* in 1859.[32] In 1861 Mill published his best-known political work, *Considerations on Representative Government*. The House of Representatives acquired the first French edition of these works.[33] In *Considerations*, he systematized his ideas about the ideal form of democratic society. In his view, democracy could only be achieved if all society's interests were included in the political system. That included women. The broader the suffrage, the fairer the system would be, able to meet the aspirations of the larger population and respect the rights of minorities. Reforming the political system must be accompanied by a reform of the educational system to universalize adult literacy, he said. The participative citizen, in Mill's thinking, had an interest in public affairs, fueled by access to books and newspapers.

As a part of the same intellectual project, the author published a book criticizing Comte in 1865; it was translated into French the following year.[34] In it, and especially in his work *The Subjection of Women*, Mill advocated equal treatment for women.[35] The French edition of that book came out in 1869, and the House of Representatives bought it.[36]

An argument repeated throughout the book compares the unbalanced power relations in marriage to the condition of slavery. Mill criticized husbands, many of them venerable men on the public scene but with unlimited powers to oppress the beings subject to them at home, their wives and children. This argument hurt the sensibilities of English public men, who saw themselves as the civilizing power responsible for suppressing the odious slave trade in the Atlantic. In Brazil, Mill's analogy between slavery and marriage resonated for women who attempted to make their living by publishing newspapers and books. Some, like journalist Josephina de Azevedo, were also abolitionists.[37]

The women's press included recurrent mentions of Mill's and Comte's ideas. As more women were educated and engaged themselves professionally in education, newspapers written by women appeared all over the country.[38] It is interesting to notice how a newspaper edited by a teacher in Minas Gerais from 1850 through the 1890s changed the way it portrayed women's social roles. In 1873 the *O Sexo Feminino* defended women's education so they could care for the home. In 1889 the editor, Francisca Senhorinha, got more ambitious and suggested women could be lawyers and doctors.[39] It became more usual to see journalists quoting Mill's books to advocate for universal education and condemn unhappy marriage as a form of slavery. This occurred in the press women edited as well as in newspapers men edited aimed at women readers.[40]

In 1868 a modest teacher from Rio de Janeiro named Anna Rosa Termacsics dos Santos published a book invoking Mill, Rousseau, and Condorcet to demand women's right to vote.[41] It is the first known female-authored book to defend suffrage. In her work, Santos also advocated for access to professional opportunities, especially public posts, so that women would no longer depend on men economically. Nevertheless, Santos did not extend the idea of liberty to the enslaved population. When it came to enslaved Black women, Santos remained silent.

Twenty years passed between the circulation of the first French editions of Mill's writing in Brazil and the triumph of the republican movement. However, ideas from a particular work can often take years to find traction. As La Capra argues, in intellectual history, it is important to understand how ideas are used at the moment and the place in which they are enunciated.[42] In this case the abolition campaign, involving literate women and public men, made it appropriate to associate slavery with domestic oppression to sustain the suffragist cause as well. Abolitionism made the association more compelling for many women suffragists. However, as seen in Santos's work, embracing the suffragist cause did not always accompany abolitionism.

Debating an Electoral Law Reform

As seen in the previous section, the issue of women's suffrage—whether universal or restricted—motivated discussion in European intellectual circles, which reverberated in Brazil. Supporters derived new arguments from Mill's works published in the 1860s, which emphatically advocated equal education for women and men. In Europe Mill was treated as a radical thinker, although he was respected for his philosophical erudition.[43]

The 1860s and 1870s were intense in France, with the publication of numerous works on the political system, as well as political analyses in magazines read throughout the French-speaking world and in Brazil.[44] In 1875, French politicians debated a new constitutional experiment, in which the jurist and politician Edouard Laboulaye played a prominent part. Attentive to the new trends, Brazilian politicians and activists divided themselves intellectually into three currents of thought. There were a small number who followed Comte's ideas and rejected integrating women into the political system.[45] Left-wing, reformist liberals found inspiration in Mill. Self-proclaimed moderate liberals preferred French authors like Laboulaye, whose ideas sounded more attainable. According to Laboulaye, individuals' political rights were not natural. Instead they were rights to be enjoyed as the social interest deemed appropriate. For Laboulaye, womanhood figured among the attributes that made an individual incapable of the suffrage because the true nature of political rights depended on social convenience.[46]

At the end of the 1870s, the Liberal Party again took up the cause of electoral system reform in Brazil.[47] It supported qualification criteria and proposed reformulating the way to carry out elections. While the debate developed in the press and in Parliament, elections in the empire continued, along with frequent and serious conflicts in the electoral parishes. In May 1879, when the House of Representatives debated the reform, radical liberal congressmen took the floor. They were not the majority, but they attended every session and voiced their opinions whenever they could. At the session on March 25, Minas Gerais congressman Martim Francisco argued that women should vote in local elections, in the same spirit of the bill his uncle Jose Bonifácio Andrada e Silva had proposed in 1831. This time, Francisco relied on Mill to argue for the education of women to make them eligible to vote. During the debates, the congressman for Bahia, Cezar Zama, seconded Francisco with similar arguments. Few congressmen cared to rebut Zama's and Francisco's speeches. Most simply chose to remain silent and let the bill follow its course.

The controversial reform resulted in a profound change in the country's electoral system by instituting voter literacy requirements. This measure showed how selectively Mill's thoughts were appropriated in Brazil. For the English author, expansions of public education and the suffrage should go hand in hand. However, most Brazilian parliamentarians preferred limiting the franchise to literate voters without democratizing access to education. The immediate effect of the new electoral rules was a reduction in the number of voters, a result of greater rigor in the qualification system in terms of income and education. Voting was also no longer mandatory but optional.

Despite dramatically reducing the number of eligible voters, Saraiva's reform opened the possibility for educated women to qualify as voters. The Saraiva Law recognized scientific titles—such as medical, law, and dentistry diplomas—as proof of voters' educational qualifications. This meant that a woman holding one of these titles could vote, provided the judges in the polling stations interpreted the term *citizen* (*cidadão*) in the constitution as extendable to men and women indistinctly. According to the suffragist newspaper *A Família*, the dentist Isabel de Souza Mattos, resident in the province of Rio Grande do Sul, requested and obtained voter registration in 1887.[48] Nonetheless, when it came the time to vote for the republican Constituent Assembly in 1890, Mattos was prevented by the enrolling board, which followed the ministry guidelines.

1890–1891: A Strange Alliance Prevented Female Voting

With the monarchy overthrown in November 1889, the republican regime called for elections to form a Constituent Assembly. Hoping for a window of opportunity, suffragists intensified their efforts. Since the mid-1870s, a growing number of non-enslaved women had pursued careers in journalism and become involved in the causes of female education and the defense of the republic. Some were also attracted to the antislavery movement, which spread in larger cities.

Since the assembly would redefine the country's institutional parameters, there was at last a real possibility of recognizing women's political rights, provided the suffragists gain parliamentary allies. Across the country, elections seated 268 constituent parliamentarians, including positivists who embraced Comte's ideas, radical liberals (also called historic republicans), moderate liberals, and a few conservatives, veterans of the empire. During the drafting of the constitution, the positivists were the most eloquent, although there were not many of them.[49] Radical liberals were the suffragists' best allies, though they were also a minority.

The drafting committee of the bill was promising. Representing twenty-one states, it included radical republican Joaquim Saldanha Marinho, who advocated universal suffrage.[50] During preparations for the assembly, the citizenship question made for a clash of ideas. There was even an attempt to resuscitate the French formula that distinguished active from inactive citizens, using a "Brazilian" versus "citizen" formula, in which the latter would be contained within the larger group of the former.[51] The proposal of explicitly distinguishing between individuals with civil rights alone and others with full rights did not advance, but it survived in a veiled way, to be brought back to life hermeneutically years later.[52] Minister Rui Barbosa, a moderate liberal, revised the constitutional draft. All 268 congressmen examined it. It did not explicitly extend suffrage to women. Constitutional commentators confirmed that the republican leaders did not embrace the idea of a truly universal suffrage.[53]

Historic republican Saldanha Marinho resumed his earlier proposal, leading the effort to pass an amendment with support from thirty-one other parliamentarians. The amendment would have enfranchised married and unmarried women who held diplomas or were teachers. Another amendment, presented by the Bahian Cézar Zama and supported by another deputy, would have extended the vote to only widowed women. The amendments were discussed twice.[54] The first time they were defeated. In the second round of discussions, Zama supported Marinho's proposal. This time, the amendments were tabled. What happened at the assembly?

Opponents of women's suffrage used varied arguments: it might threaten the family or hurt women's delicate feelings. Positivist deputy Lauro Sodré cited Comte to argue to keep women exclusively dedicated to their families. Lacerda Coutinho, from Santa Catarina, and José Moniz Freire, from Espírito Santo, both wanted to tie voting rights to eligibility for the draft. Coutinho invoked Laboulaye to argue that women did not have the same value to the state.[55] This argument later became a popular trope.[56]

Coutinho promoted a curious collection of elements from right-leaning liberalism and elements of Comte's authoritarian thinking to assert that women were incapable of dealing with public affairs and that maternity was their primary social mission.[57] He connected ideas from antagonistic philosophical currents, revealing that political debate was not always governed by ideological coherence.[58] By observing these debates, we can see that politicians made eclectic associations of ideas. They restricted the number of voters simply because they did not want to risk unpredictable elections.

Among suffrage advocates, arguments in favor of the proposals varied from an appeal to justice to a defense of representing the population. The most significant support came from Costa Machado, from Minas Gerais. On January 27, 1891, when the chances of approving anything were already declining, the congressman spoke at length; his speech was closely followed by those present, as the session's transcription remarked. Costa Machado criticized the political currents he considered responsible for rejecting the suffragist amendments—positivists and moderate liberals. Machado sustained that those blocs feared the effects of the suffrage expansion during the country's transition to the republican regime, which coincided with the recent abolition of slavery (1888). Members of the republican government worried that the poor would challenge their plans of governing for few.

1891–1932: Four Decades of Struggle

Regulating the exercise of citizenship remained a source of permanent controversy and an obstacle to enfranchising women. The term *citizen*, a masculine noun used in constitutional Articles 69 and 70, should comprise men and women. An old juridical principle from Roman law oriented the word choice in Latin American laws: *Homo est etiam femina.*[59] This meant that, following the principles of civil law, the choice of male words should imply that women were subject to the laws and protected by them as well as men. In the Iberian languages in use in Latin America, the words *ciudadano* and *cidadão* are male. That raised the question of whether a citizen's prerogatives extended to women too. There were parliamentarians at the assembly who argued that the amendments in favor of female suffrage were unnecessary because the text did not prevent women from voting. Reality, however, contradicted this interpretation. The grammatical discussion was the surface of a legal debate on the legitimate sources of law in a system formed by layers of traditions, some old and others recent. In the end, the controversies gave suffragists new angles to exploit in their campaign for the vote.

A decade of political violence and social turmoil followed the institution-alization of the republic, which frustrated many groups' expectations of modernizing access to public jobs, having a voice in public policies, even enjoying the freedoms the constitution consecrated. The 1891 charter pro-claimed freedom of professional activity and did not explicitly forbid women from voting. However, political forces showed great resistance to novelty.

Soon politicized women realized that it was no longer a matter of making statements in the press or relying on male politicians. The entire adult female population did not clamor for rights, though they made political choices in their day-to-day lives. Three remarkable activists—Myrthes Cam-pos, Leolinda Daltro, and Bertha Lutz—highlight the careers of those who did. None of them was born in the capital of Brazil, Rio de Janeiro, but they all chose Rio in which to pursue careers and find a voice in politics.[60]

Campos was one of the first women lawyers in Brazil. Others completed college before she did (in 1898), but Campos fought to be admitted to the bar and practice.[61] Initially the lawyers' association rejected her, prompting a senator to present a bill stating that women could practice any liberal profes-sion, including medicine and law.[62] Senator Pires Ferreira ultimately with-drew his bill following the advice of his peers, who believed it would be rejected on the floor, but it raised an interesting discussion, which the press covered attentively.[63] The episode tested the effectiveness of new constitu-tional devices about freedoms around professional practice, especially regarding women.

In December 1899, Judge Edmundo Muniz Barreto, president of a court in Rio de Janeiro, publicly denied women the right to practice law when Campos tried to represent a criminal in his court. Barreto quoted every-thing from the sixteenth-century Portuguese *Ordenações* to decisions held in European courts in recent years, disregarding the fact that laws were no longer valid if they collided with the 1891 charter.[64] Was freedom of profes-sional practice a principle or not?

In 1900 Campos again attempted to represent a defendant in court, only to be silenced once more.[65] In subsequent years, Campos repeatedly tried to register to vote, in vain. She wrote articles to legal journals in defense of civil rights, collaborated with the leftist press and trade unions to make suggestions for the civil law bill under discussion in the Lower Chamber, and finally managed to be admitted to the lawyers' association in 1906.[66] While these actions helped create her erudite reputation, they did not open doors to her judiciary career, which depended on political nomination. Campos was only nominated to serve in the educational administration in 1910 and was finally admitted to work in a court in 1924, both times as a clerk.

The possibility of nominating a woman to act as a judge was something that scandalized politicians and judges and affronted one of the most traditional bargaining chips in the political system. Senator Ferreira's bill sparked an interesting debate on how things could get out of hand if women were allowed to practice law. If women did not vote, could the state nominate them for public jobs, especially judgeships? Would they judge according to their emotions? Would their lack of legal autonomy jeopardize their judgment?

In response, Myrthes Campos stated that women's lack of preparation was reversible through education and that they would never lack the sense of justice.[67] Campos criticized an old tradition, perpetuated by Kant and transmitted to law schools and parliaments all over Latin America. Not until 1912 did the Brazilian Supreme Court end the matter by declaring a woman competent to represent a defendant.[68]

In 1922 Campos triumphed at a juridical congress, one of the many activities celebrating the centennial of Brazil's independence. Her thesis about the constitutionality of the women's vote won approval from most participants, overriding the vote of the president of the conference, Carlos Maximiliano Santos, a renowned jurist.[69] The event inaugurated her intermittent collaboration with the Federação Brasileira pelo Progresso Feminino (Brazilian Federation for Female Progress; FBPF), a feminist organization created that same year by Bertha Lutz and Jeronima Mesquita.[70] Winning this battle gave a new boost to the suffrage campaign. In the following years, the FBPF's publications often mentioned Campos's thesis to hammer home the idea that there was nothing in the constitution impeding women from voting. However, the war was far from over.

In a 1918 book, Maximiliano Santos had established an influential claim, arguing that the women's vote was unconstitutional because in 1891, congressmen had defeated the amendments that would have extended the vote.[71] Santos's prestige as commentator on the constitution and former minister of state weighed in his favor. In December 1927, when the Senate considered a bill to enfranchise women, the senator who reported the bill relied on Santos's reasoning. In support of the bill, feminists from the FBPF sent a petition containing two thousand signatures to the Senate, lobbied congressmen, campaigned in the press, and accompanied the session on-site.[72] All this energy resulted in frustration.

Around the country, women tried to register to vote. Judges produced decisions based on varied rules.[73] In February 1929, a judge in the city of São Paulo denied the attempt of lawyer Adalzira Bittencourt Ferrara on the grounds that the word *citizen* in the constitution referred to men only. Judge Esaú Moraes copied an extract from Santos's commentary on the constitution stating that congressmen in 1891 had no intention of enfranchising women.[74] That case attracted the attention of the press all over the country. In the previous month, a judge in the town of Niteroi, state of Rio de Janeiro, had decided in favor of a woman who wanted to vote. Myrthes Campos reproduced this last judge's ruling: "In these terms, the exposition sufficiently proves that article 70 [of the constitution], like so many other articles in the Charter encompasses both sexes. It is useless to appeal to history, which is involved in thick mist, like senator Adolpho Gordo stressed correctly in the speech he said in the Senate, on December 12th 1927."[75] Campos decided it was time for a political intervention, since the legal front had been fruitless.[76]

Feminist Leolinda Daltro tried a different approach: clientelist practices.[77] As an educator, Daltro insisted on universal education to leverage the cause of full citizenship, be it for women or poor men.[78] She made countless attempts to participate in political debates, such as with the Instituto Histórico Geográfico Brasileiro (IHGB), a prestigious organization encompassing historians, geographers, and ethnographers. The academics isolated her in an adjacent room while participants in the meetings said things she deeply disagreed with.[79]

As a teacher in the capital even before the republic, Daltro also embraced the cause of Indigenous people jeopardized by rural violence. In October 1896, she and her older son left Rio de Janeiro for a five-year journey in the hinterland of central Brazil with the mission of teaching Indigenous people to read. A single mother of five children, she depended on her own salary to provide for her family. Back home in December 1900, she used all means at her disposal to gain a position in the ministry to continue developing policies for the Indigenous populations. She had valuable experience with several ethnic groups. Daltro frequently talked to the press, hosted Indigenous people at her home, had them released from police precincts when they were incarcerated without cause, wrote petitions to the ministry, and even wrote a letter to the president of the republic asking for a job.[80] She was told the position she requested did not exist; therefore the office could not nominate her.

Following her political instinct, she went to see the president of the IHGB in October 1902 to defend the necessity of public policy assisting and protecting Indigenous people based on secular education. The members of the IHGB allowed Daltro to address the subject twice: first in 1902 and again in March 1903, when she faced the resistance of supporters of religious organizations. By 1908 Daltro had joined forces with friends to create a civil association separate from the IHGB and devoted to protecting Indigenous people.

Ideologically, Daltro breathed the atmosphere of the early republic. Although the positivists failed to institute the enlightened dictatorship many advocated, Comte's ideas continued to influence policy. Compared to the previous regime, the early republican years saw a much more interventionist state, willing to control the poor through the police. The same spirit supported, in 1910, the creation of an organ in the Ministry of Interior to execute policies for Indigenous people under the military commander Candido Rondon.[81] Daltro was not invited to participate in the initiative, despite her insistence. She managed a short audience with the minister, in which she was told that Rondon was a positivist and as such, he was against women holding public posts.[82]

In protest, Daltro rallied teachers and friends to create a party in December 1910. They called it the Feminine Republican Party (Partido Republicano Feminino), dedicated to promoting the women's vote. Under the party's label, Daltro made her students parade on the streets of Rio de Janeiro carrying flags demanding voting rights. They requested hearings with public authorities to demand resources for the women's school she directed, petitioned the House of Representatives in support of a women's suffrage bill in 1916, launched her candidacy for municipal representation in 1917, and marched in support of the first woman admitted to the federal public service in September 1918.[83]

Those were years of great agitation. In the 1920s, Daltro remained adamantly in favor of educating women and political rights.[84] Rio de Janeiro's press archives record her visits to the polls during elections. She would make a brief speech denouncing the unfair absence of women and then move on to the next precinct. Some reporters condescended. Other praised her courage, while still others mocked her.

In August 1922 the FBPF was formed. This organization of middle- and upper-class women took the flag of feminism from Daltro's hands. Among them were lawyers, engineers, writers, and a biologist named Bertha Lutz.[85] In contrast to Daltro's supporters, the FBPF was not diverse. With the exception of Almerinda Gama, a typist who joined the FBPF in 1930, there were no Black women in the FBPF.

The FBPF inaugurated a new style of feminist political action. In December 1922, it promoted a grandiloquent conference in a prestigious venue, inviting North American suffragist leader Carrie Chapman Catt to be the key speaker. Brazil was the first stop on Catt's tour of South America. At the same time, congressman Juvenal Lamartine proposed a suffrage bill. Myrthes Campos had taken part in the national legal conference in October. All these initiatives were meant to put the FBPF on the political map of the independence centennial celebrations.

With calculated moves and no noisy demonstrations, the FBPF made allies in the political system, insisting on the necessity of regenerating and modernizing representative institutions. Mirroring similar international groups, it introduced a new vocabulary to feminist political action in Brazil. Instead of asking for support for a particular school, as Daltro had, Lutz demanded new public policy in support of women's education.[86] While Daltro gave interviews to the press upon request, the FBPF developed its own lines of communication. From late 1927, the FBPF occupied a section of the prestigious newspaper *O Paiz* with news about feminism in Brazil and the world.[87] It kept permanent dialogue with parliamentarians, introducing a new agenda of state reforms aligned with international feminism. For example, the FBPF insisted on opening new career opportunities to women beyond teaching and nursing. Its members repeated the motto "Equal pay for equal work" at every opportunity.

Despite having a good relationship with politicians, the group experienced criticism. Feminism allegedly took jobs from breadwinning men. Feminist women supposedly neglected their children, if they had any. Meanwhile, leftists assailed the feminist focus on juridical equality as insufficient and elitist.[88] The struggle for the vote lasted longer than suffragists predicted; it was not easy to attract new members and keep the organization going with so many setbacks. The FBPF requested an audience with President Washington Luís. In 1929 Luís indicated a fellow politician from his state to run for the presidency. The election took place in 1930. Júlio Prestes was elected, but he never took office. In the first week of October, Getúlio Vargas led a complicated coup d'état that turned the political system upside down.

At first, FBPF's members did not know how to position themselves in the so-called revolution, as the movement's leaders insisted on calling it. It took them about six months to understand the dynamics of the new government. When they called a feminist convention in June 1931, they were surprised that Vargas agreed to talk to a delegation of activists.[89] Astoundingly, the political intervention they had desired for so long came from the hands of the most improbable leader.

Final Considerations

This chapter has discussed obstacles to enfranchising women in Brazil through two analytical lenses—ideas and political action. Starting with independence, I characterized the deep, persistent, and unequal racial and gender foundations of Brazilian society in the nineteenth century. Then I explored authors who guided how Brazilian parliamentarians expressed their positions concerning political representation, particularly the integration of women into the political system. Brazilian elites nourished cultural ties with Europe and read French authors to deal with the challenges of ruling a political system based on liberal ideas within an autocratic society. This line of investigation clarified how foreign ideas were appropriated and used to shape political factions.

I intended to show how ideas circulated between France and Brazil by taking as a proxy the House of Representative's collection of books and journals and linking them with parliamentary debates. Clearly, the enunciation of political discourses followed a cultural pattern. At first debaters would find shelter in a foreign author's ideas in vogue. They would choose authors they were more familiar with, sometimes combining conflicting intellectual schools. Then Latin American politicians and jurists quoted passages to impress their audiences. The debater's purpose was to show his familiarity with intellectual innovations. There is evidence that this pattern occurred elsewhere, such as in the courts, with serious consequences for justice, which is something I do not fully explore here, though Myrthes Campos's case shows that it possibly delayed women's enfranchisement.[90]

This exercise was crucial to explaining how congressmen debated suffrage during the 1890–1891 constitutional assembly. It permitted me to go beyond the contrast between arguments in favor of and against the proposal. By considering the ideas in circulation at that moment, I could locate congressmen's sources of inspiration. As some of the assembly's debates remained sources of law for judges years afterward, those who felt underrepresented in the political system reacted to them.

In the final part of the essay, I explored three activists who struggled for many causes, especially the right to vote. Just as understanding nineteenth-century debates needs to take into consideration cultural ties that Brazilian elites kept with France, understanding the variety of feminist action needs to consider each activist's context. Obviously, a clear understanding of the Brazilian political system needs to consider the centrality of the state in that system—even the smaller and more decentralized state that existed before Vargas required Campos, Daltro, and Lutz to use different strategies to have a voice.

Motivation is another tenet in this essay. What makes someone act politically? The historical definition of feminism states that any political action a woman conducts in defense of her autonomy and visibility in public space is a form of feminism. However, women act according to their personal backgrounds and convictions.[91] I examined three notable women, a teacher in contact with popular classes, a middle-class lawyer, and a middle-class biologist. Each developed a specific strategy to reverse the effects of gender inequality that they all experienced.

It is true that suffrage would not have become a reality if women had not agitated for it. It is also true that politically conscious women were not the sole actors involved in that decision. Vargas remains an enigma in the history of women's enfranchisement. His intellectual formation involved contact with the positivism of Saint-Simon's school of thought.[92] Vargas shared Saint-Simon's belief in centralized government. However, he showed no signs of accepting the natural inferiority of women, something Comte preached and his disciples repeated. By responding affirmatively to feminist pressure in 1932, Vargas broke the political impasse that had been dragging on for four decades already.

Nevertheless, Vargas and his closest collaborators showed no enthusiasm for the liberal representative system. He called elections in 1932 in response to his opponents' pressure. To prevent the political oligarchies from recapturing the political system, Vargas convened a commission to draft a constitution.[93] This commission was composed of ministers and a few selected members of the judiciary. After long debates, the commission elaborated a draft suggesting two forms of electoral representation: universal and corporate.[94] This combination was in effect from 1933 until 1937, when Vargas started governing as a dictator. The hybrid system expressed the deep mistrust of the liberal representative model held by many members of Vargas's government.

Ironically, when liberal feminists finally reached their most precious goal, the right to vote, politicians in Latin America were more and more suspicious of mass political participation. French authors were no longer their main sources of inspiration. Other schools of thought were already circulating, justifying an authoritarian state. Conservative thinkers appropriated Herbert Spencer´s works, Gustave Le Bon´s psychology of the crowd, and later Carl Schmitt's discrediting of parliamentary democracy. It does not matter whether the appropriation was poor or faithful. This bundle of ideas provided the intellectual basis to respond to the 1929 world crisis's effects. Feminist groups lingered for room in the representative system as sovereign individuals at a moment when countries in Europe and the Americas were moving toward a corporative form of politics, abandoning the premises of individualistic liberalism.

If enfranchisement was a justifiable goal, women's integration into the political system remains a challenge today. Despite remedial policies, women represented only 15 percent of the seats of the House of Representatives after the 2018 election. Under the intersecting lenses of gender and race, this percentage lowers even more. Afro-Brazilians and Indigenous people were never barred from office, but neither was their representation incentivized. In 1994 Benedita da Silva became the first Black woman senator. In 2018 Joênia Batista de Carvalho, an Indigenous of the Wapichana group, was elected to the House of Representatives.

Notes

1. Vargas governed the country under an exceptional regime due to the coup d'état of October 3, 1930. From November 1937 to October 1945, Vargas governed with the full powers of a dictator.
2. Marques, *Perfil parlamentar*.
3. According to the 1940 census, of the self-declared Black and biracial female population, 35.9 percent were literate, compared to 41.03 percent of the self-declared white female population. In the same census, of the self-declared "yellow-skin" female population, 48.17 percent were literate, despite representing less than 1 percent of the overall female population of the country. These numbers refer to the female population over age five. Beltrão and Novellino, *Alfabetização por raça e sexo no Brasil*.
4. Brasil, *Democracia representativa*.
5. I explored foreign relations factors that possibly contributed to Vargas's decision in an article. Marques, "Entre o igualitarismo e a reforma dos direitos das mulheres"; Barrancos, *Mujeres en la sociedad Argentina*; Osta Vazquez, "Brasil e Uruguai." For a suffrage bill under consideration in Argentinian parliament in 1932, refer to Barrancos. For the Uruguayan case, refer to Osta Vazquez.
6. Hahner, *A mulher brasileira e suas lutas sociais e políticas, 1850–1937*; Hahner, *Emancipating the Female Sex*.
7. Besse, *Restructuring Patriarchy*; Saffioti, *A mulher na sociedade de classes*; Saffioti, *Women in Class Society*.
8. Maxwell, *Naked Tropics*, chapter 8.
9. Mello, *A outra independência*.
10. Maxwell, *Naked Tropics*, chapter 8.
11. Versiani and Noguerol, *Muitos escravos, muitos senhores*.

12. Rosanvallon, "Guizot et la question du suffrage universel au XIXe siècle."

13. Lucien Jaume, *L'Individu Effacé*, 15–20.

14. Some methodological observations are necessary. Is it possible to affirm precisely that the works mentioned by congressmen in their speeches were available at the library at that time? It is not. Is it possible to ascertain that those congressmen read only books available at the library? Also, no. As congressman Rui Barbosa's library shows, politicians relied also on their personal collections. In response to the first question, very few inventories of the collection are left. A singular example is a section of the book *Synopse*, published in 1873, which provides a list of books available at the library at that moment. If the institution ever developed a system to control the acquisition of books to its collection, it was lost. It is possible that it was mislaid during the 1960 move of the capital, which was previously in Rio de Janeiro. Even so, the countless nineteenth-century books held in the library stamped with an archaic spelling—"Bibliotheca da Câmara"—reveal that the parliamentary debate was nourished by the literature at hand at the fancy bookshops on Ouvidor Street in downtown Rio, which sold imported books that the House of Representatives avidly bought. The congressional libraries also hold full collections of nineteenth-century political journals, such as the *Revue des Deux Mondes*, which was frequently mentioned in parliamentarian debates. Brazil, *Synopse*.

15. Robert Darnton, "History of Reading."

16. Louis Bonald, *Oeuvres de M. de Bonald: Melanges Literaires Politiques et Philosophiques* (Paris: A. Le Clere, 1858); Edouard Laboulaye, *Questions constitutionnelles* (Paris: Charpentier et Cie, 1872).

17. Andrade e Silva is recognized as one of the most important independence leaders, a sincere reformer though not a democrat. Manoel Alves Branco was a congressman from the province of Bahia. Maxwell, *Naked Tropics*, chapter 8.

18. Branco and Silva, Projeto de Lei de Eleições.

19. Branco and Silva.

20. Verjus, *Les cens de la famillie*.

21. *O Correio da Câmara dos Deputados*, October 1, 1831.

22. Mikkola, "Kant on Moral Agency and Women's Nature."

23. Carlos Maximiliano Santos quoted Pimenta Bueno in his commentaries on the 1891 constitution. The quotation is inserted in the part of the book on the controversy on the women's vote at the constitutional assembly. In legal reasoning at the turn of the twentieth century, the quotation implied that Santos still considered Bueno a valid interpretation. Carlos Maximiliano Santos, *Comentários à Constituição Brasileira de 1891*; J. A. Pimenta Bueno, *Direito Público Brasileiro* (Rio de Janeiro: Tipografia Villeneuve, 1857).

24. Nancy Stepan, "Race, Gender, Science and Citizenship."

25. Rosanvallon, "Guizot et la question du suffrage."

26. Comte, *Cours de Philosophie Positive*; Comte, *Système de Politique Positive*.

27. For a thorough account of political and ideological changes in play in the second half of the nineteenth century in Brazil, I refer to Alonso's 2002 *Ideias em Movimento*. The same author has recently published *The Last Abolition*, examining the abolitionist campaign in English.

28. According to Trindade, young generations of southern lawyers, such as Getulio Vargas, had their first contact with political theory and received political training by reading Saint-Simon and other conservative thinkers. Trindade, *O Positivismo*.

29. John Stuart Mill, *Correspondance inédite avec Gustave d'Eichthal* (Paris: Félix Alcan Editeur, 1898).

30. L. Levy-Bruhl, *Lettres inédites de John Stuart Mill a Auguste Comte* (Paris: Félix Alcan Editeur, 1899).

31. Comte, *Système de Politique Positive*, chapter 3.

32. V. P. Guillin, *Auguste Comte and John Stuart Mill on Sexual Equality*.

33. The oldest English-language edition to be included in the library's collection dates to 1962. It was a gift from the US Embassy in Brasilia.

34. John Stuart Mill, *Auguste Comte et le Positivisme*, 1866. (Paris: Felix Alcan Editeur, 1890).

35. There is a long controversy over the active participation of Harriet Taylor on the book *The Subjection of Women*. I acknowledge the possibility that Mill wrote this book together with Taylor.

36. Mill's books reached a large audience in Latin America. For example, in Mexico, the jurist Genaro Garcia mentioned Mill profusely in his work. In Argentina, the notorious thesis presented by Elvira Lopez in 1901 delved into the universe of ideas of the British philosopher. In Brazil, suffragist Bertha Lutz kept notes on *The Subjection of Women*. In Uruguay, the lawyer and senator Sophia Alvarez Demichelli praised the importance of Mill's ideas in her formation. García, *Apuntes sobre la Condicion de la Mujer*, 35, 54–55; López, *El movimiento feminista*; Demichelli, *Igualdad jurídica de la mujer*.

37. Azevedo published the newspaper *A Familia* from 1888 to 1897. She also authored a play titled *The Women's Vote*, which was performed during the constitutional assembly.

38. Hahner estimates that educated women were about 10 percent of the adult female population in 1872, versus 20 percent of the male adult population. The census of this same year registered 2,218 active female teachers, versus 1,307 male teachers. Hahner, *Poverty and Politics*, 110.

39. Duarte, *Imprensa feminina e feminista no Brasil*, 188.

40. Duarte, 214, 262.

41. Santos, *Tratado sobre a emancipação política da mulher e o direito de votar*.

42. La Capra, *Rethinking Intellectual History*.

43. E. Littre, "La Philosophie positive—Auguste Comte et John Stuart Mill," *Revue*

des Deux Mondes, July 1866; R. Millet, "Le Parti Radical en Anglaterre. Un Manifeste de Stuart Mill," *Revue des Deux Mondes*, January 1872.

44. Rosanvallon, *Guizot et la question du suffrage*.

45. Herbert Spencer's works were already in circulation. As to women's social role, Spencer was aligned with Comte.

46. Laboulaye, *Questions constitutionnelles*, 41, 384.

47. About the intense debate that resulted in the 1881 electoral reform, I refer to Graham, *Patronage and Politics in Nineteenth-century Brazil*, chapter 7.

48. J. Azevedo, *A Família*, August 29, 1890.

49. The positivist bloc advocated the vote for illiterate men but rejected the vote for women. Agenor Roure, *A Constituinte Republicana*.

50. Decree 510, June 22, 1890.

51. Cavalcanti, *Constituição Federal*, 287.

52. The new regime attributed the interpretation of the constitution to the Supreme Court and nullified previous laws that collided with the principles of the new constitution. However, in practice, judges continued to use old laws they claimed were still in vigor. The constitutional text itself used "Brazilian," "citizen," and "citizen with voting rights" in different articles, opening space for uncertainty. *Cidade do Rio*, December 29, 1899, 1; Cavalcanti, *Constituição Federal*, 287.

53. Roure, *A Constituinte Republicana*, 277.

54. The amendments were discussed on January 12 and January 26, 1891. Brasil, *Annaes do Congresso Constituinte*, Vols. 2–3.

55. Brasil, *Annaes do Congresso*, 2:311ss.

56. Laboulaye's ideas resonated with Roure's comments about the Brazilian constitution. Roure sustained that the modern theory of the vote considered voting a public function, very much in the same terms Laboulaye used in his 1872 work. In a book he published in Argentina while serving as an ambassador in that country, J. F. Assis Brasil, a politician from the liberal faction of the Rio Grande do Sul state, sustained, "El voto es derecho politico, cuyo ejercicio regula la sociedad en vista de la utilidad publica y con la condicion de no destruir su carater de universalidad." Roure, *A Constituinte*, 410; Brasil, *Democracia representative*, 45.

57. Roure, *A Constituinte*, 292.

58. The political scientist Wanderley G. Santos argued that the Brazilian political system at the turn of the twentieth century was incoherent, which he attributed to poor preparation on the part of politicians. My reading of the role played by ideas in the political debate goes in a different direction. Santos, "A praxis liberal no Brasil."

59. The Mexican jurist Genaro Garcia commented that the 1857 Mexican charter sustaining it did not impede women from voting: "Como nuestra Carta Magna no hizo tampoco restriccion alguna en contra las mujeres al enunciar las

personas a quienes de la ciudadania, nadie podra negar que todas las mujeres que disfrutan de la calidad de mexicanas, han cumplido 18 anos, siendo casadas, o 21 si no lo son, y poseen um modo honesto de vivir, son ciudadanas, art. 34, idem, y tienen em consecuencia las prerrogativas siguientes." In support of his argument, Garcia quoted the Roman jurists Gaius and Ulpianus. Garcia, *Apuntes sobre la Condicion de la Mujer*, 31.

60. Myrthes Campos was born in the town of Macaé, state of Rio de Janeiro, in 1875 and died in Rio de Janeiro in 1965. Leolinda Daltro was born in the state of Bahia in 1859 and died in Rio de Janeiro in May 1935. Bertha Lutz was born in São Paulo in 1894 and died in Rio de Janeiro in September 1976.

61. Silveira, "Escrever, ser útil à sociedade"; Schuma Schumaher and Erico V. Brazil, eds., *Dicionário Mulheres do Brasil—de 1500 até a atualidade* (Rio de Janeiro: Jorge Zahar, 2000), 431–32.

62. Senator Ferreira's bill was discussed in the sessions held on October 10 and 21. Brasil, Senado Federal, *Anais do Senado Federal*, 3:340–435.

63. *Jornal do Comercio*, October 8, 1899, 1; Patrocinio, *Cidade do Rio*, 1.

64. Patrocinio, 1.

65. "Justiça local. A mulher, diplomada em Direito, pode exercer a advocacia," *O Direito, Legislação, Doutrina e Jurisprudência* 28, no. 81 (January–April 1900): 420. In this issue, *O Direito* reproduced the debate held in the IAB in July 1899.

66. Silveira, "Escrever, ser útil à sociedade,"12; *Códigos civis do Brasil: do Império a República* (Brasília: Senado Federal, 2002), CD rom; Almeida, "Com ares de crónica"; Campos, "Poderá haver perfeita igualdade nos direitos civis e de família entre cônjuges?"

67. "Tribunais," *O Paiz*, September 30, 1899, 2.

68. Campos, "Comentário jurídico sobre o voto feminine."

69. "A comemoração da Independência Nacional," *O Paiz*, October 31, 1922, 5.

70. Marques, "Federação Brasileira pelo Progresso Feminino."

71. Santos, *Comentários à Constituição Brasileira de 1891*.

72. Federação Brasileira pelo Progresso Feminino, *Representação*. Marques, *Perfil parlamentar*, 28–31.

73. The Centro da Memoria da Unicamp in Campinas holds a large collection of suffragist propaganda and documents related to the FBPF in the Adolpho Gordo Collection. The same institution published the ebook *Bertha Lutz e o Voto Feminino no Acervo da CMU*, which contains a rich collection of digitalized documents.

74. "Adolpho Affonso da Silva Gordo," Centro de Memória Unicamp, https://atom. cmu.unicamp.br/index.php/adolpho-affonso-da-silva-gordo, accessed October 10, 2023.

75. Campos, "O Voto Feminino," 71. The translation is mine.

76. Campos, "O Voto Feminino," 69.

77. In this passage, I highlight aspects of Daltro's style of feminism. For further

treatment of Daltro's political figure, see Rocha, "Introdução, notas e posfacio."

78. Daltro, like other teachers, offered night school classes for workers. It was not uncommon for teachers to pay part of the expenses themselves. Rocha, "Vida de professora."

79. Daltro, *Da cathechese dos índios no Brasil*, 630.

80. Daltro, *Da catechese dos índios no Brasil*.

81. Daltro had contacted Candido Rondon in the hope that he would support her project. He replied, "A woman is the most well-formed part of humanity, and because of that, the most delicate and tender. She is, like Auguste Comte said, the intermediary between the man and humanity. If the Republic is the incorporation of proletariat to modern society, the Brazilian government's special mission is to incorporate the indigenous [*selvagens* in the original] in our society. Brazil will never accomplish its political mission while this incorporation is not fulfilled. Daltro, *Da catechese dos índios no Brasil*, 321.

82. Daltro, *O inicio do feminismo*, 46.

83. In September 1918, Maria Jose Castro Rebelo Mendes was approved on the top list of candidates for the diplomatic service. On her behalf, a habeas corpus was presented to the Supreme Court so she could accept the post. Schumaher and Brazil, *Dicionário Mulheres do Brasil*, 396–97.

84. Marques, *Women's Vote in Brazil*; Marques, *Perfil Parlamentar*, chapter 1.

85. Lutz completed a degree in biology from the Paris Sorbonne in 1918. She and her only brother attended high school in Great Britain, their mother's home.

86. In its early years, the FBPF campaigned for the admission of women in the official and prestigious high school Colegio Pedro II in Rio de Janeiro. It was the only public school that gave direct access to university. Saffioti, *A mulher na sociedade de classes*, 145.

87. Before the FBPF managed to occupy a section of *O Paiz* every Sunday, its members spoke to the press frequently. Though both Daltro and the FBPF spoke to newspapers, Daltro found space in popular newspapers while Lutz and her collaborators spoke to the middle-class press.

88. Maria Lacerda de Moura was a renowned freethinker on the left. For two years, Moura collaborated with Lutz before breaking with her in disappointment over class issues. In a 1924 book, Moura wrote: "Is juridical and political equality for half a dozen of privileged women, extracted from the dominant cast? Is it worth if most women keep on living in the misery of a millennial servitude?" (De que vale a igualdade de direitos jurídicos e políticos para meia dúzia de privilegiadas, tiradas da própria casta dominante, se a maioria feminina continua vegetando na miséria da escravidão milenar?) Moura, *A mulher é uma degenerada*.

89. Marques, *Perfil parlamentar*, 35.

90. In 1943 a former member of the Superior Court reflected candidly on the way

this court worked in the early republic: "During the first years of the Republic, the Court did not have clear its role in the regime. Many judges that integrated the court brought from the Empire a true brilliant intellectual baggage, however, unfit to understand new institutions. It was a system barely understood that was subject, in the judiciary, to disturbing application of prejudices nourished by juridical education based on Roman sources, Portuguese sources, by traditions from the old regime, as well as vulgarizing authors of French public law." Castro Nunes is mentioned by Gomes. Gomes, *La Cour Supreme dans le Système Politique Bresilien*, 17, 8n; Castro Nunes, *Teoria e Prática do Poder Judiciário* (Rio de Janeiro: Forense, 1943), 168.

91. In Besse's remarkable historiographical exercise, the author states that the dominant concept of feminism in vogue in Brazil in the 1920s and 1930s aimed at modernizing juridical institutions but failed to change gender inequalities in society. I partially agree with Besse. I believe FBPF members reacted to opportunities the political system offered them by using the means they had in hand. Susan Besse, *Restructuring Patriarchy*.

92. Trindade, *O Positivismo*.

93. Marques, *Perfil parlamentar*, chapter 2.

94. Employee union representatives selected eighteen names; employer unions, seventeen; liberal professions, three; public service, two. In total, forty representatives of these corporate bodies were elected to serve in the assembly.

CHAPTER FIVE

History and Interpretations of Women's Suffrage in Argentina

ADRIANA MARÍA VALOBRA

IN SEPTEMBER 1947, ARGENTINA'S LAW 13010 extended the suffrage to women and gave them representation in Congress. Legislation from 1912, the Sáenz Peña Law, had made voting both secret and obligatory for men. Law 13010 made it the same for women. A provincial constitutional reform in San Juan in 1927 meant that women had already been voting there since 1928. In both San Juan and Santa Fe, women also participated in municipal elections.

These milestones are part of women's suffrage history in Argentina, which can be divided into two periods. During the first, early suffragists put together an array of organizations, alliances, and strategies to procure their rights. Despite abundant research on this period, there are still significant gaps in basic information. There are also readings of the history that lack sophistication. For example, suffragist strategies have been grouped together under the umbrella of political maternalism.[1] I have used it myself, but with insufficient data, turning maternalism into an acritical, catch-all explanation. The second period took place in the context of Peronism. In this case, the historiography has been linked to discussions about populism and has privileged certain aspects of that narrative: (1) the leadership of Perón and Evita; (2) Evita's conservative ideas about women; and (3) the manipulation of the electorate, especially women, in favor of Peronism.

In my view, it is necessary to enrich the image of political maternalism from the early twentieth century as a homogenous strategy to gain the suffrage, qualify some of the assertions regarding Evita's supposed maternal conservatism, and include tensions relating to developmentalism that emerged after 1955, connecting them to women's political activism. I also want to underscore the importance of questioning some of the assumptions that have emerged from connecting the study of women's suffrage to narratives on populism. Among these are simplified views about electoral outcomes, looking at women's actions as mere reproductions of propagandist assertions, and an instrumentalist conceptualization of Evita. These three assumptions have tended to deprive women of agency and portray them instead as weak puppets.

This chapter examines the strategies suffragists used to win the suffrage. They made alliances with male leaders who supported them either in an individual or party capacity and who, when elected, put forward legislation and attempted to persuade opponents in the legislature. They created all-female organizations that launched visibility campaigns, including mock elections—a distinctively Argentine performance—individual actions in court, press releases and conferences, and radio broadcasts.[2] Parliament played a central role due to the crucial need for legislation to achieve the goal.

Women's Suffrage before Women's Suffrage

At the conclusion of the nineteenth century, Argentina adopted an agro-export economic model and created the basis for consolidation of the nation-state. That process was not without internal conflicts. Various movements emerged—some that resisted the nation-state and others that sought recognition as citizens. After that time, suffragism grew and strengthened as a demand for political rights in a country based on an exclusivist and fraudulent system of representation. Near the end of this period, coinciding with World War II, suffragist demands began to include ideas related to the tension between democracy and totalitarianism. This added an antifascist element due to suffragists' rejection of Hitler, Mussolini, Franco, and similar figures in the Americas. Some sectors identified Perón as an expression of totalitarianism, and rejection of Perón unified a heterogeneous group under the umbrella of anti-Peronism.[3] Critiques of leaders identified with demagoguery and the mobilization of the masses predated anti-Peronism, however. They date to the election of the first president under universal manhood suffrage, Hipólito Yrigoyen.[4]

LEADERSHIP AND IDEOLOGY

One of the most important moments in Argentine women's history is one that has yet to be confirmed with documentary evidence. Domingo Faustino Sarmiento (governor of San Juan province and later president) is credited with having granted women municipal suffrage, landing him a place in history as a visionary of political modernization. Nevertheless, we have yet to find a single historical document that confirms this idea, despite its broad acceptance in the historiography.[5] It is true that San Juan was the first to consider municipal suffrage, in 1878, but Sarmiento was then neither governor nor president. In the constitutional debates of 1878, legislators agreed that women would vote in municipal but not provincial elections. One deputy said it was better to include language that "women and men" can vote in municipal elections. The rest of the deputies considered women to be included in the category "tax payer," so it was not necessary to clarify "women and men." For that reason, the language in the constitution appears only in masculine form. Women were supposed to know when the grammatically masculine nouns were meant to be inclusive and when they were not.[6] Women were to understand that the masculine noun *contribuyente*, meaning "taxpayer," included them, but the masculine noun *citizen* excluded them from provincial and national suffrage. Some doubt that the 1878 constitution was ever implemented at all.[7]

Another study proposes an earlier date, with the provincial constitution of 1856,[8] but the evidence has yet to be found either in the articles of the legislation or in the debates. Others claim that municipal suffrage occurred with a 1912 reform, but it does not appear in the written constitution in 1912 but rather in Article 21 of the municipal Organic Law in 1913, after which we have evidence of women actually voting.[9] Obviously, until we have reliable data, we cannot credit Sarmiento with municipal women's suffrage. All we know—until new evidence appears—is that San Juan is the first place women received formal recognition of this right in Argentina. Even so, the women who received the franchise could only vote in their capacity as taxpayers, not citizens, which was not on its own considered adequate qualification. We also have no idea whether a suffrage movement existed in San Juan.

In addition to the specific experience of this province and of certain men who as individuals expressed their support for recognizing women's civil rights, the International Workers Socialist Party (later the Argentina Socialist Party) began including this demand in its platform from about 1894. In a similar vein, beginning near the turn of the century, there were women's groups who demanded suffrage who allied themselves, variously, with the socialists and freethinkers, as well as with the Unión Cívica Radical (Radical Civil Union).[10] At this point we see the emergence of women's leaders who articulated an ideology that has been encapsulated under the blanket term *first-wave feminism* but that was in reality far more nuanced. As Karen Offen and Joan Scott have suggested was true for other latitudes,[11] strategies that stressed equality and difference coexisted in the struggle for not only social rights but also political rights. For this reason, throughout the period, we find feminists who demanded equal political rights as well as state protection for women workers to diminish the inequality and oppression of which women were victims in the labor force. We should also recall that women, especially married women, did not enjoy full civil rights. Despite successive reforms, women received equal parental authority over their own children only in the 1980s.

The story of the feminist and freethinker Julieta Lanteri is perhaps one of the best to give us a sense of how stubborn the first suffragist figures had to be. By taking her demands to court, she managed to persuade a judge that no constitution prohibited women from voting, and she was able to procure the municipal vote for Buenos Aires in 1911.[12] Through de Lanteri, we see the emergence of the tip of an iceberg: the history of women's mobilization for their rights—meager though they were.[13] In general, we have tended to speak of a feminist movement as though it were unified and homogeneous. Feminists agreed that women should demand civil rights that recognized their status as individuals with autonomy, discernment, and will. They also agreed on the right to secondary—not just for teachers—and higher education. Primary education was mandatory, but it was not successfully extended throughout the national territory until the 1940s. The lack of full civil rights was connected to the exercise of political rights. Even though, in the electoral law, illiteracy did not disqualify Argentines from the suffrage, suffragists considered education key to civil culture in general. On political rights themselves, however, the women's movement was very diverse and divided. Cecilia Grierson, the first woman doctor, opposed suffrage because she did not feel that it was the right moment, given women's situation at the time.[14] Alicia Moreau de Justo, Julieta Lanteri, and Elvira Rawson de Dellepiane, of the Radical Civic Union (all doctors and pillars of Argentine suffragism), as well as María Abella de Ramírez, a Uruguayan teacher and freethinker who lived in La Plata, Argentina, all favored equal political rights—at least at the end of 1910. The nuances among their positions were subsequently erased by the idea that they all employed political maternalism, a posture that argued for political rights on the basis of women's real or potential motherhood.[15] Without denying the existence of political maternalism as a strategy, we should recognize that some leaders, such as Alicia Moreau of the Socialist Party or Julieta Lanteri of the National Feminist Party, were more focused on recognizing women's individuality, a key aspect relative to their autonomy as citizens. They believed the state had an obligation to protect maternity, but they were far less emphatic about maternalism as an argument to demand political rights.[16] We also have to take into consideration the lapse of four decades between the movement's beginnings and the achievement of its goal. Different strategies were employed over time. This is simply an area that requires further research.

It is worth distinguishing between municipal and national suffrage in Argentina, since taxpayer status is what qualified voters at the municipal level, which is not the case at the national or provincial level. The passage of the Sáenz Peña Law (Law 8871 of 1912 with national scope) is considered exceptionally important within Argentine historiography since it proposed to mend the existing fraudulent electoral system. It would bring legitimacy to a government via new electoral methods and obligatory voting for an expanded male electorate. The law also explicitly blocked women from voting. In effect, its passage made it such that the voter rolls would be based on military service and not on voluntary registration on the part of the citizenry. In this way, the law ensured that political rights would be quintessentially masculine, making it a step backward when viewed through the lens of women's history.

PARLIAMENTARY DEBATES AND PROVINCIAL CONSTITUTIONS

The year 1919 was a critical one in suffrage history, when new action strategies were unveiled. In the twentieth century, Elvira Rawson brought a draft of a national law to Unión Cívica Radical legislator Rogelio Araya, who in 1919 brought forward the first proposal for national women's suffrage. What followed was a succession of the same, none of which passed but that continued to press for the relevance of the subject. In a parallel fashion, Lanteri and others pushed to be included in the military conscription lists in order also to be included as voters, but they were denied. Later, in an act that even some suffragists criticized, Lanteri ran for Congress (March 1919), winning 1,730 votes. It was the first time a woman had run for office in Argentina, and she was able to do so because the law had failed to specifically prohibit women's candidacies[17] Together with other activists, she formed the National Feminist Party, made up entirely of women, the only one of its kind in Argentina. This organization mobilized to support Lanteri's candidacies in 1920, 1924, and 1926, each time winning men's votes, as men were the only ones with voting rights.[18] Alicia Moreau founded the National Feminist Union, and Elvira Rawson founded the Pro-Women's Rights Association. Through these organizations, they stayed in contact with leaders from all over the world while they lobbied legislators to support proposals on women's rights. In 1920 Moreau, Lanteri, and Rawson were candidates in mock elections, performances suffragists put on at the same time legitimate, male elections were being held. The goal was not only to draw the public's attention to women's lack of rights but also to demonstrate women's capacity to participate electorally.

Another milestone occurred 1921 in Santa Fe province, where a constitutional reform would have granted women's suffrage had the governor, Enrique Mosca, not vetoed it. We know something of the activities of leading suffragists in Santa Fe, especially Alicia Moreau, but we still lack a thorough local study. A decade after Mosca's veto, the incoming governor, Luciano Molinas of the Democratic Progressive Party, finally implemented the 1921 reformed constitution, permitting women to vote in some cities in Santa Fe beginning in the 1930s.[19] Recent studies show that, before Molinas, a 1927 municipal reform allowed women to vote not only as taxpayers but also if they were teachers or had similar professional careers.[20]

A third milestone brings us back to San Juan province, where in 1927, under the government of Aldo Cantoni, a reformed constitution permitted women to vote in provincial and municipal elections. While the municipal vote was still restricted to property owners and taxpayers, the provincial vote was opened to all who, by birth or adoption, were of age and could claim residency.[21]

A coup in 1930 eclipsed national politics. The new national government, elected in 1932, ruled by outlawing competition and persecuting political enemies. If fraud failed to deliver an electoral win, it would nullify the election. Argentine democracy in 1932 was reduced almost to the status of a mere formal democracy. The economy grew, but wealth was not distributed equitably. In this context, the Chamber of Deputies gave preliminary approval to a law giving women political rights. Pressure from the socialist bloc—which did have representatives—was key to this achievement, but full passage failed in the Senate, where the law was never debated.[22] Numerous legislative proposals were put forward, some by new suffragist groups like the Argentine Women's Union, a heterogeneous group that included the writer Victoria Ocampo and the leader of Unión Cívica Radical, Ana Rosa Schlieper de Martínez Guerrero. Despite Schlieper's international renown as president of the Inter-American Commission of Women, she was unable to persuade the government to grant women political rights.

Suffragists were no longer only freethinkers or leftists: now new groups, especially Catholics ones, emerged. In the 1930s, the church began to fear the spread of leftist ideas among women, which led some Catholic groups to boost their own suffrage activity. Thus a number of arguments emerged to qualify voters—by age or civil status, for example—but none prospered.[23]

Suffragists generally repudiated the military government that ascended to power in 1943. There were a few exceptions, such as the lawyers Lucila de

Gregorio Lavié and Blanca Cassagne Serres, who drew close to Juan Domingo Perón. Perón, a member of the new military government, would soon climb to power as executive.[24] In this context, Perón first attempted suffragist mobilization. According to several authors, Perón's early attempts at suffragist mobilization signaled that women's political rights "were assumed by the same officialism that sought to mobilize women in order to incorporate them into political practice."[25] Perón had the support of the Argentina Association for Women's Suffrage, a Catholic group led by Carmela Horne de Burmeister that had been pushing a restricted vote for literate women since the 1930s. Some studies have signaled that it was never clear that Perón planned to decree women's suffrage in 1945.[26] Discussions of a possible decree said nothing about whether the vote would be restricted or universal, voluntary or obligatory. Most suffragist organizations rejected what they considered machinations that would permit reactionary forces—which for them meant Perón—to manipulate women.[27] They also noticed that generating voter rolls with the required documentation could take months, if not years, which would conveniently postpone the promised general elections for the de facto government. Finally, they did not approve of gaining the vote by decree from a military government. They wanted an act of Congress.

Norms, Representations, and Practices around Women's Voting

The legislation came during Perón's first government, a period known for socioeconomic redistribution, centralization of leadership, and political persecution. Its passage was accompanied by protests from Peronist women and union groups under the leadership of Evita, the president's wife. Other groups also pressured Congress. Some were affiliated with communism, others with radical leaders such as Clotilde Sabattini, a history professor, political newspaper columnist, and daughter of a prominent leader of the Radical Party. Once the law passed, women voted in national elections for the first time in 1951.

It is true that a law extending political rights to women was included in a process of Peronization, and especially Evitization, where it remained. As soon as the law was passed, both Evita and the president sought to capitalize on the political possibilities that women's enfranchisement offered, as did all the other political parties. Nevertheless, we should recognize that previous governments had repeatedly failed to pass women's suffrage, even when it was a goal of their campaigns. Not until Peronism was an Argentine government willing to experiment and run the risk with the source of its political power in this way.

LEADERSHIP

From a symbolic point of view, women's suffrage has undoubtedly been associated with the figure of Evita, despite the fact that her comments on the matter were missing from the historiography for a long time. On the other hand, even when studies on Evita's radio speeches do point to nuances relating to her female audience, most of them end up dwelling on the more conservative aspects of her discourse. Some studies consider that this single maneuver managed to procure Evita's "own political function" within the party, implementing "a campaign in favor of a measure already being undertaken, which even acquired the character of a vigorous struggle against supposed enemies."[28] Other studies argue that Evita's mark on women's political rights has been exaggerated in the literature because her radio speeches dedicated to the topic were concentrated in 1947. Most research on women focuses only on the period from 1946 to 1952.[29] Those arguments return to the idea of opportunism regarding her action. Other scholars consider that, while her language may have emphasized tradition, her practice did not.[30] Bianchi and Sanchís observe the same duality,[31] while others view her speeches as traditionalist but observably distinct from many in the same genre.[32] Bianchi examines Evita's radio speeches on political rights, going more deeply into maternalism than other scholars to highlight her originality and her rupture with tradition.[33]

It is clear that Evita did not have, at least publicly, a background in the suffragist struggle. Nevertheless, her words had a significant impact on her audience. Prior to her visit to Europe, she had given radio talks on the topic. Those messages constructed the category of *ciudadana* ("citizen," but gendered female) in such a way that sexual identity was privileged over the condition of citizenship. She tended to use *woman* or *women* more often than *ciudadana* or *ciudadanas*. She articulated the characteristics of model motherhood and stressed roles within the family that implied a women's relationship to men (mother, sister, wife, daughter). The same followed for gendered words that described women's social and economic roles as laborer (*obrera*), worker (*trabajadora*), housewife (*ama de casa*), and so on. Women legitimized their civic activity by defending not their own rights but the rights of others.[34] Political rights also became unidimensional in her speeches since they referred, almost exclusively, to the act of voting.

In the radio messages from 1947, suffrage also had a definite emphasis on women's liberation from patriarchal structures (which were unacceptable in relation only to the domestic space, not to the tasks associated with it) and on what women's participation in the system might bring. These speeches also proposed something unusual: not only to bring household problems into the public space—something that was already a part of suffragist rhetoric—but also to bring politics to the dining room table to reflect there on the ways that politics could attend to the problems of the people.[35] This idea was entirely disruptive. It contradicted the accepted notion that politics should never invade the domestic arena. Some believe that Evita contrived a discourse that mitigated the radical nature of women's political action by wrapping it in conservative trappings.[36]

Evita's return from her European tour coincided with the moment Congress began to discuss women's political rights. According to Marysa Navarro, the trip produced a political transformation in Evita.[37] On the old continent, in addition to learning about the dramatic aftermath of the war, she also learned about women's mass mobilization and organizing. Upon her return, she led the call for the Chamber of Deputies to take up the new law. Then she mobilized women to demand it. This juncture gave suffragism a new face under the rhetoric of Evita and Peronism.[38] It also changed the suffragist political geography, since most feminists who had been fighting for suffrage up to that point found themselves opposing Peronism. Suffragists did not oppose the 1947 law, passed by a duly elected Congress, the way they had opposed Perón's 1945 decree, although the distinction between the two moments is frequently overlooked. Nevertheless, they had not dreamed of winning their goal under a government like Perón's, so they henceforth dedicated themselves to women's civic education to prevent what they saw as an effort on the part of the president to manipulate women's choices.

PARLIAMENTARY DEBATES AND PASSAGE OF
THE LAW GRANTING POLITICAL RIGHTS

It is important to review parliamentary debates following the elections of 1946, during Peronism's early days, to see how the proposal for women's rights changed over time before its passage. I will focus on the law granting political rights to women (13010/1947).[39]

As soon as he was elected, "Peron returns to the question of women's political rights. In his first message to Congress (26 June 1946), he announces his support for women's suffrage and declares it one of the most essential measures for the new government to resolve. The first Five Year Plan (October 1946)" also took up the question.[40] Once in session, both houses of Congress put forth proposals. The discussions in both chambers demonstrate that positions varied widely, even among members of the same party. In 1946 debates began in the Senate. Although there were only senators representing the ruling party, the discussion produced divergent points of view. The original proposal, which included civil and social rights for women along with political rights, was discarded in favor of one that addressed political rights exclusively. Legislators also focused entirely on voting and dismissed almost as absurd the idea that women could run for and be elected to office. Despite this, they held to the conviction that women's political rights would be the same as men's.[41] In the Chamber of Deputies, debate was hurried due to the legislative calendar. Discussions were heated because in addition to deputies from the ruling party, there were representatives from the second strongest party, the Radical Civil Union, and the conservative Democratic National Party. There was agreement on the general principle of extending political rights to women (there were no socialist deputies). Differences emerged not only among the different parties—Peronists, radicals, and conservatives—about also among the Peronists themselves. Some Peronists sided with the conservatives, who preferred to extend the vote only to certain groups of women, while others allied with the radicals, who argued for full equality. In reality, the disagreement related largely to conflicts among the parties regarding the anticipated symbolic harvest the legislation might yield. The law ultimately passed in the midst of a scandalous discussion and the withdrawal of opposition legislators. Women obtained universal and obligatory suffrage under equal conditions with men.[42]

From this perspective, discourse analysis of the parliamentary debates in the lower chamber under Peronism confirms that the debate in 1947, no less than the emergence of Peronism itself, can be understood as an attempt to overcome "the crisis of liberal consensus."[43] New notions of democracy that now included the masses might have stifled dissent, but they did not completely nullify forms of representation.[44] The opposition lent itself to the political game in relation to this law in particular, simultaneously affirming its agreement while insisting on the opportunism of Peronism, doubting the authenticity of the rhetoric on rights, and elevating that of women's obligations.[45] The idea of citizenship was not only modeled on the working class but also borrowed "features belonging to the maternal role like disinterestedness and abnegation and exalting them in defense of women's rights from the perspective of maternalist feminism. . . . Since civic virtue did not derive from formal education, the vote was stripped of its pedagogical function and the breach between the model of the good citizen and women or illiteracy disappeared."[46] Recall that the idea of maternalism was superimposed on Evita's emphasis on family in her radio speeches. Perón, Evita, and the minister of the interior, Ángel Borlenghi, played central roles in promulgation of the law, which took place on September 23. It was the first time a first lady played a central part in the promulgation of a law, which doubtless reinforced her political position. The most liberating aspects of women's suffrage, according to her radio speeches, were softened in the act of promulgation. The idea the women would somehow cleanse politics with their virtue persisted, and women were advised not to place their trust in the men who had always run things, with the exception of Perón.

In summary, women's suffrage—which had a long history of proposals coming from different sectors with different objectives—was part of a larger transformation of the political system, and it cannot be understood without considering how the system was transforming itself in response to recent crises.

Interpretations and Conceptualizations

Argentina is a singular case in Latin American suffrage history due to its early passage of universal and obligatory manhood suffrage in 1912 with the Sáenz Peña Law, which made electoral participation at the national level broader over time. Women's suffrage at the national level also differed from that in other countries because it was both universal and granted on equal conditions with men. Elsewhere, electoral qualifications and voluntary voter registration reduced both the male and female electorate. Argentina is similar to other countries in that its history through the first half of the twentieth century was marked by fraud, political conflict, and the exclusion of some sectors from elections, either by force or by the choice of some parties to abstain from the political process. It also stands out against countries like Costa Rica and Uruguay, which experienced institutional stability. It not only had the first military coup to overthrow an elected government in Latin America, but its history alternated between civilian and military governments right through to the last dictatorship, which lasted from 1976 to 1983.

The short synthesis of the history of women's suffrage in Argentina suggests several inferences. First, I would like to point out that I have proposed a reformulated periodization that differs even from my own previous periodizations. We should constantly rethink periodization. We should ask ourselves whether the history of women's suffrage followed the same pattern as phenomena such as the municipal, provincial, and national vote. This history points to the importance of understanding often neglected local processes. We also need to undertake a profound revision of the nature of the vote. The municipal vote was property-based. So should we consider it to have been an antecedent to universal suffrage without regard to class? This is important because we do not want to construct a teleological history of the vote. Nevertheless, we should also recognize that in the case of women's suffrage, both legislators and suffragists understood the municipal vote as a tool for civic education that would permit women to begin the exercise of political citizenship at a level where they likely already had practical knowledge, such as their own city.

Another aspect that is often linked to the passage of women's suffrage is populism. As Homero Saltalamacchia has observed, the category "populist" has been stretched out to include widely divergent cases. However, the cases share a context in which there has been a "crisis of representation."[47] Along these same lines, Gerardo Aboy Carlés reminds us that the category, aside from having been ambiguously defined, has also been used condescendingly and in juxtaposition with "democracy,"[48] a category that has definitely received better press in the social sciences. Democracy, however, should include not only the Western liberal variety but also diverse empirical realities. If we complement these considerations with an analysis from Aníbal Viguera, we can organize research on populism into two perspectives: one that privileges a "certain kind of participation or political subjugation" and another that underscores "social and economic policies that will determine the nature" of populism. Although the two categories are not mutually exclusive, "most definitions fall into one or the other"[49]

In the case of women's suffrage, interpretations have tended to revolve around the question of political dominance; they have therefore emphasized the nature of leadership. Celso Rodríguez identified Cantoni's government as a populist antecedent to Peronism,[50] and several studies have followed this analysis.[51] In this view, the populist leaders (Cantoni and Perón) opportunistically used the women's vote to expand their electoral support. In both cases, women, having received the suffrage, repaid the leaders by voting for them en masse. These same ideas were taken up by other authors, who added that San Juan's populism might have had "indisputable personal leadership" in Cantoni but that Peronism both theoretically and practically removed "any instance of deliberation in politics" in favor of "an idea of an enlightened 'driver' with providential knowledge of national doctrine."[52] In this view, Peronism was populist, with a theory of leadership that nullified any possibility of deliberation on the part of the voter.

The functionalist sociologist Gino Germani's thesis lies at the base of many of these explanations. Germani followed the "theory of modernization" and understood Peronism as a transitional phase between a traditional society and a fully modern one. Nevertheless, political modernity (democracy) should accompany socioeconomic modernity. According to Germani, Argentina modernized socioeconomically but politically maintained an irrational, authoritarian mobilization.[53] Thus populism arose as a "'deviation' from the model that was considered normal."[54]

Undeniably, Peronism had authoritarian tendencies, especially after the 1949 constitutional reform. However, we should ask what sort of deliberation was possible prior to Peronism given the fraud, suppression, and persecution that characterized Argentine politics both before and following Peronism. This is to say that to look at Peronism as though it were exceptional in this sense is shortsighted. We should also ask why the women's vote has been viewed in a certain light under Cantoni's and Perón's governments while references to municipal and provisional proposed extensions have been ignored, as well as the actual extension in Santa Fe. Indeed, little attention at all has been paid to women's suffrage under governments after 1955.

One consequence of the theory of leadership analysis has been the assumption of electoral manipulation, especially with respect to the women's vote. According to this point of view, the charismatic leader emphasizes symbolic, simplistic value statements to gain the favor of "available" irrational masses to the point where they may follow a leader who does not best reflect their own interests.[55] Cases categorized as "populist" are seen to owe their electoral victory to women's suffrage.[56] We should consider, however, that each time the vote was extended to women, either at the municipal or provincial level, it was assumed that those responsible for the extension were looking to capitalize on women's votes. The same analysis is not generally applied, however, regarding passage of the Sáenz Peña Law, which is especially noteworthy given the levels of electoral fraud during the entire first half of the century, when only men were voting. An analysis of electoral results does not support the conclusion that Peronists won by manipulating women's votes. Far from insisting that the women's vote was responsible for Perón's victory, we should understand that he would have won even if women had not voted at all. Generally speaking, we see a similar pattern of voting between men and women with regard to Peronism.[57] Additionally, in Perón's case, when Law 13010 passed in 1947, the constitution did not permit presidential reelection. That change came later, in 1949. Thus we cannot attribute a law passed in 1947 to a possible reelection campaign strategy. Of course, we could argue that Perón planned to change the constitution in order to win reelection and that women were fundamental to a strategy in which he intended to manipulate them in his favor. There has been no evidence to suggest that this was the case, however. At present, scholars have only connected two events as though there were causality: Perón supported women's suffrage; then he was reelected; therefore he must have done it in order to be reelected. Thus women are responsible for his victory. These ideas have been so persistent as to have served as the basis for attempts, in 1956, to nullify the law that granted women political rights. That proposal came from conservative leader Reynaldo Pastor of the Junta Consultiva Nacional (JCN)—an institution made up of representatives from the different parties supporting the military government in reconstructing the political bases of the country, uprooting Peronism. Socialist Alicia Moreau de Justo and Unión Cívica Radical member Oscar López Serrot also served on the JCN, and they vigorously opposed the effort to re-disenfranchise women. In the end, the law granting political rights was not abrogated, although the Peronist divorce law was, but the episode is a good reminder that achieving rights is no guarantee of maintaining them. Thus we must ask not only how political rights were won but also how they were sustained.

Another aspect that is frequently linked to this issue is the use of the figure of Evita as a strategy to manipulate women in Perón's favor. Some studies have suggested an instrumentalist vision with regard to both the passage of the law and the figure of Eva Perón. In these perspectives, the role of Evita goes beyond Manichean interpretations.[58] The views on populism that focus on leadership have reinforced a profoundly sexist view of women, assigning them a greater susceptibility to influence. Regardless, as we have seen, political maternalism was in any case a strategy that went beyond demanding women's suffrage. In reality, Evita used references to motherhood less than others had in earlier periods. Her statements questioned men's roles and their control over women, except of course Perón. If Evita did express a demand regarding women's political rights, it was on the eve of her first national act, in which she encouraged women to choose well, which for her meant to vote for Perón. By contrast, her positions were less conservative and exclusionary than many that followed Peronism's overthrow. As Cavarozzi observes, "Developmentalism also constituted a reaction against the mobilizing component of populisms, accusing them of having excessively increased the weight and influence of mass organizations; in this other sense, the developmentalist discourse opposed democracy and popular participation."[59]

In the specific case we have analyzed here, a state modernization project concerned with following international standards favored social protection and security for women. This was combined with the emergence of a dynamic Catholic group in women-focused areas of government, which moderated and restrained the more liberal proposals that had come before.[60] The long view this chapter has adopted allows us to analyze the twists and nuances that women's suffrage acquired over time and in historical interpretations. I have also attempted to highlight the many possibilities for further research and how the complexities of the processes under study require a critical eye, well-founded arguments, and interpretative creativity as we continue to contemplate the history of women's suffrage in Argentina.

Acknowledgments

I would like to thank the compiler for inviting me to participate in this volume and for the opportunity to converse with her and Patricia Harms in Colombia on a panel where we exchanged the first drafts of our work. I am especially grateful to Stephanie for opening her home to me and offering me her friendship. I also thank Donna Guy for her constant encouragement and the opportunities to debate. My thanks also go to Dora Barrancos, Sol Calandria, Gisela Manzoni, Rosario Gómez Molla, Nadia Ledesma Prietto, and Esteban Barroso, who made substantive comments on this version of the chapter.

Notes

1. Nari, *Políticas de maternidad y maternalismo político.*
2. At the risk of incurring an endogenous national vision of the development of women's suffrage history, I should point out that much must be left out in the interest of brevity. It is true that suffragists maintained important relationships with other parts of the globe and that the recommendations of international organizations were, at various junctures, important. Nevertheless, the Argentine government mistrusted especially US intentions and US-led pan-Americanism, which lessened the impact of that influence. I develop the

relationship to the international arena in "Los derechos políticos en Argentina y los vaivenes internacionales y nacionales." See also, Vignoli, "El Consejo Nacional de la Mujer en Argentina y su dimensión internacional"; Marino, "Marta Vergara."

3. García Sebastiani, *Los antiperonistas en la Argentina peronista.*

4. Nállim, *Las raíces del antiperonismo,* 18.

5. Valobra, "Una historia para el voto femenino municipal en San Juan."

6. Solar, "La mujer sufragante en San Juan."

7. Ramella de Jefferies, "El régimen electoral de San Juan en la década de los años 1880."

8. Videla, *Historia de San Juan.*

9. For more on this debate, see Valobra, "Una historia para el voto femenino municipal en San Juan."

10. Lavrin, *Women, Feminism, and Social Change.*

11. Offen 1991; Scott, *Only Paradoxes to Offer.*

12. Bellota, *Julieta Lanteri*; Deleis et al., *Mujeres de La Política Argentina.*

13. Barrancos, *Inclusión/Exclusión*; Barrancos, "Socialismo y sufragio femenino." Lavrin, *Women, Feminism, and Social Change.*

14. Vignoli, "El Consejo Nacional de la Mujer en Argentina y su dimensión internacional."

15. Nari, *Políticas de maternidad y maternalismo politico.*

16. Terzaghi, "Trabajo Final Integrador Miradas de Alicia Moreau sobre Ciudadanía."

17. Barrancos, *Inclusión/Exclusión.*

18. Demichelli, *Igualdad jurídica de la mujer,* 267.

19. Valobra, "Elogio de la mujer que vota."

20. Videla, "Elecciones, partidos y conflicto social a finales de los años veinte del siglo XX en Rosario."

21. Ramella de Jefferies, *El radicalismo bloquista de San Juan.*

22. Palermo, "El Sufragio Femenino en el Congreso Nacional."

23. Barrancos, "Sociedad y género"; Barrancos, *Inclusión/Exclusión*; Palermo, "El Sufragio Femenino en el Congreso Nacional"; Palermo, *Los derechos políticos de la mujer.*

24. Guy, "Suffrage in San Juan."

25. Bianchi, "Peronismo y sufragio femenino," 262.

26. Valobra, *Del Hogar a las Urnas. Recorridos de la Ciudadanía Política Femenina.*

27. Bianchi, "Peronismo y sufragio femenino," 262.

28. Bianchi, 267.

29. Lobato, *Eva Perón.*

30. Navaro, *Evita: Mitos y representaciones.*

31. Bianchi and Sanchís, *El partido peronista femenino.*

32. Plotkin, *Mañana es San Perón.*

33. Bianchi, "Peronismo y sufragio femenino."

34. Valobra, "Los discursos de Eva Perón."

35. Valobra, "Los discursos de Eva Perón."

36. Barry, "Evita."

37. Navarro, *Evita* (1994).

38. Guy, *Las mujeres y la construcción del Estado de Bienestar.*

39. I make no reference here to the legislation on the Statute on Political Parties (September 1949). Neither, due to space considerations, do I include references to the reform of 1948. For further analysis, see Valobra, *Del Hogar a las Urnas,* 61–62; Barrancos, *Inclusión/Exclusión,* 148.

40. Bianchi, "Peronismo y sufragio femenino," 267.

41. Valobra, *Mujeres en espacios bonaerenses;* Valobra, *Del Hogar a las Urnas.*

42. Valobra, *Mujeres en espacios bonaerenses.*

43. Palermo, "El Sufragio Femenino en el Congreso Nacional," 171.

44. Aboy Carlés, "Las dos caras de Jano."

45. Valobra, *Del Hogar a las Urnas.*

46. Palermo, "El Sufragio Femenino en el Congreso Nacional," 173; Palermo, *Los derechos políticos de la mujer.*

47. Saltalamacchia, "Para qué sirve el 'populismo'?" 2.

48. Aboy Carlés, "Las dos caras de Jano."

49. Viguera, "'Populismo' y 'neopopulismo' en América Latina," 50.

50. Rodríguez, *Lencinas y Cantoni, el populismo cuyano en tiempos de Yrigoyen.*

51. Hammond, "Suffrage in San Juan," 3.

52. De Privitellio, "Sociedad y sufragio femenino en la reforma constitucional de San Juan," 70.

53. Germani, *Política y sociedad en una época de transición,* 335.

54. Viguera, "'Populismo' y 'neopopulismo' en América Latina," 51.

55. Viguera, 51.

56. The notion of blaming women for electoral results was also present in San Juan in 1928, and it reappeared whenever a Cantonista-style candidate won an election.

57. In 1946 the proportion of Peronist votes was 50.1 percent. If we look only at male voters from 1951 and the fifteen electoral districts from 1946, the proportion of the Peronist vote increases to 61.1 percent. The difference can be explained by various things, including changes in elector districts and the direct vote, as well as gender. This means that Peronism increased its participation even without the women's vote or the new districts. Original research based on data published in Argentina, Ministerio del Interior, *Confirmación electoral de la voluntad justicialista del pueblo argentino,* Buenos Aires: Ministerio del Interior de la República Argentina, 1951. If we look only at female voters, Peronism would have won in 1951 with 64.1 percent of the vote, which increases in 1954.

58. Palermo, "Sufragio femenino"; Palermo, *Los derechos políticos de la mujer*; Valobra, "Los discursos de Eva Perón."
59. Cavarozzi, "'Desarrollismo' y las relaciones entre democracia y capitalism dependiente en 'Dependencia y Desarrollo en América Latina," 156.
60. Valobra, "Representación política y derechos de las trabajadoras en Argentina."

CHAPTER SIX

Women's Suffrage in Colombia

GUIOMAR DUEÑAS VARGAS

ON AUGUST 27, 1954, COLOMBIAN women won the right to vote, but the bill that granted them access to the voting box was actually sanctioned by the plebiscite of December 1, 1957, convoked by the National Front.[1] Powerful political adversaries opposed women's suffrage, but there had also been an unwavering women's mobilization since 1933. Several feminist international conferences demanding political rights for women on the continent also contributed to the final success.

Women's path to citizenship in Colombia reveals some unique characteristics. First, it came rather late in comparison with other Latin American countries. Second, it was obstructed by the conservative presidential regime that stretched from 1886 to 1930, which put an end to some progressive liberal educational policies in support of women. It was again obstructed, during the postwar years (1946–1953), when conservatives and the church planted the fear of communism and advocated for confining women in the home. Liberals, on the other hand, enacted important reforms, endorsing higher education for women and promoting the reform of the civil code in favor of married women. Women's full citizenship, in the form of voting rights, was strongly opposed by the Catholic Church.

Toward the end of the nineteenth century, while many countries in the region enjoyed a period of economic bonanza, the spread of liberal ideas, and new opportunities for educating women, Colombia entered a period of unwavering conservatism known as La Regeneración (1886–1898), which affected women in significant ways. A new constitution drafted by Rafael Núñez and Miguel Antonio Caro ratified the alliance between the Catholic Church and the state, proclaiming the birth of a new country under Catholic principles and granting the church social control of family life, education, and cultural direction. The "natural" difference of the sexes in matters of rights and duties, which benefited men, was ratified by the constitution of 1886. Citizens were "males over 21 years of age, with a defined profession, skill, legal occupation, or any other legitimate form of subsistence." Women belonged to the home. Women's roles were seen to be more altruistic than those of men: to raise good Christians and to preserve the flame of love within the family. Their education was entrusted to convents and not to the state. Placing women above the muddy scenario of politics was an efficient way to deprive women of the rights and duties of citizenship.

Educating Women

In Colombia, as in the rest of the continent, public education of women became linked to the process of state modernization and secularization initiated by liberals elsewhere. Feminist critique of the traditional social order was linked to advanced public education systems as found in countries such as Argentina, Uruguay, and Chile. Under the conservative regime, Colombia went backward. Gains obtained under the previous liberal governments, such as the founding of normal schools for men and women—initiatives that provided a good source of legitimate work outside the home for middle-class women—suffered a setback under the conservative regime. In fact, the abrupt rupture with the liberal educational model occurred concurrently with enforced religious instruction at all levels: Decree 544 of June 1888 mandated the teaching of dogmas of the Catholic faith in every public and private institution of basic, *normalista*, arts and crafts, and higher education. To gain admission to any academic program of the National University of Colombia, the candidate had to have previously passed a religion course.[2]

The new regime inaugurated in 1886 ended liberal attempts to secularize schooling. In fact, since the founding of the Colombian republic, the leaders had relegated the education of women to convents and other religious institutions, but with the inception of the conservative government, women's education acquired a higher purpose: to create "agents of Christian civilization" and guardians of faith and tradition.

Elite women, in general, submitted willingly to the values promulgated by the new regime. Some were against the participation of women in politics. Soledad Acosta de Samper, for instance, a member of the liberal elite who wrote frequently about the education of women, represented the country in several international women's conferences and was the wife of one of the liberal scions of Colombia; she opposed the participation of women in politics and wrote eloquently against the "absurd" emancipation of the fair sex. Women, she said, should not aspire to public positions and should not dispute with men in the "public arena," which she claimed had been degraded and sullied. She believed that women were called to superior tasks. They were the moral conscience of society, promoting its most transcendental values. The role of women should be to educate their children to serve the country and to help their husbands participate honestly in the public service: "Women should be the guardian angels that help men to make the morally right political decisions. Women's mission should be to purify the moral environment and enhance the morals of husbands and children to enable them to do well as citizens."[3] This entrenched social belief hindered the advance of Colombian women, who had to wait for the fall of the conservative government and the rise of the liberals to gain access to secondary and higher education. Liberals also contributed to the reform of the civil code in favor of the economic independence of married women.

The development of manufacturing, urban growth, and social change that occurred in the 1920s required women workers in factories. Labor and education, as Asunción Lavrin writes in relation to the Southern Cone countries, brought women into the light of the public debate.[4] Textile factories in Antioquia—the hub of industrialization in the country—provided employment for women. The factory was also a school for their political awareness and for the formation of female social leaders. The sweatshop environment, the grueling working conditions, the triple-shift status of mother/wife/worker, low salaries, and long working hours led women to protest in Bello, Antioquia. In 1920 labor rights activist Betsabé Espinal led a strike of four hundred female workers. This was the first protest organized by women in the country, and it was a great triumph. The strike led to a 40 percent salary increase, a nine-hour workday, and protection against sexual harassment. The experience resonated elsewhere. The influence of María Cano, an activist from Antioquia who fought for social justice for workers, spread throughout the country. Channeling the workers' discontent in Antioquia, she became the leader of the struggle for social justice in the factory. Initially advocating for the miners of Remedios, Antioquia, she expanded her goals in favor of the workers of the recently created textile factories. Just as in the early days of the Industrial Revolution in England, these workers lacked labor protection and were untrained, unorganized, and unable to fight for better salaries and decent conditions of work. She cofounded the Socialist Revolutionary Party (PSR), becoming its spokesperson in the public plaza; the workers called her La Flor del Trabajo. She was the leader of several workers' strikes in defense of basic civil rights and just salaries.[5] While women in the sweatshop became active advocating for their rights as workers, middle-class women in major urban centers were questioning their subjugation as married women, as ratified in the civil codes, and demanded access to higher education and the opportunity to hold public service appointments. Issues such as the latter attracted the attention of the liberal representative Absalón Fernández, who presented a bill asserting the right of women to hold public employment.[6]

Early suffragists, such as Georgina Fletcher, Ofelia Uribe de Acosta, Clotilde García Ucross, and Lucila Rubio de Laverde, found allies among some progressive liberals. They were the pioneers of the women's movement in the country, and they represented what many studies of the feminist struggle in Colombia define as the first phase toward citizenship.[7]

Women's Legal and Cultural Achievements: 1930–1957

The period 1930–1957 was decisive for women's aspirations. The liberals took power after a prolonged conservative hegemony and governed until 1946. The ensuing decade, which began in a state of siege, ended in dictatorship. Women navigated throughout these years, negotiating their claims with liberals, conservatives, and the dictator Gustavo Rojas Pinilla, who came to power in 1953.

Under the leadership of Alfonso López (1934–1938 and 1942–1946), the liberal republic took shape. In his governing plan, "Revolution on the March," López reformulated the role of the state in new terms, promoting peasant access to vacant lands and backing the creation of labor unions. In the economic sphere he endorsed trade and the production of coffee, which became an important source of revenue for the country.[8] Concerning women, the liberals were no more enthusiastic than the conservatives before them about extending their political rights. Nevertheless, the liberals did try to address the dependent status of women within the family and produced some modifications to the civil code (1932), allowing women control of their own wealth and their own professions. The new civil code of 1936 removed the differential punishment for adultery for men and women, which had previously been more severe for the latter.

In 1930 Carlos E. Restrepo, minister of government of the new liberal regime, sponsored the first initiative to reform the civil rights of married women. He focused specifically on their property rights. Feminists who had been discussing the need to change laws concerning the patrimonial rights of married women found an opportunity to collaborate with the new government in addressing legal limitations married women had been suffering with respect to their husbands. This issue was part of the agenda of the Fourth International Feminist Conference in Bogotá (1930), an event organized by the energetic Georgina Fletcher with the financial help of the recently inaugurated president, Enrique Olaya Herrera (1930–1934). Married women could not administer their own property, whether it was owned before marriage or acquired during it. Husbands were entitled to administer everything. If a woman worked, her wages belonged to her husband. She was obliged to live wherever her husband wished, and she could not operate a business in her own name.

Women had to break open their domestic prisons before fighting for a spot in the public world. At the Fourth International Feminist Conference, Ofelia Uribe de Acosta delivered a paper titled "Régimen de Capitulaciones Matrimoniales" (Economic Marriage Contract), which became a civil code reform proposal to grant married women the freedom to administer their own properties. The request presented to the House of Representatives was not approved in 1930 but was approved as Law 28 in 1932. There were tempestuous reactions from the entire social spectrum. The feminist proposal had pinched a sensitive nerve in the political body. In her fascinating book *Una voz insurgente* (An Insurgent Voice), Ofelia Uribe de Acosta vividly described some of the most vociferous foes of the project while it was being defended in the Chamber of Representatives: "The struggle was incredible, and the controversy was ugly. Men, who in the past had enjoyed the political cavorting of a group of 'playful dolls' turned very serious and ended annoyed with the 'horrible old age feminists.'"[9]

She continued, "Prominent conservative senators left the session in which the new project was being discussed to prevent a quorum for its approval, not without leaving a negative vote against it, on the ground that it would contribute to the destabilization of the family and because it would go against the conjugal union, the foundation of Catholic marriage."[10]

Representative Luis Muñoz Obando felt obliged to reproach women for acting in "such an irrational way": "Women in Colombia insist on smashing the crystal that protects them. If the project becomes law, they will become victims of unscrupulous men who would take away their children's patrimony. What would they do without their husbands, the managers of the marital society, men who are the intelligence and strong arms upon which the family patrimony rests?"

Women from the balustrade yelled, "We don't want tutors," to which the representative responded, "But you will [have them], whether you like it or not."[11]

The representatives' reactions frightened many women, who slowly began to leave the chamber. Only Clotilde García de Ucrós rallied a group of women to remain, and they valiantly burst through the balustrades of the Senate to exert pressure on the congressmen. Five hundred women demanded the approval of the project.[12]

Further legislation (Decree 1972; December 1, 1933) allowed women to obtain university degrees and access to government jobs; it was finally approved in the constitutional reform of 1936, under the presidency of Alfonso López Pumarejo. While it was considered a great women's achievement, some high-profile people didn't find it prudent legislation. Germán

Arciniegas, a well-known public intellectual, had tried to prevent the admittance of women to the National University of Colombia, arguing "women are not competent to enter certain occupations and professions that belong and correspond to men."[13] In 1938 the city of Tunja's high school stopped admitting females "because the girls did better than the boys and that caused problems."[14] Nevertheless, the possibility of appointment to high government posts allowed women with university degrees to thrive. It also brought about the ire of journalists like Enrique Santos Montejo (aka Calibán), who from the liberal newspaper *El Tiempo* launched a systematic attack on any initiative in favor of women.

Battles for Female Suffrage: 1944–1953

During this period, feminism and the civil and political emancipation of women were thoroughly debated by men and women—conservatives, socialists, and liberals—in national newspapers and feminist publications. The rhetoric of liberals and conservatives was not radically different, however: women were morally superior to men; the political world was a volatile and dangerous arena, unsuited to women; women in general were not interested in acquiring political rights; Latin women were more inclined than others to stay home and take care of men; feminist demands were contrary to the national culture, and so on. Most men and even many women from all walks of life feared the potential destruction of the domestic sphere if women were allowed to participate in politics.[15]

The period was dominated by the decline of liberal hegemony and the rise of conservative politics. Women entered the fray during this convulsive period. The first generation of feminists led the advance into the public arena, interacting with powerful men, sharing activities, exchanging ideas, and helping form new activist groups, while liberals were still in power, more specifically during the second term of the liberal Alfonso López Pumarejo. Cities such as Tunja, Bucaramanga, Medellín, and Cali became sites of feminist activity; Ofelia Uribe de Acosta had moved to Tunja and, with the gifted feminist Inés Gómez, initiated the radio program *La hora feminista* (The Feminist Hour). The goal of these feminists was to reach an educated audience on topics that concerned women's rights. They traveled around the country to promote women's groups. In 1944 Ofelia Uribe with Inés Gómez, Carmen Medina de López, Mercedes Arenas de Lara, Alicia Solano Sanabria, and Leonor Barrete founded, edited, and distributed the magazine *Agitación Femenina*.[16] Ofelia Uribe stated up front in the first issue that the purpose of their publication was to shake the general opinion in favor of women's citizenship. In those years the political struggle between the traditional political parties was putting the country on the threshold of civil war, and Uribe de Acosta wanted to enhance the power of women to bring in some common sense: "We want to contribute in the making of our nation to moderate the insane whirlwind of the partisan upheaval."[17] She published the feminist magazine *La Verdad* (1955) and the book *Una voz insurgente*. Uribe de Acosta remained loyal to a liberal conception of politics. She, like many feminists of her generation, struggled to extend the benefits of the modern world, in terms of education, intellectual development, political aspirations, and job opportunities, to married women. Men of her time, whether conservative or liberal, favored the vision of a secluded wife committed entirely to motherhood and domestic affairs. She wrote, "[The] modern woman is a good mother and homemaker, but she also should look around to learn about the changes taken place in the world and act consequently."[18]

Through her writings, Uribe de Acosta kept reiterating that the modern world required new roles for women: "They [women] have to change the home conditions of patriarchal epochs exploring the new opportunities a changing world offered, and by learning about new conceptions of womanhood."[19] She said that men should not be afraid, because a well-informed wife would provide a better education to her children and would be a more efficient homemaker. She wrote about the moral crisis of Colombia and the need to allow new pressure groups to participate in the running of the state, with new modern criteria, new thinking, and acting with the community in mind. These groups were encouraged to introduce, immediately, educational plans for children and adults. Citizenship would allow women to be a moralizing force at the service of the community: "We, the new citizens represent a great reserve for acting with a pristine sense of the social and political reality, to contribute to the restoration of this agonizing democracy. I think we feminists are obliged to pinpoint to our sisters, the course of action to enjoy the rights we have conquered with such great difficulty."[20]

Between 1944 and 1953, women's organizations worked to expand the political education of the female sex throughout the country. In 1944 Rosa María Moreno Aguilera and Ilda Carriazo founded the feminist group Union Femenina (Feminine Union), comprised mainly of well-educated middle- and upper-class women. The initial group of seventy included university students, medical doctors, lawyers, teachers, and nurses. The main objective of the group was to support women who worked outside the home.

Advocacy and militancy were not limited to upper- and middle-class women. The Federación Femenina Nacional (Feminine National Federation), founded in 1945, opened sections in Atlántico, Antioquia, and Valle del Cauca.[21] It changed its name to Alianza Femenina de Colombia (Colombian Feminine Alliance) to expand its goals and to allow women from different socioeconomic standings to be a part of the political discussion. The Second World War offered women the opportunity to amplify their demands in the Primer Congreso Nacional de Mujeres (First National Women's Conference), held in February 1945. Organized by Mercedes Abadía, Lucila Rubio de Laverde, and Matilde Espinosa, the multi-class event included peasants, workers, and students. Its main focus was on issues such as citizenship for women, the defense of democracy against fascism, and the centrality of maternity. In 1946 the Segundo Congreso Nacional Femenino (Second Feminine Conference) discussed the incongruent position of women, who were able to hold high state positions notwithstanding lacking citizenship. Lucila Rubio de Laverde delivered the inaugural speech, acknowledging women's political rights and their role in bringing peace to the country. According to Rubio de Laverde, women had other responsibilities in addition to their domestic chores. She, just like Ofelia Uribe, addressed the fallacy of feminism versus home. She asserted that, contrary to the false belief that politics destroyed the private dominion and endangered femininity, the mother dignified life at home. The housewife who knew her political rights would have a better understanding of her real mission on earth.[22]

The condition of women was also a topic of concern to conservatives and to women loyal to traditional political doctrines and Catholic teachings. Both rejected suffrage, but men were more radical in identifying the destruction of the home with the political empowering of women.[23] For con-servative women, home was a place for fulfillment: the site in which they complied with the sacred duties of maternity. Josefina Canal de Reyes edited the magazine *Mireya*, the purpose of which was to "fulfill feminine concerns and the National and family ideals." *Letras y Encajes* (Letters and Lace) was the first magazine published by women. Founded in Medellín in 1929 by a group of elite women and directed for many years by Teresa Santamaría de González, it sought to enlighten women in the fields of religion, literature, art, history, and home economics.[24]

The emancipation of women was at the center of discussion among social-ist and liberal feminists when the liberal regime was under threat. Lucila Rubio de Laverde, who had worked closely with Ofelia Uribe since the 1930s—presenting proposals, publishing magazines, creating women's groups, and spreading the feminist agenda throughout the country—wanted to move the discussion of the role of women in the public sphere into the open while the liberals were still in power. Rubio de Laverde, Ofelia Uribe, and most socialist and liberal feminists defended the idea that women deserved a place in the public sphere to be better homemakers and better fellows of society. Rubio de Laverde, who had a strong sense of the opportu-nities women had under the liberal regime, sent a well-written document to President López Pumarejo asking for his intervention in favor of a constitu-tional reform to put an end to sexual discrimination in the public sector. In response, López sent the following statement for discussion in the Chamber of Representatives: "Citizenship is the necessary condition to elect and to be elected, and to perform public services that require authority and jurisdic-tion. A Colombian woman of legal age may be elected but cannot vote until female suffrage has been approved with the restrictions established by the law."[25] The reaction against the legal project was thundering. The political scene at the end of the Second World War was not favorable for any feminist demands. Latin American countries positioned themselves on the side of the "free world" in the fight against communism and sought to protect the fam-ily and enhance the authority of the father in the private home. Some liber-als, looking backward, questioned women's earlier gains. In 1944 López Pumarejo's minister of education, Antonio Rocha, said that "unless we force the *campesino* (peasant) back to his plot and women back to the home the integrity of the nation will be in jeopardy."[26] The proposed law presented to the president to address sex discrimination in the workplace by Lucila Rubio de Laverde, a socialist, was condemned at the pulpit and in the press.

Caliban, the above-mentioned journalist from the liberal newspaper *El Tiempo*, who regularly attacked feminists' activity in his column "Danza de las Horas," conducted a poll to prove that women's suffrage was unpopular among city dwellers. Not surprisingly, the poll revealed disapproval of the proposal. Caliban, as demonstrated in *Agitación Femenina* by Ofelia Uribe and other feminists, had used flawed methodology and had thereby manipulated the results. But Uribe and her friends knew very well that women, intimidated by the men of their households and the Catholic Church, did not dare disobey their husbands. Uribe de Acosta knew that feminists could not count on mass support from most women. She and her small group of committed suffragists would need to prepare for a long struggle, pressing for changes that would extend to women who, at least at that moment, may not have been in a position to support them.[27] Caliban's antifeminist attitude is revealed in "Danza de las Horas": "Now, when our ladies again demand equal rights, they should read *Women and Men* published by Amram Scheninfeld. There, the author destroyed the legend of the seemingly biological equality among the sexes, which began spreading after World War I. While women repel diseases better than men, men are endowed with all the ability to dominate and succeed in any physical and spiritual activity. No female has matched a male in athletic pursuits among all animals."[28]

Alberto Lleras Camargo, the liberal state minister, was not eager to support his president's law proposal either, reiterating instead the murky character of the political realm and contrasting it not with the innate purity of the "weaker sex" but with the emotionality of women, which could not contribute to the progress of the nation. When the results of Caliban's poll were published, he happily declared the lack of public demand to advance the legal project/process in favor of the emancipation of Colombian women. Some journalists, using humorous critiques, commented on the aspiration of women. The conservative Julio Abril, in his column "The Feminine Vote Question," wrote:

The equality of rights demanded by women Is debatable. Rights involve duties. Men, working in the public service, for instance, get their salaries and deliver them immediately to the state coffers through the taxes paid for the consumption of liquor. Now, the spinster that earns a salary . . . nobody knows how she spends it. This is what a friend of mine was figuring out in relation to a female colleague who was a spinster . . . and adding to that, she was an ugly spinster: How does she spend her salary? She doesn't smoke, she doesn't drink . . . and she doesn't like women!"[29]

Political Turmoil and Women's Triumph

Women's mobilization suffered a slowdown with the return of the conservatives Mariano Ospina Pérez (1946–1950) and Laureano Gómez (1950–1951) to the presidency and the assassination of Jorge Eliécer Gaitán (April 9, 1948), which engulfed the country in flames. It also saw the first phase of political violence during the electoral campaigns. The 1953 military coup by General Gustavo Rojas Pinilla, which dethroned Laureano Gómez, opened the road for women's citizenship.

The assassination of the populist leader Jorge Eliécer Gaitán, who had criticized the oligarchy—the upper echelons of the traditional parties—and had advocated for those without power, was followed by an outburst of mass rioting, turmoil, and death, referred to as El Bogotazo, a generalized insurrection that immersed the entire country. Violent behavior had disturbed the country since the rise of the conservatives to power, but it became rampant and explosive after Gaitán's murder. This was the beginning of a historical period called La Violencia (1948–1964), characterized by a bloody partisan confrontation in the countryside. Gaitán's political movement resembled many populist parties that arose in many countries of Latin America throughout the twentieth century.

Its adherents were members of the new urban and popular sectors, expanding in ranks thanks to rural–urban migration. Women's rights had figured among Gaitán's projects. In 1935, as mayor of Bogotá, he asked the legislators to grant women the right to vote.[30] In Colombia women from all walks of life became fervent Gaitanistas. Arturo Alape, a chronicler of the

Bogotazo, described the participation of marketplace women in the popular protest that followed Gaitán's murder. Marketplace women, or followers of Gaitán, took to the street to participate in the riot; "Alfonso Araujo (a bystander) was held by his arm by a marketplace woman, ostensibly a popular leader . . . when the shooting began, the woman holding Araujo got shot and fell to the ground . . . the marketplace was a frightful site because it was a sincere Gaitanista stronghold. Women and men looking distraught armed with knives and sticks yelling, 'To the Palace'! 'To the palace'!"[31]

These episodes of unrest marked a point of departure during La Violencia, which reached a climax under Laureano Gómez's presidential term. Intensely traditional and religious, Gómez acted as a crusader for orthodox Catholicism to guide the governance of the country. He wanted to erase any vestige of liberalism and liberal ideas, which he blamed for the erosion of the Catholic faith in the country and the anticlerical disposition of the liberal government. The climate of the cold war provided him with a string of ideological arguments to "reconstruct" the country under the banner of Catholicism. Catholic doctrine returned, as under the regime of the Regeneración, as the foundation for public education.

The educational reform approved in the constitutional reform of 1936, which sought the secularization and modernization of society, was bitterly criticized by Gómez. Historian James D. Henderson writes of this period, "Convinced that Liberalism had corrupted the nation's youth, he [Gómez] launched a program of 're-Christianizing' the nation's educational establishment by injecting heavy doses of religion into the curriculum and firing teachers who were not confessing Catholics."[32] Gómez found support in the ultraconservative clerical side of the church for his fight against communism, Protestantism, and anti-secularism, and to justify the repression of liberals. Moral campaigns against pornography, prostitution, communism, Protestantism, and religious tolerance were entrusted to Acción Católica (Catholic Action), a lay association founded to spread the Catholic faith.[33] Gómez wanted a corporatist state following the Spanish model of governance under General Francisco Franco, believing that corporatism would eliminate the belligerent political environment he attributed to universal suffrage.[34] Traditional womanhood was invoked as the savior of the patriarchal home, and married women were called the backbone of Christian traditions. The role of the family in rescuing the world from the claws of communism after the Second World War was a priority for Pope Pious XII, whose thoughts about the *doctrina familiar* was captured in the Malines Code. For Pious, the family was the cornerstone of society and had precedence over the state.[35] Married women could be elected to municipal councils. They would be elected not as individuals, however, but as members of their families, which meant that their votes were merged with their husbands' votes.

Relations between liberal and conservative leaders stood at an all-time low throughout Gómez's presidency. The Violencia grew worse with each passing day, which led to the nonviolent coup d'état of army general Gustavo Rojas Pinilla on June 13, 1953. The Asamblea Nacional Constituyente (Constitutional National Assembly) dissolved the corporatist reform promoted by Gómez and confirmed the general as the new president of the nation in August 1954. The Comisión de Estudios Constitucionales (CEC; Commission of Constitutional Studies) was asked to write a new constitution for the country. Supported by members of both traditional parties, Rojas Pinilla promised to bring peace and amnesty to insurgents who had reached the outskirts of Bogotá.

Populism and Suffrage

Female suffragists in Colombia had sought the support of the liberals to further their cause, and under a liberal president they gained the right to administer their own wealth, access to higher education, and access to public service appointments, but it was under a military conservative/populist regime that they obtained the right to vote. Rojas Pinilla belonged to a generation of leaders in Latin America, including Juan Domingo Perón, Getulio Vargas, and Lázaro Cárdenas, who sought to dominate the national political scene after World War II, vilifying the oligarchies and looking for the support of the working and lower middle classes. They also had in common paternalistic attitudes and nationalistic sentiments. Although Rojas Pinilla acted as a populist, he came to power not to scourge the oligarchy but to stop the violence that traditional leaders couldn't. Both liberals and conservatives enabled Rojas Pinilla to take power while they—away in Spain—sought a convivial solution to share power again. They soon returned (1957) with a novel political solution: the National Front, an agreement to share power, allowing each party to govern in turns of four years.

Rojas Pinilla was a colorless leader; he lacked the fervor that Jorge Eliécer Gaitán inspired among the common people. Gaitán had used his charisma and eloquence, his ability to condemn traditional elites, and his talent to identify himself with oppressed people.

The gender dimension of politics changed under the "populist" regimes. These leaders represented a new masculinity; they were charismatic, visible, and gifted orators. The names of their political movements—Gaitanismo, Varguismo, Peronismo—encompassed personalistic styles of male governance. They expressed interest in the feminine element of their societies and were committed to enhancing essentialist notions of women's roles as mothers and daughters. As in similar regimes, and seeking support from women and families, Rojas Pinilla launched social programs targeting families, children, and women from the popular sectors. Inspired by the social doctrine of the Catholic Church, Rojas Pinilla created Secretaría Nacional de Asistencia Social (SENDAS). Its programs and activities were designed to help families from the lower sectors, under clearly defined Catholic and paternalistic principles. It seems his model for the creation of SENDAS was Argentina, under Juan and Eva Perón, where women, as mothers, became the targets of reformist social programs. Rojas Pinilla wanted his daughter María Eugenia to become the Colombian Evita. She would enhance his demeanor of benevolence toward women. María Eugenia met Eva Perón in 1954 during an official visit to Argentina, where she more than likely talked to her about the Eva Perón Foundation.[36] The creation of SENDAS, in September 1954, occurred three months after the repression of a student protest against the military regime of Rojas Pinilla in which two students from the National University of Colombia were killed. It can be interpreted as a strategy to avoid further social discontent.

Rojas Pinilla needed to placate the general dissatisfaction with his regime and to gain the support of the popular sectors. He and his daughter targeted poor families—especially women—to expand his electorate. Women of all walks of life also sought the opportunity to obtain political gains.

The National Popular Alliance, the general's political movement, and women activists of different political persuasions—socialists, liberals, and conservatives—called for suffrage in a single voice. They organized a campaign to promote the vote throughout the country. The goal was to discuss and debate women's full citizenship in every corner of Colombia. Related documents were discussed among various women: peasants, professionals, homemakers, workers, students, teachers, and members of the clergy. After the CEC was installed on December 1, 1953, a memorandum asking for women's full citizenship had support from Ayde Anzola Linares, Ismenia Mujica, Isabel Lleras, and three thousand additional women. It was submitted to the plenary on February 23 of the following year.[37]

By this time, the emergence of women as political actors was beyond question. The international climate favored them. The United Nations conference (1952) endorsed women's political rights, reminding reluctant countries like Colombia that it was their obligation to allow women to participate in the direction of their nations. In Colombia the new regime encouraged women to present and discuss their proposal to the CEC. Liberal and socialist activists had the opportunity to voice claims for better salaries, infant protection, and education; conservatives stressed the need to preserve Catholic principles, the search for peace, and education in political matters.[38] The liberal Esmeralda Arboleda and the conservative Josefina Valencia de Hubech were the main advocates for women's rights at this crucial time. They, along with other feminists, wrote a memorandum asking to include the demand for women's rights in the CEC.[39] Rojas Pinilla endorsed the project and nominated Esmeralda Arboleda, Josefina Valencia de Hubech, and Teresita Santamaría as members of the Asamblea Nacional Constituyente (ANAC; National Constitutional Assembly). The proposal was studied and presented to the plenary by the distinguished scientist Luis López de Mesa. Then women made their own defense, and finally Ángel Vallejo made the motion to illustrate to the audience the importance of women's claims for political equality for the entire country. After four plenaries, the project passed, but not without opposition. Some congressmen wanted to grant rights gradually. Many complained about "the lack of intellectual formation of women," but the main objection was the abandonment of the home. In her speech, Esmeralda Arboleda defended a comprehensive vote—a vote "without any limitations." She assured the congressmen that women's claims "are not to defeat men, but to form them, to work with them and for them, to work together in the hardships of raising a family and to build the nation."[40] She addressed the many ways that fratricidal war had affected women from all walks of life and how they, as citizens, could contribute to bringing peace and prosperity to the nation. Her intervention met with general approval. The project was approved by the plenary, as Legislative Act No. 3, on August 27, 1954, but access to the ballot box had to wait until December 1957. Esmeralda Arboleda, as Patricia Pinzón de Lewin shows, played a central role in the successful battle for citizenship, begun by the early suffragists of the 1930s. A lawyer from the University of Cauca, she began her private practice focusing on labor law in Cali. She moved to Bogotá, where she became interested in the suffragist movement. There she met activists such as Josefina Valencia, María Currea, and Bertha Hernández, the wife of President Mariano Ospina. They wanted to take advantage of the political moment and in April 1954 founded the multi-class feminist movement Organización Nacional Femenina (ONF; National Feminine Organization) to work for issues such as gender equality, education for both sexes, and protection of female workers. These demands appeared in Arboleda's successful defense in the CEC.

Having the proposal passed into law produced important political gains for Rojas Pinilla. The military regime allowed women to attain high positions in the government. Josefina Valencia de Hubech, a member of the Popayán conservative elite and sister of future president Guillermo León Valencia, became governor of Cauca and minister of education. Rojas Pinillas's daughter María Eugenia Rojas continued as director of SENDAS.

But the honeymoon was short.

While Rojas's ambitions increased, he was not able to maintain enough faithful followers. He could not deliver on his promises of peace and prosperity; economic and political elites turned against him. In 1955, unable to bring order and peace, Rojas Pinilla declared a state of siege in the country. This allowed him to tighten the repressive measures against his former allies from the traditional parties and to suppress any criticism of his dictatorial regime. Press censorship produced the temporary closing of the national newspaper *El Tiempo* in August 1955, the restriction of political freedoms and feminist demands, the closing of Ofelia Uribe de Acosta's journal *La Verdad*, and the violent dispersion of public protests against the dictatorship by students and women. Esmeralda Arboleda, making public her lack of support for the general's dictatorial tendencies, was chastised by Rojas Pinilla and removed from the ANAC. In May 1957 a massive mobilization of Colombians forced the general to relinquish power in favor of a military junta. The traditional parties then called for a plebiscite to legitimize the National Front. The same referendum granted the right to vote to Colombian women on December 1, 1957.

Conclusions

Women in Colombia began to discuss their place in society and their political rights during the Liberal Republic (1930–1946). The main foci of their debate were inclusion in the state and equality both in the private domain of the family and in the public domain of civil society. Regardless of social class or political persuasion, women suffrage activists called for inclusion in the body politic not primarily in defense of their own roles in politics but to change the civil law that had essentially enslaved women to their husbands.

Through changes in the law, women sought to empower themselves within the family and society, where they sought public recognition of their intellectual abilities. Nonetheless, the right of citizenship was still elusive. Liberals backed some feminist demands, but they worried about "destructive" effects in the home that might stem from the political empowerment of women. Conservatives who opposed any notion of women's rights in the public sphere argued that the family was the basis of the state. Their idea of family, however, was patriarchal, with no thought of equality among family members. They said the greatest female mission was to be a mother, and motherhood placed women above men, so women should not have any grounds for complaints.

Full political rights for women were demanded after a period of obscurity, repression, political violence, fear, and church dominion had oppressed the country between 1946 and 1953. In search of their own voice, suffragists found an ally in Gustavo Rojas Pinilla, the general who overthrew Laureano

Gómez and his conservative regime. Rojas was a populist leader. Looking to enlarge his political clientele, he enabled women to defend their full political rights project before the Colombian constitutional assembly. In this context, women activists focused on achieving the right to vote, and they succeeded.

Motherhood remained an overarching theme in the defense of women's rights. Women's activity, whether social or political, was deemed an extension of maternity during the 1930s and continued as such in 1953. Esmeralda Arboleda, as spokeswoman in the constitutional assembly, defended the demands of women with arguments, discussed collectively in the ONF and other women's groups, that centered on the sanctity of motherhood, supporting the ability of women to take over social policies concerning infants, women, and the elderly. Arboleda's veneration of maternity is captured in her words before the CEC: "To us women, our relations with God, with society and the fatherland have a name: the name of our children. Through her son a woman can govern the world in the best possible way. Colombian feminism doesn't want to defeat men, but to work with them and for them, shoulder by shoulder with the purpose of making a home and the fatherland."[41]

Colombian women fought and won the right to participate in the political arena in 1953. Women's reevaluation of sexuality and gender relations is a battle still being fought to this day.

Notes

1. The National Front was an agreement to share power, allowing each party—conservative and liberal—to govern in turns of four years between 1958 and 1974.
2. González Rey, "La educación de las mujeres en Colombia a finales del siglo XIX," 251.
3. Acosta de Samper, *La mujer*, 5.
4. Lavrin, *Women, Feminism, and Social Change*, 1–14.
5. Marín Taboada, "María Cano," 157.
6. Velázquez Toro, "La República Liberal," 188–89.
7. Luna and Villareal, *Historia, género y política*, 79–82.
8. Palacios, *Between Legitimacy and Violence*, chapter 3.
9. Uribe de Acosta, *Una voz insurgente*, 195.
10. Uribe de Acosta, 195.

11. Uribe de Acosta, 195–96.
12. Uribe de Acosta, 196.
13. Henderson, *Modernization in Colombia*, 260.
14. Henderson, 260.
15. For more on the negative reactions of liberals and conservatives, see Velázquez Toro, "La República Liberal," 219–26.
16. *Agitación Femenina* was the country's leading broadcaster about feminism and the right of women to vote between 1944 and 1948. Men and women of different political persuasions and social statuses had the opportunity to air their opinions, guide the audience on themes that began to resonate, and generate heated debates.
17. "Adelante!" *Agitación Femenina*, October 1944, 1.
18. Uribe de Acosta, *Una voz insurgente*.
19. "La mujer en la hora actual" *El Radical*, January 17, 1942, in Luna and Villareal, "La feminidad y el sufragismo," 209.
20. Uribe de Acosta, *Una voz insurgente*.
21. Luna and Villareal, "La feminidad y el sufragismo," 197–200.
22. Luna and Villareal, 205.
23. Luna and Villareal, 199.
24. "Feminismo en Colombia: una historia de triunfos y tensiones," *Sentiido*, https://sentiido.com/feminismo-en-colombia-una-historia-de-triunfos-y-tensiones, accessed August 30, 2023.
25. Uribe de Acosta, *Una voz insurgente*, 202.
26. Henderson, *Modernization in Colombia*, 260.
27. Uribe de Acosta, *Una voz insurgente*, 214–15.
28. Enrique Santos (Calibán), "Danza de las Horas," *El Tiempo*, October 24, 1944.
29. Ofelia Uribe de Acosta, *Una voz insurgente*, 211.
30. Henderson, *Modernization in Colombia*, 261.
31. Cited in Luna and Villareal, *Historia, género y política*, 99.
32. Henderson, *Modernization in Colombia*, 352.
33. See the complete description of the Gómez government and its effects in society in Velazquez and Reyes, "Proceso histórico," 229–67.
34. Bushnell, *The Making of Modern Colombia*, 216.
35. Gonzáles Moral, Ireneo, *Códigos de Malinas*.
36. Lola and Villareal, "SENDAS."
37. Lola and Villareal, "SENDAS," 128.
38. Luna and Villareal, *Historia, género y política*, 129–30.
39. Velázquez Toro and Reyes, "Proceso histórico," 249.
40. Pinzón de Lewin, *Esmeralda Arboleda*, 144.
41. Pinzón de Lewin, 136.

LIBERAL DELAY

Examples: Mexico, Chile, Nicaragua

In this scenario, self-described liberals claimed to support women's suffrage but then blocked or delayed extending the franchise out of fear that it might give conservative rivals a strategic advantage. Liberals promoted women's suffrage discursively, and sometimes politically, but fell short of enacting it, resulting sometimes in decades of delay. They knew conservative women had formed organized and well-funded opposition groups and feared their electoral impact. Instead of acknowledging their fear of female agency, however, liberal leaders targeted supposed feminine vulnerability to malign conservative—particularly clerical—influence. Liberal leaders had to choose between their ideals and political expediency. They worried that giving the vote to women would be the same as placing their own political futures in the hands of the clergy.

Liberals had introduced republicanism to the hemisphere and had historically presented themselves as standard bearers of modernity. Yet these would-be champions of individual rights were typically fearful of extending the electoral franchise beyond groups of elite men. They saw themselves as dragging their populations, often unwillingly, into the modern age. Influential European ideologies like positivism and social Darwinism melded with liberalism during the late nineteenth century and into the twentieth under different names. These innovations worked to justify women's exclusion on various grounds, including the preservation of the family and women's alleged biologically determined intellectual inferiority.

In the cases of Mexico and Nicaragua, regimes morphed from liberal to authoritarian. They delayed extending the suffrage to women until they had effectively limited the ability of the electorate to determine political outcomes in general. With that accomplished, women's suffrage could be extended as a nod to modernity and openness without genuinely putting authoritarian regimes at political risk.

CHAPTER SEVEN

"Laughter in the Chamber"

Mexico's Long Road to Women's Suffrage

STEPHANIE MITCHELL

IN 1917, AS THE REVOLUTIONARY delegates to the constitutional congress in Querétaro briefly considered the question of women's suffrage, there seemed a broad consensus that feminism had not yet had much impact in Mexico. Delegate Félix Palavacini remarked that tighter language restricting citizenship to men might be advisable, given the possibility that women might in the future organize to demand political rights. His colleagues, according to notes in the *Diary of Debates*, quite literally laughed off his suggestion. Twenty years later, President Lázaro Cárdenas found himself in the position of introducing a constitutional amendment not to clarify men's exclusive rights but to extend them unequivocally to women. He did so in response to just the sort of women's movement that Palavacini had feared. According to that amendment, women should have voted for the first time in the momentous 1940 presidential election. All the major candidates in that election, as well as members of the press, assumed that they would. Nevertheless, Mexican women had to wait another fifteen years for that opportunity. The same individuals who had promoted the mass mobilization of women and proposed the amendment that would have granted them full citizenship blocked the promulgation of their own legislation on the very eve of the election. For this reason, the Mexican case fits the parameters of the Delayed Liberal Scenario.

Feminism in Mexico: Nineteenth-Century Beginnings

According to Silvia Arrom, reforms to the Mexican Civil Code in 1870 and 1884 "often repeated ancient patriarchal provisions almost verbatim."[1] Minor changes to colonial law gave female heads of household slightly more authority, and separation (but not divorce) became easier, but the new laws continued to make married women legally subject to their husbands.[2]

In the words of Carmen Ramos Escandón,

> The liberal oligarchic state subsumed women's rights and restricted them, making the family the first sphere in which the state exercised control over women. . . . The regulation of women's rights within the family reinforced and redefined a turn-of-the-century Mexican paradigm of female behavior that included submission, the idealization of maternity, and the repeated equating of femininity with a disinterest in political life or in politics.[3]

Yet the same period saw the first examples of women's political mobilization. Women participated in the regional affiliates of the Gran Círculo de Obreros de México from 1872. By 1875 there were twenty-five such regional groups, mostly from Veracruz, Puebla, México, and the Federal District, where the textile industry was strong.[4] A group of women appeared at the First Workers Congress, in 1876, but were not permitted to participate on the grounds that "propriety prohibits letting women participate in public tasks. . . . A woman's stage is her home."[5] Nevertheless, by 1895 women made up 17 percent of the economically active population.[6] Nationally, industry had been expanding since the 1830s, and women's employment increased until 1907, when economic crisis forced many workers, particularly women, out of the workplace.[7] As they entered the industrial workforce, some women joined unions and participated in strikes. Women strikers' demands included, in addition to pay increases and reduced working hours, gender-specific demands such as maternity leave and child care.[8] Justo Sierra served as minister of education under President Porfirio Díaz. Sierra felt that "the woman" was morally superior to "the man" but that this moral superiority "was linked with her association with submissive and emotional values, her withdrawal from the public world and lack of understanding of it, and her role in uncritically reproducing it."[9] Nevertheless, Sierra's educational reforms unintentionally opened new opportunities for women. According to Julia Tuñón Pablos, female teachers "were the main protagonists [in the Porfirian feminist] struggle."[10]

In 1910 the Mexican Revolution began, ending the long period of stability under virtual dictator Porfirio Díaz. For most women, the war did not signal a new era of women's liberation. On the contrary, it entailed a tightening of patriarchal control and increased restrictions on personal freedom. For women living in rural villages, a passing army portended rape or abduction. Enedina Román, an ordinary woman who lived her entire life in the district of Uruapan, Michoacán, is a good example of how most rural women experienced the revolution. As an old woman, she remembered when the Villistas, the Carrancistas, and later the Cristeros passed through her town, but she struggled to distinguish one army from another in her memory. Her strongest recollection was that all three armies stole food and "killed lots of people."[11]

During the armed conflict, a few women participated in the fighting as soldiers (*soldadas*) and many more as camp followers (*soldaderas*). There is little to suggest that either of these roles was significantly different from the activities of women in previous wars, except in scale. However, some prominent women's leaders, such as Juana Belen Gutiérrez and Hermila Galindo, did enter politics during and because of the armed struggle. In this respect, women's participation in the armed conflict did mark a change from the past. The war, together with the rise of international feminism, set the stage for some women to become politically active in new ways after the fighting ended.

Martha Rocha observes, "The process of turning the revolution into a masculine, patriarchal event began as soon as the bullets stopped flying."[12] Venustiano Carranza, the general who eventually emerged victorious among the various competing revolutionary factions, did not wait even that long. He began stripping female officers of their commissions in 1916, declaring, "All the military appointments given to married or single women [*señoras y señoritas*], whatever may be the services that they have given, are declared null and void." After the war, out of some sixty thousand applicants, only about 450 women were successful in obtaining recognition for their military service.[13] Revolutionary legislation also prevented women from benefiting directly from land reform or citizenship rights. Women were expected to profit from the revolution, of course, but primarily in their capacities as daughters or wives of male citizens.

Some early legislation did explicitly revoke juridical patriarchal constraints. The 1917 Ley de Relaciones Familiares equalized conditions for divorce, and a new *código civil* in 1928 made the profound statement, "La capacidad jurídica es igual para el hombre y la mujer."[14] The new code introduced many significant changes: it allowed women to leave their parents' home at the same age as men, increased women's rights with regard to their children, and permitted women (with the written permission of their husbands) to be employed or take up a profession.[15] Thus women's *civil* rights increased dramatically with the revolution; their *political* rights, however, were purposefully left vague.[16] According to the letter of the 1917 constitution, all Mexican citizens had the right to vote, and the requirements for citizenship did not refer to gender. Nevertheless, Article 37 of the electoral law of 1918 defined electors as "all male Mexicans older than 18 if they are married, and older than 21 if they are not."[17]

Expansion of the Women's Movement

Though excluded from the rights of citizenship, women in the post-conflict period entered into a period of unprecedented activism and political activity. Culminating in the presidency of Lázaro Cárdenas (1934–1940), the era of the "social revolution" offered unprecedented opportunities for resource mobilization, which accounts for the scale of women's activism during this period.[18] Many students of social movements agree that the role of the state is often crucial. As Steven Buechler explains, "[Resource mobilization theory recognizes] the central role of the state in facilitating, obstructing, or otherwise mediating the process of movement mobilization. Mobilization occurs when political opportunity structures become more favorable for a given group, and the state is frequently the major actor shaping these opportunity structures."[19] In the case of the revolutionary women's movement, the state had a significant role in facilitating, and sometimes leading and directing, the organization of women.

Some Constitutionalist military leaders, including Francisco J. Múgica and Salvador Alvarado, made feminism an explicit part of their revolutionary program. As military governor of Tabasco, Múgica sponsored the first Mexican feminist congress in 1915.[20] Alvarado led two more in Yucatán in January and June 1916.[21] For Alvarado, the congresses were a strategic move designed to promote grassroots support for his (especially anticlerical) policies.[22] He determined the agenda beforehand by presenting the participants with specific questions, which set the tone of the debates:

1. What social means should be employed for the manumission of the woman from the yoke of tradition?
2. What is the role of primary education in women's emancipation, since the goal of education is preparation for life?
3. Which arts and occupations should be promoted in the State whose tendency would be to prepare women for the intense life of progress?
4. Which public functions can and should women undertake in order to be leaders as well as followers?[23]

The discussions that ensued illustrated the kinds of ideological differences among women's activists that would continue through the 1920s and 1930s. A few of the women present advocated birth control, sex education, secular schooling, and liberal divorce legislation. Most of the participants were shocked by such proposals, however. For example, the majority rejected Hermila Galindo's views regarding the female libido. Galindo's contribution, "La Mujer en el Porvenir," argued, "The sexual instinct rules women with such irresistible force that no hypocritical artifice is capable of destroying, modifying, or diminishing it. To struggle against sovereign instinct is to destroy health, corrupt morality, demolish the grandiose work of nature, and affront the Creator with the most atrocious of blasphemies."[24] One of the delegates provoked a round of applause by suggesting that Galindo's paper ought to be destroyed.[25] In fact, very little consensus could be established, even on more conservative women's issues.

Fewer than half of the delegates bothered to appear for the vote on whether to endorse women's suffrage, and of those who were present, only one third were in favor of the resolution.[26] Finally, the participants presented the governor with a vague statement to the effect that "in the future," women should be able to hold public office, as long as doing so would not require a "vigorous physical constitution," avoiding direct reference to the vote. In other words, it would seem that, as with many revolutionary reforms to come, would-be reformists were often out of step with the values held by the groups of people they intended to assist. A few years later, revolutionary governor Felipe Carrillo Puerto alienated even Yucatán's most progressive women by endorsing sex education in schools (including providing information on birth control) and passing a law permitting easy divorce.[27] Carrillo Puerto acted under the influence of his sister Elvia Carrillo Puerto, who, like Galindo, was exceptional in her feminist views. Most of the feminist legislation passed under both revolutionary governors, including limited suffrage, was later repealed.

Far more enduring were Carrillo Puerto's experiments with popular mobilization as a means to prop up his Yucatecan Socialist Party. He created a web of pro-party *ligas de resistencia,* many of which were explicitly designated as women's leagues. This strategy was copied by other Constitutionalist governors in the short term and later by national leaders. Tomás Garrido Canabal, who dominated Tabasqueño politics from 1922 to 1935, modeled his network of support for the Partido Socialista Radical Tabasqueño on the ligas de resistencia.[28] Women participated in the ligas de resistencia, as well as in antialcohol Garridista leagues and the League of Atheist Teachers.[29] The Partido Feminista Revolucionario de Tabasco was created in 1931, dedicated to the "cultural elevation of rural and working class women, achieving the economic stability of both [groups of women], as well as their social betterment."[30] The following year, with the support of Garrido, women voted in Tabascan state elections. Progressive governors in Chiapas and San Luis Potosí also permitted women to vote for short periods during the 1920s and early 1930s.

Perhaps most importantly, the national government and the revolutionary party that controlled it ultimately adopted the practice of mobilizing groups of workers and peasants to create bases of political support. As in Yucatán, agents of the state (particularly teachers) organized women as well as men.[31] This, more than any other factor, accounts for the growth of the organized women's movement in the 1920s and 1930s. Just as popular mobilization in the labor and agrarian sectors reached new heights during this period, the numbers of grassroots women's organizations soared. As was true of the agrarian and labor movements, the line between autonomous social mobilization (such as Zapatismo) and state-prompted mobilization (such as the Yucatecan ligas de resistencia) was often indistinct. For example, the local agrarian leader Primo Tapia from Michoacán organized women into *ligas femeniles* before any state officials did. Although these organizations were autonomous in the sense that they were not state developed, they were not formed autonomously by *women.*

In the rural feminine leagues, suffrage was almost never a priority, if it was mentioned at all. The personal experience of Mónica Cruz, a relative of Primo Tapia, is instructive. When asked why she decided to become involved in the agrarian women's league, Cruz explained how *agrarismo* was a family affair. She became involved "because my uncle Primo was involved in all that. He was my mother's first cousin. My Mama Acalia, my aunt Rosita, my aunt María and my uncle Joaquín—they were all siblings. My Mama Acalia was my uncle Ezequiel's mother. María de la Cruz was Pedro López's sister. My aunt Tila and my Aunt Rosita . . . she was my uncle Primo's mother. The whole family. . . . Everybody with the agrarian struggle."[32] She fully and proudly identified with agrarismo as a political ideology. When asked what the *agraristas* were about, she replied, "They were fighting to win the land. . . . And there I was, right there among them!"[33] Yet when asked about the women's league specifically, she replied, "Well, we had to organize ourselves. I don't really remember about that. We had regular meetings. Everyone gave five *centavos*. . . . They talked about what they were going to do, and in general how things were going." Women's leaders in Mexico City claimed to represent Cruz when they demanded women's suffrage, among other things. It seems these claims to representation were tenuous, even for Cruz, who belonged to a particularly active organization.

Ironically, however, this doesn't mean that rural women's organizing was not important to the eventual achievement of suffrage. It is hard to imagine that self-identified "national" leaders would have had much success had they not been able to point to a numerically significant base who could reasonably be classified as members of a national women's movement. Sarah Buck Kachaluba believes that "women's action, even when it was primarily in needs-based organizations, such as the feminine leagues . . . , contributed as much, if not more, to the acquisition of the vote, as suffrage campaigns."[34]

The National Movement

Early feminist activity, especially in Yucatán, was important in another respect, in that several Yucatecan women's leaders from the early post-conflict period, most notably Elvia Carrillo Puerto, went on to become prominent at national and international levels. Elena Torres, a Yucatecan schoolteacher and friend of Hermila Galindo's, was one of the first women to try to incorporate Mexican feminists into the international women's movement, which had been rapidly developing since the first international women's congress in Paris in conjunction with the 1878 World Exposition.[35] Although relatively small numerically at first, women's organizations were often able to exert considerable influence on their home countries and, after the formation of the League of Nations, international politics. The early feminists based their organizations on networks of friendship. They were often able to use each other's political and media connections to create the appearance of international pressure on national governments to take women's issues seriously. The three most powerful international women's organizations, the International Council of Women, the International Alliance of Women, and the Women's International League for Peace and Freedom, each had press committees, and their conventions usually made front-page news in host cities, such as Paris and New York.[36] When attendees returned from gatherings, their participation reliably generated prominent coverage in their home countries' national press.

Mexican feminists involved themselves in the burgeoning American side of the movement early. Indeed, the national and transnational movements developed simultaneously and in relationship with one another. For example, in 1919 Elena Torres cofounded one of the first national women's organizations in Mexico City, the Consejo Feminista.[37] Three years later, she attended the international First Pan American Conference of Women, held in Baltimore, Maryland. At this conference, Torres was elected vice president for North America of the new organization, the Pan-American League for the Elevation of Women. After returning to Mexico, she proceeded to organize a congress to integrate the efforts of feminists from the United States, Mexico, and Cuba. The congress was held in Mexico City in May 1923. Attendees included delegates from the US League of Women Voters, the Women's International League for Peace and Freedom, the Parent Teacher Association, the YWCA, and the American Birth Control League, as well as several Mexican states and various incipient Mexican feminist organizations.[38]

Sofía Villa de Buentello, founder of another early Mexican feminist organization, the Unión Cooperativa "Mujeres de la Raza," was another participant in the pan-American congress. In 1925 she organized another international congress in Mexico City, designed to unite Iberian and Hispanic American women.[39] More than one hundred delegates attended from Spain, Guatemala, Cuba, Nicaragua, and Panama, as well as various Mexican states.[40] The meeting revealed divisive ideological splits among feminist leaders. As was the case in Yucatán a decade earlier, the most prominent women leaders came from different and at times irreconcilable ideological backgrounds. After a heated debate between Buentello and María del Refugio "Cuca" García, cofounder of the Consejo Feminista, over whether social problems related to marriage were determined by morality or economics, Buentello declared the conference over.[41] In its coverage of the conference, *El Universal* reported that the congress spelled "The Defeat of Feminism."[42]

El Universal's conclusions were premature. Six years later, the first of three important national conferences, sponsored and promoted by the ruling revolutionary party, took place in Mexico City. The conferences were important for three reasons. First, they returned the issue of women's rights to the national media headlines, which gave educated, urban, revolutionary leaders the impression that a vigorous, if divided, women's movement existed. Second, attendees at the conferences confronted and ultimately resolved the issues that had prevented the formation of a politically unified feminist movement. Third, the most important national women's organization of the social revolutionary period emerged from the conferences.

On September 28, 1931, the same newspaper that had earlier announced the defeat of feminism advertised a "national conference of women workers and peasants" to be held in Mexico City during the first week of October. The conference was to address six issues: cooperation between women workers and peasants, women in farming, the development of a nationalist campaign, the establishment of a Peasant Family Bank, defining women's political and economic situation, and the establishment of a protective organization for children. The conference brought delegates from across the republic, as well as a number of national and regional women's organizations representing a broad ideological spectrum, including the governing party's Partido Femenista Revolucionario, the Liga Anticlerical Mexicana, the Asociación Cristiana Femenina, the Club Liberal de Mujeres Reformistas, and several representatives from communist groups.[43]

The congress began amicably, as participants presented papers on themes related to the six topics on the agenda, such as Cuca García's "The Infancy Issue" and René Rodríguez's "Security of the Female Laborer." All went smoothly until María Ríos Cárdenas gave a talk on the "Organization of Women in the Social Struggle," in which she announced her plan to create a national women's federation. She argued that women needed an all-female national organization that would agitate for their rights *as women*. She argued, "Although unionism has achieved many benefits for workers, it has not resolved women's problems. We need purely female associations that would represent our own work, and that would work for us."[44]

She told the assembly, "Only the woman understands her problems, and hence, only she is equipped to solve them!"[45] Her proposal unleashed a fierce ideological debate between the communists and supporters of the revolutionary government, the Penerristas, named after the initials of the governing party. The debate became the central feature of the leadership of the women's movement for the next four years. Ríos Cárdenas later recalled the events that followed her proposal: "The assembly divided into two large factions: that of the extremists, commanded by Professor María del Refugio [Cuca] García, and that of the moderates, led by Licenciada Florinda Lazos León."[46] Ríos Cárdenas's "extremists" were communist feminists, specifically Cuca García, Concha Michel, and Consuelo Uranga, who represented both the National Apparel Union and the United Confederation of Unions of

Mexico. Following the party line, they argued that women's oppression was the result of capitalist class exploitation. The best way to defend the rights of women, they asserted, was through class struggle in cooperation with proletarian men in mixed-sex unions. Penerrista Florinda Lazos, who had organized the congress, together with half a dozen or so other women representing organizations that were affiliated with the ruling party, supported Ríos Cárdenas's proposal. They favored the creation of a national organization that would focus on women's gender-specific needs. The argument became heated, and some communists eventually left the room in anger.[47]

The second conference, in 1933, followed a similar pattern, but it illustrated a shift in tone. While communists and Penerristas continued to feud, the organizers of the second conference seemed less concerned with appearing too strident in their defense of women's rights. Florinda Lazos had opened the first congress with a speech that alluded to "women's liberation" but focused on emphasizing that Mexican women would never abandon their traditional roles: "Mexican feminism does not arise with the same difficulties of North American feminism. . . . There is no view to abandon the home, because the history of the Mexican woman does not permit such an idea. The feminism that we represent today is formed by women . . . who are classically domestic [hogareñas]."[48] Blanca Lydia Trejo's keynote speech in 1933 had an entirely different tone. Whereas Lazos had said, "We do not reproach men," Trejo felt no such inhibition: "It is necessary to take strategic action from beneath the tyrannical dominion of men and to raise a cry of protest for their having left women relegated to oblivion, as confirmed by the fact that we are legislated by partial laws. . . . The women's vote must be recognized . . . it is of nature's essence that women should be permitted to occupy public posts in order to achieve a better society and a stronger and nobler fatherland."[49]

As before, Excelsior, El Nacional, and El Mundo reported on the conferences daily. Their editorialists again delighted in observing ideological divisions. Police intervened repeatedly (ostensibly to keep order but more likely to harass communists). Consuelo Uranga and Florinda Lazos León locked horns again on the issue of class versus gender. Uranga declared that feminism, like reformism, was a "bourgeois theory" that served only the interests of the bourgeois class. Lazos de León responded: "Communism is not adaptable to the idiosyncrasies of our people. Reformism is achieved through culture. . . . Feminism has a reason to exist because mixed-sex organizations only work for the strongest, which are the men, and when women demand their rights, the leadership [of mixed organizations], who are unfamiliar with feminine psychology and physiology, fail to take them into consideration."[50]

Despite these profound disagreements, there was considerable consensus on most issues, such as promoting a fair minimum wage with equal pay for equal work; organizing, educating, and protecting working-class women; extending state protection of children; and protesting against international imperialism.[51] There was still, however, little agreement on the issue of women's suffrage. Florinda Lazos argued against demanding the franchise, contending that women did not need to vote directly because they could do so indirectly, through the votes of the men in their families. María Rodríguez did not dispute women's right to political participation in principle, as Lazos did, but stressed the reigning inefficacy of the suffrage in Mexico. Consuelo Urango responded in favor, pointing out that if many women were unprepared to exercise political rights, then so were the vast majority of men, and this was no reason to disenfranchise women.[52] Despite the lack of consensus, the resolution to call for women's suffrage did pass.

If Gerda Lerna had observed the shifts that occurred between the three national conferences of the early 1930s, she would have argued that the participants were gaining what she termed "feminist consciousness." At the third and final conference, participants unanimously and without any discussion approved María Ríos Cárdenas's proposal to demand the abolition of restrictions on women's suffrage.[53] The communists continued to face off against government supporters on many issues. Chaos reigned as the vote approached to decide the leadership of a new commission (to organize a fourth congress in Cuernavaca, which never took place). Police threatened to open fire if the shouting participants did not bring order to the proceedings.[54] This final conference signaled the end of the rift, however. Soon after, the Comintern announced a policy shift that eventually led to the unification of leading Mexican feminists.

From 1929, following the Comintern's 1928 "left turn," the Central Committee of the Mexican Communist Party (PCM) had repudiated all "reformism," arguing that successful reform in favor of the poor would only delay the fall of capitalism. In Mexico as elsewhere, communist parties struggled to maintain their membership levels; participants isolated themselves from precisely those individuals and organizations closest to them ideologically. In 1934, as Cárdenas took office, the PCM promoted the slogan "Neither Calles nor Cárdenas."[55] Communist faithful were to reject revolutionary alliances in the interest of hastening the total collapse of the bourgeois system. Then, in 1935, perhaps in response to its dwindling global impact, the Comintern announced a new "popular front" strategy, which reversed course completely, directing communists to influence reformist regimes from within rather than attacking them from without. By 1937 the "Neither Calles nor Cárdenas" slogan had been replaced by "Unity at All Costs."[56] A felicitous byproduct for Mexican feminism was that communist feminists made peace with Penerristas. In fact, many went to work for the government.

In the end, those who had most strongly opposed an autonomous women's movement spearheaded that same endeavor, following the third and final Congress of Women Workers and Peasants. Cuca García emerged as leader of the effort to create a united front among women of different ideologies, classes, and ethnicities. The organization was called the Frente Único Pro-Derechos de la Mujer (FUPDM). Communists dominated the leadership of the organization, but the dozen or so founders included Penerristas and at least one practicing Catholic.[57] An FUPDM poster reflected the new "popular front" ideology of the PCM: "The Frente Único Pro-Derechos de la Mujer . . . offers you the achievements that organized women have been accomplishing, without distinction regarding political or religious creeds, as our goals are about economic improvement, cultural evolution and the acquisition of political rights."[58] From its inception, the goals of the FUPDM were as broad as the demands presented at the Congress of Women Workers and Peasants.

Having a broad definition of the organization's aims carried a strategic advantage that lay at the heart of the popular front strategy. It allowed women of widely divergent ideologies to come together in a single organization, which in turn led to the possibility of a wider membership than would otherwise have been possible. As Adelina Zendejas later commented, "The goals were very concrete and so broad that they were important to everyone: who was going to be against the struggle for lowering the cost of living, against the installation of medical services that would give attention to maternity, against the principle of equal pay for equal work? . . . These things were important to everyone: Catholics, Protestants, communists.[59]

This same strategy had worked for suffragists in the United States, where the largest organization demanding the franchise was not a suffragist organization at all but the Women's Christian Temperance Union (WCTU). The success of the WCTU was partly due to the flexibility of its objectives. Although the leaders of the WCTU petitioned politicians for the vote on behalf of the entire organization, individual chapters were free to choose from a variety of objectives that included temperance, public hygiene, and protection of children. The FUPDM's brand of feminism was so broadly defined as to encompass a wide range of opinion. The "feminist principles" of the FUPDM were:

1. Become strong in numbers.
2. Become respectable through self-improvement.
3. Gain an audience by speaking with the voice of reason.
4. Gain others' attention by being conscious of your personality.
5. Become likeable for your positive values.
6. Join in solidarity with all human causes.
7. Become indispensable through your efficient co-operation.
8. Become master of yourself through control of your emotions.
9. Gain respect of others through the rectitude of your comportment.
10. Make a firm commitment to solidarity with the Frente Único Pro-derechos de la Mujer, an indispensable condition for success.[60]

Thus the FUPDM, like the US WCTU, allowed maximum participation with minimum ideological commitment.

The FUPDM came closer than any other organization to achieving unity among Mexican women's activists. Other ostensibly "national" organizations were unwilling to give up their individual identities to merge with others and so remained numerically insignificant. Most had little presence outside the capital. New organizations were formed continuously throughout the 1930s.

Many of them claimed to speak on behalf of "the Mexican woman," yet few ever achieved a substantial membership. According to Verna Carlton Millan, one of the FUPDM's leaders, the organization acquired a membership of fifty thousand women in eight hundred affiliated regional chapters.[61] As happened with the WCTU, individual chapters often chose to emphasize social concerns at the local level, such as antialcoholism, public health, or maternity care for poor and working-class women. At the national level, however, the leadership soon placed political equality for women at the forefront of the agenda. What emerged, then, was a constellation of local, grassroots women's organizations mobilized around any number of themes, including child welfare, nutrition, hygiene, anticlericalism, unionism, and land reform, but nominally all members of a single group. The FUPDM often piggybacked on other mass mobilization efforts. Indeed, many FUPDM members were involved in grassroots mobilization through their jobs as rural schoolteachers. Thus a women's agrarian league could double as an FUPDM chapter in a way that allowed both the state's agrarian organizers and the FUPDM to count the same women as contributing to their membership. For the FUPDM, this carried a strategic advantage, since it could use high membership numbers to make demands regarding women's issues, especially in the struggle to assert women's political rights.

The Grassroots

The problem of quantifying women's mobilization during the Cardenista heyday is complex. While the FUPDM's success at grassroots organizing was remarkable, the popular mobilizing capacity of the state and its affiliated state and regional organizations was astonishing.[62] In 1937, when Sara Godina López, Virginia Godina, and Concha Michel founded the Instituto Revolucionario Femenino, which ostensibly combined the forces of all progovernment women's organizations, they claimed that throughout Mexico, some three hundred thousand women belonged to revolutionary women's organizations.[63] While they had every reason to exaggerate their numbers, the figure is plausible given the vigorous efforts and notable successes of the various state-run entities charged with the task of mobilizing women.

These included the Ministry of Education, the Department of Agriculture, the Department of Indigenous Affairs, the ruling party, and its local and regional affiliates, including labor and peasant organizations. The numbers of women organized into single-sex labor unions, agrarian leagues, and other progovernment organizations was doubtless very high indeed.[64] At the grassroots level, however, participation in any of these groups meant little beyond a signature or thumbprint affixed to a document confirming membership. It would be hard to ascribe with any accuracy any single ideological motivation to the tens or even hundreds of thousands of women who affiliated, with widely varying degrees of sincerity, with revolutionary women's organizations. We can certainly not equate participation in women's organizations with support for, or even knowledge of, the suffrage movement.

The Struggle for Citizenship

The FUPDM, the Instituto Revolucionario, and other "national" women's organizations failed to represent in any meaningful way the opinions of most Mexican women.[65] Nevertheless, they claimed to. Thus feminist leaders in major cities could point to two pieces of evidence that women's rights were gaining an unstoppable momentum: (1) high-profile participation in an increasingly prominent international women's movement; (2) mass participation of hundreds of thousands of ordinary Mexican women. In 1937 leaders of the FUPDM manipulated both perceptions when they decided to focus their attention on gaining the suffrage. That spring, two leaders of the FUPDM, Soledad Orozco and Cuca García, ran as candidates in congressional primaries. (The party had recently permitted women to vote in internal party elections.) Had a woman become a PRM candidate for office, however, she would have advanced to the general election, which would have tested the constitutionality of women's citizenship more broadly. Both women lost their bids for the party nomination, but the FUPDM managed to turn their losses into a rallying cause for women's suffrage.[66] Again claiming to speak on behalf of Mexican women in a broad sense, the FUDPM and other suffragist organizations in Mexico City and in prominent provincial cities urged the president to affirm women's citizenship. As telegrams poured in both domestically and from abroad, Cárdenas relented and proposed legislation to amend the constitution. Citizenship would belong to both *mexicanos* and *mexicanas*. Under pressure from Cárdenas, the legislation passed both houses of Congress and was sent to the states for ratification. After a successful campaign led by the FUPDM, in which a majority of states ratified the constitutional amendment, the legislation was ready to become law. In spring of 1939, politically active women throughout Mexico prepared to cast their first ballots in a presidential election. Women supporters of all three major candidates, Francisco J. Múgica, Juan Andreu Almazán, and Manuel Ávila Camacho, formed all-female electoral campaigns aimed entirely at would-be female voters.[67] There was widespread anticipation that women would be participating in the election, which many viewed as a referendum not only on the leftward-leaning policies of the Cárdenas administration but also on the legitimacy of the revolutionary party. Domestic challenges included an economic downturn, capital flight, the rising popularity of Spanish-inspired fascism, and a unified, well-financed political opposition. Seeming victories, such as the petroleum expropriation and the successful repression of the Cedillo Rebellion, ironically strengthened the hand of conservatives, who used their quiescence as a bargaining chip to demand concessions from President Cárdenas. From abroad, Mexico faced an antagonist looking to retaliate for the petroleum expropriation, coupled with the rise of fascism in Europe. The revolutionary party's position in the 1940 election was therefore anything but secure.

Congress resumed its ordinary session on August 22, a day before the world was stunned to learn of the Hitler–Stalin pact. World War II began just over a week later. Congress continued to sit through December, but the bill granting citizenship to women languished without publication. There was no public debate deciding to delay, but neither did Congress move to publish the bill in the *Gazeta Oficial*, which would have officially enacted it into law. Under normal circumstances, this final step in the legislative process was pro forma, but not here. At the conclusion of the December session, the question was settled. Congress would not meet again until a week after the election.

No records have been found regarding exactly how or by whom the decision was made to prevent women from voting in 1940, and scholars have long
argued over what really happened. Nevertheless, the basic contours are
clear. In Catholic countries across Latin America and Europe, presumptions
about women's supposed natural conservatism and tendency toward
increased religiosity influenced decisions about extending the franchise.
There is compelling evidence that this was also true in Mexico in 1939–1940.
The Senate committee first charged with examining the legislation advised
altering the amendment "with the object of preventing the influence of religious groups of whatever creed, upon the exercise of these rights." Facing
criticism, however, the president of the Senate returned the bill to the committee, whose members agreed with Cárdenas's position at the time: "It is
true . . . that the workingwoman is at the present time a decided and convinced ally of the revolutionary regime of Mexico and therefore is very far
from serving later as an instrument of the conservative forces which still
operate in our national community,"[68] Nearly all arguments during the Senate debates, for and against women's suffrage alike, centered on the issue of
women's religiosity and conservatism. There is no compelling reason to
imagine that any other consideration prevented the publication of the
amendment in December 1939. National and international events had simply
made the gamble much more risky. As Congress first considered placing the
bill on the agenda for promulgation, Franco's forces captured Madrid, ending the years-long siege and dooming the republic. That victory emboldened
Mexican sympathizers, called *sinarquistas*. Mexico, under Cárdenas's leadership, was one of the only Western nations to have provided support to the
Spanish Republic. Its grinding defeat was a blow, and one that was connected to the question of the women's vote. In 1931 two Spanish feminists,
Victoria Kent and Clara Campoamor, had debated whether to extend the
franchise to women or whether women's piety and conservatism posed too
great a threat. Campoamor prevailed; women voted in the 1933 election,
helping to deliver a conservative victory and hammering the first nail in the
coffin of the republic. Now, as Cárdenas read the headlines coming from
Madrid, he had to decide whether to proceed with women's suffrage in frag-
ile revolutionary Mexico. It is foolish to suggest, as some have, that the decision to delay promulgation of the law could have been made without

Cárdenas. Congress did not act independently of and in opposition to the wishes of the president in 1930s Mexico. We may never know the full story, but we can surmise that Cárdenas concluded that the risk to the revolution was too great.

Conclusion

Mexico is a perfect example of the Delayed Liberal Scenario: the political element most aligned with suffragism was responsible for delaying the extension of women's suffrage. The revolutionary state strongly supported women's mobilization, fostered development of a cadre of feminist leadership, and sponsored national congresses that gave way to a mass movement that was at least nominally suffragist. That same state opened the doors to women's suffrage by permitting women to participate in internal party elections, which led to the proposal, passage, and ratification of a constitutional amendment that would have guaranteed equal citizenship to men and women. Nevertheless, the same institutions and indeed some of the same individuals that had earlier championed suffrage also quashed the women's vote on the very eve of one of the most critical elections in Mexican history. While it's impossible to prove, it is almost certain that the reason has to do with the widespread presumption of women's conservatism. Historian Gabriela Cano observed the paradox between the way the Mexican Revolution both "favored" and "obstructed" the advance of women's suffrage. Mexico became one of the Americas' holdouts, waiting until well after the Second World War to enfranchise women. "The fear of conservatism—real or imagined," she writes, was a "decisive element" in that delay.[69]

Revolutionaries were afraid with good reason: Catholic women's activism during the same time period surpassed revolutionary activism, and Catholic women were responsible for some of the most effective antirevolutionary organizing.[70] In 1939 revolutionaries were hard-pressed to win victories among voting men. As long as the suffrage was at all effective in determining electoral outcomes, and as long as the revolutionary state was associated with anticlericalism, they could ill-afford doubling the electorate with voters who were likely more conservative still. During the tumultuous 1930s, elections did not adhere to anything like a liberal democratic ideal, but they did still matter.[71] By the presidency of Adolfo Ruiz Cortines, they did not. Within a decade the Partido Revolucionario Institucional had become, as a recent popular film has parodied, the "perfect dictatorship." Regular elections ensured the overt appearance of democracy, while the party controlled politics from the national to the local level. The term *presidencialismo* developed to describe the subordination of all branches and levels of government to the federal executive. Presidential succession was determined by *dedazo*, or "big finger," as each outgoing president personally selected the next. In 1947 Miguel Alemán tested the waters by permitting women to vote in municipal elections. His successor, Ruiz Cortines, took office in 1952 after having included women's suffrage in his campaign platform. When he followed through on his promise, he made no reference to Cárdenas or the earlier amendment to the constitution. Instead of winning the right to vote through the hard work of suffragist organizing, Mexican women received the suffrage as a gift from on high. They first used their right in 1955, although their impact would be difficult to gauge given the extent of fraud that by then predetermined every electoral outcome.

Some scholars have criticized the movement of the 1930s for having made itself dependent on patronage from the ruling party, thus depriving itself of the ability to exercise effective criticism from the outside. Others have observed that, post-1940, suffragists shifted their tone away from the rights-based arguments that dominated the earlier movement in favor of difference-based arguments like maternalism. Surely, however, it mattered very little what approach suffragists tried. As long as those in power stood to lose that power by enfranchising them, they were doomed to fail. Only once electors of any gender no longer posed a threat to the ruling party would universal suffrage be achieved.

Notes

1. Arrom, "Changes in Mexican Family Law in the Nineteenth Century," 306.
2. See also Rojina Villegas, "Capacidad de la mujer," 14–15; Varley, "Women and the Home in Mexican Family Law," 241–43.
3. Ramós Escandón, "Women and Power in Mexico," 89. Little work has been done to disaggregate the category "women" by class or ethnicity during this period. Since many poor couples were in relationships sanctioned by neither the church nor the state, it is possible that poorer women failed to experience a

significant change in their civil rights as a consequence of the new civil code.

4. Towner, "Monopoly Capitalism," 96.

5. Quoted in Tuñón Pablos, *Women in Mexico*, 80. Her translation.

6. Towner, "Monopoly Capitalism," 90.

7. Towner, 90.

8. Tuñon Pablos, *Mujeres que se organizan*, 17.

9. Vaughan, "Women, Class, and Education in Mexico," 140.

10. Tuñón Pablos, *Women in Mexico*, 79.

11. Interview with author, 1998. In reality, there were sometimes few distinguishing characteristics among the different armies. Sometimes the same local bands roamed under various political labels, occasionally with no extra-local affiliation at all. See Purnell, *Popular State Movement*, 52.

12. Purnell, *Popular State Movement*, 17.

13. Martha Eva Rocha, "The Faces of Rebellion: From Revolutionaries to Veterans in Nationalist Mexico," in Mitchell and Schell, *Women's Revolution*, 16.

14. Juridical capacity is equal for women and men.

15. Gabriela Cano, "Feminism," 483; Macías, *Against All Odds*, 119–21; Soto, *Emergence of the Modern Mexican Woman*, 99.

16. As other chapters in this volume make clear, grammatical ambiguity was common in Spanish and Portuguese constitutional definitions of citizenship.

17. Spota Valencia, *La igualdad jurídica*, 274.

18. This theory rests on the premise that discontent among underprivileged people is common while social movements are not. Thus social movements are not the direct result of discontent. Grievances are a necessary but not sufficient condition for collective action. Articulated movements designed to overcome social inequities occur when groups of people who share a specific grievance are able to mobilize assets such as money, political connections, organizing and leadership abilities, and access to media.

19. Buechler, *Women's Movements in the United States*, 6.

20. Tuñón Pablos, *Women in Mexico*, 94. The only precedent in Latin America for a meeting of this kind was a congress held in Buenos Aires in 1910.

21. See Ramírez et al., "El Primer Congreso Feminista de Yucatán."

22. Macías, *Against*, 70.

23. Congreso Feminista de Yucatán, *El Primer Congreso Feminista de Yucatán*, 129–31.

24. She had probably read August Bebel's *Woman in the Past, Present and Future*.

25. Macías, *Against*, 74.

26. Macías, 78.

27. Macías, 92–94.

28. Martínez Assad, *El laboratorio de la revolución*, 12–13.

29. Martínez Assad, 178.

30. Martínez Assad, 181.

31. Their reasons for doing so were similar to their reasons for organizing men.

Revolutionary leaders needed bases of popular support to offset the power of opposition groups. They particularly feared women because they thought women were naturally more conservative than men. Paradoxically, women were thought to be at once weak, thus susceptible to influence from reactionary priests, and powerful, thus capable of harming revolutionary organizations.

32. Author interview with Mónica Cruz, Naranja, Michoacán, November 1999. Mama Acalia is the woman who raised her rather than her biological mother.

33. Author interview with Mónica Cruz, Naranja, Michoacán, November 1999.

34. Sarah Buck, "The Meaning of the Women's Vote in Mexico," in Mitchell and Schell, *Women's Revolution*.

35. The first important period of international feminist activity took place between 1915 and the First World War.

36. Rupp, *Worlds of Women*, 209–10.

37. Soto, *Emergence of the Modern Mexican Woman*, 103.

38. Macías, *Against*, p. 96.

39. Macías,108, 110.

40. Carmen Ramos Escandón, "Challenging Legal and Gender Constraints in Mexico: Sofía Villa's Criticism of Family Legislation 1917–1927," in Mitchell and Schell, *Women's Revolution*, 58.

41. The participants continued with the agenda anyway. In the end, the assembly decided on a number of resolutions, demanding suffrage, higher taxes on alcohol, and special judicial procedures for women. Ramos Escandón, "Challenging," 59.

42. Soto, *Emergence of the Modern Mexican Woman*, 108.

43. Aguascalientes, Sinaloa, Oaxaca, Guanajuato, Hidalgo, Nuevo León, Puebla, Chiapas, Querétaro, Tamaulipas, Morelos, and Veracruz. Barragán and Rosales, "Congresos Nacionales de Obreras y Campesinas," 24.

44. Barragán and Rosales, "Congresos Nacionales de Obreras y Campesinas," 25.

45. Ríos Cárdenas, *La mujer mexicana*, 36–37.

46. Ríos Cárdenas, 38.

47. For discussion of these congresses, see Tuñon Pablos, *Mujeres que se organizan*, 34–35; Ríos Cárdenas, *La mujer mexicana*, 36–49; Barragán and Rosales, "Congresos Nacionales de Obreras y Campesinas"; Macías, *Against*, 128–30.

48. Barragán and Rosales, "Congresos Nacionales de Obreras y Campesinas," 24–5.

49. Barragán and Rosales, 32.

50. Barragán and Rosales, 36.

51. Ríos Cárdenas, *La mujer mexicana*, 79–80.

52. Barragán and Rosales, "Congresos Nacionales de Obreras y Campesinas," 38.

53. Barragán and Rosales, 44. Different sources give different estimates as to the number of participants, ranging from four hundred to six hundred.

54. Ríos Cárdenas, *La mujer mexicana*, 117.

55. Carr, *Marxism and Communism in Twentieth-Century Mexico*, 8–9.

56. Carr, 48.

57. Tuñón Pablos, *Mujeres que se organizan*, 76–77.

58. FUPDM poster, 544/1, Archivo General de la Nación-Acervos Presidenciales-Lázaro Cárdenas del Río, Mexico City.

59. Tuñón Pablos, *Mujeres que se organizan*, 73–74.

60. FUPDM poster, 544/1, Archivo General de la Nación-Acervos Presidenciales-Lázaro Cárdenas del Río, Mexico City.

61. Millan, *Mexico Reborn*, 164–65. This figure is often repeated and hard to verify. The 1930s were a great era for inflating numbers of mass membership. Given the FUPDM's strategy of taking advantage of already existing organizations in the provinces, however, the figure is plausible.

62. Ultimately, the FUPDM also affiliated and merged with the ruling party apparatus. It became part of the Popular Sector of the newly organized PRM.

63. Letter, Godina López, Godina, and Michel to Cárdenas, July 21, 1937, 544.6/24, Archivo General de la Nación-Acervos Presidenciales-Lázaro Cárdenas del Río, Mexico City.

64. Back-of-the envelope calculations derived from hard numbers confirm the plausibility of the institute's claim.

65. The meteoric success of Catholic Acción Femenina groups suggests that far more Mexican women identified conservatively than as revolutionaries.

66. See Mitchell, "Revolutionary Feminism."

67. See Mitchell, "Death of a Revolution."

68. Morton, *Woman Suffrage in Mexico*, 31–32. His translation.

69. Cano, "Debates En Torno Al Sufragio," 8.

70. The Damas Católicas, for example, were effective agents against the state during both Cristero Wars in the 1920s and 1930s. Acción Católica's rosters far surpassed those of progovernment agrarian and labor leagues. Revolutionary organizations only ever represented a minority of the public, whether male or female, although there was wide regional variation.

71. Butler's *Popular Piety and Political Identity in Mexico's Cristero Rebellion* is an especially useful look at how this *voto morado*, or Catholic vote, shaped elections in the 1930s.

CHAPTER EIGHT

Women's History

*Historiographical Proposals on How Women
Obtained the Suffrage in Chile*

CLAUDIA MONTERO AND MARÍA PAZ VERA

THE HISTORY OF CHILEAN WOMEN'S suffrage is not simple. A range of factors must be taken into account, including economic, political, social, and cultural transformations that gave rise to the process of modernization; the kind of political system that the country adopted; the strength and form that liberalism acquired; and the history of the women's movement, which included a diverse array of manifestations. We have placed Chile in the Delayed Liberal Scenario because the woman's vote was achieved piecemeal over many decades beginning in 1870, when the first voices begin to demand the suffrage, until the 1940s, when it was finally achieved.

Advances in women's history have made it possible to write the history of Chilean women's suffrage. Gaviola's pioneering *Queremos votar en las próximas elecciones* proposed a periodization commencing in the nineteenth century that was able to hold the complexities and contradictions inherent in the history.[1] It also hypothesized that, despite political differences, activists developed an associative spirit from the early twentieth century that made possible a consciousness of how many problems they shared in common. This process culminated in the formation of two organizations that historians have judged to be vital to the history of the women's movement: the

Movimiento pro Emancipación de la Mujer Chilena (MEMCH) in 1935 and the Federación Chilena de Instituciones Femeninas (FECHIF) in 1944. Together they formed a united front in favor of the vote. Kirkwood's *Ser Política en Chile* is another important early analysis.[2] It modified Gaviola's periodization to establish a period from the turn of the twentieth century through 1931, labeled "Origins," in which the first dissident voices, clubs, organizations, and an "anonymous political presence" emerged. Kirkwood's second period, "Ascent," from 1931 to 1949, was characterized by a democratic opening and a generalized struggle that resulted in the vote.[3]

Erika Maza's contribution followed. It observed that suffrage was delayed because of the strength of Chilean Catholicism.[4] Anticlerical liberal forces were among the most fearful of extending the vote to women, while the first public support and the first legislative proposals came from Catholic conservatives, who foresaw an electoral advantage. Thus we are left with a contradictory scenario in which political Catholics and the Chilean ecclesiastical hierarchy opted for progressive and pragmatic positions with respect to women's political rights.

After a decade of historiographical silence, Asunción Lavrin published *Mujeres, feminismo y cambio social en Argentina, Chile y Uruguay 1890–1940.*[5] This invaluable comparative work revised Chilean suffrage history, providing a detailed contrast between the activities of women's organizations and their legislative initiatives, and the early twentieth-century political context in which they took place. Javiera Errázuriz then argued that women voted later in Chile because neither politicians nor public opinion considered suffrage to be important until the 1930s.[6] Women, she thought, obtained the vote less through the efforts of suffrage activists and more because of political opportunism. She noted that *El Eco de las Señoras de Santiago* clearly rejected suffrage in 1865, whereas by the 1930s and 1940s, women's groups passionately supported it. Men's attitudes showed a similar evolution, from silence throughout the nineteenth century to near unanimous acceptance by the 1940s, when the absence of the women's vote was seen as a smear on Chile's democratic image.

Finally, María Rosaria Stabili, like Edda Gaviola, saw a fundamental unity, especially between Catholic and secular feminist groups, in spite of wide divergences of opinion on the importance of political as well as civil and social rights.[7] She added that there was also agreement to avoid confrontation with those who wielded political power, with a preference instead to obtain rights through a gradual process of dialogue. Each of these historians is important for understanding how the women's movement's capacity for social and political action has been revealed over time.

Political scientists have also weighed in. Miguel López and Ricardo Gamboa have placed Chile among those countries that extended the vote to women only once the interests of the elite had been satisfied.[8] The philosopher Alejandra Castillo has also contributed, focusing on the relationship between political parties and women's political participation.[9] She explores the contradictions between the supposedly universal ideology that nineteenth-century politicians claimed to embrace, on the one hand, and the exclusions they accepted and considered only natural, on the other. Although her work does not refer specifically to the process that led to women's suffrage, her insights permit us to deepen our understanding of other time periods and their contradictions.

To truly understand Chilean women's suffrage, we should develop a panoramic view of the history of voting in Chile, one that is not limited to considering women's exclusion alone. For this reason, this chapter aims to analyze factors that explain the particular characteristics of women's suffrage history in Chile while considering the larger context of the expansion of the suffrage, in which the women's vote figured as only one facet among many.

This chapter considers several dimensions of this history's complexity. First, we must distinguish among three distinct phenomena: the women's movement, the feminist movement, and the suffragist movement, which are explained later. A whole series of activists from diverse social and political spaces in these three movements organized to demand political rights, and they intersected. The demand for the vote was therefore neither unitary nor unified. It also changed over time. Nevertheless, we do see continuity. For example, one of the arguments that different groups repeated, and that remained constant over time, was the moral superiority of women as mothers and molders of citizens. Second, we must recognize the role of women's suffrage in the context of the wider history of the broadening of the suffrage generally. Although the process was slow for many men, women were excluded until well into the twentieth century. That exclusion exposes a contradiction within the liberal political system. This system permitted women's political activity, including women's political parties, which existed since the 1920s, but failed to recognize women as subjects with full political rights. Women's demands for equality undermined the system in the sense that those who installed liberalism (men) did not want to accept its principles when it came to confronting the uncertainty that gender equality would assuredly represent, putting everything they had achieved at risk.

Chronology and Context for Women's Political Participation in Chile: The Road to demanding Political Rights

The history of voting in Chile began with the independence movement in 1810, when the first electoral law was promulgated. Exclusion characterized that law and every other until well into the twentieth century. Only male members of the elite were eligible to vote. This group alone elected the first Chilean Congress in 1811, excluding all women along with most other Chileans. Liberals triumphed in 1828 in the environment of strong competition between liberals and conservatives that characterized the newly independent republic. Provincial assemblies and the capital nullified those elections, however, after liberals were defeated on the battlefield. In 1831 the conservative government exerted strong control over new elections for city officials, deputies, and electors for the presidency. Congress convoked another constitutional convention, resulting in the constitution of 1833, which remained in force for nearly a hundred years. It left an authoritarian mark on a political system that permitted the continued exclusion of multiple social groups. Nevertheless, authors like Eduardo Posada consider Chile to have developed important democratic values, given that the period from 1833 to 1970 was characterized by regular elections and peaceful transitions of power. Breaks with this pattern of institutional stability were both exceptional and short.[10]

A new electoral law promulgated in 1834 extended the suffrage to men over the age of twenty-five who met certain economic requirements. Voters were required to reregister every three years. A literacy requirement was added in 1840, and in 1869 a system of review boards, composed of the wealthiest male members of each municipality, was established to monitor voter registration.[11] The 1870s, however, saw the introduction of direct elections for senators, and, importantly, a reform passed in 1874 presumed that a literate elector already possessed the necessary assets to vote. In 1875 a group of literate women took advantage of this last change to register in the newly created voter rolls, arguing that they had met the requirements of the law.

These electoral reforms translated into an expansion of the electorate, permitting the incorporation of some sectors of the popular classes, and they passed in a Congress that was composed of a majority from opposition parties, among whom figured conservatives, radicals, and "advanced" liberals. All shared the common goal of limiting the power of the government to control both electoral processes and the electorate.[12]

Nineteenth-century political practices did not consider women as subjects. For this reason, the Chilean imaginary did not consider them to be political actors. Their labor was reproductive in every sense. Recommendations for appropriate conduct included being a good mother, a good homemaker, and good companion for one's spouse.[13] The need to systemize women's education in order for women to fulfill their roles as molders of future citizens is what led to the establishment of the first (private) girls' schools after 1845.

One milestone in suffrage history was an 1865 speech given by Abdón Cifuentes (1836–1928): lawyer, teacher, writer, editor, and member of the Conservative Party.[14] He articulated, for the first time, problems posed by women's exclusion from public affairs. His argument recognized social inequality and marginalization affecting the "weaker half," who required greater protection. He declared that women, as a moral reservoir for the nation, had much to bring to politics:

And this is precisely what we have in sight to request now, in favor of the woman, nothing more than a quite restricted right to vote. We should put together exactly which conditions correspond to the right to cast a ballot with a cultivated understanding and an upright conscience; the vote of an intelligence that knows what is right for her country infinitely better than many men to whom the law concedes this right; the vote of a heart with unrivaled love for her fatherland, who can serve it even with heroism.[15]

In the same year, we have one of the first examples of a group of women (con-nected to the conservative elite and the ecclesiastical authorities) participat-ing in the public sphere with the publication of the first women's political journal, the *Eco de las Señoras de Santiago*. It appeared in the context of the debate over religious freedom, in which it had been proposed that Catholi-cism as a state religion should be eliminated from the 1833 constitution. The nineteenth-century press was a privileged space characterized by exclusion and the dominance of intellectuals. It is not accidental that the first women's journal in Chile should have been political and published by elite, conserva-tive women. As members of the elite and also part of the small percentage of the population that was literate, these women assumed that they were enti-tled to contribute their opinions. At the same time, they were conscious of their gender and knew they were trespassing on forbidden territory.[16] The following appeared in the first issue: "Why then should we remain cold spec-tators of the political drama that the Chamber of Deputies has begun, and which may well have for its theater the entire Republic? Because we are ladies? No."[17] They questioned politicians from a position they had occupied precisely because they were Catholic women and members of the elite. Moral superiority granted nobility to their cause. Their intervention had as its object the conservation of order that religion offered. They seized on the common understanding of feminine power that the labors of wife and mother conferred. Catholicism had given them a specific and fundamental role in the nation: the formation of the citizenry. Despite the fact that defending tradition broke with norms that defined women's roles as private, the action of these women marked the beginning of women's activism, which eventually led women to make a wide range of demands.[18]

The diverse periodizations that exist to capture the history of the wom-en's movement in Chile all recognize the last quarter of the nineteenth cen-tury as a moment in which women's public action began. The changes that accompanied the process of modernization—urbanization, greater access to education, cultural transformations—all altered behavior and made room for new political actors, new social subjects.

Chilean liberalism hastened the process of modernization. Liberals required a new order to promote the necessities of the elite, put an end to colonial tradition, and achieve new forms of legitimacy, one that would appear simultaneously rational and universal. Nineteenth-century Chilean liberalism was broadly characterized by consensus among different political forces about republicanism, with divergences regarding the appropriate level of representation of civil society. That in turn generated constant debate about the balance of power between the executive and the legislature. There was also agreement that liberal principles should be introduced via a process of reform, not through revolution. This ended armed uprisings and also resulted in a strengthened executive under conservative rule from 1830 to the 1860s.[19]

Claims to universalism, however, shifted the boundaries of politics beyond the interests of the elite and opened the doors to a new world to be enjoyed by all potential subjects.[20] The processes of installing and legitimizing the modern republic soon revealed an ambivalent character, in which liberals contradicted their own founding principles.

Despite gendered norms that impeded their political activity, women discovered ways to be present in discussions about the public good. As was true for their masculine peers, nineteenth-century intellectuals did not see a great distinction between politics and culture; they became politicians, writers, and cultural agents. In the same way, women who entered the world of political action also developed a field of mutually complementary activity. They were writers, journalists, teachers, translators, painters, cultural agents, and editors, as well as political activists. For example, the liberal Catholic autodidact Martina Barros (1850–1944) did not limit herself to the cultural spaces to which she had access as a woman—salons and *tertulias*. She was also a collaborator with the Academia de Letras at the Universidad Católica, and she published articles in the press, held conferences, and wrote her memoirs.[21] In 1872 she translated for the first time into Spanish John Stuart Mill's *The Subjection of Women*. She titled it *La esclavitud de la mujer* and incorporated a prologue of her own, which was published in the *Revista de Santiago*, edited by Augusto Orrego Luco and Fanor Velasco. In it, we can see how questions about women's political exclusion were beginning to formulate:

Society tells the woman that marriage is her only destiny, declaring her unfit for anything other than wife and mother in the name of a certain difference that nature establishes between the woman and the man. But it forgets logic in spite of denying her all rights by virtue of that nature which it arbitrarily attributes to her, all receive them yet the woman born on a throne and by an inconceivable aberration, while it finds it natural, logical, and simple that a queen should preside over the supreme tribunal of justice of a nation, it would find it ridiculous and grotesque should a women administer justice over a small neighborhood.[22]

The ideology that legitimized independence conferred certain characteristics on Chilean republicanism, such as love of country, virtue, and the rights of citizens, among which figured universal suffrage.[23] According to Alejandra Castillo, this ideology was fundamental to the emergence of a feminist discourse at the conclusion of the nineteenth century due to its emphasis on the ideas of liberty and equality among citizens. She cites Jocelyn Holt to point out, "The Creole aristocracy appropriated a radical language, mitigated and softened its revolutionary impact, but it was not able to prevent other groups from eventually accessing the same language, making it their own, and fulfilling the revolutionary character that was implicit in it."[24] Women felt themselves to be citizens with the right to vote since the constitution itself gave suffrage to "todos los chilenos." According to Castillo, "It wasn't possible to avoid the eventual demand for equality." The lawyer and liberal politician Jorge Enrique Costa (1870–1918) affirmed that the constitution of 1833 and successive electoral laws establishing citizenship had conceded the same rights to women as to men.[25] He based his argument on the civil code, which stipulated that laws should apply to both sexes unless nature manifestly limited them to one alone, declaring, "The definitive text of the electoral law of 12 February 1915 and its antecedents, by prohibiting women from the exercise of the right to vote, is contrary to the provisions of the Constitution."[26] This brings us to another milestone, the attempt by a group of women to register to vote in San Felipe, la Serena, and Casablanca, in 1875. This occurred a year after the promulgation of a new electoral law undermining state control of elections, making them at the same time much more competitive. The law established the secret ballot and moved control over elections from municipalities to review boards, constituted by the wealthiest city residents and in some cases accompanied by ecclesiastical authorities. Since there was no explicit prohibition, women saw no reason why they could not register to vote, so long as they complied with the requirements set forth by the law. Some were approved to vote. According to Errázuriz, the phenomenon was considered not to be dangerous because it was anomalous. Therefore it did not merit public debate.[27] Alejandra Castillo argues that women made their own promise of equality. They entered and intervened progressively as actors in the public sphere, extending the republican ethos contained within the constitution of 1833 and illuminating the conflict between universalizing tenets and exclusions that were assumed to be natural to the practice of politics.[28]

On the other hand, Stabili notes how paradoxical it was that these suffragist actions came from women who did not share a liberal democratic ideology.[29] They were women from "good families," Catholic, and close to the Conservative Party. She posits that this "progressive" posture of the Catholic Church and the politicians who represented it can be explained by the protagonist role that women had enjoyed within that institution since the colonial period. That role, in turn, is connected to representations of the Virgin Mary, the model mother, from whence came the idea that "the woman performs the tasks assigned to her with full autonomy from men, which is possible thanks to the power that is conferred upon her by her condition of motherhood. For this reason, it is this religious vision of the world and of social relationships where the upper class Chilean woman finds the foundation for reaffirming her own autonomy and dignity."[30] We will find this same argument, with some nuances, throughout the history of the demand for the vote, regardless of political faction.

It is possible that the entire episode was part of the Conservative Party's electoral strategy. In 1876 it did not field a candidate for president but allied itself with sectors of the Liberal Party who supported the candidacy of Benjamín Vicuña Mackenna. Ostensibly, this was to combat government intervention in elections, although the party worked at the same time on mobilizing adherents in defense of Catholicism.[31] The women's group's attempt to gain the suffrage might have figured among these strategies. Stabili considers this possibility plausible, but she argues that we cannot reduce the suffragist demands to "manipulation" by the Conservative Party. Maza also attempts to understand the contradiction that this support from clerical conservatives implied. She notes the weakness of connections between anti-clerical parties and women's organizations, which she attributes to the exclusively masculine character of the spaces and practices of sociability, such as political party clubs, Masonic lodges, and fire brigades.[32]

Polemic gave way to the express prohibition of women's suffrage in the reform of the electoral law of 1884. A group of young deputies from diverse parties proposed a women's suffrage bill, which Congress rejected. This mobilized the opinion of those women most critical of the patriarchal order, such as Martina Barros, who lamented that women remained "in the HONORABLE company of the demented, domestic servants, those whose crimes merit a jail sentence, and those convicted of fraudulent bankruptcy."[33] She promoted making suffrage the highest priority for women.

In the midst of social transformation caused by modernization, the Amunategui Decree passed on November 6, 1877. It opened higher education to women. Despite the removal of legal impediments to study, women still faced innumerable incidents of discrimination as they pursued their degrees, which is why the first female doctors, Eloísa Díaz and Ernestina Pérez, did not graduate for ten more years, in 1887. Fields such as journalism were easier because there already existed publications by and for women in which authors reflected on the place of women in society.[34]

After 1900, women's participation in the public sphere diversified. Now we must distinguish between the women's movement, the feminist movement, and the suffrage movement. The first contained the other two because it included all expression of women's activism, from the struggles against social inequality to those who worked to maintain the status quo. The feminist movement included organizations that developed feminist discourses, such as liberal feminism, socialist feminism, and anarchist feminism. The suffrage movement concerned only the period during the struggle for the vote. It discursively united feminist activists with members of the general women's movement.

By the start of the twentieth century, the first organizations of women workers had already been formed. Once they became part of the labor force and found themselves in factories, they could not be obviated as partners in the labor struggle. This produced a series of cultural changes, such as the modification of relationships inside the family and a greater social visibility for women.[35] More research will be required to allow us to consider how racially and ethnically different women behaved, since race and ethnicity have been virtually ignored in Chile since the beginning of the twentieth century. For now, we are only able to comment based on differences in social class.

Working-class women's activities were accompanied by the development of socialist feminism, which affirmed the existence of a double oppression: by gender and by social class. Asunción Lavrin points out, however, that liberal and socialist feminists rapidly found ways to accommodate each other's differences to avoid open confrontation. In this way, they unified lines of action to address women's legal subordination.[36]

The autonomous movement of working class women is visible from 1905 with the publication of *La Alborada* (1905) in Valparaíso and its successor, the feminist newspaper *La Palanca*, in Santiago in 1907. In the 1910s, the first feminist centers in Iquique were formed. These were the Centros Belén de Sárraga, under the influence of the Spanish freethinker Belén de Sárraga and the socialist leader Luis Emilio Recabarren. Their ideology stressed anticlericalism (in response to the kind of education offered by the church), women's emancipation, and rights for working-class women. The Consejo Federal Femenino was formed in 1917 within the Gran Federación Obrera de Chile, with the object of improving the cultural level and organizing action of women workers. In 1921 the Unión Obrera Femenina followed. It called on women workers to unite to fight against capital.[37] Thus we see that the apogee of the Chilean labor movement included the participation of women workers.

In a parallel fashion, women from the conservative elite posited a feminine mandate for charity. They began with public actions that transformed into political ones. María Angélica Illanes believes that charity institutions were part of a project to inject tradition into a context in which the process of modernization was altering the status quo.[38] She argues that elite men asked their wives to be mediators to reconstruct an order that had been fractured by the modern class consciousness that workers had acquired. This request was based on the conception of women as a "neutral sex"—possessing no power and unable to participate in the public sphere, they were able to be closer to one another and share the inequality of the patriarchal system. Beginning in 1910 this would form the context for the creation of a series of women's organizations, such as the Asociación de la Juventud Católica Femenina, founded in 1921; the Liga de Madres Cristianas, founded in 1923; the Unión Patriótica de Mujeres de Chile, founded in 1925; and the Archicofradía de Madres Cristianas y Acción Nacional de Mujeres de Chile, also founded in 1925. Another view demanding a public hearing came from women who questioned the social role the patriarchy had assigned to them. The Club de Señoras (1916) and the Círculo de Lectura (1915) were both founded to advance women's cultural and intellectual development. Women's organizations created their own public spaces for intellectual and cultural discussion out of necessity. They wanted to educate themselves and develop a civic spirit, defining themselves as social subjects in the social and cultural space. Their cultural impact was important, yet they extended their labor into the political realm and began a discussion of citizenship rights for Chilean women.[39] Organizations like the Consejo Nacional de Mujeres de Atacama and the Consejo Nacional de Mujeres were founded in this spirit in 1919.

Organizing permitted these women to glimpse what an important weapon the vote could be for entering the political system and acting from within. The vote, therefore, was not an end unto itself but rather a means for achieving specific demands.[40] Women from this group developed "liberal feminism," a European ideological perspective that proposed the necessity of granting women the same civil and political rights as men. Equality lies at the base of this idea. It presupposed that reason was common to all humanity; men and women possessing the same abilities should also possess the same rights. Asunción Lavrin observed that liberal feminism developed in Chile and Latin America in a particular way. Latin Americans added to the demands for civil and political equality the necessity for gender-specific legal protections, fundamentally concerning maternity. Lavrin called this combination "compensatory feminism."[41] Alejandra Castillo names Martina Barros as a precursor to liberal feminism for having questioned hierarchy and tradition in favor of action guided by reason. Nevertheless, she did so while vacillating between positions that permitted theoretical equality while limiting it in practice. Chilean liberal feminism fluctuated between "a restricted model of democracy and a model of extended participation, between a revindication of civic rights and a revindication of political rights; between the defense of the privileged domestic sphere and the defense of women's presence in the public sphere; and finally, between affirming the equality of the sexes and justifying women's confinement in the private sphere of the family."[42]

In 1915 a new electoral reform established a unified voter registration roll that was renewable every nine years. In 1917 conservative deputy Luis Undurraga presented a proposal for women's suffrage. He did so acknowledging that it was a "strange" topic, indicating that it was not important to public opinion. He took up the same argument that Abdón Cifuentes had employed in 1865, which shows that the conservatives were the only ones concerned with women's suffrage for fifty years. Regardless, their concern did not necessarily have anything to do with the defense of republican principles but rather with adding votes for Catholic women, elites, and adherents of the Conservative Party. Errázuriz posits that we can see in Undurraga's argument the tension between the republican principles of equality and universality and the limits of the legislative system. He argued that women should exercise political rights as pillars of society and sustainers of values.[43]

Regardless of why conservatives supported women's rights, they undertook concrete action in favor of Catholic and conservative women's activism. This was a far cry from the liberal, anticlerical world, in which no one under any circumstance considered promoting women's rights. Their refusal had the same foundation as that which motivated conservatives to defend women's suffrage: the assumption that women would vote for the Conservative Party.[44] Although we have seen that by the early twentieth century, women of all social classes and political persuasions were participating in public life, formal politics was still the preserve of the elite, which made it apparent that conservative women would be the best organized and most active. We can add to this the influence of the Catholic Church, which was allied with the Conservative Party, making liberal anticlericals fearful that women would follow political directives from the pulpit. Only international pressure forced anticlerical leaders to consider recognizing political rights for women.

The exclusivity of the Chilean political system engendered a crisis of participation in the 1920s. Indignation in the face of corruption, power plays that impeded parliamentary action, and the breakdown of the state stoked pressure for democratization.[45] The Radical Party achieved a parliamentary majority in the elections of 1918, helped by the achievement of labor consolidation into broad groups with international reach, such as the Chilean chapter of the IWW and the Federación Obrera de Chile (1919). Students also organized and radicalized around the call for democracy. Among the various women's groups, the importance of the vote now became mainstream. New divisions, including those based on gender inequality, emerged from the crisis and gave rise to new political parties.[46] Among these figured the Partido Cívico Femenino, in 1922, which advocated pragmatic reforms around women's education and civil and labor rights for women. The party also made specific demands, such as a liberalization of the civil code, protective legislation for women workers, and other social reforms, such as controlling prostitution and alcoholism.[47] The Partido Demócrata Femenino was founded in 1924 along similar lines.

The atmosphere of crisis of the 1910s proved auspicious for a presidential candidate like Arturo Alessandri, a charismatic liberal democratic leader. His unusually dynamic campaign brought broad support from the popular classes. Its reformist discourse implied a fracturing of the liberal alliance, which had always leaned to the right. Despite all this, Alessandri's government failed to generate substantive changes. Although Alessandri failed to achieve a parliamentary majority in 1921, there were still signs of changes to come in the first Mapuche member of the Chamber of Deputies and a significant number of new middle-class deputies.[48] Then, in 1922, the Consejo Nacional de Mujeres introduced a bill to address women's political and civil rights.

Halfway through the 1920s, the political crisis showed no signs of lessening, which increased tension and quashed any efforts to compromise in the legislature. The period 1924–1925 was an extremely tense time that included a military intervention, accelerating discussion in Congress.[49] Thus, with pressure from the military in the Senate, social legislation finally passed, but Alessandri was forced to resign at the same time. The sense of political crisis seemed permanent until, following two military juntas, Alessandri resumed power in 1925 and, without recalling Congress, decreed a new constitution.[50] This inclined the balance of power in favor of the executive and created a presidentialist regime that established the separation of church and state; added social reforms such as worker protections, social security, and housing; and affirmed state responsibility for public health.[51]

Castillo notes that the new constitution meant continued exclusion from public life for women. The emancipating discourses of the late nineteenth century had discredited arguments about women's intellectual and biological inferiority, however, and the more recent emphasis on equality had opened a space to appeal for political rights. Suffragists now extended the same argument: we are all citizens. There was no longer a logical reason to exclude women, yet the exclusion endured.

The idea of the universal applicability of the law, however, eventually translated into promises for gradual increases in political rights: women would vote first at the municipal level (effective from April 13, 1926, although with many restrictions); then women could stand as candidates for election at the same level. Later women would be able to vote in elections for deputies, senators, and the president. Then they would be allowed to stand for legislative office and to serve as jurors, until finally they could be named ministers or elected to the presidency.[52] Castillo observes, "The horizontal utopia conferred by the democratic ideology had thus transformed into a gradual promise, in a game of trial and error whose rules were established by the *masculine republic*."[53]

The 1930s marked a new phase in the women's movement. The world crisis affected Chile especially, and the radicalization of politics made women unite to launch a definitive campaign for the vote. Workers, conservatives, and liberal feminists were strengthened within their own organizations as well as through other groups with national reach that aimed to integrate the various factions. Women literally took to the streets, organizing the first large-scale protests and street parades while founding new women's organizations. In 1933 we see the creation of the Comité Nacional Pro Derechos de la Mujer, which unleashed a suffragist campaign that put pressure on political structures through propaganda, conferences, and street actions. Made up of leftists and members of independent parties, the MEMCH emerged in 1935. Its objective was to create a progressive feminist consciousness, demanding economic, social, and juridical emancipation. It advocated for democracy, education, and vocational training, among other objectives. It was the first group to achieve a massive and continued presence. It also maintained international connections with other women's organizations.

The municipal vote passed in 1931, and the right to be elected to municipal posts in 1934. According to Errázuriz, this was a good solution for radicals and liberals who wanted to observe the electoral effects of women's participation while initiating women's sectors within each of their own parties. The achievement of the municipal vote was a legislative advance, but it also laid bare prejudices about women's roles in society and politicians' fears about the effect women's suffrage could have on elections.[54] In 1935 women's political parties ran candidates for municipal offices and won important victories. MEMCH engaged in frenetic suffragist activity, organizing events in theaters and attending international conferences.

The 1935 elections mobilized just 9 percent of the new voters, of whom more than 50 percent preferred the Conservative Party, which made it the party with the strongest electoral base.[55] Without considering what percentage had participated, liberal and leftists politicians reinforced their fear of approving women's suffrage more broadly.[56]

Numerous women's organizations joined the coalition effort Frente Popular, dedicated to broadening democracy, after its creation in 1936. For the first time, activists glimpsed the real possibility of winning the vote, and they added other demands. The Frente Popular also looked to be able to capture women's votes, so it undertook a campaign directed at women in support of the candidacy of Pedro Aguirre Cerda, who included women's suffrage among his campaign promises. Subsequent municipal elections saw an increase in the number of registered women voters, which changed the percentage of ballots cast for each party. The Conservative Party lost votes and the Radical Party ascended.[57] In this context, newly elected president Pedro Aguirre Cerda declared in 1938, "We are going to recognize all rights. Everything, exactly the same as for men. It is a form of disloyalty to keep half of the human race in chains."[58]

In 1937 a delegation from Democracia Unificada introduced a motion in the Chamber of Deputies to extend the vote to women. The debate took place over four years and suffered a setback when the suffragist ally President Aguirre Cerda died, which brought negotiations to a standstill until new conditions emerged. This, together with problems relating to the outbreak of the Second World War, stifled demands for the vote. Even feminist discourse focused more on addressing social problems than clamoring for suffrage.

During the 1940s, the fight for the vote intensified. Women occupied public spaces in every sense, protesting in the street, on the radio, and in the newspapers. Feminists from diverse perspectives joined forces, pressuring Congress and the Chilean state to comply with international agreements that required recognizing women's political equality. Law 6.825, granting the armed forces control over safeguarding elections, passed in 1941, the same year in which Elena Caffarena and Flor Heredia, with support from Pedro Aguirre, prepared a bill on the requirements for citizenship with voting rights.[59] These activities influenced Pedro Aguirre Cerda's message on reforming the 1929 electoral registry law, Law 4554.

According to Errázuriz, the political class during the 1940s began to argue for women's suffrage both to democratize and to comply with international obligations. Chile had always boasted of being a "civilized" country, more advanced than its Latin American neighbors, which made it hard to justify a democratic system that excluded more than half the population and that ignored international agreements to which it was a party.[60] Those international agreements included recommendations on women's political rights from the fifth Pan-American Conference, held in Santiago in 1924, and the eighth, held in Lima in 1938. There Chile joined the Inter-American Commission on Women (created in 1928), which was charged with achieving full civil and political rights for women throughout the continent. The exclusion of women became a real problem, one requiring a solution, when it became a source of international embarrassment. Of course, even international humiliation proved insufficient, since in 1941 a majority of legislators declared themselves to be in favor of women's suffrage while it still took eight more years to pass. Politicians were clearly inconsistent, claiming to believe one thing while their actions showed otherwise.

In 1944 FECHIF was formed, with the purpose of uniting all women's organizations behind the suffrage effort. Beginning in the second half of the 1940s, under the presidency of Gabriel González Videla, political instability pushed the suffrage movement to one side, despite the support of First

Lady Rosa Markmann. In 1945 Senator Horacio Walker introduced a new proposal with support from diverse political parties. Its rationale was identical to Aguirre Cerda's from 1941: the need for justice (meaning democratization) for a sector of the population that, "due to its culture, sensitivity, abnegation, and clear sense of responsibility, will permit the woman to contribute to the advancement of national life."[61] Women's moral superiority was a ruse to disguise the real reason, which was to avoid putting republican institutions at risk. When faced with a challenge to democracy, the Radical, Communist, and Socialist Parties strongly defended women's suffrage in that it was necessary to amplify their electoral base. The Conservative Party weakened its support because it had concluded that the women's vote no longer would favor the party. In 1946 the Commission on Constitution, Legislation, and Justice announced that the women's vote would be obligatory, like men's, proposing January 1, 1948, as a start date to give women time to prepare to fulfil their "new" civic duty. With this, the commission went against the principle of gradualism from 1925, making it once again obvious that it was fear, not principle, that had delayed full participation.[62]

In 1947 the FECHIF congress took place in Valparaíso at the Universidad Federico Santa María. Starting in 1948, under the motto "We want to vote in the next elections," it increased pressure on Congress and the González Videla government. International scrutiny and accusations of a deteriorating democracy brought dispatch to the recently proposed legislation from December 1948 following the Law for the Permanent Defense of Democracy, which declared the Communist Party illegal.[63] The law passed on December 15, 1948, in an extraordinary session of the Chamber of Deputies. On January 8, 1949, the president signed it, and on January 14 it was published in the *Diario Oficial*, promulgating it. Chilean women now had full political rights in time to vote in the 1949 parliamentary elections.[64]

Chilean women's suffrage became a reality as the government was experiencing instability. It was an effort to arrest the effects of the deterioration of democracy implied by the Ley Maldita, as the law prohibiting the Communist Party was popularly known. Errázuriz argues that the Chilean political scene was more efficacious than all the women's suffrage campaigns.[65] She adds that the argument never was to grant rights to women for their own sake but rather in their capacities as mothers and formers of citizens.

This analysis does not discount the agency of the women's movement, but it recognizes that the political system characterized by masculine politics was the fundamental factor in determining women's suffrage. This phenomenon may explain why women's political action becomes blurry after women achieve the vote—why we talk about a feminist silence. Emphasizing institutional politics in the history of women's suffrage has impeded our understanding of the new forms in which women engaged in politics, whether inside of party apparatuses or autonomously.

Recognizing the impact of masculine institutions on the history of women's suffrage ought to push us to reexamine our parameters for analysis to identify forms of political action that went beyond institutions, which in this case implies lifting the veil on women's political activity after 1950, when,

for the first time in the annals of Chile, a woman presents herself as a candidate for Senator of the Republic. This is a new case for us since only one year ago we received political rights as though they were a snack that was just sitting on the table; but those who have for half a century been preparing that morsel, fighting against obstacles men put in their paths, who saw, repeatedly, legislation discussed in Congress only to be placed again in the sepulcher of its archives, who we were afraid might die, as has happened to others, without ever realizing this ideal to which we dedicated the greatest energies of our souls, we know that it is not a morsel put on the table beforehand, but rather something built up with titanic effort by pioneers: Martina Barros de Orrego, Inés Echeverría de Larrain, Delia Matte de Izquierdo, Elvira Santa Cruz and many others who, defying the storm, went forth on the battlefield waving the banner of women's right to vote and be voted for to represent the people in Parliament. . . . But today's women, those who have received the right to vote, do not know and have not been able to value this privilege and have run *to stand in line for the parties that yesterday fought us*, that fought us for years and years, finally giving us the vote when they could no longer avoid it, it is a triumph that was already ripe, only now falling from the tree . . . and now that the test is at hand, in the face of the possibility of defeat for the only woman who has ever dared to rise up, throwing down the gauntlet to the political parties, the painful conviction that this defeat could come at the hands of those same women torments us, to place the name of a man in the ballot box . . . and to arrive at this point we have battled for half a century.[66]

Conclusion

This chapter has reviewed the literature on the history of women's suffrage in Chile and concluded that it was a process characterized by the Liberal Delay. The chapter has attempted to give a panoramic view of the phenomenon, including gendered arguments that justified women's exclusion, factors that made this case special within the general context of the broadening of the electorate, of which women's voting was but one aspect. We can see that it was a multidimensional process. On the one hand, we recognize the intersectionality of those female subjects who demanded the vote; there was no unified position among women, and their demands changed over time. Differences emerged among women according to social class: working class, middle class, and elites. Working-class women tended to identify with socialists, while elite women favored conservatives, although we cannot establish a general rule. Sadly, we are still unable to say much about the role of race or ethnicity within the women's movement, which must remain an open question. On the other hand, in the Chilean case, it is vital to understand the larger process of the expansion of the electorate, wherein women lagged behind well into the twentieth century. This speaks of the contradiction within the liberal political system, which permitted women's political activity but failed to recognize their status as subjects with full political rights. Thus the history of Chilean women's suffrage can been understood as a contradiction of modernization, which is reflected in the way women's political participation was made invisible after 1950.

Notes

1. Gaviola, "*Queremos votar en las próximas elecciones.*"
2. Kirkwood, *Ser política en Chile.*
3. Kirkwood, 68–69.

4. Maza, "Catolicismo, anticlericalismo y la extensión del sufragio a la mujer en Chile."

5. Asunción Lavrín, *Mujeres, feminismo y cambio social en Argentina, Chile y Uruguay 1890–1940* (Santiago: Centro de Investigación Barros Arana, 2005).

6. Errázuriz, "Discursos en torno al sufragio femenino en Chile 1865–1949."

7. Stabili, "Las Res-Públicas de las mujeres."

8. López and Gamboa, "Sufragio femenino en Chile."

9. Castillo, *El desorden de la democracia.*

10. Posada Carbó, "Las prácticas electorales en Chile 1810–1970."

11. Posada Carbó, 186.

12. Fernández, "Conformación de partidos políticos en Chile."

13. Vicuña, *La belle époque chilena*, 129.

14. Senator in three periods from 1888 to 1912 and deputy in four between 1887 and 1882. In 1871 he was minister of justice, religion, and public instruction. During the 1880s, he fought hard, both in the press and in the legislature, against the wave of liberalism reflected in passage of the so-called secular laws. This dispute led him to develop, together with other leaders of Catholic conservatism, various mechanisms for defending their beliefs, such as the Unión Católica de Chile, which at the end of the 1880s founded the Pontificia Universidad Católica. "Abdón Cifuentes Espinosa," Historia Politica, www.bcn.cl/historiapolitica/resenas_parlamentarias/wiki/Abd%C3%B3n_Cifuentes_Espinosa, accessed September 17, 2023.

15. Cifuentes, "Acerca del derecho electoral de la mujer."

16. Montero, "Trocar agujas por la pluma."

17. *El Eco de las Señoras de Santiago* 1, no. 1 (1865): 1.

18. Montero, "Trocar agujas por la pluma."

19. Jacksic and Serrano, "El gobierno y las libertades."

20. Castillo, *El desorden de la democracia*, 24.

21. She is considered one of the precursors of feminism in Chile. Her principal works were the publication of Mill's *The Subjection of Women* (1869), conferences, and press articles on political and civil rights for women, women's education, and other subjects. She also wrote an extensive volume of memoirs, *Recuerdos de mi vida* (1942). She brought her liberal ideology to the political and literary spheres of her era.

22. Barros, *Prologo a La esclavitud de la Mujer*, 50–51.

23. Castillo, *El desorden de la democracia*, 26.

24. Castillo, *El desorden de la democracia*, 27.

25. Representing the Partido Liberal, he participated in general elections from 1912 to 1915. He was vice president of the House and a member of the Permanent Commission on Public Instruction, the Permanent Commission on Elections, and the Permanent Commission on Legislation and Justice. "Jorge Enrique Cost Rogers," Historia Política, https://www.bcn.cl/historiapolitica/

resenas_parlamentarias/wiki/Jorge_Enrique_Costa_Rogers, accessed September 17, 2023.

26. Costa, *La Mujer*, 7.
27. Errázuriz, "Discursos en torno al sufragio femenino en Chile 1865–1949."
28. Castillo, *El desorden de la democracia*, 23
29. Stabili, "El sexo de la ciudadanía."
30. Stabili, "El sexo de la ciudadanía," 153.
31. Eduardo Posada Carbó, "Las prácticas electorales en Chile 1810–1970," 195.
32. Maza, "Liberales, radicales y la ciudadanía de la mujer en Chile (1872–1930)."
33. Quoted in Errázuriz, "Discursos en torno al sufragio femenino en Chile 1865–1949," 12.
34. They also published newspapers.
35. Hutchison, Elizabeth, *Labors Appropriate to Their Sex.*
36. Lavrín, *Women, Feminism, and Social Change*, 4–5.
37. Gaviola, *"Queremos votar en las próximas elecciones,"* 31–35.
38. Illanes, "Maternalismo popular e hibridación cultural en Chile, 1900–1920."
39. Vicuña, Manuel; *La belle époque chilena*, 129–81.
40. Errázuriz, "Discursos en torno al sufragio femenino en Chile 1865–1949."
41. Lavrín, *Women, Feminism, and Social Change*, 15–18.
42. Castillo, *El desorden de la democracia*, 68.
43. Errázuriz, "Discursos en torno al sufragio femenino en Chile 1865–1949."
44. Errázuriz, 14
45. Collier and Sater, *Historia de Chile.*
46. Samuel J. Valenzuela, "Orígenes y transformaciones del sistema de partidos en Chile," *Revista Estudios Públicos* 58 (1995): 53, http://www.cepchile.cl.
47. Veneros, "Dos vertientes," 53.
48. Collier and Sater, *Historia de Chile.*
49. In September 1924, a group of ranking military officers entered the session and unsheathed their swords, intimidating the legislators.
50. The constitution of 1925 was written by a consultive commission, which drafted a proposal that was submitted to a plebiscite and promulgated on September 18 of the same year. Maria Aylwin et al, *Chile en el Siglo XX*, 119.
51. Halperin Donghi, *Historia Contemporánea de América Latina*, 336.
52. Castillo, *El desorden de la democracia*, 56–57.
53. Castillo, 57
54. Errázuriz, "Discursos en torno al sufragio femenino en Chile 1865–1949."
55. Errázuriz.
56. Errázuriz.
57. Maza, "Liberales, radicales y la ciudadanía de la mujer en Chile (1872–1930)," 185.
58. Errázuriz, "Discursos en torno al sufragio femenino en Chile 1865–1949."
59. Maza, "Liberales, radicales y la ciudadanía de la mujer en Chile (1872–1930)," 189.

60. Errázuriz, "Discursos en torno al sufragio femenino en Chile 1865–1949."

61. *Boletín de Sesiones Ordinarias, Senado* 53 (June 20, 1945): 476.

62. Errázuriz, "Discursos en torno al sufragio femenino en Chile 1865–1949," 21.

63. González Videla's government was marked by a political crisis stemming from his own cabinet. The president, without congressional support, feared the power of the Communist Party—hence the law proscribing it, which was known as the Ley Maldita, or Accursed Law. The event discredited Chilean democracy.

64. Gaviola, *"Queremos votar en las próximas elecciones."*

65. Errázuriz, "Discursos en torno al sufragio femenino en Chile 1865–1949," 23.

66. Vera Zouroff, "Una mujer al Senado," *Revista Mujeres de América* 9 (1950).

CHAPTER NINE

The History of Women's Suffrage in Nicaragua

An Incomplete Story

VICTORIA GONZÁLEZ-RIVERA

WESTERN AND CENTRAL NICARAGUA GAINED independence from Spain in 1821 and forcibly "incorporated" the Caribbean Coast, which had been colonized by the British, into the Nicaraguan nation in 1894. The inhabitants of the two different regions have had very different histories. One of the differences relates to women's right to vote.

While this chapter focuses almost exclusively on the experiences of urban women in western and central Nicaragua due to the sources available, it is important to note that the liberal politician Modesto Armijo Lozano (1886–1968) wrote in 1912 that women on the Caribbean Coast had acquired the right to vote in 1894, as part of accords reached in the meeting of Miskitu mayors that took place in Bluefields to ratify Nicaraguan governance over the region.[1] This is also mentioned by the Nicaraguan scholar Jorge Eduardo Arellano, who cited a brief note published in a 1933 Managua newspaper under the section "Correspondence from Bluefields" that stated, "So much has been published in the newspapers from the capital about the feminine vote that we think it is of interest . . . to remember the decree from the Mosquitia that established the right to suffrage for both men and women."[2]

Indeed, on February 27, 1895, Nicaragua's National Assembly had approved the November 20, 1894, decree from the Mosquito Convention, which stated in Article 5, "The right to suffrage is extended to men and women who are eighteen years old."[3]

How did women on Nicaragua's Caribbean Coast gain the right to vote so early? And were they in fact able to exercise suffrage before 1957, which is when women in the rest of Nicaragua were able to vote? We do not know the full answers to these questions yet. However, we do know that no women signed the Mosquito Convention decree that granted women the vote in its Article 5 and that the same decree stated as Article 1, "The Nicaraguan Constitution and its laws will be obeyed by the 'pueblos mosquitos.'"[4] The brand-new liberal 1893 constitution of Nicaragua did *not* contain an article that granted women suffrage. Therefore we must assume that the constitution of 1893 trumped the 1894 Mosquito Convention decree and that the Nicaraguan National Assembly approved the latter (including Article 5) precisely because it was nullified by the constitution. But in 1896 the constitutional law professor J. Hernández Somoza wrote the following in a constitutional law textbook he authored: "Here [in Nicaragua], women in the Mosquitia . . . can carry out the role of electors and our [Nicaraguan] Constitution establishes [in theory] universal suffrage, as we can see when we study Article 20 of the Constitution that governs us; although it excludes woman."[5] Professor Hernández Somoza did not discuss how or why women on the Caribbean Coast could be "electors" given that, as he himself noted, the Nicaraguan constitution excluded women from voting. We know, however, that in the 1928 presidential elections that took place under US supervision, women in the port city of Bluefields, the capital of the former Mosquito Kingdom, did not vote.[6]

It is important to understand the context in which this short-lived opportunity for women took place. In the early 1890s, like now, the region was populated by different Indigenous peoples, among them Miskitus, Mayangnas, and Ramas. Other major groups in the area were Garifunas, Creoles, and mestizos. Additionally, there were a few hundred white folks from the United States and Europe. And the British and US governments were still actively vying for political and economic power, even though the mestizo Nicaraguan government had gained official control over the region in 1894.

The inhabitants of the Caribbean Coast rebelled repeatedly against the Nicaraguan government during this period, often with outside support. The United States at the time was considering building a canal that would cut across the area, hence its extensive involvement. Additionally, US corporations and white US Americans living there had many economic interests on the Caribbean Coast. As a result, white settlers (with the backing of the US government) often supported the demand for local autonomy made by Indigenous peoples and Creoles, rejecting the Nicaraguan government's takeover of the region since they believed it would threaten their own economic interests.[7] The ongoing insistence on local autonomy is most likely what fueled the article in the 1894 Mosquito Convention decree that granted women the vote, a vote that was perhaps never exercised since no explicit mention of women actually voting between 1894 and 1928 has been found. There is also no evidence to suggest that women's suffrage on the Caribbean Coast was related to "traditional," or precolonial, roles of Indigenous women in local governing councils. That said, it is crucial to mention that those decades were not characterized by democratic politics and free elections but rather by dictatorial leadership, widespread state violence, and British and US military intervention, which often made voting a moot point. Imperialism impacted the course of Nicaraguan women's history on the Caribbean Coast, a subject rarely addressed by historians, by oppressing any expression of political equality on the part of women, and this should not be understated.

Women in the western and central regions of Nicaragua did not gain the right to vote in the 1890s, but it was not because efforts were not made to pass a law granting them suffrage. In fact, the president of the assembly that approved the decree from the Mosquito Convention in 1895 was Francisco Montenegro, a "visionary fanatic"[8] and liberal legislator who, in 1893, had made an unsuccessful yet "vigorous" push for women's suffrage[9] under the liberal president José Santos Zelaya López (1853–1919), in power from 1893 until 1909, the year in which he was deposed with assistance from the US government.

The Nationalist Liberal Party (PLN), the main liberal party in Nicaragua, paid lip service to the political and legal emancipation of women from the nineteenth century onward. But the PLN failed to make women's suffrage a reality until the 1950s, when two things happened: the party mobilized liberal women in partisan organizations, and it was absolutely impossible to delay the vote for women due to local and international pressure.[10]

Part of the reason for the delay was that liberals were not a monolith. Many liberal men had reservations when it came to giving women the vote, particularly because they agreed with pro-suffrage conservatives who believed that, if given a chance, women would vote on behalf of conservative candidates and the Catholic Church. Ironically, when women finally were able to vote and be elected, in 1955, the liberal Somoza government wanted this achievement to be an example of Somocista "modernity" and "progress."

While the Liberal Party had formally endorsed the vote for women in 1913,[11] the Conservative Party did not publicly support women's suffrage until years later, once its leaders thought it could benefit them and the Catholic Church. But conservatives were also not a monolith. Individual conservatives continued to speak out *against* suffrage even though their party was pushing *for* suffrage during the "Pact of the [liberal and conservative] Generals" that took place in 1950, an agreement that ultimately facilitated a change in the law and allowed women to vote. Even General Emiliano Chamorro Vargas (1871–1966), the long-standing Conservative Party leader (Nicaraguan president from 1917 to 1921 and then again in 1927) and the one who appears to have insisted that suffrage be included as part of the pact, wanted restrictions on the vote for women: "The feminine vote . . . must be voluntary and not obligatory . . . its obligatory nature . . . would tear women away from the duties of home."[12]

Contrary to a common narrative, women were not "granted" the vote by the liberal general Anastasio Somoza García (1896–1956) and/or the conservative general Emiliano Chamorro. After a discouraging defeat in 1939 at the hands of liberal representatives, independent suffragists along with partisan liberal and conservative ones regrouped in the 1940s and mounted fierce campaigns for their cause. Their campaigns were able to garner the male support they needed to eventually make the dream of suffrage for all in Nicaragua a reality.

Suffragists had hoped to help shape Nicaragua's political future through the vote, and in fact that did happen. But voting under a repressive decades-long right-wing dictatorship (1936–1979), which among other things curtailed free speech and conducted fraudulent elections, was a huge disappointment for politically independent suffragists, those aligned with the Conservative Party, and those who favored the breakaway Liberal Independent Party (PLI). Only those who supported the Somocista PLN were able to become part of the expanding Somoza state apparatus and thrive in the long-lasting patron-clientelistic system they helped create.[13]

While the suffrage movement in western and central Nicaragua intersected with the feminist movement, not all suffragists were feminists. In fact, it is often hard to know whether a suffragist identified as a feminist. Sometimes it is even hard to know whether a woman activist who wrote favorably of feminism and suffrage self-identified as a suffragist and/or a feminist. To complicate matters, after the vote, the Somoza government promoted its own version of history, one that displaced suffragists and feminists and instead centered the contributions of Somocista women *only as* Somocista women. This version was so successful that by 1979 Nicaragua's first wave feminism had been forgotten in Nicaragua and abroad, and the leftist Sandinista revolution, which brought an end to the forty-three-year-old dictatorship, was given the credit for politically "awakening" Nicaraguan women.[14]

The history of women's suffrage in Nicaragua thus far has privileged the urban, western region of Nicaragua, but there are still many gaps in that history. As was the case in other countries, most suffragists in Nicaragua belonged to the minority mestizo, urban, and middle/upper classes. Many, if not most, saw themselves as superior to working-class peoples, rural peoples, Indigenous peoples, Afro-Nicaraguans, and peoples on the Caribbean Coast. In other words, although suffragists in Nicaragua did *not* advocate for restricting the vote to literate, property-owning, or mestiza women, their history is intertwined with the enshrinement of an inherently anti-Indigenous and anti-Black mestizo nationalism that came to dominate Nicaragua in the mid-twentieth century.[15]

Additionally, while we have chosen in this volume to classify the history of women's suffrage in Nicaragua under the Delayed Liberal Scenario, the delay in women's right to vote is impossible to understand without also addressing the profoundly negative impact of the long-standing US military intervention on *both* the Caribbean and the western/central regions, a topic discussed in depth later in this chapter.[16]

Antecedents: Women, Work, and Maternalist Rhetoric

In western Nicaragua, most women before the Spanish conquest worked in open-air markets called *tiangues*. In fact, women (trans and cis) were the only locals allowed in these markets, as they were the ones in charge of commerce there. After the conquest, these markets were no longer women-only or Indigenous spaces. However, the historical links between femininity, indigeneity, and local commerce can still be seen today in western Nicaragua: many contemporary urban working-class women continue to work in or near open-air markets and/or in sales as part of the informal economy.[17]

Historically then, urban working-class women's employment outside the home in western Nicaragua was accepted and sometimes even expected.[18] It was considered "traditional." Middle-class urban women's employment (as teachers, nurses, telegraph operators, receptionists, secretaries, attorneys, judges, medical doctors, pharmacists, and so on) would not become the norm until the mid-twentieth century, with the opening of universities to female students and the expansion of state services under the Somoza dictatorship. In 1950 women made up 14 percent of the nation's economically active population.[19] By the late 1970s "women, who made up 30 percent of the economically active population in Managua, . . . constituted 70 percent of the service workers, 55 percent of the sellers and merchants, 37 percent of the office workers, [and] 24 percent of the artisans and operators."[20]

Unlike other right-wing dictatorships in Latin America and elsewhere, the Somoza dictatorship did not spend a great deal of time promoting a narrow maternalist rhetoric or a constricted understanding of women's maternal roles.[21] Moreover, the Somozas realized that most Nicaraguans were working class and that many working-class women needed to contribute, partially or fully, to the financial support of their children, particularly in a country where female-headed working-class households had been common for generations. Women constituted 23 percent of heads of households in 1977 and 25 percent in 1985.[22] Although we do not have exact figures for earlier periods, almost 40 percent of all Nicaraguans in the 1920 census were illegitimate, suggesting that many of them had been raised in female-headed households. Additionally, that same census revealed that only 15 percent of all Nicaraguans were married. (Approximately 69 percent of the population was over 20 years of age.[23]) Given these numbers, I contend that for generations, many Nicaraguan working women have understood mothering *itself* as contributing to the financial support of their children.[24]

The Somozas sought the political support of working-class maternal breadwinners in exchange for facilitating their employment.[25] The Somozas also took advantage of the fact that women were paid lower wages than men for similar work, which meant that working women subsidized the expansion of state services and the agro-industrial export sector in the mid-twentieth century.[26] As was the case elsewhere, women also tended to be segregated in lower-paying fields. As early as 1921, Granada conservative J. D. Mondragón justified women's low wages in the following manner: "Woman needs only two things. To be clean and to be powdered. Once she is clean and her hair is done, she is ready to work. Hence she can adapt, more than man, to the small salaries."[27]

Nineteenth- and early twentieth-century middle-class feminists also largely rejected a narrow maternalist rhetoric, such as one, espoused by some Nicaraguan clergy, arguing that in addition to focusing exclusively on being good mothers and wives, women and girls should rarely leave their homes.[28] Only some suffragists (mostly affiliated with the Conservative Party) stressed women's maternal roles as a primary reason women should have the right to vote.[29]

The Rights of Single and Married Women after the End of Enslavement in Western and Central Nicaragua

The enslavement of people of African ancestry was legal in western and central Nicaragua until 1824, creating unfathomable legal differences between enslaved and non-enslaved peoples. There was also a legal difference between enslaved women and enslaved men, since only the children of enslaved women were automatically enslaved. After 1824, however, single women over the age of twenty-five in western and central Nicaragua in theory had most of the legal rights that men of the same age and social class had.[30] They could own, administer, and inherit property. They could write their own wills. They could also litigate and serve as witnesses without having to ask anyone for permission. *Married* women, on the other hand, had limited juridical capacity.

The restrictions on married Nicaraguan women after independence were largely a continuation of colonial policies and could be found in the civil code. Article 132 of Nicaragua's 1867 civil code, based on the Chilean civil code drafted by Andrés Bello, stated, "The husband owes the woman protection and the woman owes the husband obedience."[31] Out of 2,524 articles in the code, this was one of only two that included the word *obedience*. The other, Article 222, stated that legitimate children owed obedience to their father and mother but "were especially subjected to the father."[32] These articles remained intact when the civil code was amended in 1871.

The crux of the matter was that although married women could own property and inherit it, and in fact owned half of the goods acquired in a marriage due to the existence of community property (*sociedad conyugal*), their husbands were legally tasked with administering their property unless other arrangements, such as a prenuptial agreement, had been made.[33] Moreover, a woman needed her husband's authorization for most legal activities, including participating as a litigant and working outside the home.[34] Article 140 specified, "Woman cannot, without the authorization of the husband, enter into any contracts, nor can she end an earlier contract . . . nor accept or decline a donation, inheritance . . . nor can she . . . mortgage or pawn."[35] Adding insult to injury, Article 141 stated, "The husband's authorization must be given in writing."[36]

A separate section of the civil code dealt specifically with women who worked outside the home. Article 153 stated, "If the married woman exercises a profession or any industry, like being the director of a private school, a teacher at a school, an actress, delivers babies, rents out rooms, is a wet nurse; the general authorization of the husband for all the acts and contracts related to her profession or industry will be assumed, as long as the husband does not protest."[37]

Additionally, a totally separate article in the civil code dealt exclusively with married market vendors. Article 154 stated, "The married woman who is a market vendor is subject to the special rules dictated in the Commerce Code."[38] The 1869 commerce code added additional restrictions to married women who wished to engage in commerce.

By 1914, the commerce code placed no constraints on married women who wished to engage in commerce.[39] Earlier, in 1904,[40] the civil code had eliminated previous restrictions on married women's rights, including the order that women obey their husbands in almost everything, a legal concept known as *potestad marital*. But the civil code maintained the husband as head of household and as the one who had authority over minor children through *patria potestad*, a concept that would not disappear until the 1980s under the Sandinista revolution. Moreover, while the word *obedience* disappeared from the 1904 civil code, this new code provided a definition of civil marriage that did not necessarily benefit women.

Article 94 of the 1904 civil code proclaimed, "Matrimony is a solemn contract in which a man and a woman unite for life, and has as its object procreation and mutual aid."[41] The emphasis on procreation (based on Catholic doctrine, which would eventually change with the reforms of Vatican II in the twentieth century) would solidify the heterosexual nature of marriage for years to come. And it underscored the fact that secular laws were not necessarily less patriarchal than Catholic ones.

Around the time the word *feminist* was first used in Nicaragua, in 1905,[42] married women in Nicaragua had the right to administer their own property. Civil marriage and the possibility of divorce had become a reality in 1904.[43] State-funded secular primary education for boys and girls was mandatory, and women could attend a university without having to first petition the government. What women did not have was the right to vote and be elected.[44]

Women's gender alone was what prevented them from being full citizens with voting rights.[45] In fact, the idea of women having political rights was so inconceivable to most male politicians that they did not feel a need to specify in the early constitutions that only men could be citizens. As was true elsewhere, the 1858 constitution did not specifically state that only men had that right. Women would eventually be explicitly excluded from citizenship in the 1939 constitution. They then became passive citizens under the

1950 constitution and full citizens, with voting rights, in 1955, after the constitution and the electoral law were reformed.[46]

The Early Years of the Suffrage Movement

Pro-independence elites in Nicaragua drew a connection between republicanism and women's emancipation. An 1837 editorial published in the official newspaper *Aurora de Nicaragua* stated, "During three centuries of slavery and tyranny . . . the fair sex was submerged in ignorance, causing notable damage to society; and if that conduct was indispensable for upholding an oppressive regime, it is no longer necessary now that we are ruled by a republican system."[47]

Although the early nineteenth century saw the rise of liberal arguments on behalf of the education of women, between 1821 and the 1860s, political conflicts and foreign intervention prevailed in Nicaragua, making it hard to consolidate liberalism and enact many changes on behalf of women and girls. The last decades of the nineteenth century would witness increased advocacy on behalf of women's education and see the emergence of bitter discussions over women's suffrage in Nicaragua. These debates became especially heated from the 1870s and 1880s onward. At that time, a stronger and more defined liberalism, with an anticlerical and equal rights rhetoric, gained a strong foothold. It challenged the conservative, Catholic traditions that had prevailed from 1857 to 1893, the years after the William Walker invasion of 1856.

The nineteenth-century liberal reforms that characterized other Latin American countries happened rather late in Nicaragua. As noted earlier, it was not until 1893 that the liberal legislator Francisco Montenegro proposed the first bill that would have granted western and central Nicaraguan women suffrage, with no success.

Over the course of the nineteenth century and the early decades of the twentieth century, there emerged a tenuous and sometimes ambiguous relationship between feminists and liberals. Additionally, the feminist movement became consolidated under the leadership of one woman, the educator Josefa Toledo de Aguerri (1865–1962). And despite the broad vision of the movement's leader, only the issue of female suffrage gained prominence within feminism.

In spite of the support liberals as a group gave (and said they would give) to the struggle for women's political rights, individual liberal men had mixed feelings about women's participation in politics. For instance, Max Jerez, a well-known writer for the liberal León newspaper *El 93* (named for the year Zelaya came to power), said in a 1916 editorial that his journal supported female suffrage. But he and his colleagues did not think it was appropriate for women to participate in political rallies or clubs until they were indeed able to vote.[48]

The mixed messages expressed by liberals like Jerez contributed to the delay of the franchise for women, who, he noted, were widely organized in clubs and pro-suffrage female associations. Nevertheless, these ambivalent liberals did not completely succeed in their efforts to prevent women from participating in politics and government.[49]

In addition to participating—albeit minimally—in the PLN, women were able to be part of the state's bureaucratic apparatus. When Toledo de Aguerri became general director of public instruction (education) in 1924, she was part of the first group of Nicaraguan women to officially enter the world of government. That same year, the feminist Juanita Molina de Fromen (1893–1934), Toledo de Aguerri's friend, was named assistant secretary of public instruction, a position she declined.[50]

It was also during this period that Toledo de Aguerri founded Nicaragua's first feminist journals: *Revista femenina ilustrada* in 1918 and *Mujer nicaragüense* in 1929. Feminist journals and organizations flourished during the 1920s and 1930s, many of them influenced directly by feminist activism taking place throughout the world.[51]

Like many other feminists, Juanita Molina de Fromen had opposed the presence of the US Marines in Nicaragua. Nonetheless, like other suffragists, she maintained a friendship with presidents José María Moncada (1870–1945), who held office from 1929 through 1932, and Juan Bautista Sacasa (1874–1946), who held office from 1933 to 1936. Both Moncada and Sacasa were elected in the US-supervised elections discussed below. The latter took office in January 1933, as the marines were leaving Nicaragua.

Liberal politicians listened to, recognized, and applauded feminists when the Liberal Party returned to power in 1929. Molina de Fromen, in fact, had high hopes for the passage of suffrage during the Moncada administration. On March 21, 1930, Molina de Fromen sent Alice Paul (1885–1977), a leading US suffragist and founder of the National Woman's Party, a letter on this subject. Molina de Fromen wrote,

> Great news from Nicaragua! On the 19th Mr. Fromen and I were received by . . . General . . . Moncada . . . and were informed . . . that he has submitted to the Chamber of Representatives and the Senate here a proposal to amend the Constitution . . . to the effect that [the] VOTE BE GRANTED TO ALL WOMEN WHO CAN READ AND WRITE.
>   . . . President Moncada is a man of unusual foresight and greatly interested in the welfare of the Nicaraguan women, realizing that this amendment to the Constitution, if passed by Congress, will mean the regeneration of our women since new ambitions and possibilities will enter into their lives.[52]

Molina de Fromen wanted Paul and other feminist leaders in the United States to write a letter to Moncada "and also to the Presidents of the Senate and the Chamber of Representatives, asking them to pass the said amendment." Molina de Fromen felt that the letters "would be of great help." Unfortunately, we do not know whether Paul and others were able to write letters of support or the details of President Moncada's efforts on behalf of women's political rights. We do know that these efforts failed.[53]

Moncada's 1930 proposal for women's suffrage in Nicaragua stands out because it appears to be the only one that sought to grant the vote to only literate women, at a time when only about 30 percent of the overall population could read and write.[54] The sources do not reveal whose idea it was to limit the vote in this way. That said, Moncada had very mixed feelings about women's involvement in politics, which might explain the proposed restriction.[55]

The Impact of US Intervention

In retrospect, it is clear that Nicaraguan suffragists had a very slim chance of obtaining the right to vote in the 1928 and the 1932 elections, since these were held under the jurisdiction of the US government during its military occupation. And crucially, at least one of the high-level white men overseeing the occupation was an outspoken anti-suffragist.

US secretary of state Henry L. Stimson (1867–1950) traveled with his wife, Mabel Wellington White Stimson (1866–1965), to Nicaragua in 1927. During that trip she met with Nicaraguan women and reported back to her husband. Strangely, given that it was not true, the conclusion Henry Stimson reached was that "they are not invested with suffrage."[56] Although we do not know which women Mabel Stimson met with, we do know that the liberal suffragist María Cristina Zapata Mallie de Montealegre (1883–1971) met with Lou Henry Hoover (1874–1944), the pro-suffrage wife of US president Herbert Clark Hoover (1874–1964), when the Hoovers visited Nicaragua soon after the 1928 election.[57] It is likely that Mabel Stimson, like Lou Henry Hoover, met with Zapata and/or other suffragists.

The Stimsons were very familiar with the struggle for suffrage in the United States since Mabel was the sister of Elizabeth Selden Rogers (1868–1950), a prominent suffragist in the United States. Once, according to Alice Paul, Henry Stimson even helped a suffragist procession in Washington, DC, by providing the necessary cavalry that allowed it to take place.[58] In spite of all that, Henry Stimson was an active and vocal anti-suffragist.

In 1915 he wrote a very long and public letter to a leader of the anti-suffrage movement in the United States, Alice Hill Chittenden, to be published in the *New York Times*. He note, "Suffrage is not in any sense a natural right, such as we call the right to life or liberty or the pursuit of happiness. No class of the community can insist upon the right to vote as it could upon the right to live. . . . I am opposed to woman suffrage because I believe it would throw an additional strain upon the efficiency of . . . government."[59]

Given Stimson's known opposition to granting women the vote, in addition to the fact that the United States was in Nicaragua to promote US interests and not those of suffragists, there was no public debate among the invaders over the possibility of granting Nicaraguan women suffrage in time for the 1928 elections. Indeed, electoral politics in Nicaragua during this period were greatly complicated by the marine occupation. And feminists did not appreciate this added complication.

Feminist María Gámez (1876–1940) corresponded with US feminist Doris

Stevens (1888–1963). In a June 1932 letter to Stevens, dated months before a US representative would formally refuse to back woman suffrage in time for the November 1932 elections, Gámez was already critical of the US Marines' position on female suffrage. She confided in Stevens that the electoral law drafted by army brigadier general Frank Ross McCoy (1874–1954) in preparation for the 1928 election had been inherently flawed. Gámez argued that McCoy had ignored women's constitutional right to vote (since there was nothing in Nicaragua's constitution that prohibited women from voting), which was, in Gámez's words, "inexcusable in an American, given the degree of culture North Americans have regarding women's rights."[60] María Gámez's criticism of McCoy as someone who should have known better, given women's right to vote in the United States and the supposed US support for women's rights abroad, was literally lost in translation. Doris Stevens read a watered-down version that stated simply that McCoy's actions were "inexcusable for a man of North America in connection with the rights of women."[61]

McCoy, who was known as "the Mussolini of Nicaragua,"[62] could have allowed women to vote in Nicaragua in 1928 but was unwilling to do so. Not surprisingly, other men on McCoy's team, such as General Matthew B. Ridgway (1895–1993), were not very receptive to promoting women's rights either. Ridgway would famously go on to oppose the admission of women into the US military academies.[63]

While all hope was lost for the 1928 elections, feminists thought they had a chance of voting in 1932; hence the proposal submitted by Moncada in 1930 discussed earlier. Those hopes were dashed, however, when, according to the *New York Times*, Clark Howell Woodward (1877–1967), the US admiral in charge of supervising the November 1932 presidential and congressional elections in Nicaragua, formally denied suffrage to women a few months before the elections, suggesting that feminists submit their request at a later, and presumably more convenient, time:

> Admiral C. H. Woodward of the United States Navy, chairman of the Election Mission, in a letter . . . to Señora María A. Gómez [Gámez], a feminist leader in Managua, announced that while he was in sympathy with her proposal that women [be] permitted to vote he could not

accede to her request that they be allowed to do so in the November elections.

He advised Señora Gómez to present the project of permitting women's suffrage to the next Congress.[64]

María Gámez, however, was not to be stopped by Woodward's antifeminist intervention in Nicaraguan politics. Feminists had the support of the liberal representative Ildefonso Palma Martínez (1900–1978), who had already submitted a suffrage bill before Congress in June 1932, a few months before Woodward's announcement. Representative Palma Martínez presented before Congress the "Bill in favor of the vote for women in Nicaragua" in late June 1932. That proposal stated, "The right to vote belongs to Nicaraguans, men and women twenty-one years old or older; those who are eighteen can also vote, if they are married or know how to read and write."[65]

The law would have granted women the vote as early as 1933. While women would not have been able to vote in the 1932 US-supervised elections, they would have been able to vote in municipal elections soon after that and in presidential elections in the mid-1930s.

Since the political climate was dire, Gámez had not been very optimistic about winning the vote in 1932. She had written in a June 17, 1932, letter to Doris Stevens that she doubted Palma Martínez would be successful, even though the bill had the support of quite a few representatives.[66] When the 1932 bill failed to pass, Gámez and Palma Martínez simply waited a few months after the elections and tried again in 1933.

Another politician who supported female suffrage during this period was the liberal politician, medical doctor, and diplomat Rodolfo Espinosa Ramírez (1876–1944). In a speech delivered in August 1932, he had commented that "nothing would be more just . . . than to see the Nicaraguan woman deciding with her vote the national destinies in the 1936 election."[67] Espinosa would go on to become vice president under the medical doctor Juan Bautista Sacasa, who served as president from 1933 to 1936.[68] He affirmed his support for woman suffrage in December 1933.[69]

In early January 1933, soon after Sacasa had taken office, Ildefonso Palma Martínez presented his bill before Congress for a second time.[70] The bill was defeated twenty to three.[71] Possibly in response to the defeat, in 1933

Angelica Balladares Montealegre de Argüello (1872–1973), president of the recently formed Nicaraguan Feminist League, published a pamphlet in support of the vote, titled "Feminist Decalogue, i.e. Ideals and Work Programs That the Nicaraguan Feminist League Tends to Realize."[72] The Nicaraguan Feminist League, along with other suffragist organizations, continued to work for suffrage during this decade, albeit to no avail.

US interference in Nicaraguan elections and Nicaraguan politics clearly had a detrimental effect on women's rights at a time when popular support for the vote was increasing. Even Augusto C. Sandino (1895–1934), the liberal nationalist and anti-imperialist leader that the US Marines were there to defeat, thought highly of feminism in the 1930s. In a letter dated June 10, 1933, to the liberal activist and suffragist María Cristina Zapata, in response to her condolences after the death of his wife, Sandino wrote, "My wife died in childbirth . . . [but] our daughter Blanca Segovia will carry an inheritance of love in her veins and for that reason will lead Nicaraguan feminism in her era. May you and your Interamerican Committee of Women receive my personal goodwill."[73] The US Marines left Nicaragua without defeating Sandino, giving their stand-in, Anastasio Somoza García, the task of killing Sandino, which he accomplished in 1934.

As is often the case, for the people who oversaw this round of US military occupation in Nicaragua, it was just a line in their curriculum vitae—"Nicaragua 1927–1933"—as they moved on to bigger and better assignments. The fact that the occupiers radically changed the course of an entire country's history *for the worse* was most likely not even a blip on their radar. Nicaraguans, meanwhile, continued and continue to suffer the seemingly endless effects of the US meddling in their affairs. While only Sandino and his forces took up arms against the marines, it must be noted that suffragists also took a stand and refused the "favor" of US imperialism.

The Struggle for Suffrage in the Late 1930s, in the Aftermath of US Intervention

In 1936 the newly installed liberal Somoza administration seemed particularly receptive to feminist concerns. Anastasio Somoza García's wife, Salvadora Debayle Sacasa (1895–1987), belonged to many women's organizations.

Moreover, she and her family were personally acquainted with Josefa Toledo de Aguerri. The first lady's father, the medical doctor Luis H. Debayle (1865– 1938), had shared a strong friendship with Toledo de Aguerri based on their mutual devotion to the arts and their service to the poor.[74]

Perhaps due to this long-standing friendship, feminists received encouragement from the extended Somoza family even before Somoza García's ascent to power. In October 1933, Nicaragua's acting minister to the United States, the medical doctor Luis Manuel Debayle Sacasa (the son of Luis H. Debayle), gave a speech to a group of National Woman's Party (NWP) members at their headquarters in Washington, DC.[75] This was the same organization that Juanita Molina de Fromen was involved with. In fact she gave a speech to the NWP around the same time.[76]

Luis Manuel Debayle Sacasa (1894–1983), Anastasio Somoza García's brother-in-law, was familiar with the feminist arguments for suffrage in his country. He summarized them in his presentation: "The Feminists in Nicaragua claim that, inasmuch as the Constitution does not mention sex as a qualification or hindrance to citizenship and its prerogatives, the custom which has excluded women from the vote and, in general, from the right to hold office, has no fundamental basis."[77]

A few years later, in 1939, Somoza García drafted a new and controversial constitution. The most radical article of the new constitution proclaimed that the Nicaraguan state had no official religion. In retaliation, the Catholic Church excommunicated several congressional representatives, including Guillermo Sevilla Sacasa (1908–1997), a main supporter of the new article and Somoza's future son-in-law.[78] Erroneously believing the climate was ripe for feminist change, Toledo de Aguerri participated in the presentation of yet another petition before Nicaragua's Constitutional Assembly on February 23, 1939, urging the Somoza government to make good on its promise, and to grant women suffrage.[79]

Thinking they had considerable support within the seemingly radical Somocista regime, feminists used tactics in this suffrage drive that were different from those used in the 1893 campaign. If during the nineteenth century and early twentieth century men tended to speak for women, this certainly was not the case in 1939. In the "Feminist Petition to the Constitutional [Assembly] Demanding Woman's Rights as Citizen of the Republic," drafted by Toledo de Aguerri, women spoke quite forcefully on their own behalf.[80]

Many independent feminist groups and organizations were involved in drafting this petition, and Josefa Toledo de Aguerri belonged to almost all of them. It was after this attempt failed at winning the vote for women that Josefa Toledo de Aguerri started to be displaced by a new generation of women's rights activists who identified primarily as suffragists. This second generation of suffragists included many of Toledo de Aguerri's former students. Unlike their teacher, however, many of the former pupils tended to be fiercely partisan. This characteristic would radically change the face of women's activism, facilitating the emergence of the Somocista women's movement in the 1950s.[81]

The worldwide economic depression, the devastation caused by the 1931 Managua earthquake, and the conflict between secular liberalism and Catholicism at a time when the Catholic Church was actively organizing women all had a negative effect on the struggle for women's suffrage.

The power of the Catholic Church in Nicaragua was the reason the anticlerical liberal representative Guillermo Sevilla Sacasa gave for his antisuffrage vote in 1939. Although he conceded that feminists had a long history of independent activism, he believed most women would be manipulated by their confessors into voting against their own interests. According to journalist Ignacio Briones (1928–2009), Sevilla Sacasa was so opposed to the vote that he gave the order to ignore feminist protests outside Congress. Briones claimed that Somocista liberals, expecting feminists to continue their protests and in agreement with conservative "accomplices" of the regime, formed groups "of fanatics that were in charge of ridiculing and even offending the women suffragists. In that infamous task they arrived at the sidewalk of the Escuela Normal de Señoritas [which Toledo de Aguerri administered], with posters in which they asked the young women if they would have rather been born men. And they nicknamed them 'Dykes' [*marimachas*]."[82]

Whether most women would have voted for conservative candidates had they been able to vote in 1939 is impossible to tell, although it appears that the Conservative Party believed exactly that and thus supported this particular campaign for the vote. What is clear is that the Liberal Party believed it had nothing to win by giving women the vote at that time, even though party members had just ratified their support for female suffrage in January of that same year during their convention in León.[83]

The Struggle for Suffrage in the 1940s and 1950s

In 1944 the Liberal Party once again "declared [itself] in favor of . . . woman suffrage."[84] Then, in 1945, Representative Roberto González, a liberal who had distanced himself from the Somozas, "presented a bill . . . to grant women equal right with men to vote in national and local elections."[85] The liberal legislators Enoc Aguado (1883–1964) and Adolfo Altamirano Brown also supported the bill.[86] But Somocista liberals defeated the bill, arguing once again that it was not yet the right moment to grant women the vote and that women's dignity could be placed in jeopardy if they were able to vote. In fact, liberals argued, they were voting against woman suffrage as a sign of "respect towards women and the home."[87]

Although the 1945 bill was defeated and two of Nicaragua's most important feminists, Juanita Molina de Fromen and María Gámez, had died, suffrage continued to be discussed in legislative sessions. It would be brought up again in the 1948 and 1950 constitutional debates, with positive results only in the latter debate. According to the *New York Times*, the 1950 constitution was "criticized by leading Nicaraguan women inasmuch as suffrage rights would not be exercised until [the elections of] 1964. Some women [petitioned] Congress for reconsideration of the article and immediate suffrage."[88] As a result, yet another bill proposing suffrage was brought before Congress in May 1953, this time introduced by the conservative legislators Juan Munguía Novoa and José Antonio Artiles.[89] That effort also failed. The liberals in power, who theoretically supported the vote, continued to be wary of women voters, even in 1953, since they felt women could not be fully trusted to vote for the PLN. That would soon change with the formation of a women's wing within the PLN in 1954.[90]

After submitting the proposal for suffrage nine times, in 1893, 1930, 1932, 1933, 1939, 1945, 1948, 1950, and 1953, women finally gained the vote on April 20, 1955, and voted for the first time on February 3, 1957. How did it happen?

One of the factors that influenced the eventual outcome was that in 1945 suffragists decided to renew and centralize their efforts by organizing the "Central Feminine Committee Pro-Woman's Vote."[91] Moreover, many other women were lobbying for the vote, often within their political parties. In short, women's organizing made an important difference.

To understand how women's activism helped them finally gain the vote, the following must be stressed: independent feminists like Josefa Toledo de Aguerri continued to be active in the 1950s, *and* suffragists of all political persuasions joined together in the Central Feminine Committee. Equally important, however, is that partisan women's organizations (often led by suffragists), such as the women's wing of the PLN (the Ala Femenina del Partido Liberal), were founded in the early 1950s. Male politicians of all political leanings were enthusiastic about creating women's wings in their organizations. By 1955 they understood that to fully take advantage of women's political potential, they needed to give women the right to vote.[92]

In 1950, when liberal attorney Joaquina Vega presented before Congress the "Exposition in Favor of the Vote for the Nicaraguan Woman" on behalf of the Central Feminine Committee and the Nicaraguan Feminist League, the vote that would eventually approve suffrage was only five years away.[93] In 1953 an article in *La Prensa* noted the extent of women's organizing and lobbying: "Since various feminist organizations requested it, it will not be until Thursday that the bill to grant the Nicaraguan woman the active vote will be presented for consideration. . . . Those organizations want to take advantage of the time to conduct intense propaganda work and try to bring many supporters to . . . Congress. . . . Doña Chepita de Aguerri's signature is first, followed by many more."[94]

In 1953 the Central Feminine Committee made its widest suffragist appeal yet, not to the legislators but to "all the Feminine Associations, and all the women of goodwill, to attend . . . the National Congress and support the petition this committee has sent demanding the exercise of the feminine vote."[95] This type of grassroots effort helped women achieve the vote. However, it was women's partisan organizing that would prevail in the long run.

Who Were the Men Who Supported Suffrage?

Male legislators played a significant role in the push for suffrage, and a subset of them were married to suffragists. The liberal medical doctor Roberto González Dubon (1895–1959), for instance, was married to Mercedes Lopez Roig (1903–?), one of the more than seventy-two suffragists who signed the "Exposition in Favor of the Vote" that Attorney Joaquina Vega presented to Congress in 1950. The conservative attorney Eduardo Abellino Conrado Vado (1906–2000) was married to María Encarnación Gómez Saballos, who also signed the document. The liberal attorney Ildefonso Palma Martínez (1900–1978) was married to Inés Ibarra; he also signed the "Exposition."[96]

The liberal medical doctor and mason Rodolfo Espinosa R., who was among the legislators who supported suffrage in the 1930s, was married to Leonor de Mezzerville Ossaye (1877–1935), a teacher of French at Josefa Toledo de Aguerri's Colegio de Señoritas. She died before suffrage was passed in Nicaragua, but her sister in Costa Rica, the very famous feminist and suffragist Esther de Mezzerville Ossaye (1885–1971), lived long enough to see all women in Central America achieve the right to vote.[97]

Several of the younger liberal legislators, such as Palma and González, left the pro-Somoza PLN and joined the PLI, which had been founded in the 1940s. The conservative legislator Conrado Vado also opposed the Somoza dictatorship, at least in the 1940s, and suffered greatly for it. This is not to say, however, that there were no liberal pro-Somoza legislators who supported suffrage before 1953. The attorney Mariano Valle Quintero (1910–1979) was one of them. He gave a speech on behalf of women's suffrage in deliberations on the vote in 1950 even though his party's leaders opposed the vote at that time.[98]

Of course, being married to suffragists did not necessarily turn men into suffragists. Moreover, the individual political opinions of most people change—if only slightly—over time, and some individuals presumably started out against suffrage and eventually changed their minds.

Conclusion: The Legacy and Importance of Women's Suffrage in Nicaragua

I have argued elsewhere that in several important ways, the legacy of first wave feminism in western and central Nicaragua was nondemocratic and that this contributed, in part, to its erasure from the national imaginary. Power struggles were common among first wave feminists, and they were ultimately unable to create transparent organizations that held periodic elections. As expected, some of the conflicts among feminists were partisan ones, based on real differences regarding the significance they attached to suffrage. But there were also disagreements over how some feminists exercised leadership.

Ironically, Josefa Toledo de Aguerri's longevity and personality most likely were two of the factors that prevented a more dynamic and democratic feminist movement from emerging. Like all other organizations of the period, the many groups she founded centralized power and lacked procedures to derive consensus and foster new leadership. It is said that to last as long as she did in the public limelight, Toledo de Aguerri had a forceful personality. Indeed, she was called a "benevolent dictator" by those close to her. Eventually, Toledo de Aguerri was relegated in Nicaraguan memory to being a "teacher of generations." Few of her former students remembered her as a feminist, or even a suffragist, in the late 1990s.[99]

Understandably, the fact that so many suffragists and/or feminists were members of the nation's political and economic elites, and that they espoused the racism and classism that permeated their social class, has made their story uninteresting and even repulsive to some Nicaraguans. That so many suffragists and/or feminists went on to support the Somozas and benefit greatly from Somocismo has also made their stories seem to be simple ones of privilege.

Additionally, since voting in fraudulent elections under the Somozas was understood to be a farce by so many Nicaraguans, the story of how women achieved the right to vote has not received the attention it deserves. It certainly has not attracted the academic attention that the story of women who took up arms against the Somozas has gotten. However, the struggle for women's suffrage (in western and central Nicaragua *and* on the Caribbean Coast) is central to any story told about women in Nicaragua. It reveals the contradictions and complexities in women's lives.

Specifically, the history of suffragists in western and central Nicaragua reveals the ways in which many elite women made enormous sacrifices to bring greater rights (such as the vote) to other women while benefiting simultaneously from the (class and racial) oppression of those same women. This kind of nuanced story usually gets told only about elite men. But the story of elite women who oppressed others is an equally important human story, which is also about incredibly flawed and contradictory human beings who sometimes did great things.

Notes

1. Cited in Cobo del Arco, "Populismo, somocismo y el voto femenino: Nicaragua, 1936–1955," 153. All translations are my own.
2. Eduardo Arellano, *Maria Cristina Zapata*, 91.
3. "Aprobar el siguiente decreto de la Convención Mosquita," Enrique Bolaños Biblioteca, https://sajurin.enriquebolanos.org/docs/CLR%20-%201893–1895%20-%2026.pdf, accessed September 25, 2023.
4. "Aprobar el siguiente decreto de la Convención Mosquita."
5. J. Hernández Somoza, *Curso de Derecho Constitucional Nicaragüense* (Managua: Tipografía Nacional, 1896), 78.
6. "El lenguaje de los números. Elecciones supervigiladas," Enrique Bolaños Biblioteca, https://sajurin.enriquebolanos.org/docs/4.pdf, accessed September 19, 2023.
7. Letter from US consul S. C. Braida to Lewis Baker, Bluefields, March 21, 1894. *The Executive Documents of the House of Representatives for the Third Session of the Fifty-Third Congress, 1894–1895* (Washington, DC: Government Printing Office, 1895), 256–58, https://babel.hathitrust.org/cgi/pt?id=uc1.31210011005293&view=1up&seq=281&skin=2021&q1=mosquito. See also p. 267.
8. Francisco Montenegro was called a "fanático visionario" by the conservative Enrique Guzmán (1843–1911). Franco Cerutti, ed., *Enrique Guzmán: Escritos históricos y políticos*, Vol. 3 (San José: Libro Libre, 1988), 53.
9. "Diario Político y de Variedades," *El 93*. September 1, 1916.
10. See González-Rivera, *Before the Revolution*, and Montenegro, "El voto femenino en Nicaragua."
11. Cobo del Arco, "Populismo, somocismo y el voto femenino," 155.
12. Montenegro, "El voto femenino en Nicaragua."
13. See González-Rivera, *Before the Revolution*, and Baltodano Marcenaro "Ciudadanas por y para la dictadura."
14. See González-Rivera, *Before the Revolution*, 2011.

15. For more on the "triumph" of mestizaje in Nicaragua, see Jeffrey L. Gould, *To Die in This Way: Nicaraguan Indians and the Myth of Mestizaje, 1880–1965* (Durham, NC: Duke University Press, 1998). See also Juliet Hooker "'Beloved Enemies': Race and Official Mestizo Nationalism in Nicaragua," *Latin American Research Review* 40, no. 3 (2005).

16. As is true with other countries covered in this book, Nicaragua might have been classified differently. Many of the elements of the imperialism scenario appear in Nicaragua's history as well. It is important to keep in mind that the classification system presented here is a somewhat artificial tool for illuminating certain aspects of history that are shared by some countries and not others. We do not want to overstate the case.

17. See González-Rivera and Kampwirth, *Diversidad Sexual en el Pacífico y Centro de Nicaragua*.

18. For more on rural women's employment, see Teresa Cobo del Arco, "La exclusión de las mujeres de Nicaragua durante la primera mitad del siglo XX," in Dalla Corte, *Homogeneidad, Diferencia y Exclusión en América*, 237–48.

19. Ruchwarger, *People in Power*, 199.

20. Vilas, *Sandinista Revolution*, 103.

21. González-Rivera, *Before the Revolution*, 2011.

22. García and Gomariz, *Mujeres centroamericanas ante la crisis*, 329.

23. *Censo General de 1920. Administración del General Chamorro* (Managua: Tipografía Nacional, 1920).

24. González-Rivera, *Before the* Revolution, 2011.

25. González-Rivera, 2011.

26. González-Rivera, 2011; Cobo del Arco, "La exclusión de las mujeres de Nicaragua durante la primera mitad del siglo XX."

27. J. D. Mondragón, "Rebelión de la mujer," *La Tribuna*, August 14, 1921.

28. See, for example, the exhortations of Monsignor José Antonio Lezcano y Ortega (1865–1952) in González-Rivera and Kampwirth, *Diversidad Sexual en el Pacífico y Centro de Nicaragua* 2021, 199–200.

29. González-Rivera, *Before the Revolution*, 2011.

30. Although legal racial distinctions technically disappeared after independence, the 1920 census still differentiated by color categories: Black, white, *trigueño*, *cobrizo*, and yellow (*amarillo*). *Censo General de 1920*.

31. *Código Civil de la República de Nicaragua 1867*, 24.

32. *Código Civil de la República de Nicaragua 1867*, 33.

33. Carmen Diana Deere and Magdalena de Leon, "Liberalism and Married Women's Property Rights in 19th Century Latin America., *Hispanic American Historical Review* 85, no. 4 (2005).

34. *Código Civil de la República de Nicaragua 1867*, 24.

35. *Código Civil de la República de Nicaragua 1867*, 24.

36. *Código Civil de la República de Nicaragua 1867*, 24.

37. *Código Civil de la República de Nicaragua 1867*, 26.
38. *Código Civil de la República de Nicaragua 1867*, 26.
39. *Código de Comercio de la República de Nicaragua 1914*.
40. The 1904 civil code is sometimes referred to as the 1903 civil code.
41. *Código Civil de la República de Nicaragua 1904*, 17.
42. For the earliest use of the word in Nicaragua, see Benjamín Cuadra's antifeminist thesis *Situación jurídica de la mujer nicaragüense* (Granada, Nicaragua: Tipografía de "El Centro Americano," 1905), 16, 18.
43. *Constitución y Leyes de Reforma de la República de Nicaragua 1893–1894–1895* (Managua: Tipografía Nacional, 1896), 149–50.
44. González-Rivera, *Before the Revolution*.
45. Nicaraguan women who married foreigners lost their Nicaraguan citizenship.
46. González-Rivera, *Before the Revolution*, 49.
47. "Instrucción Pública," *Aurora de Nicaragua* 2 (1837): 2.
48. González-Rivera, *Before the Revolution*, 33.
49. González-Rivera, 34.
50. González-Rivera, 34.
51. González-Rivera, 34.
52. Juanita Molina de Fromen to Alice Paul, March 21, 1930, MC 199, Box 102, Folder 1337, Alice Paul Papers, Schlesinger Library, Harvard University, Cambridge, MA.
53. Juanita Molina de Fromen to Alice Paul, March 21, 1930, MC 199, Box 102, Folder 1337 Alice Paul Papers, Schlesinger Library, Harvard University, Cambridge, MA.
54. "Cuadro General del Censo de la República de Nicaragua por Instrucción y su Porcentaje," Censo General de 1920, https://ccp.ucr.ac.cr/bvp/pdf/censos/nc1920.pdf, accessed July 9, 2021.
55. For more on Moncada's sexist views, see González-Rivera and Kampwirth, *Diversidad Sexual en el Pacífico y Centro de Nicaragua*, 182–183.
56. Henry L. Stimson, *American Policy in Nicaragua* (New York: C. Scribner's Sons, 1927), 54.
57. Eduardo Arellano, *María Cristina Zapata*, 76.
58. "Conversations with Alice Paul: Woman Suffrage and the Equal Rights Amendment," Online Archive of California, https://oac.cdlib.org/view?docId=kt6f59n89c&doc.view=entire_text, accessed September 19, 2023.
59. Henry L. Stimson, "Suffrage Not a Natural Right," *New York Times*, June 12, 1915.
60. Letter from María Gámez to Doris Stevens, June 17, 1932, MC 546, Doris Stevens Papers, Schlesinger Library, Harvard University, Cambridge, MA.
61. Letter from María Gámez to Doris Stevens.
62. A. J. Bacevich, *Diplomat in Khaki. Major General Frank Ross McCoy and American Foreign Policy, 1898–1949* (Lawrence: University Press of Kansas, 1989), 126.

63. Albin Krebs, "Matthew B. Ridgway Dies at 98," *New York Times*, July 27, 1993.
64. *New York Times*, September 27, 1932, 12. María Gómez was actually María Gámez, daughter of Nicaragua's pioneer historian and liberal politician José Dolores Gámez Guzmán (1851–1918). Poet Helena Ramos first alerted me to this mistake.
65. Letters from María Gámez to Doris Stevens, June 17, 1932, June 27, 1932, MC 546, Box 83, Doris Stevens Papers, Schlesinger Library, Harvard University, Cambridge, MA. The second letter had the bill in favor of suffrage as an attachment.
66. Letters from María Gámez to Doris Stevens.
67. Espinosa Ramírez, as quoted in Borge de Sotomayor, *La mujer y el derecho*, 62.
68. Espinosa Ramírez would also serve as mayor of Managua and foreign minister under liberal president José Santos Zelaya. Olga Madriz de Mézerville, "Descendencia de la Casa de Mézerville a los 109 años de su llegada a Costa Rica," *Revista Electrónica de la Academia Costarricense de Ciencias Genealógicas* 3 (May 2007): 46, http://www.geocities.ws/picasso2k/pdf/revistas/ACCG-revista003.pdf
69. Borge de Sotomayor, *La mujer y el derecho*, 62.
70. Cobo del Arco, "Populismo, somocismo y el voto femenino," 156.
71. "Nicaragua Bars Votes for Women" *New York Times*, January 8, 1933, 3.
72. Borge de Sotomayor, *La mujer y el derecho*, 62.
73. Eduardo Arellano, *Maria Cristina Zapata*, 86–87.
74. González-Rivera, *Before the Revolution*, 43.
75. Debayle, "The Status of Women in Nicaragua."
76. Letter from Gunnar Fromen to Doris Stevens, December 22, 1934, MC 546, Box 83, Doris Stevens Papers Schlesinger Library, Harvard University, Cambridge, MA.
77. Debayle, "The Status of Women in Nicaragua," 238.
78. Cole Chamorro, *145 años de historia política*, 122–23.
79. Toledo de Aguerri, *Educación y feminismo*, 25.
80. Toledo de Aguerri, 21, 24.
81. González-Rivera, *Before the Revolution*.
82. Briones "Las mujeres nicaragüenses ayer y hoy."
83. "Ask Vote for Nicaraguan Women," *New York Times*, January 20, 1939, 9.
84. "Nicaragua Liberals Act: Convention Favors Presidential Re-Election and Woman Suffrage," *New York Times*, January 11, 1944, 5.
85. "Women's Vote Bill in Nicaragua," *New York Times*, May 9, 1945, 14; see also Cobo del Arco, 2008, 157.
86. "El somocismo, llevado de pura fuerzas a conceder el voto a las mujeres," *La Prensa*, February 7, 1954.
87. As quoted in Cobo del Arco, "Populismo, somocismo y el voto femenino," 157–58.

88. "Nicaraguan Women Seek the Vote," *New York Times*, August 17, 1950, 17.

89. "Voto de la Mujer," *La Prensa*, May 28, 1953. See also, "Reglamentación del voto femenino va al Congreso," *La Prensa*, May 23, 1953, 1, 3.

90. See González-Rivera, *Before the Revolution*; Cobo del Arco, "Populismo, somocismo y el voto femenino," 2008; Baltodano Marcenaro "Ciudadanas por y para la dictadura"; Montenegro "El voto femenino en Nicaragua."

91. "Acta Constitutiva del Comité Femenino Pro-Voto de la Mujer de Nicaragua," *La Nueva Prensa*, January 10, 1946, 12.

92. See González-Rivera, *Before the Revolution*; Cobo del Arco, "Populismo, somocismo y el voto femenino"; Baltodano Marcenaro "Ciudadanas por y para la dictadura"; Montenegro, "El voto femenino en Nicaragua."

93. Vega, "Exposición Del Comité Central Femenino."

94. "Voto de la Mujer," *La Prensa*, May 28, 1953.

95. "Voto de la Mujer."

96. Vega, "Exposición Del Comité Central Femenino," 9–10.

97. Madriz de Mézerville, "Descendencia de la Casa de Mézerville," 6–49.

98. "Vigésima Novena Sesión de la Asamblea Nacional Constituyente," *La Gaceta* 188 (September 7, 1950).

99. González-Rivera, *Before the Revolution*, 2011.

Scenario IV

PERCEIVED CONSERVATIVE STRATEGIC ADVANTAGE

Examples: Ecuador, Peru

The Conservative Strategic Advantage Scenario is the inverse of the Delayed Liberal Scenario. If liberals claimed to support feminism and feminists but feared the consequences of enfranchising conservative women, conservatives defended traditional roles for women yet sometimes saw potential advantages to enfranchising them. In this scenario conservatives, who may have been responsible for persecuting progressive feminists, as in the Peruvian case, took advantage of a presumed political advantage by enfranchising women. This section discusses Ecuador and Peru, but it is possible that Honduras and El Salvador belong in this category as well.

Prior to 1919, Catholic women's organizations regularly engaged in charity as well as movements for social welfare reform, but they did not advocate for women's political rights. On the contrary, Catholics everywhere argued for the preservation of women's traditional roles. In 1919, however, Pope Benedict XV grudgingly acknowledged that voting rights for women were a "social necessity in some countries, that is in order to counter the generally subversive votes of the socialists."[1] In 1931 Uruguayan Damas Católicas leader Nélida Madoz de Barthesagui wrote, "No party is in more need of votes than the Catholic, and we must counteract the effect that Freethinker women will bring to other parties."[2]

Here it is important to avoid duplicating two tired tropes, both of which stem from the period of the suffrage movements. The first originated with progressive feminists themselves, who viewed conservative women as either insufficiently informed or victims of ideological manipulation. In this sense, ironically, conservatives were sometimes more ready to acknowledge women's full rationality and political agency than liberals. However, women's supposed special vulnerability to manipulation proved to be such a compelling narrative that it was adapted to other political contexts, such as Peronist Argentina, and hauled out whenever it was convenient to explain any unfavorable electoral dynamic. The notion persists to this day.

The second trope has to do with the presumption of Latin American women's conservativism in particular. During the formation of the pan-American feminist movement, US suffragists reproduced and recontextualized imperialist assumptions about the relationship between themselves and their Latin American counterparts. The US view that Latin Americans were passive in the pursuit of women's rights, often expressed in racialized renderings of the cliché of the "naturally" conservative Catholic Latin American woman, penetrated early historiography on feminism. This assumption, like that of women's supposed manipulability, has proved challenging to dislodge. These disclaimers notwithstanding, conservatives who opposed feminism on principle did sometimes see women's suffrage as strategically useful. Conservative women should not be construed as passive or manipulated. Their political agency and electoral power should not be interpreted any differently than that of any other group.

Notes

1. Pollard, *Unknown Pope Benedict XV*, 174. Pius XII later issued similar instructions to women to counteract the perceived communist threat.
2. "Graciela Sapriza, "El voto femenino en Uruguay, 1900–1932," in Barry, *Sufragio Femenino*, 69; my translation. Original text: "Ningún partido está más necesitado de votos que el católico y hay que contrarrestar el efecto de los nuevos votos que aportarán a los demás partidos las mujeres librepensadoras."

CHAPTER TEN

Without Consideration of Their Sex?

The Uneven Path to Female Suffrage in Ecuador, ca. 1883–1940

ERIN E. O'CONNOR

IN 1924 MATILDE HIDALGO DE Procel petitioned the electoral board in her home canton of Machala, Ecuador, so that she could register to vote. She based her appeal on the fact that an individual had to be over twenty-one years of age and literate to vote in Ecuador; the law said nothing about being male. This unprecedented request set off a series of events, summarized by Minister of Interior Francisco Ochoa Ortiz:

> Matilde Hidalgo de Procel presented herself and asked to be registered in order to exercise the right to vote in elections. The board consented to this petition, registering the said señora on May 2 of this year; But as it was an unusual act, the president of this organization consulted my office regarding the legality of the procedure. To that query I answered on May 8 that there was no legal prohibition for women to be inscribed in the Electoral Register; And that consequently the said señora should be registered, as she had requested in the exercise of her rights.
>
> The Council of Machala . . . asked me to consult with the State Council on the legality of [this request], since [they were] of the opinion that

there was no express law granting political rights to Ecuadorian women, nor any rule to abide by. This consultation was copied to the State Council and at its meeting on June 9 of this year, [the Council] unanimously decided that women have the right to register to vote, and to vote and be elected, if they meet the other requirements demanded by our Political Constitution; That is, that citizenship is a right that corresponds to and can be exercised by both men and women.[1]

Hidalgo registered and voted that year. Five years later, the 1929 constitution included the phrase "without consideration of their sex" in its description of age and literacy requirements for voting. Ecuador therefore has the distinction of being the first country in mainland Latin America to grant (literate) women the right to vote in national elections.

A particular point of pride for many middle- and upper-class Ecuadorians was the idea that women had gained the vote without strife. In October 1929, a report in the Quito daily newspaper *El Comercio* contrasted the Ecuadorian path to the vote with the contentious British suffrage campaign headed by Sylvia Pankhurst, remarking, "In Ecuador [the right to vote] has not been the cause of any sacrifice [on women's part]. Nor has it been requested, nor has it been fought against. It was recorded in the fundamental letter perhaps unconsciously."[2] While Ecuador lacked a robust women's suffrage movement, it was hardly the case that women were passive recipients of the vote or that its passage came without conflict. Discussions of female suffrage began in the 1880s and continued even after the right was officially granted to literate women in 1929. Arguments for and against the women's vote evolved in relation to changes in politics, society, and the economy, and Ecuadorian women took an active part on both sides of these debates.

Until recently, most historians presumed that Ecuadorian women gained the right to vote in national elections as part of a conservative political strategy, often citing Rafael Quintero's 1983 book on populism and the rise of the modern state in Ecuador.[3] Quintero claimed that women's movements were too weak to influence debates on the female vote and that Matilde Hidalgo de Procel's actions had only a local rather than a national impact on the question. He instead proposed that the highland landowning class, working through the Conservative Party, played the decisive role in granting women the right to vote in national elections. Highland elites expected literate middle- and upper-class women to side with conservatives due to the influence that church officials held over them. Taking this view as fact, Quintero proposed that women helped bring conservative presidents to power in the 1930s. He based his claim on the fact that more women registered to vote in the (conservative) highlands than along the (liberal) coast and that there was a greater increase in female than in male voting during the period.[4]

Newer studies have called Quintero's analysis into question. Mercedes Prieto and Ana María Goetschel indicated a variety of factors, including women's own demands and actions, which culminated in the 1929 law granting women the right to vote. They further contend that conservatives were not the sole advocates of female suffrage in the 1920s because many liberals supported women's right to vote. Liberal resistance to female suffrage, they claimed, only developed as a result of the political volatility of the 1930s. Most important, Prieto and Goetschel maintain that far from upholding conservative aims, female suffrage questioned dominant gender norms and blurred the boundaries between public and private spheres.[5] Similarly, Raquel Rodas Morales examined the history of female suffrage within the context of feminist movements, arguing that even if women did not have direct input in political debates over suffrage, their struggle for the vote mattered. In her view, "Women won the vote, it was not granted to them."[6] Unlike Prieto and Goetschel, Rodas analyzed the ways in which female suffrage both challenged and employed dominant concepts regarding masculinity and femininity.[7] Neither of these studies definitively disproves the Conservative Strategic Advantage: conservative support was crucial to the passage of female suffrage, and conservative backing likely rested on a widely held assumption that women were inherently more conservative than men. Nevertheless, these works provide a nuanced understanding of female suffrage in Ecuador that pays close attention to women's agency and to the changing political climate over the course of time.

Recent scholarship on the women's vote highlights several problems with Quintero's analysis. Quintero assumed rather than proved that only a large and unified women's movement could influence the debate over female suffrage. His readiness to view women as pawns in political conflicts certainly

reflected male politicians' assumptions, but it reinforced gender stereotypes without presenting rigorous historical analysis.[8] Even if more highland than coastal women registered to vote in the 1930s, that is not definitive
proof that those who registered were conservative. Despite these limitations, Quintero's discussion of female suffrage remains relevant insofar as
it reminds us not to overstate the importance of allowing literate women to
vote. Most Ecuadorians, including most women, were still disenfranchised
by the literacy requirement tied to the vote, and many people who were eligible to vote found it difficult to register or have their votes counted.[9]
Although Indigenous peoples were the group least likely to have access to
education, literacy rates were also low among the urban and (especially)
rural poor more generally.[10] Finally, although many liberals supported
female suffrage when it came to a vote in 1929, they had previously used
gender stereotypes to deny women the vote (and would do so again in the
1930s).

This essay builds upon existing scholarship by focusing on how discourses on the women's vote changed over time. Rather than look at how
female suffrage challenged dominant gender norms, I explore how dominant gender norms shaped both legislative and feminist arguments about
suffrage. I am also interested in how concerns about gender and voting
compared with those about race and class. Central questions explored:
How did dominant gender norms and laws shape discourses on female
suffrage? Why did these debates begin within the Delayed Liberal Scenario
and end with discussions and practices that better fit the Perceived Conservative Strategic Advantage? How might concerns over race and class
have influenced deliberations regarding the women's vote? I contend that
liberal and conservative politicians' shifting positions over time were not
based solely on their ideological differences or power struggles with each
other, or even on the relative stability of the state. Their stances on the
female vote were also shaped by the rise of feminist, Indigenous, populist,
and leftist movements in the 1920s and 1930s. Liberal and conservative
politicians played these different groups off each other, while activists
took advantage of contradictory political discourses whenever possible.
The checkered history of suffrage in Ecuador reflects a broader pattern in
many Latin American countries in which legislatures granted the right to

vote either to literate women or to men across class and race lines—but not to both groups at once.

Citizenship, Gender, and Race in the Nineteenth Century

The first five Ecuadorian constitutions, drafted from 1830 to 1869, did not explicitly exclude women from voting. Citizenship and voting requirements stipulated only that one had to be of majority age, know how to read and write, and have anywhere from two hundred to three hundred pesos in property. This oversight was common throughout the Atlantic world in the late eighteenth and nineteenth centuries, when women's exclusion from politics was assumed rather than debated and civil codes reinforced husbands' rights to rule over their homes and control their wives' economic and civil interests.[11] The 1860 Ecuadorian civil code, for example, identified married women as legal dependents and gave husbands control of all marital goods as well as the responsibility to represent their wives' civil and financial interests. A wife could act directly on her own behalf only with her husband's—or, in his absence, a judge's—authorization (permission that could be revoked at any time). The explanation given for these limited female rights in the public sphere in the 1860 civil code was that "the husband is the master of conjugal society, and as such he freely administers his wife's worldly goods."[12] Women were important to the nation, but in their capacity as wives and mothers, with husbands or fathers serving as mediators between the state and the family.[13]

However, nineteenth-century politicians were concerned with the continuation of racial inequality through the collection of Indian tribute, a head tax aimed at Indigenous men between the ages of eighteen and sixty. Tribute was a holdover from the Spanish colonial regime, in which Spanish and Indigenous peoples had differing rights and obligations before the state. Both liberals and conservatives loathed the continued collection of tribute because it contradicted their proclaimed goal of equality before the law. Nevertheless, they kept the tax in place until 1857 because it accounted for a large portion of government revenue in difficult economic times.[14] Although they did not discuss it openly, government officials' debates over Indigenous

men's status in the new nation were rife with gender concerns. Many officials calling for the abolition of tribute contended that the tax not only got
in the way of equality before the law but also kept Indigenous men from
fulfilling their patriarchal duties to provide for their families. At the same
time, political and intellectual elites justified Indigenous men's political and
social marginalization by describing them as childlike and in need of protection and guidance.[15]

The first time that Ecuadorian legislators discussed the women's vote
was 1883. In the middle of a debate over whether to do away with literacy
restrictions for voting, a conservative legislator observed that the law did
not explicitly ban women from voting and thus opened a discussion of
women's rights under the constitution. The 1869 constitution stated that in
order to vote, one had to be a citizen (*ciudadano*), at least twenty-one years
old (or married), and able to read and write. Legislators in 1883 centered
their debate over women on the meaning of the term *ciudadano*: in the plural, *ciudadanos* could mean either men or men and women; the question
was whether the singular term *ciudadano* was equally ambiguous or clearly
indicated a man. Some legislators feared that without identifying suffrage
as an exclusively male right, women would have a loophole through which
they could vote. As Luis Felipe Borja put it, "In the Constitution everything
must be clear and determined, so that there is no place for interpretation.
. . . Therefore, it should read expressly 'all Ecuadorian men.'" Borja insisted
that women's specific exclusion did not undermine their rights because
"they are not called, by nature, for politics but for the home."[16] Not all
assembly members agreed that it was necessary to clarify that only men
could vote. Nicolás Arizaga, for example, thought that adding "male"
would be both redundant and in bad taste, because it was already clear
that women did not belong in politics.[17] Despite their different interpretations on wording, Borja and Arizaga agreed that there was a palpable
danger that any woman who transgressed the private/public divide to participate in politics threatened to become a *marimacho*, a "mannish" and
"unnatural" woman.[18] Following the debate, the assembly voted to add
wording to clarify that only men who were over twenty-one and literate
were eligible to vote.[19]

Liberals and Gender in the Early Twentieth Century: Rights but Not Votes

When coastal liberals came to power in 1895, they reopened the question of women's and Indigenous people's rights before the law. Eloy Alfaro was particularly concerned with addressing women's rights, which he identified with the broader liberal mission in an 1897 speech:

> Nothing today is so painful as the condition of woman in our country, where she is relegated to domestic work, [and] constrained in her sphere of intellectual [activity] and even more in the manner in which she can independently and honestly earn a living. . . . In Ecuador, especially, nothing has been done to improve woman's condition; it is not right that an illustrious Assembly composed of liberals should close its sessions without having even initiated reform in this cause.[20]

It was during Alfaro's presidential terms (1895–1901, 1906–1911) that the legislature passed laws to establish civil marriage and divorce, expand public education, and allow women the right to maintain control of wealth they brought into marriage.

Alfaro's position on women's rights was inspired by US laws advancing women's education and the right to work. He was also responding to women who supported the liberals' rise to power, most of whom fought simultaneously for the liberal cause and for their own advancement.[21] Yet if Alfaro was rewarding women for their support and was perhaps genuinely concerned with women's plight, his call for gender reforms was also self-serving. Women were pivotal to the liberal goal of building a strong secular state that could challenge the power of the Catholic Church; civil marriage laws cut into the church's social control, while educational reforms advanced secular over religious schooling.[22] Moreover, liberal emphasis on women's supposed "liberation" did not necessarily challenge dominant gender norms. Alfaro himself assured legislators that educational and work reforms for women would enhance rather than undermine women's roles in the domestic sphere as wives and mothers.[23] Similarly, women who wanted to take advantage of a 1911 law that allowed them to maintain control of goods that they brought into marriage had to declare their intent in a public (notarized) document and register any immovable assets in the public registry. The default legal arrangement was still to have husbands administer and control all marital goods. There is no doubt that many liberal legislators supported these reforms as a means of improving women's lives, but the changes fell far short of recognizing women as independent and equal individuals before the law. Instead, legislators assumed that women would assert their right to economic independence or divorce only if their husbands failed to fulfill their patriarchal duties to provide and protect.[24] They expected that in most cases women would remain under their husbands' supervision.

The tension between advancing women's rights and maintaining patriarchal order was evident in the 1910 debate over female suffrage. Although the 1906 constitution did not state that one had to be male to vote, its wording was based on a 1904 debate in which legislators decided that women's exclusion from the vote was already presumed.[25] When the proposal to extend the suffrage to women came before the Chamber of Deputies in 1910, a few legislators argued for universal suffrage, but most of the bill's supporters considered extending the vote only to women who could read and write. Nicolás López, for example, strongly identified (literate) female suffrage with the Liberal Party's emphasis on individual rights and equality before the law when he declared,

> Woman is called upon to share responsibility for the family in the home, therefore why would she not enjoy equally in civil and political rights with man? Will it be the liberal party that will deny this right, against the text of the Constitution, created by those who called themselves liberals, a text that states that to be a citizen, one simply has to prove a capacity to read and write, without referring to sex?[26]

In the same passage, López also claimed that opponents of the bill disliked it because it "does not conform to antiquated ideas, outdated ideas from the colonial period, in which women were considered inferior to men in every way."[27] His arguments identified liberals as both defenders of women's rights and as the only party that could modernize the nation.

The bill's opponents insisted that the women's vote would lead to political and social upheaval. Ángel Borja Cordero was particularly adamant when he claimed that the woman's vote would be "a bloody mockery of citizens' rights, because if it is not possible for all men to vote, are we going to permit women to do so? I insist that this proposal is a joke, and that we cannot allow it to pass to a second debate."[28] He expanded on his opposition to the women's vote by declaring, "To remove woman from the sacred obligations of the home and mix her up in public affairs, about which the poor little things don't know anything in the least; to throw them into the maelstrom of our corrupt politics—this is nothing less, Mr. President, than to beg for the moral corruption of the Ecuadorian woman, who carries the banner of morality in South America."[29]

Borja Cordero's argument rested on dominant gender norms that identified women with the home, and his concern was echoed by other critics of the proposal. They argued that crossing from the private into the public sphere would corrupt women, and since women upheld national morality, their downfall threatened society at large. Borja Cordero even cautioned that because women were under the direct power of men, they would vote however their husbands, fathers, or brothers told them to vote.[30] Opponents of the bill emphasized that even the most civilized nations did not grant women the right to vote in national elections, suggesting that it was not a matter that needed consideration in Ecuador. At the same time, they raised the specter of militant suffragettes in England to call upon their colleagues' fears of the marimacho, implying that the vote might create a similar group of purportedly unnatural women in their own nation. The bill's supporters tried to reassure their colleagues that women would not abandon the home or other feminine virtues if granted suffrage rights, but the opposition prevailed.

The 1910 suffrage debate shows that it is too simple to say that liberals either did or did not want to give women the right to vote. It was, after all, a group of liberals who proposed extending the vote to women in the first place, while another group joined the conservative opposition to defeat the bill. Instead, the 1910 debate over female suffrage reveals a tension among legislators about exactly what it should mean to liberate women. Liberals from different regions and with distinct agendas came together fairly easily when advancing women's rights dovetailed with their shared goal of limiting the power of the church, though even then some legislators were wary of straying too far from Catholic teachings.[31] However, legislators from both parties supported dominant gender norms that identified women with the home. To pass laws increasing women's rights or independence, lawmakers had to offer compelling arguments about how and why such changes would not overturn patriarchal structures. Female suffrage crossed a line between public and private spheres, threatening patriarchal order by granting literate women rights that many men did not enjoy.

Multiple Feminisms and the Question of the Vote

The expansion of feminism in the early twentieth century was likely related at least in part to liberal reforms, even if women's presumed "emancipation" fell short of transforming gender norms. Liberal policies also indirectly fostered feminism by providing women with more education and work experiences, which in turn gave women—particularly middle-class women— greater knowledge of politics and experience in the public sphere.[32] Although Ecuador lacked a well-organized suffrage movement, Ecuadorian feminists engaged actively with the question of voting rights. Historian Ana María Goetschel noted that there were multiple feminist discourses and agendas in early twentieth-century Ecuador. Some of them sought equality with men and political rights; others focused on gender complementarity rather than equality, calling for women's social and educational advancement but not political rights. Both types of feminists wanted to improve women's conditions in Ecuador, and both worked within the constraints of the power structures and discourses of their times.[33] These various viewpoints led to multiple and conflicting feminist stances on the question of the female vote.

On one end of the spectrum of feminisms and voting rights was Zoila Rendón. Her 1925 essay on women, society, and politics asserted that a woman should develop her faculties and intelligence but "without deviating from her destiny and by embracing the purpose for which she was created. We do not intend to make ourselves equal to men in their steely character, their warrior spirit, their love of politics."[34] In her view, this did not mean that women had to be apolitical but rather that "woman is capable of being more political than man without leaving her family and social environment, where she acts through her education and virtue. But when, due to political mistakes, she leaves the gentle pleasures and solicitous care that the mother gives to her husband, children, and friendships, and throws herself into the public sphere, it sours all her delicacy of heart, turning it to restlessness before the contradictions of political parties and political turbulence."[35]

Although Rendón stressed that women belonged in the home rather than politics, she was adamant in her belief that a woman deserved to be treated as a "man's companion, not his slave" and that women had the right to education and dignity. She also believed that women could better advance their interests by winning over men's hearts through their work in the home than they ever could through the ballot box.[36] Rendón warned that if women tried to win rights by becoming like men, they would simply reproduce men's defects at the expense of their own good qualities, such as feminine delicacy and sensibility.[37] Like most middle-class feminists—including those with more liberal views than her own—Rendón focused mainly on white mestiza women who could afford to stay at home. She did not closely consider the needs and realities of working-class, Indigenous, or Afro-Ecuadorian women in terms of either their need for paying work or ways in which they were denied the right to claim female respectability.[38]

Other feminists argued that women should be allowed to vote because they were just as qualified as men to cast ballots. Zoila Ugarte de Landívar, a prominent feminist and one of Ecuador's first female journalists, used her position with the newspaper La Prensa to question why women were being denied the right to vote on matters vital to their own interests, particularly when the electoral law did not directly prohibit them from voting. She argued that women were neither intellectually inferior to men nor less prepared than men to vote; at one point she suggested that any men who were unprepared to vote should have the right taken away from them.[39] Hipatia Cárdenas de Bustamante made similar points, questioning why women were so harshly criticized if they showed interest in public matters. In her view, women had the same patriotic duty to be politically involved as men did.[40] She further argued that women's religious commitment should not be used against them, stating, "If we ardently defend our faith and beliefs, we too can come through heroically for the Patria."[41] In fact, she suggested that only women could root out societal cancers and regenerate the nation.[42]

Cárdenas had to walk a fine line in her discussions of private versus public spheres. She often bemoaned that women were relegated to the home, and she rejected the idea that women were more likely than men to vote as priests told them to: "The reasons given to rescind the women's vote? The same as always: that women are not prepared, that they are sheep following priests and friars, etc. This would mean that men are [prepared] and that they are not under anyone else's management or suggestion. . . . [Men] can also be [influenced by] the priests and, in any case, they are easily [led] by any charlatan that calls himself 'leader.'"[43] Cárdenas's frustration highlighted one of the key reasons for the Delayed Liberal Scenario in the history of female suffrage: the stereotype of the ultra-religious woman who would side with the church on every issue. In Ecuador as elsewhere, deeply ingrained beliefs about gender convinced liberal politicians that the women's vote would undermine their goal to build a secular state. Like their conservative counterparts, liberal men seemed incapable of imagining that women would have the same diverse set of political beliefs that men did. Yet although Cárdenas sharply criticized men's proclaimed reasons for denying women the vote, she also carefully proposed that women's involvement in politics would not be at odds with their duties in the home. She even went so far as to claim that the great triumph in her own life had been educating her children.[44]

The development of leftist parties in the 1920s and 1930s offered Ecuadorian women political options beyond the long-standing liberal–conservative divide.[45] Among the women drawn to the left was María Luisa Gómez de la Torre, the only woman present at the founding of the Ecuadorian Socialist Party in 1926. Gómez de la Torre was a teacher who elected to work in schools for either boys or poor girls rather than taking the typical route of working in middle-class girls' schools. She was also politically active: she founded a union for teachers in the 1930s, and in the 1940s she worked with Indigenous leader Dolores Cacuango to establish bilingual schools for Indigenous children. Gómez de la Torre was similarly unconventional in her personal life, as she never married or had children. Along with her friend the famed Ecuadorian leftist feminist Nela Martínez, she challenged both gender norms and socioeconomic structures. Anthropologist Kim Clark observed that Gómez de la Torres's unusual choices earned her a reputation as an "unsightly" or bad feminist, in contrast with supposedly "good" or "aesthetic" feminists who sought rights without challenging dominant gender paradigms.[46]

Politics as well as feminism set the scene for the 1929 passage of female suffrage. On July 9, 1925, a group of young military officers overthrew the government in a bloodless coup. Known as the Revolución Juliana (the July Revolution), the takeover resulted in a progressive movement to modernize the Ecuadorian state. Physician Isidro Ayora rose within the movement to become president in 1926. During the late 1920s the government focused on social reforms and created an interventionist state by expanding both public health and social welfare programs. Ayora was friends with Matilde Hidalgo de Procel, whose successful petition to vote occurred only a year before the coup that eventually put Ayora in power.

The Path to Female Suffrage, 1924–1929

When Matilde Hidalgo petitioned for the right to register to vote in Machala in May 1924, she was doing what she had always done when she faced exclusion based on her sex: seeking inclusion anyway. This method had allowed her to attend a boys' high school when no girls' school was available in her home province of Loja, enroll in the medical school at the University of Azuay, and become the first Ecuadorian woman to earn the title of medical doctor. None of these achievements had been easy. Hidalgo faced obstacles, often was not taken seriously, and sometimes lost friends. Nevertheless, she persisted. Her specific circumstances made many of her achievements possible: her wealth and whiteness were crucial, as was the fact that her brother and later her husband supported her in these endeavors. Even so, each of her accomplishments resulted from her own hard work and determination.[47] The same personal resolve that made Hidalgo the first female doctor in her country also made her the first woman to vote in Ecuadorian national elections, and thus the first woman to vote in national elections in Latin America.

Hidalgo's feat, though personal, came out of the convergence of several historical circumstances. First, Hidalgo's petition came at a time when many Ecuadorian feminists argued for political rights, and even though she did not refer to these demands, her actions took place within an environment of expanding feminism. Second, although the liberal-era gender reforms were limited, their rhetoric opened a path for women to demand political rights. Third, Hidalgo's home location of Machala was along Ecuador's southern coast, and coastal liberals tended to be more supportive of women's political rights than highland liberals. This allowed her petition to move up from the local to the national government level. Fourth, Hidalgo's actions were a continuation of a long-standing debate among Ecuadorian statesmen over whether the wording in the constitution could be used to grant women the right to vote. Even though Hidalgo's interpretation had consistently been on the losing side of legislative votes, the woman's vote clearly had some support among male government officials. The fact that many Western nations had granted women the right to vote by the 1920s might also have influenced officials' reactions to Hidalgo's petition, since the Ecuadorian debates over female suffrage often referenced women's political status in Europe and the United States. Finally, there is the matter of what Matilde Hidalgo did *not* do. She did not demand the vote for all womankind; nor did she overtly challenge dominant gender norms. Instead, she made use of a loophole in the constitution to assert her individual right to vote. This, combined with her marital and maternal status (she was eight months pregnant with her first child when she petitioned for the right to vote), made her request more palatable to men in power.[48]

Evidence of rising support for female suffrage can also be found in Pedro Undurraga Fernandez's 1927 doctoral thesis on women and politics, in which he advocated for the female vote. Undurraga echoed statements that both Zoila Ugarte and Hipatia Cárdenas made about the double standard regarding men's and women's moral and intellectual capacities when he wrote, "With man, we do not discuss whether he is rational and free; but there are some who debate women's liberty and ability to reason. It seems to me that such a commonsense thing does not deserve attention and debate."[49] Undurraga dismantled various claims about women's inferiority to men and then, like Hidalgo, noted that although Article 13 of the constitution placed age and literacy requirements on voting and office holding, it was silent on gender. He closed his arguments by stating: "The current position on the law completely contradicts the broad democratic principles established in our constitution. It is also unjust because it deprives the exercise of sovereignty to fifty percent of the inhabitants of the [national] territory, given that Art. 10 of the Constitution 'assures all inhabitants of the Republic: equality before the law and equal distribution of public positions.' It is not possible to consider women equal in order to make them pay taxes and not [to allow them] to enjoy the benefits that the laws establish."[50] Undurraga based his argument for the female vote squarely on liberal ideals of equality before the law. While he believed women were equal to men in intelligence and morality, he also identified them with the home and motherhood. However, rather than view women's domestic nature as an obstacle to their right to vote, he saw it as a strong argument in their favor: "It is difficult for me to conceive what actually happens, that in a society where the mother is responsible for the education and moral formation of the child . . . she cannot participate in electing those who govern and appoint teachers. This is one of the most important reasons that woman has to participate in public matters."[51]

When the constitutional assembly discussed voting rights in December 1928, conservative members led the call for women's right to vote, but the proposed law passed in an assembly that had more liberals than conservatives. Prieto and Goetschel have rightly indicated that the female vote was therefore not an exclusively conservative goal, as Quintero had proposed.[52] Yet without conservatives shifting to support female suffrage, Ecuador might have continued on the Liberal Delay path of the earlier suffrage debates.[53] Gauging conservative motives more precisely is difficult, however, because the representatives spent more time discussing educational criteria for voting than they did on extending the vote to women. Conservative representative Crespo Toral, for example, suggested that only individuals who had a primary education should be eligible vote. A Dr. Vega agreed, adding that voters should also have to demonstrate a basic understanding of government organizations and functions and that individuals should have to have at least a secondary education to be eligible to hold an office. Although his apprehension might have been based partly on an assumption that many women did not understand politics, Vega was particularly concerned with "the sad ignorance in which our campesinos are mired, for example, who could not explain a political work of any significance." He suggested that neither the rural population nor many of the urban poor had the minimum level of culture necessary for voting. Other legislators pointed out that it would be difficult to verify primary education, which could in turn be an impediment to voting rights. In the end, they maintained the literacy requirement without making it more specific.[54]

Although conservatives did not elaborate on their reasons for supporting the women's vote in 1928, it is possible to weigh the historical factors that were most and least likely to have influenced them. It is doubtful that feminists convinced conservatives to support the women's vote, given that the women who wanted this right were more often associated with liberal or leftist politics. However, changing international contexts might have played a role in altering conservatives' stance on the role of women in politics. Not only had many Western countries granted women the right to vote by the late 1920s, making the expansion of female suffrage seem inevitable, but Pope Benedict XV's acceptance of the female vote might have swayed conservatives in particular.[55] New political developments within Ecuador might also have prompted conservatives to alter their view of the female vote. Particularly important was the recent creation of the Socialist Party, whose members, although not large in numbers, had already made connections with Indigenous activists in the highlands and labor movements along the coast.[56] Vega's concern with "ignorant" campesinos is especially telling in this context; political elites had long identified rural coarseness and lack of education specifically with Indigenous peoples, and by the 1920s many Indigenous workers in the north-central highlands were politically active. The rise of leftist and Indigenous movements may have made conservatives more willing to support female suffrage, especially because gender norms identified (middle- and upper-class) women as deeply religious and therefore possible supporters of conservative agendas.[57]

The shift to the Conservative Strategic Advantage Scenario was not complete, however. In addition to the liberal support for the women's vote in the assembly, editorials in the liberal newspaper *El Día* celebrated women's expanding horizons as an indicator of modernity and expected women to vote with even greater conscience and enthusiasm than men.[58] Editorial pieces in more conservative-leaning newspapers often argued that women were not prepared for the vote and that female suffrage could endanger the stability of home life in Ecuador.[59] Most editorial pieces accepted the female vote once the law was passed, though some of the more conservative newspapers downplayed women's roles in the events leading up to the law's passage. In retrospect, 1929 marked not the culmination of the debate over female suffrage but rather an important transitional moment in the discussions of gender and politics in Ecuador.

The Question of Whether to Rescind Women's Right to Vote in the 1930s

Soon after literate women gained the right to vote in national elections, Ecuador fell into economic and political turmoil. The Great Depression sent the economy into a tailspin, significantly weakened the political influence of coastal agro-export elites, and generated popular discontent. With a deteriorating support base, and facing opposition from across the political spectrum, Isidro Ayora resigned in August 1931. Ecuador had 17 different governments between 1931 and 1940, during which time both leftist activism and conservative populism were on the rise.[60] Economic and political upheaval led to a reopening of the debate over female suffrage, particularly in 1937–1938, when a new elections law was under construction.

The 1930s debates over female suffrage returned to well-worn arguments. In a speech at a women's school, Humberto Mata emphasized that *el verdadero feminismo* (true feminism) sought to "redeem woman, not just allow her to enter lines of work in which she will suffer the same penalties as men, not just to learn to organize home life and improve her fulfillment of maternal duties, but also to push society toward a better future." He warned that women should not embrace feminism in order to vote on matters that fell outside of their particular interests and knowledge.[61] Mata's claims echoed the opinions of Zoila Rendón, advocating greater rights for women while strongly associating women with the domestic sphere. At the other end of the spectrum, Hipatia Cárdenas pushed back against the campaign to rescind women's right to vote. She remarked that it was not just older conservatives and liberals who opposed female suffrage but that young leftists were also wary of granting women political rights.[62] She thought that the plan to retract women's right to vote was the greatest insult to women in her time.[63]

By the time a commission began working on the new Law of Elections in 1937, the debates over suffrage were intense and varied. Several contributors to *El Día* questioned whether a woman who could sign her name necessarily understood political matters well enough to vote, whereas they proposed that some illiterate (male) workers might have good judgment in political matters. One opinion piece suggested that there would be no ill effect from allowing an Indigenous man who "knows his value as a man" to vote.[64] Another contributor argued that individuals should have to meet a higher standard to vote—such as having an academic title or having graduated from a military or normal school—and trusted neither underprepared women nor "coarse" campesinos with the privilege of voting.[65] Such arguments, which had been part of a minority opinion in the 1929 legislature and newspapers, gained traction in the 1930s.

As usual, women were split with regard to female suffrage in the 1930s. Hipatia Cárdenas continued to champion the cause of the women's vote. She wrote to the president of the Commission on Electoral Law, equating the women's vote with the well-being of Ecuadorian democracy.[66] She also held liberal men accountable for attacks against the female vote, noting that the new proposal "reveals the fear that men, especially Ecuadorian liberals, harbor against the free expression of the popular will." Cárdenas argued that all women should be allowed to vote, showing that at least some feminists looked beyond their own middle-class interests.[67] María Luisa Calle, however, claimed that women lacked the discipline and sense of duty necessary for voting. She also argued that women had failed to prove themselves prepared for political rights and "instead of contributing to the enhancement of politics or moralizing public dealings . . . nothing has been achieved by the female element taking part in militant politics or public concerns."[68]

Why was female suffrage more heatedly debated in 1937 than before its passage in 1929, especially when women had accounted for only 12 percent of voters in the 1933 elections? Mercedes Prieto and Ana María Goetschel observed that the political upheavals of the 1930s led some liberal and leftist men to rethink the women's vote because they assumed that women were vulnerable to clerical influence.[69] In short, they feared that women would be "a decisive force in favor of traditionalist policy."[70] Although concerns about women's penchant for tradition and loyalty to the church can be found throughout the early twentieth century, they seemed to become reality with populist José María Velasco Ibarra's election to the presidency in 1934.[71] Historian Ximena Sosa traced how Velasco Ibarra gained female voters through his advocacy of female education and with his rhetoric on morality. Velasco Ibarra argued that Catholic morality needed to be revived in Ecuadorian politics, and although he presented himself as the father figure qualified to accomplish this goal, he also considered women "moral guardians of society" who would help him to carry out his agenda. His commitment to expanding female education also strengthened his position in elections, because many women were only eligible to vote due to the schooling they received because of his policies.[72]

Many women responded positively and became ardent supporters and campaigners for Velasquista populism. While women may not have been the reason for Velasco Ibarra's electoral victory in 1934, they certainly helped. Velasco Ibarra recognized that women were a potentially powerful interest group because, unlike men, they were not required to vote. He could therefore gain an electoral advantage if he inspired more women to vote than his opponents did.[73] In essence, Velasco Ibarra combined populism with the Perceived Conservative Strategic Advantage Scenario to seek women supporters. His success in doing so was a pivotal reason that his opponents revived concerns associated with the Delayed Liberal Scenario to try to repeal women's right to vote.

If liberals were concerned with women's support for conservative candidates, both liberals and conservatives were increasingly alarmed by leftists and Indigenous activism. Many Indigenous men and women on state-owned haciendas engaged actively in politics during the 1920s and 1930s, joining forces with leftist intellectuals to improve their work conditions and to fight the racism they faced on a daily basis. Although government officials typically blamed socialists for agitating Indigenous workers, historian Marc Becker has shown that leftist–Indigenous partnerships were often formed out of mutual respect.[74] Government attitudes and responses to Indigenous demands were paradoxical. The 1929 constitution established that collective interest groups—including Indians—would be allowed their own "functional representatives" in the legislature. However, unlike other groups, Indigenous people were not allowed to elect their functional representatives; instead, white mestizo men selected them.[75] Anthropologist Mercedes Prieto asserted that such half-hearted promises to represent Indigenous peoples amounted to "subjecting Indians while promising them a voice."[76] At the same time, Ecuadorian officials often responded to Indigenous actions and demands by sending police and military forces against Indigenous protestors, even when protests were peaceful.[77] Politicians were divided over the question of whether to grant Indigenous men the right to vote: although leftists and (some) liberals argued that indigenous men should enjoy the suffrage, conservatives and (some) liberals thought that the poor would be too easily influenced by political bosses, particularly Indigenous peons who were under the control of estate owners.[78] Such arguments ran parallel to those aimed at denying women the right to vote, underscoring the multilayered power differentials within Ecuadorian politics. Ecuadorian politicians considered middle- and upper-class women unfit to vote because of they were inherently domestic and dependent on men while they claimed that Indigenous peoples were coarse and easily controlled by their bosses. These arguments were, at core, circular: they sought to disqualify people who were in low positions within patriarchal social hierarchies, which would in turn ensure that they remained dependent and weak vis-à-vis wealthy white and mestizo men.

While Velasco Ibarra courted female voters and liberals feared women's political potential, leftist politicians sought gender equality in theory while ignoring women's concerns in practice. They were more focused on revisions of the Ecuadorian labor code or the defense of Indigenous hacienda workers' demands than they were on upholding Ecuadorian women's political rights. Some women rose to prominence within the Communist Party, but they typically did so without challenging their male peers on gender issues. A good example of this can be found in the life of Indigenous activist Dolores Cacuango. Cacuango was the daughter and wife of hacienda debt peons who worked tirelessly on behalf of Indigenous laborers. She rose to a leadership position within the Ecuadorian Communist Party and was a cofounder of the Federation of Ecuadorian Indians. Despite her reputation as a "mother" to the Indigenous movement (both in her life and in historical memory), Cacuango focused on addressing inequalities based on ethnicity and class rather than gender.[79]

Where Dolores Cacuango adopted the Communist Party's silence on gender issues, Nela Martínez found alternative means to address women's needs. Martínez was born to a wealthy landowning family, but from an early age she was drawn to leftist politics as a means of addressing class and race inequalities. Though she rose in ranks of the Communist Party, she was unable to tackle the problem of gender discrimination through her work there.[80] Rather than ignore women's problems, Martínez joined ranks with women from across the political spectrum to form the Asociación Femenina Ecuatoriana (Ecuadorian Women's Association, or AFE) in 1938. The AFE sought to appeal to women across class, race, and political divides and to promote "mutual respect for the political and religious convictions of members and among all citizens generally." According to its statutes, the AFE's goals were to advance solidarity among all Ecuadorian women; encourage women in the conscientious exercise of their civil rights; fight for economic, social, and political equality; and struggle to achieve direct legislative representation for Ecuadorian women.[81] Women's marginalization across the spectrum of Ecuadorian politics created the conditions that made development of the AFE possible: having met obstacles within their own parties, women who joined the AFE were willing to set aside their ideological differences to address the practical needs of women across class and race lines.

It was therefore not only general political turmoil that led to Ecuadorian women's tenuous position vis-à-vis the vote but rather a perfect storm of political conflict and agitation from both above and below. Economic crises and political upheaval created an atmosphere in which laws and rights were in a continual state of debate from 1929 to 1944. Not only were liberals, conservatives, and leftists vying for power, but the 1930s ushered in a populist era through Velasco Ibarra's rise to power.[82] At the same time, feminists and Indigenous activists embarked on political movements either on their own or in conjunction with existing political parties. In short, both politics and feminism were becoming more diverse, which meant that no one party or movement could rely on the so-called woman's vote.

It was the combination of political instability and expanding social movements that made the woman's vote seem especially dangerous. Male politicians' concern had less to do with the actual impact of the women's vote—given that literate women accounted for a small percentage of the overall population—and more to do with the potential implications of allowing women to vote. Women's right to vote challenged dominant gender norms that identified women with domesticity, and male politicians across much of the political spectrum worried that this would threaten the social order. If women could vote, it made it harder to justify denying a political voice to other dependent groups. Indigenous activism of the 1930s added to middle-class and elite men's fears of social and political upheaval. Only Velasco Ibarra managed to encourage women's political participation while reinforcing patriarchy and social hierarchies; he did so by combining conservative family values with tangible benefits for literate women. His success reignited debates over gender and politics and left literate women in a politically precarious position during the 1930s.[83]

Conclusions

Although contemporary scholars, similar to Ecuadorian politicians of the 1930s, normally focus on either female suffrage or the voting rights of the poor, these rights were often granted or denied in relation to each other. Ecuadorian debates over the women's vote raised questions about whether or not to expand the vote to men of all classes and races. Whereas legislators denied literate women the right to vote in 1910 in part because there were men who could not vote, lawmakers in 1929 asserted that literate women were more deserving of the vote than purportedly "ignorant" men in the countryside. The debate over literate women versus illiterate men's preparedness to vote returned in the 1930s, but female suffrage ultimately prevailed. Voting rights were linked to literacy until 1979, ensuring that suffrage remained a privilege of the minority rather than a right that all citizens enjoyed. Moreover, although the law required all literate men to vote, voting remained optional for literate women until 1968. These questions about the readiness of literate women versus uneducated men to vote helped to justify the continuing control that middle- and upper-class men exerted over Ecuadorian politics.

Like male politicians, Ecuadorian feminists had diverse opinions on both voting rights and the relationship between the public and private spheres. But feminist concerns differed from those of legislators in fundamental ways. Men used the division between the domestic and public spheres to question whether women should be allowed to influence politics. Ecuadorian feminists debated not whether but *how* women should influence politics: some of them believed the vote was necessary while others thought that women could better impact politics through their roles in the home. Many men feared that a woman who voted would become a marimacho and reject all forms of femininity. Feminists either rejected that notion or, if they worried about the impact voting would have on a woman's character, assumed that women would lose their moral superiority by entering the political fray alongside men. These differences were subtle but significant; whereas male politicians tended to think of the threat to gender norms in black-and-white terms, feminists concerned themselves with the extent to which gender roles could be altered while still maintaining the well-being of both the family and the nation.

These debates intensified in the 1930s because both politics and feminism were increasingly wide ranging. In the first decades of the twentieth century, liberals and conservatives dominated Ecuadorian national politics. By the 1930s, however, there were both leftist and populist challengers in the quest for national political power. Indigenous activists aligned themselves with leftist leaders to make demands of the state and to have a voice in politics. It is not surprising that feminism—complex from its beginnings—further diversified alongside other political changes and challenges. After all, Ecuadorian women were divided by class and race; they lived in different regions of the country; some lived in cities, others in the countryside; some were literate, others were not. New party options allowed women additional avenues for expressing their unique views, problems, and goals. At the same time, party leaders from across the political spectrum—though not the populist Velasco Ibarra— tended to address women's concerns as an afterthought in the 1930s, which brought women from various backgrounds and viewpoints together in the Alianza Femenina Ecuatoriana to advance the needs of women and families. Male liberals were in a particularly difficult position in the 1930s, facing challenges to power from both conservative populism and leftist movements.

While not all liberal leaders sought to revoke female suffrage in the 1930s, those who did were quite vocal, whereas male leftists mostly remained silent on the question of women's rights.[84]

Although female suffrage in Ecuador was not preceded by a long or highly organized suffrage movement, male legislators were influenced by feminist arguments and actions when they expanded voting rights to women in 1929. If there was a clear strategy in debates over women's right to vote (and here I include the discussions over whether to rescind that right in the 1930s), it had less to do with a conservative–liberal divide and more to do with a middle- and upper-class male strategy to maintain dominance over all aspects of the political process. Some political leaders advocated universal suffrage, but they held few seats in the national government. Most politicians wanted to limit the expansion of voting rights to groups they considered either inferior to themselves or dangerous to their political goals; officially, however, they argued that these groups were not qualified to vote. The argument in favor of granting literate women the right to vote was strategic insofar as it helped to build a case against allowing the majority of poor, uneducated Ecuadorians a political voice.

Notes

This essay could not have been written without the work of a number of Ecuadorian scholars. Most importantly, I have been influenced by and rely upon multiple works by Raquel Rodas Morales and Ana María Goetschel, as well as the pioneering work of Jenny Estrada.

1. This document appears in full in Estrada, *Matilde Hidalgo de Procel*, 93–94.
2. "La mujer y el sufragio," *El Comercio*, October 11, 1929, 3.
3. Quintero, *El mito del populismo en el Ecuador*.
4. Quintero, 241–46.
5. Prieto and Goetschel, "El sufragio femenino."
6. Rodás Morales, *Historia del voto femenino en el Ecuador*, 14–16.
7. This analysis is evident not only in the discussion of the path to female suffrage but also in Alexandra Quezada's analysis of later suffrage debates and women's experiences of voting in *Historia del voto femenino*.
8. In fairness to Quintero, *El mito del populismo* was published when Ecuadorian women's history was still quite new and gender analysis was not yet fully developed. However, some early histories suggested greater complexity and agency in Ecuadorian women's history than he recognized.
9. Quintero, *El mito del populismo en el Ecuador*, 221–38, 247–48.

10. It is difficult to determine the various ethnic populations of Ecuador in the early twentieth century precisely, especially because of the fluidity of categories and individual identities. The 1942 census estimated that Indigenous peoples and mestizos each made up 40 percent of the total population, followed by whites (10 percent), with Afro-Ecuadorians and "others" making up 5 percent each. See Clark and Becker, "Indigenous Peoples and State Formation in Modern Ecuador," 10.

11. See Roisida Aguilar's essay in this volume regarding Peru. For a broader discussion of Latin American gender and politics in the period, see Elizabeth Dore, "One Step Forward, Two Steps Back: Gender and the State in the Long Nineteenth Century," in Dore, *Hidden Histories*, particularly pages 9 and 15. See also see Rebecca Earle's essay "Rape and the Anxious Republic: Revolutionary Colombia, 1810–1830," in Dore, *Hidden Histories*, 147–71.

12. República del Ecuador, *Código Civil de la República del Ecuador*, Article 1734. See Articles 124, 128, 130, 134, and 136 for further details on limitations on wives' actions in the public sphere.

13. Further discussion of women and nineteenth-century Ecuadorian state formation can be found in O'Connor, *Gender, Indian, Nation*, chapter 3. Dore notes a similar general pattern throughout Latin America in "One Step Forward, Two Steps Back," page 15, where she writes, "Male elders represented both the family to the state and the state inside the family."

14. There was an attempt to establish a head tax on all adult men in the early nineteenth century, but it met with resistance from whites and mestizos, who felt that it lowered them to the same status as Indians.

15. The classic discussion of the debate over tribute is Van Aken, "The Lingering Death of Indian Tribute in Ecuador." For a discussion of gender and tribute debates, see O'Connor, *Gender, Indian, Nation*, chapter 2.

16. Asamblea Nacional Constituyente de 1883, cited in Rodas Morales, *Historia del voto femenino en el Ecuador*, 58, 60.

17. Rodas Morales, 61.

18. Rodas Morales, 60, 63. The term *marimacho* referred not simply to a tomboy but rather to a woman who rejected femininity altogether and was perhaps suspected of being a lesbian.

19. For a summary of this debate, see Prieto and Goetschel, "El sufragio femenino," 302.

20. Alfaro, "Mensaje del Presidente de la República," 33–335.

21. Romo Leroux G., *El movimiento de mujeres en el Ecuador*, 28.

22. Although educational reforms were not exclusively aimed at women, they expanded women's access to education and relied heavily on women as teachers in public schools.

23. Alfaro, "Mensaje del Presidente de la República," 335.

24. For a fuller discussion of gender laws in the liberal period, see O'Connor, *Gender, Indian, Nation*, 87–99.

25. Rodas Morales, ed., *Historia del voto femenino en el Ecuador*, 78.
26. República del Ecuador, *Anales de Diputados*, 217 (for Barrera's argument in favor of universal suffrage), 218 (for López's discusión of women and rights).
27. República del Ecuador, 217–18.
28. República del Ecuador, 216–17.
29. República del Ecuador, 219.
30. República del Ecuador, 227.
31. Their resistance was evident in the 1902 and 1910 civil marriage laws, which allowed divorce. After some debate, the 1902 law allowed divorce only in cases that the Catholic Church would have approved for formal separation—such as a husband's failure to provide or a wife's adultery. The 1910 law, which allowed couples to divorce based on mutual consent, was much more hotly contested.
32. For an especially good discussion of how middle-class female teachers engaged politics and developed an "alternative public sphere," see Goetschel, *Educación de las mujeres*.
33. Goetschel, "Estudio Introductorio," 20, 25.
34. Rendón, *Condición social y política de la mujer*, 17–18.
35. Rendón, 32.
36. Rendón, 34.
37. Rendón de Mosquera, *La mujer en el hogar y en la sociedad*, 95.
38. One should not presume that Rendón de Mosquera's ideas were rejected by all working-class women. She was an occasional contributor, in the 1920s and 1930s, to the Guayaquil labor magazine *La Aurora* and contributed at least twice to *La Mujer Ecuatoriana*, a magazine published by the working-class Centro Feminista "La Aurora" in Guayaquil. Both magazines reflected the views of the artisan class, many of whom sought to earn middle-class respectability themselves. I touch upon this in my essay "¿Mujeres o trabajadoras? Exploración de la historia de la hegemonía de género en los movimientos obreros del Ecuador, entre 1895 y 1938," in progress.
39. On September 9, 12, 14, and 23 of 1910, Zoila Ugarte de Landívar wrote several pieces on this subject (under the title "Plumadas") in her capacity as a writer for the periodical *La Prensa*. Passages from these appear in Rodas Morales, *Historia del voto femenino en el Ecuador*, 106–9. A decade later, María Luisa Lecaro Pinto (writing as "Sor Marisa") made a similar call for women's equality in "La mujer y sus derechos," which appears in Goetschel, *Orígenes del feminismo*, 161–62.
40. Cárdenas de Bustamante, *Oro, rojo, azul*, 39.
41. Cárdenas de Bustamante, 43.
42. Cárdenas de Bustamante, 51.
43. Cárdenas de Bustamante, 34–35. Though Cárdenas's essay is not dated, the wording suggests that it came from the 1930s, when Ecuadorian politicians

contemplated revoking women's right to vote. See the essay for details about the 1930s debates.

44. Cárdenas de Bustamante, 51–52.
45. The Ecuadorian Socialist Party (Partido Socialista del Ecuador, or PSE) was established in 1926. The party splintered in 1931 when a group of more radical leftists founded the Ecuadorian Communist Party (Partido Comunista del Ecuador, or PCE).
46. Clark, "Feminismos estéticos y antiestéticos," 93–97.
47. Biographical material on Matilde Hidalgo's life is based on Estrada, *Matilde Hidalgo de Procel*.
48. Clark, "Feminismos estéticos y antiestéticos." See particularly her contrast between Hidalgo and María Luisa Gómez de la Torre on page 101.
49. Undurraga Fernandez, "Los Derechos Políticos de la Mujer," 3.
50. Undurraga Fernandez, 60.
51. Undurraga Fernandez, 7–8.
52. Prieto and Goetschel, "El sufragio femenino," 310–11.
53. Thanks to Stephanie Mitchell for insights that have deepened my analysis of this moment and its importance in the history of female suffrage in Ecuador.
54. A few legislators, such as Moncayo Andrade, argued against giving women the right to vote, claiming that women themselves had never sought it. For the debates, see Asamblea Nacional Constituyente (ANC), December 14, 1928, pp. 248–51, Archivo Palacio Legislativo, Quito.
55. For a discussion of the changing stance of the Catholic Church, see the introduction to this volume.
56. For connections between the left and Indigenous peoples, see Becker, *Indians and Leftists*, chapter 2. For the left and workers, see Milk, *Movimiento obrero ecuatoriano*, 66–69, 104; Pineo, *Social and Economic Reform in Ecuador*, 141–43; Robalino Bolle, *El sindicalismo en el Ecuador*, 100–103.
57. Concern with socialism was also one reason why Pope Benedict XV had supported female suffrage.
58. *El Día*, January 22, 1929, and January 9, 1929, respectively.
59. For a good discussion of these different perspectives, see Prieto and Goetschel, "El sufragio femenino," 307–9.
60. Cueva, "El Ecuador de 1925 a 1960," 96–103.
61. Mata, *Feminismo?*, 50, 52. This was a publication of the Ministry of Public Education.
62. Cárdenas Bustamante, *Oro, rojo, azul*, 34–35.
63. Cárdenas, 23. Also see Lcda. María Esther Martínez Macías, "La mujer y el sufragio," in Goetschel, *Orígenes del feminismo*, 173–80. Martínez focused on the fact that it was only by having the right to vote that women could advance both their own interests and those of the nation. She, like Cárdenas, also pointed out that men's economic dependence on employers or susceptibility to

church influence did not disqualify them from voting; thus women's economic dependence on men or priests should not disqualify them either.

64. "Elecciones libres," *El Día*, January 24, 1937, 3.

65. Nelson, "El derecho del Sufragio," *El Día*, January 22, 1937, 3.

66. Cárdenas Bustamante, *Oro, rojo, azul*, 68.

67. Cárdenas, 86–87.

68. María Luisa Calle, "La mujer, la política y los prejuicios confesionales," *El Día*, January 4 1937, 3.

69. Prieto and Goetschel, "El sufragio femenino," 320.

70. "El voto femenino," *El Día*, March 12, 1937, 3.

71. This was just the beginning of Velasco Ibarra's long career of populist politics in Ecuador; he was president in 1934–1935, 1944–1947, 1952–1956, 1960–1961, 1968–1972.

72. Sosa-Bucholz, "Changing Images of Male and Female in Ecuador," 49, 52, 56–57. Sosa notes that although historians typically label Velasco Ibarra a conservative, he identified himself as a Catholic liberal.

73. Sosa, "Changing Images of Male and Female in Ecuador," 48.

74. Becker, *Indians and Leftists*, especially chapter 2.

75. The 1938 constitution maintained functional representatives for corporate groups but eliminated them for Indigenous peoples. (They were reinstated in the 1940s.)

76. Prieto, "A Liberalism of Fear," 119–30.

77. Becker, *Indians and Leftists*, 19.

78. "El voto calificado," *El Día*, January 23, 1937, 3; also see Prieto, "A Liberalism of Fear," 205–15.

79. Rodás Morales, *Crónica de un sueño: Las escuelas indígenas de Dolores Cacuango*; Becker, *Indians and Leftists*.

80. For more on Nela Martínez's life, see Martínez, *Yo siempre he sido Nela Martínez Espinosa*.

81. Alianza Femenina Ecuatoriana, *Estatutos de Alianza Femenina Ecuatoriana*, 8–10. In practice, the AFE seems to have straddled the leftist aims for class equality of some of its founders with a middle-class feminist focus on domestic changes among the poor.

82. Populist Velasco Ibarra held office five times in all: 1934–1935, 1944–1947, 1952–1956, 1960–1961, and 1968–1972.

83. These debates continued into the 1940s, particularly with the 1944 "May Revolution," in which citizenship and voting rights were reexamined.

84. Both Liberal Party and Socialist Party manifestos called for women's political advancement before 1929. Once literate women achieved the suffrage, both parties (as well as the newly formed Communist Party) were silent on gender—as if the vote alone, and for a minority of women, had resolved political gender inequalities.

CHAPTER ELEVEN

Collective Action for Women's Suffrage in Peru

Political Contexts, Women's Organizations, and Public Actors

ROISIDA AGUILAR

The spirit of our woman lacks reflection; it is emotional, frivolous, and joyful, and it wouldn't know what to do with the right to vote in political processes. Instinct would inhibit her from such a fastidious function, but the exploitation of the priest, the husband, the brother, the boyfriend, or the male friend would lead her to act in accordance with their interests. Only if the vote were reserved for a few grave, dishpan spinsters, deviant by fate due to the course of life for their sex, or for those who, due to special mental or personality conditions, are able to overcome the level what social law has fixed as the sphere of action for the feminine sex.[1]

Such was the pronouncement of the editorial page of the journal *Variedades*, one of the most important in Peru, in response to rumors that the Commission on Electoral Reform in the Chamber of Deputies was planning to concede the vote to women meeting certain conditions, including literacy.[2] In Peru in 1923, women's suffrage was imagined to be "a joke born from the constant humor of idle *limeños* [people from Lima]. . . . [S]omething like that would be unacceptable" because women lacked preparation, were "subjugated by religious sentimentalism." Nevertheless, leaders such as María Jesús Alvarado Rivera and Zoila Aurora Cáceres Moreno, who had identified the injury to Peruvian women that stemmed from their marginalization to the private sphere, demanded civil and political rights, despite adverse conditions.

This chapter investigates how and under what conditions Peruvian women obtained the suffrage. The period under study extends from 1911, when María Jesús Alvarado gave a conference at the Sociedad Geográfica de Lima, to 1956, when the first women voted in a general election.

Antecedents: The Civil Condition of Women and Enlightened women in the Late Nineteenth Century

The social condition of Peruvian women did not changed with independence. The oft-proclaimed liberty did not include women. On the contrary, the first institutional plans for constitutions and a civil code reinforced masculine dominance by relegating women, especially married women, to the private sphere. These institutions endured through the first decades of the twentieth century. The roots of the struggle for women's political and civil rights date to the late nineteenth century. In the 1870s female writers such as Mercedes Cabello de Carbonera (1845–1909), Clorinda Matto de Turner (1852–1909), Lastenia Larriva de Llona (1848–1924), Teresa González de Fanning (1836–1918), and Carolina Freyre de Jaimes (1844–1916) formed the "first generation of enlightened women in Peru," according to Francesca Denegri.[3] They employed literature as a space in which to explore and make known the deleterious effects of patriarchy on marriage, the family, education, and work.

Several trends favored this awakening. The first was the entrance of civilian elites into politics. The military held onto the reins of power until 1872, when civilian forces united under the banner of the Partido Civil triumphed in a bloody election. The second was a new vogue for literary salons like those organized by the Argentine María Manuela Gorriti, where both women and men (such as intellectuals Ricardo Palma and Manuel Gonzáles Prada) attended. The War of the Pacific between Chile and Peru (1879–1883) failed to dampen feminists' enthusiasm. In fact, the opposite may be true. If we look at publication dates, we observe that some sharpened their critiques, as was the case with Clorinda Matto de Turner, who held a series of partisan soirees in 1886.[4] Her polemical novels *Aves sin Nido* (1889), *Índole* (1891), and *Herencia* (1894) revealed the near enslavement of Indigenous Peruvians as well as abuses by political and religious authorities. Her works were subsequently banned under the government of Nicolás de Piérola. The clergy excommunicated her, while others in power censured and humiliated her, forcing her into an Argentine exile from which she never returned.

The first civil code in Peru, promulgated in 1852, consigned women to the "protection" of "another," in the same way that it did minors, orphans, and, until 1854, slaves. Unmarried women were under the protection of a father, brother, or "other," while married women were subject to their husbands. A wife was obliged to obey her husband and reside where he decided, while a husband had to permit his wife to live in his home and to provide her with necessities "according to his abilities and situation."[5] A wife could not administer wealth she received as an inheritance.[6] In the case of separation, children could remain with the mother only until their third birthday, at which point they could be "torn from her arms to go with their father."[7]

In the 1880s, Felisa Moscoso de Carbajal expressed a reality that many women experienced daily: "scandalizing society with crimes that are deplored every day and in which the woman always has the worst part, because as wife, or as victim of a criminal love, she suffers horrible. . . . The man always finds an excuse for his deviations and is easily pardoned. For the woman, censure is more acrid, the criticism more cruel, and she bears the greater responsibility: she is condemned before she is even heard; And why not, if her accusers and judges are all men?"[8] Women writers from across the spectrum—conservative Catholics, liberals, and members of the opposition—began to demand better conditions for women.[9] They attributed the country's backwardness to its marginalization of women and prescribed education as the path to progress: for women, the nation, and the world.[10] In the words of Mercedes Cabello de Carbonera, "Educate the woman, enlighten her intelligence, and you will have a powerful and universal motor for progress of world civilization."[11] Teresa González de Fanning also advocated for education but argued that it should be more practical:

Education in Peru suffers from a grave defect: the lack of practical application, both in that which is offered to the people and that which the elevated classes receive. . . . Instruction should be in relation to the aptitudes and necessities of the educated and according to the social environment in which they must live. . . . If rich, then they should learn how to manage and preserve their fortune; if poor, then let them be taught how to achieve subsistence and obtain an independent position; and in any case, according to their own personality, so that knowledge obtained might never serve as an obstacle to marriage.[12]

In this way, nineteenth-century women moved from literature to politics. But even the most important of them did not gamble on equal political rights, although they were aware of the movement in England, Switzerland, and the United States.[13] Mercedes Cabello said it would be "absurd," "risible," and "impossible for women to take part in the political movement of nations"; it would be "as bad for her as it would be for humanity" because "giving her political rights would only embitter her character and increase the effervescence of political passions, converting the domestic hearth into a new breeding ground for discord and distaste. . . . What would the woman achieve the day she had political rights? Nothing. She would do no more than wrap herself in that drama of political passions, where astuteness and falsehood play principal roles and where the tempered soul of the man feels the bite of the asp of treason that hides beneath the false mask of patriotism, to wound the heart."[14] Corinda Matto observed that the "raucous" public sphere was a place "where everyone betrays everyone else."[15] This point of view expressed reality. The struggle for power had led the country through prolonged periods of political crisis, in which institutional instability from civil wars and coups d'état had become a constant.

Although these writers did not support women's political rights, they contributed to the struggle for those rights because they laid its foundations. Maritza Villavicencio argued that they preferred to emancipate women through culture "instead of thinking about opening terrain for the struggle over women's social revindication."[16]

Birth of Peruvian feminism

Following the War of the Pacific, Peru began its economic recovery under the presidency of Nicolás de Piérola (1895–1899).[17] His government's reforms inaugurated a period of relative stability that Jorge Basadre has termed the "Aristocratic Republic."[18] During this period and the following under Augusto B. Leguía (1919–1930, known as the Oncenio de Leguía because it lasted eleven years), critiques emerged from the new working class, from Indigenous groups, and from students. In the cities, leadership for these movements came from sindicalists, anarchists, and radicals familiar with political events abroad, such as the Russian and Mexican Revolutions and the First World War. They organized strikes and work stoppages to ask for better wages and a shorter workday, among other demands. In the country-side, Indigenous people rose up in protest against abuse and the expansion of the giant estates that were eating up their communal lands.[19] Women and men together contributed to the 1918 passage of José Matías Manzanilla's proposal for an eight-hour workday for women and children, which was extended to all in 1919.[20] Students achieved the reform of the university in the same year.

In this context, the journalist and writer María Jesús Alvarado Rivera emerged. A positivist motivated by the ideas of Condorcet and J. S. Mill, she defended oppressed groups: Indigenous peoples, workers, and especially women. In 1908 Alvarado advocated education for working-class children so they would know their rights and be able to defend themselves, as well as become good patriots.[21] In 1910 she sent a paper to the First International Women's Congress in Argentina, calling for a reform of women's education. She argued that education was a necessity of life for women and that they should have access to the professions and the highest functions of the state.[22]

On October 28, 1911, Alvarado presented a paper titled "Feminism" to the Geographic Society of Lima. In it she responded to a Chilean antifeminist who had pronounced in *El Comercio* that "women's subordination was natural and eternal." The article argued, "The woman was born exclusively for the hearth." It also made fun of English suffragists.[23] Alvarado responded that feminism was "one of the most important sociological questions of the age" and that it was developing in the "civilized world." She also refuted the assertion that women's subordination was natural, arguing that it was instead the product of the "depressed" place society had assigned them. A democratic society that abolished privilege, she contended, could not continue to hold women in a position of inferiority. Feminism, she said, aimed for equal civil and political rights "in order to intervene directly in the national destiny as an apt, intelligent member of the State."[24] Her statement marked a milestone in the history of Peruvian feminism.

In 1914 Alvarado founded the organization Evolución Femenina, whose principles included "a broad women's culture, that Domestic Economy be based on women's education; to dignify women's work; the defense of her rights; equality of civil rights between men and women; a campaign against social vices; a stimulus for women to fulfil their social obligations; to intensify and orient feminine patriotism towards the beneficent labor of the country; and pacifism."[25] In 1915 she founded the school Moral y Trabajo, "for the protection of the proletarian, feminine youth." She also achieved recognition for women's work to be included in the Sociedad de Beneficencia Pública, which was an important step for women's rights. In 1923, together with members of the Liga Peruana de Laboradoras Pacifistas, she took advantage of the formation of a commission to reform the civil code of 1852 to demand recognition of women's civil rights and the rights of illegitimate children. The same year, she received a visit from Carrie Chapman Catt, the president of the Pan-American Women's Suffrage Alliance, as part of that organization's Latin American tour.[26] In March they together founded the Consejo Nacional de Mujeres, with the objective of obtaining women's suffrage.[27] Catt's subsequent letter to a friend revealed something of the racism she found among Peruvian feminists, to say nothing of her own: "We had heard much about conditions in Perú before our arrival. Everyone predicted failure. The organizing difficulty was a wholly new one. [Women of the upper middle classes] will not associate. All the university women, doctors, etc., are not only middle class but mostly of decidedly mixed blood. The pure Castilian woman would die before she moved equally herself with those of color."[28] Religion was another important factor. Peru was a very Catholic country, and the church enjoyed good relations with those in power.

Conservatives and Catholics opposed any kind of feminine independence. According to them, what women needed was "protection." Liberation would bring only suffering, they said. During her visit, Catt noticed that clerical emissaries had observed her sessions at the university, intimidating some of the possible orators.[29]

It is perhaps for this reason that Alvarado was silent regarding the struggle for equal political rights. She may have been biding her time until conditions improved, especially among the middle and lower classes. She wrote, for the inaugural speech of Evolución Femenina in 1914, "We are not going to throw ourselves into an unconsidered feminism. . . . We are not going to demand reforms that cannot be adapted to the environment. . . . We are not, then, going to undertake a revolution whose innovations would fail in an adverse environment; we are only going to promote an evolution in the feminine mentality toward the superior culture that dignifies, liberates, and prepares for life's struggles, and for the fulfillment of the high social obligations that human progress demands today of the woman as well as the man."[30] Nevertheless, at the Second Pan-American Conference, held in Lima from December 21, 1924, to January 6, 1925, Alvarado made a general call for women's full legal equality. The League of Catholic Women objected vehemently.[31] Alvarado had allowed equipment at her school, Moral y Trabajo, to be used to print student and labor manifestos denouncing the forced recruitment of the poor to build roads and the pollution of the environment stemming from operations of a US company, Fundación de Oroya. For this reason, Leguía ordered her detained and incarcerated in the remote district of Santo Tomas. Her school was closed and its press destroyed. She finally left the country and lived in exile in Argentina for eleven years.[32] Her removal, along with that of many other members of the opposition, meant that another group of activists would have to take up the struggle.[33]

Institutional Framework for Women's Political Condition

Within the institutional framework of political rights, women did not exist. The 1860 constitution defined electors as citizens who could read and write, or owned property, or paid taxes, or managed a workshop.[34] Again, as occurred elsewhere, a reform in 1895 removed all restrictions except for literacy, which endured until 1979, when Peruvians finally achieved universal suffrage.

The constitution of 1933 was the first in 112 years of republican government to mention the word *woman*. At that time, women were permitted to vote in municipal elections, which were not considered to be political. This right, however, did not recognize women's status as citizens. The constitutions of 1860 and 1920 both defined "citizens" as "Peruvians" (*peruanos*) having achieved the age of majority or having married as minors. As was true throughout Latin America, it was not necessary to clarify that *citizen* referred exclusively to men.[35]

Feminismo Peruano Founded

The organization Feminismo Peruano was founded under adverse conditions. Augusto B. Leguía had reformed his own constitution to permit his reelection. At this time, writer Zoila Aurora Cáceres had published in a variety of Latin American newspapers under the pseudonym Evangelina.[36] Following her separation from her husband, Guatemalan writer Gómez Carrillo, she continued her literary career, saying it allowed her to "think, feel, and say everything freely." She wrote, "Through literature I was able to gain access to the public sphere and earn acceptance in the world of the 'citizens.'"[37]

Cáceres founded a number of societies, including schools and unions, demonstrating her desire to achieve multiple goals: to liberate women from the private sphere by making them financially independent through education and professionalization, to fight for women's civil and political rights, and to advance the interests of women workers.[38] She also cofounded, together with María Jesús Alvarado, the Comité Femenino de la Lucha Pro-Abaratamiento de las Subsistencias to combat hunger and price increases on basic necessities.

Feminismo Peruano was created to obtain "the most progressive social evolution," which included "social equality" and "equality before the law." It strategically avoided affiliation with any political party in order to attract

Peruvians of all religious and political persuasions. "Peruvian feminists" could include "everyone who sympathizes with the group's principles: nationalist, republican, democratic, and unwilling to admit differences among social classes."[39] Almost all its members, however, came from the privileged classes, and almost all were in the capital, with a small presence in Cuzco and Piura.[40]

Not everyone supported Cáceres. Notably, Magda Porta, a poet, story-teller, and founding member of Alianza Popular Revolucionaria Americana (APRA), followed her party's line and supported a restricted vote for women who worked or studied, which would have eliminated most Catholic and conservative potential female voters.[41] According to Asunción Lavrin, the two ideological groups were called "las viejas" (the old ladies) and "las jóvenes" (the young—the *apristas*).[42] The writer and journalist Dora Mayer went so far as to advocate for Indigenous suffrage, at least for men, despite widespread illiteracy. For Mayer, Indigenous men were part of the nation and therefore ought to vote. She nevertheless opposed women's suffrage because she thought it would deprive women of femininity.[43]

Cáceres intensified her activism between 1930 and 1933 after a coup over-threw Leguía's government. It was a moment of democratic transition and institutional reorganization that proved favorable for demanding women's rights. When Sánchez Cerro proclaimed Leguía's overthrow from the city of Arequipa, he promised to reconstruct the country on a foundation of elec-toral freedom. He affirmed that he would maintain "with invincible will, the banner of liberty and right."[44] Feminismo Peruano took advantage of the same rhetoric to demand that the revolutionary government liberate women from the "most cruel injustice" and decree women's suffrage.[45]

The members of the 1930 Commission on the Proposal for the Electoral Statute declared themselves in support of women's suffrage, but when it came to the vote, many either absented themselves or voted against it. When the new law was passed the following year, it obligated voter registration for all "male Peruvians who can read and write and who are in full exercise of their civil rights."[46] The word *male*, it would appear, was added to prevent women from trying to register for the elections of the Constituent Assembly. Decades later, the renown historian Jorge Basadre, who sat on the commis-sion, called the failure to extend the vote to women an "unpardonable error."[47] Cáceres called out the members of the commission, especially the apristas, for their failure to adhere to their own principle of equality. "All laws with restrictions are odious and contribute to bitterness that becomes harmful, particularly in Peru, where we have more than enough concerns with our racial problems."[48] It is likely that the progressive members of the commission were telling the truth when they said they supported women's suffrage but were fearful that many Peruvian women would vote against progressive politics if given the chance.

Maritza Villavicencio calls Feminismo Peruano a "solitary voice amid highly adverse conditions," not because Peru lacked women's organizations but because most of them did not promote suffrage. They were cultural or beneficent societies that were either unwilling to diverge from their founding principles, as was the case with the Legión Femenina Pro-cultura, or failed to see the importance of the vote, such as the Consejo Nacional de Mujeres, even if they had been founded to obtain it.[49]

First Debate on Suffrage in the Constituent Congress

Zoila A. Cáceres, through an alliance with the press, had managed to make known national and international events that favored women's suffrage in the pages of El Comercio, La Prensa, La Crónica, La Patria, La Sanción, La Idea, La Noche, El Perú, Últimas Noticias, El Pueblo, and La Libertad. Some of these papers even opened a section called "Feminismo Peruano" to inform society on the advances of the suffrage movement. Cáceres kept women's suffrage in the public eye through conferences, meetings, visits, and interviews.[50, 51] She also maintained an active correspondence with intellectuals and politicians, pressuring them to come out in favor of women's suffrage.[52] Her efforts paid off with the first debates in Congress on legislation to extend the suffrage. Of the 145 representatives in Congress, approximately 20 percent participated in the debate, which took place from December 26, 1931, to January 12, 1932. There were three main divisions. The conservative Partido Descentralista del Perú (PDP) opposed the extension outright; apristas supported a qualified and restricted vote; some members of the dominant (populist and authoritarian) Unión Revolucionaria (UR) supported full equality for literate women, although others were opposed.[53]

The conservative argument posited that nature had made men and women different and that differentiated social roles flowed logically from those differences. Men, some legislators argued, were born in a state of liberty that protected them from external influence, while women were not. Manuel J. Bustamante de la Fuente (PDP) argued that "nature since primitive times has charged women with the preservation of the specie, the home, the family, and its traditions."[54] Francisco Pastor (PSP) contended that women had been consigned to the home and family because they were "more sentimental and emotional" and it was only there that they could "affirm their virtues." Manuel Ignacio Frisancho (PSP) opposed suffrage because he believed a majority of women looked through the "prism of clericalism," which meant the "stagnation and paralysis of all progress." Víctor Colina (PDP) claimed that women had received an "essentially mystical education," which implied that "the women's vote for us would become a vote for the religious," which would entail "expanding the electorate of ultramontane conservatism."[55]

The same legislators approved of other types of women's public activity at the local level, however. The independent representative Emilio Abril Vizcarra noted Elvira García y García's successful Asylum for Orphaned Children in Cusco, for example.[56] Teaching was also suitable, according to Francisco Pastor of the PSP, who lauded Gabriela Mistral's efforts at primary instruction because "[the mother is] the first teacher in the home and because pedagogically, education should follow a maternal educative process."[57] Pediatric medicine and puericulture were also appropriate, according to Pastor: "This would be the modern, scientific, and humane idea of the woman's conquest, and not a grotesque equality with men." If absolutely necessary, women's participation should be gradual, as had occurred in England.[58]

Apristas preferred to deny the vote to women of the upper class while supporting suffrage for lower- and middle-class women (who, they thought, would be more likely to support them politically). They proposed to extend the vote to women who worked, which they defined as remunerative labor undertaken outside of the private sphere. "To say that a woman who works inside her house is a worker," according to aprista delegate Luis Alberto Sánchez, "is simple demagogy."[59] The aprista Luis E. Heysen added, "We differ regarding who should receive citizenship, the little doll, or little society girl, who being idle, does not produce and being idle is at the same time subject to outside influences, clerical influences, if you will. . . . We oppose the vote for the little doll, the little salon girl."[60] Peru, according to these apristas, "should be a republic of workers." Manuel Seoane explained, "If we believe that democracy rests on the economy and the principle foundation of the economy is work, the worker is the one who ought to have the right to create the system that will govern that democracy."[61] If women "bearing arms and the instruments of their own liberation concur with the citizens, with manual labors and intellectuals, the middle class, workers and peasants, in the transformation of the Peruvian State, [it will be] no longer an oppressive state, but rather a state of liberty, justice, and economic equality," said Luis E. Heysen Inchaústegui (APRA).[62]

Some advocated unrestricted access to the vote, basing their arguments on the defense of "equity, justice, and social utility."[63] They said there was no reason to establish a difference between men and women because both shared an interest in the development of the state. Women should have the vote because it would be "one of the best ways to channel the ascent of patriotism among women in the country and to interest them in public affairs, which are generally neglected in Peru.[64] Other legislators followed J. S. Mill's philosophy, which demanded women's suffrage on equal terms with men. Lucio Fuentes Aragón (UR) argued that women had demonstrated sufficient patriotism in the War of the Pacific and had contributed to the downfall of Leguía's dictatorship and Sánchez Cerro's election.[65]

Representatives from the Socialist Party, such as Hildebrando Castro Pozo and Luciano Castillo Coloma, maintained that the fundamental distinction in society was not between those who worked and those who did not but "between bourgeois and proletarians, between those who owned the means of production and those who possessed nothing more than the strength of their arms."[66] To reserve the vote for those who worked during a period of high unemployment could "in practice reclaim it for the bourgeoisie, for the owners, and deny it to the proletarians."[67] They claimed to be unafraid of the possibility that women might be "completely religious" because they believed the issue could be resolved with secular teachers and instruction.[68] The socialists proposed unrestricted, universal suffrage, including women's suffrage and the right to be elected for congressional and municipal office.[69]

Representative M. Arébalo, who originally had showed little interest in the debate, put forth a lone proposal to extend only the municipal vote to women. He reasoned that there were more women than men, and to concede the full suffrage "would create a privilege for the woman with detriment for the male."[70] Women, he noted, were still legally subject to their fathers and husbands for purposes of civil law. They should not be able to decide matters of national import when they could not even act in civil, individual, and private matters. Finally, he said, the Peruvian woman was essentially religious. To give her full voting rights would result in a clerical government that would risk the "natural evolution of our institutions."[71] The independent Catholic representative Víctor Andrés Belaúnde moved Arévalo's proposal after both restricted and full suffrage had been voted down. The proposal passed.[72] The constitution of 1933 would include Article 86: "Literate citizens will enjoy suffrage rights; and, in municipal elections, Peruvian women over the age of majority [twenty-one years], married women or women who have been married, and mothers who have not yet achieved the age of majority."[73] It is noteworthy that the constitution conceded suffrage rights without acknowledging that women were citizens.[74] In any event, no municipal elections took place for decades—until 1963. Sitting government ministers appointed mayors and councilmen.

Feminismo Peruano concluded its activities with the recognition of municipal suffrage. During its existence, it had enjoyed foreign, especially British, support from prominent figures like Margaret Bonfield, minister of labor of the United Kingdom, and Eleanor Rathbone and Mary Agnes Hamilton, both British members of Parliament.[75] Several years passed with little suffragist agitation. In 1936, however, a reform to the civil code of 1852 finally brought some relief, including a woman's right to divorce, which conservatives had previously been able to prevent. María Emma Mannarelli dryly observes that long-lived opposition to divorce stemmed from "the fear women might choose it" and from "the masculine zeal for control.[76] Suffrage activism resumed with the Eighth American International Conference, which took place in Lima on December 9–27, 1938.

The Eighth American International Conference and women's suffrage rights

The Eighth American International Conference permitted Peruvian suffrag-ists to demand their rights not only from the highest level of Peruvian politi-cal authority but also on the international stage. General Oscar R. Benavides had assumed the presidency following the death of the incumbent, army commander Luis M. Sánchez Cerro, ostensibly to serve out the remainder of the six-year term. Benavides remained in power until 1939, however, after suspending scheduled elections in 1936. Both military governments devel-oped policies of repression toward every kind of opposition party. A prohibi-tion against parties with international affiliation in the 1933 constitution justified purges of the Communist Party of Peru as well as APRA, whose lead-ers were persecuted, jailed, and deported. Using Dahl's classification, we can categorize Peru as a regime with a "closed hegemony."[77]

At the conference, Cáceres returned to the stage, again arguing that women should vote and be voted for "in order . . . to defend their interests as mother, wife, and worker. To protect their children, ensure the integrity of the family and to collaborate with men in patriotic causes."[78] Women, she pointed out, were subject to the law and obliged to pay taxes. It was only right they should have the same rights as men.[79]

The Consejo Nacional de Mujeres submitted a "Memorial to the Peruvian Woman," which read, "We address you to ask in the name of the Peruvian woman in general that she be granted the full political vote. Not because we want to mix actively in political life but because when the occasion presents itself, we aspire to be able to use it to sustain the institution at the base of our national life . . . [a]nd also to support, where they already exist, and to obtain where they do not yet exist, broad laws for the protection of the woman and child."[80] The Comité Nacional Pro Derechos Civiles y Políticos de la Mujer, presided over by Elisa Rodríguez Parra de García Rosell, sent a memo to the president of the conference, Carlos Concha, requesting, if a treaty or convention were not possible, "that [the conference] conclude with a final recommendation to the represented Government a modification of their laws in the sense of extending to all the women in America equality before the laws with respect to men, in the sense of an equivalence of rights and duties in the political and civil life of the peoples."[81] The writer and journalist Elvira García García, who had declined to support Cáceres's project in the early 1930s, now joined the campaign in favor of the vote. "Outdated prejudices," she wrote, "should be destroyed." She felt confident that "today's woman, conscious of her rights and responsibilities, can face whatever the future may bring."[82] Not everyone was yet persuaded, however. Hortensia Málaga de Cornejo Bouroncle published an article making the case that women should avoid entry into the political life of the nation out of patriotism, "until we are perfectly conscious of our CAPACITY, DISCIPLINE, MORALS, AND SOLIDARITY." Otherwise, premature suffrage would be "a total failure."[83] As had always been true in the past, the great majority of Peruvian women did not involve themselves in collective action for political rights. It continued to be a concern primarily of intellectuals and professionals from the middle and upper classes.[84]

The Inter-American Commission of Women sent a proposal for the establishment of a formal convention to the Commission of Women's Political and Civil Rights. Argentine delegate Susana Larguía, secretary of the Argentine Union of Women, appealed to recent changes in women's roles, noting, "Today's woman has greater responsibilities, on a greater field of action. Her femininity is no longer a luxury sheltered by ignorance and confinement."[85] Chilean delegate Graciela Mandujano added that "every kind of protection, every kind of collective paternalism, is odious, whether is it from group to group, national to nation, sex to sex."[86] For Mandujano, the vote was nothing more than a "symbol" of citizenship, which, if granted, would confer "dignity" and "the possibility of defending ourselves individually."[87] The Dominican delegate, Minerva Bernardino, excoriated countries with "shameful codes inspired by the ancient font of Roman law and modeled on the narrow and reactionary framework of Napoleonic law."[88] She warned that if their petitions were not accepted, "the cause of feminism, like any other movement that arises from the live and palpitating entrails of the people, is destined to triumph fully."[89]

In the end, as in prior conferences, the proposed convention was not accepted. Neither did the memorial from the Peruvian delegation receive consideration, despite the fact that a majority of the delegates considered themselves to be "fervent defenders" of the feminine cause. The five thousand signatures Cáceres presented on behalf of Feminismo Peruano and the four thousand from Esther Festini de Ramos Ocampo of Consejo Nacional de Mujeres del Perú counted for nothing.[90] Nevertheless, their labors contributed to the signing of the Declaration of Lima in Favor of Women's Rights, which affirmed a woman's right to "equal political treatment," "to enjoy equality in civil order," "to the most ample opportunities and protection in the workplace," and to "the broadest protection as a mother."[91] The female delegates were not satisfied.

The Lima press had made public the women's demands from the conference. Most papers declined to support them overtly, with the exception of *La Crónica*, which published an editorial marking a shift in the struggle: "[Women's rights have] ceased to be a topic of political frivolity and have become a serious equation, it is no longer a question of incorporating the woman in political and civil life, with prerogatives that would serve no purpose if she were not integrally prepared. It concerns, on real bases, the way to extend to the woman what, in all truth, is hers. Her legitimate rights. The rights of the woman."[92] The conference also served to connect leaders from across the Americas who were involved in the same cause. The delegates created a web of representatives from different women's organizations, which would empower them in their own national struggles. For example, members of forty-three different Mexican women's organizations sent an inspiring greeting to the delegation from the Unión Continental Femenina de Cuba, congratulating them on their work as "vanguards" at the conference.[93]

The Recognition of Political Rights and the Movimiento Cívico Femenino during El Ochenio de Odría[94]

By the postwar period, most countries in Latin America had recognized women's political rights, either of their own accord or as a result of having signed international agreements following the Second World War. In the Ninth International American Conference (1948), participating countries adopted an agreement to neither deny nor restrict the right to vote and be voted for on account of sex. The conference's American Declaration of the Rights and Duties of Man affirmed that all persons were equal before the law and that they had the same rights and duties regardless of race, sex, language, creed, or any other distinction.[95] In a similar fashion, the United Nations' Universal Declaration of Human Rights stipulated that all human beings are born free and equal in dignity and rights. It declared that political power should be chosen by the people, expressed by means of authentic elections with universal, secret, and equal suffrage.[96]

By the 1950s, many South American countries had already recognized women's suffrage, at least for the (sometimes small) portion of the female population that was literate: Ecuador in 1929, Brazil and Uruguay in 1932, Argentina and Venezuela in 1947, Chile in 1949, and Bolivia in 1952. Others, including Peru, Colombia, and Paraguay, continued to resist demands for women's political participation. In Peru, the expansion of citizenship took place within a context of profound social change: massive migration from the countryside to the city and the consequent appearance of slums, industrialization and an increase in the proletariat (fueled by increased demand for exports following World War II and the Korean War), and a revitalized peasant movement.[97] In 1948 General Manuel Arturo Odría Amoretti had taken power in a coup that overthrew José Luis Bustamante y Rivero. In 1950 he legitimized his government by holding elections in which, after he imprisoned his opponent, Ernesto Montagne, he ran as the only candidate. Radical parties like APRA and the Peruvian Communist Party (PCP) could function only clandestinely, having been barred from participation since 1933. Odría toughened his persecution of communists and apristas on the grounds that they put the "democratic system" at risk.[98]

Efforts to obtain women's suffrage in Peru continued during the 1940s and 1950s in the form of bills to reform Articles 84, 86, and 88 of the constitution of 1933.[99] These bills were presented to Congress on the initiative of several women's organization and some legislators. In 1941, for example, Elisa Rodríguez Parra de García Rossell's Comité Nacional Pro-Derechos Civiles y Políticos de la Mujer was behind a bill presented by Dante Castañola. It sought to reform Article 86. It was admitted for debate but never emerged from committee.[100] In 1945 Senator José Antonio Encinas and Emilio Romero moved a bill that originated with María Jesús Alvarado, who was once again in charge of Evolución Femenina. She sent a letter to the congressional Commission on the Constitution. citing the UN Charter: "The capacity of the woman throughout all epochs of history, as oppressed as she has been, [has been demonstrated]; her aptitudes for modern life in multiple activities affirmed . . . cooperating alongside the man in various functions that require greater physical strength, intelligence, and technical knowledge, surpassing in many cases the work of the male."[101] The following year, in the context of the democratic aperture of the government of José Luis Bustamante y Rivero (1945–1948), Magda Portal, having recently returned from exile, presided over the First Congress of Aprista Women. Portal had publicly expressed that the moment for women to manage their own affairs had arrived. To her consternation, however, the aprista leader Haya de La Torre continued to affirm that the woman's place was in the home. Her disillusionment increased when, at the Second Congress of the Aprista Party, in 1948, her petition to permit women to vote in internal party elections was ignored, leading her to quit the congress and later the party.[102]

The year 1953 saw two constitutional reform bills. One, from Francisco Pastor, the deputy who had opposed women's suffrage in 1932, proposed the modification of Article 84. The other, from Osores Villacorta, addressed Articles 84, 86, and 88. It would have granted women citizenship (Article 84), suffrage (86), and voter registration (88). Neither bill passed.

Women's suffrage finally came from the executive in 1954. President Manuel A. Odría, celebrating the sixth anniversary of his coup d'état, declared that there was no "reason why the Peruvian woman should be in inferior conditions with respect to others on the Continent and in the World, [and that it would be] the work of the Restored Revolution to extend full rights of citizenship to the woman."[103] The move was seen as an electoral strategy with an eye toward 1956; there were clear signs the president intended to pursue reelection then. The day after making the declaration, the Chamber of Deputies received an executive bill formulated by the Ministry of Government and Police that proposed the reform of Articles 84 and 86 with the objective "of conceding to Peruvian women equal rights as citizens."[104] The bill did nothing to remove literacy restrictions, which continued to disenfranchise the vast majority of poor and Indigenous Peruvians.

A majority in Congress promptly asserted that it was no longer time to discuss, as in the past, whether women did or did not have equal rights with men to participate in public life because they had already overcome the notion that "politics were only for men."[105] On the other hand, deputies like

Luis Osores Villacorta advocated for the extension of not only political rights but also social and economic rights so "that woman should never the be object, on account of her sex, of any kind of discrimination."[106] He continued to portray women's entrance into political life as an opportunity for the moral salvation of politics. "The woman," he claimed, "should continue to improve the moral tonic of the country's political struggle; because . . . it is evident in woman a sense of justice, an inclination towards piety, and a fervent desire for everything that means national aggrandizement; and this tonic, this note that the woman should impress on public life, should indisputably be of great moral encouragement."[107] The bill modified the 1933 constitution (after being debated in two ordinary legislative sessions in both chambers) with the promulgation of Law 12391 on September 7, 1955. The law summarized the three changes, making women citizens, granting them suffrage, and making them eligible for voter registration (Articles 84, 86, and 88, respectively).[108] A group of female intellectuals, professionals, and representatives of women's organizations attended the debates. They included María C. Moreno, director of the journal *Cultura Americana*; the professor Eloisa Peralta Torres; and María Luisa Montori, president of Movimiento Cívico Femenino del Perú.[109] Twenty-four more years would pass before the constitution of 1979 declared universal suffrage.

Many have speculated about the reasons Odría chose to enfranchise some women in 1955. Most assume it is because he wanted their support, yet he did not stand in the 1956 elections. Many believe he initially intended to run but changed his mind. If that's true, that would support the hypothesis that electoral politics motivated the decision to expand the franchise. We cannot be sure. What is certain, however, is that he favored groups that tended to oppose APRA, such as the women who created the Movimiento Cívico Femenino del Perú.

Movimiento Cívico Femenino del Perú

Women were eligible to register to vote for the 1956 presidential and congressional elections. Of a total of 1,575,741 registered voters, 34 percent (531,541) were women and 66 percent (1,044,200) were men.[110] This indicates that there was broad interest among literate women in participating in politics, especially when we consider that both parties of the masses, the APRA and the PCP, were excluded from the ballot.[111] If women had voted as a group, it is clear they would have had the voting power to sway the election.

Odría appears to have been behind the creation of the Partido Restaurador, whose candidate, Hernando de Lavalle, he initially supported.[112] When it became apparent that Lavalle would lose, he negotiated an agreement with Manuel Prado Ugarteche of the Movimiento Democrático Peruano (MDP). He agreed to switch his support to the MDP in exchange for impunity. APRA had separately negotiated an agreement with the same party, combining unlikely bedfellows behind a single candidacy, whose subsequent victory was therefore unsurprising.

The Movimiento Cívico Femenino del Perú was organized in Lima during the congressional debates of 1955 along the lines of the US League of Women Voters.[113] It was ostensibly nonpartisan and aimed to "awaken in the Peruvian woman a consciousness of her responsibilities in the civil arena and provide her with the means to prepare herself to act with efficiency."[114] Women were told they should not only vote in favor of "apt and honest" candidates but "also, and above all interest themselves and collaborate according to their aptitudes in order to complement the civic work of men.[115] The organization promoted these goals through the press, on the radio, and in talks, conferences, and short courses.

The Movimiento Cívico claimed to want every Peruvian woman, regardless of social class, to be able to contribute to the "common good."[116] Nevertheless, the movement was another association of women from the middle and upper classes and had no reach beyond the capital. According to Elsa Chaney, its members were Catholic, and many were involved in Catholic Action. Chaney believes that one of its members was part of a Catholic group that was founded to counter aprista women.[117] Matilde Pérez Palacio (the first treasurer of the Movimiento Cívico) had been secretary of the Comité Organizador de la Acción Católica de la Juventud Femenina and had worked with a journal at the Universidad Católica, where she had also founded the school of journalism. Thus, as was probably Odría's intention, his 1955 suffrage extension had the immediate effect of strengthening the hand of anti-aprista Catholic conservatives.[118]

The Movimiento Cívico was aggressive in putting forward candidates for Congress. Of the freshmen members elected in 1956, three were members of the Movimiento Cívico and four had graduated from the Universidad Católica. Matilde Pérez Palacio Carranza worked at the university as director of the Instituto Femenino de Estudios Superiores, a post she held from 1941 to 1970. She entered Congress having participated in a number of women's organizations, including the Consejo Nacional de Mujeres.

Political rights came to Peruvian women during a moment of worldwide feminist retreat.[119] Peru was no exception. Nina Flores, secretary general of the Frente Nacional de Mujeres, wrote a letter to Congress that gives a sense of the environment: "There is nothing more satisfactory or that fills the spirit with more renewed hope than to testify to a spontaneous act of justice. President Odría is interested in granting us a right that had previously been delayed without genuine justification. More meritorious and humane is General Odría's gesture because, with its motive of observation and understanding of the current political process, it prevents our women from becoming instruments of professional agitators, dragging them into the streets to solicit a right, in the midst of boisterous protests."[120] Nevertheless, we should not discount the struggle that had, since the start of the twentieth century, raised the consciousness of Peruvian society about equal political rights.

Nine women, mostly from the provinces, were elected to Congress in 1956—4 percent of the total number of representatives.[121] An article in *El Comercio* titled "Woman's Triumph" declared that "the prejudice of masculine superiority is dead. Good and dead, and we'll have to bury it."[122] In reality, women have still not achieved equality of opportunity for participation in politics, despite having applied the mechanism of positive discrimination in the form of gender quotas. In the application of the quota laws, women continue to be marginalized because they appear at the bottom of the list of candidates, especially at the municipal and regional levels, which explains why many women candidates fail to be elected.

Conclusion

The Peruvian suffrage movement developed in three periods. María Jesús

Alvarado inaugurated the first in 1911 with her speech before the Lima Geographic Society, which lay the foundations for Peruvian feminism. It was a moment of social change that gave rise to a labor movement and an Indigenous rights movement as well. Zoila A. Cáceres and her organization Feminismo Peruano led the second wave in 1931–1933, culminating in the achievement of the municipal vote. However, political instability due to coups d'état contributed to a long delay before municipal elections were held, undermining the meaning of the attainment. In 1938 suffragists took advantage of the Eighth International American Conference to situate their demands within an international context. They secured a statement of principles in the form of the Declaration of Lima in Favor of the Rights of the Woman but fell short of obtaining promises of action. This activity took place in the setting of the military government of General Oscar R. Benavides, who continued his predecessor's repression of the political opposition. The final period took place during the dictatorship of Manuel A. Odría Amoretti, who introduced his own legislation to reform the three articles of the 1933 constitution that impeded women from voting. By then, the only other countries in the Americas that still had no form of women's suffrage were Colombia and Paraguay. However, even that extension failed to include most poor and indigenous Peruvians, who were barred from participation by literacy restrictions until 1979.

Notes

1. *Variedades* 19, no. 799 (June 1923): 799.
2. Clemente Palma was editor. He held a doctorate in letters (1897) and later worked as a lawyer. He represented Lima in the Chamber of Deputies from 1919 to 1930. Tauro del Pino, *Enciclopedia ilustrada del Perú.*
3. Denegri, *La Primera Generación de Mujeres Ilustradas*, 11–12.
4. Rama, *La ciudad letrada*, 119.
5. *Código Civil de 1852* (Lima: Impr. del Gobierno, Eusebio Aranda, 1852), Articles 16–17, 175–177. This version is available in the Biblioteca Nacional de Perú, in the research reading room. Women's legal subjugation was common throughout the hemisphere.
6. *Código Civil de 1852*, Articles 33–34.
7. *Diario de los Debates del Congreso Constituyente de 1931. T. I. (28 November 1931 to 23 January 1932)* (Lima: Congreso Constituyente, 1931), 421.

8. Moscoso de Carbajal, *Felisa: Ligeros pensamientos consagrados a la mujer,* in Villavicencio and Zegarra, *Del Silencio a la Palabra.*

9. Asunción Lavrin notes that Peruvian women at the end of the nineteenth century had diverse social conditions. Lavrin, *Women, Feminism, and Social Change,* 4.

10. In Peru in 1919 there were 3,006 primary schools with 181,211 students. By 1929 this number had risen to 3,553 primary schools with 308,450 students. By that time, secondary education had been extended to women. Of the thirty-six national schools, twenty-nine were for males and seven were for females. (Basadre, *Historia de la República del Perú,* 142). In 1920 state secondary schools registered 3,350 male students with only 144 females. In 1933 there were 8,310 males and 1,130 females (Contreras, Mistis y campesinos, Table 11). Only men attended university since only recently, in 1908, had Law 801 permitted women to obtain academic degrees. There were exceptions. In 1875 María Trinidad Enríquez entered the School of Law in Cuzco, becoming the first university-educated woman in Peru. She was barred from graduating, however. Years later other women enrolled at the Universidad Mayor de San Marcos. They included Laura Rodríguez Dulanto, who entered in 1895 to study medicine, and Esther Festini, who enrolled in the Faculty of Letters in 1899. Basadre, *Historia de la República del Perú,* 105–6.

11. Mercedes Cabello de Carbonera, "Influencia de la mujer en la civilización," in Villavicencio and Zegarra, *Del Silencio a la Palabra,* 65.

12. Teresa González de Fanning, "La Educación Femenina," in Villavicencio and Zegarra, *Del Silencio a la Palabra,* 108.

13. In 1874 Carbonera wrote, "Hace tiempo que en los principales centros de civilización, la mujer trabaja con empeño para obtener derechos políticos. En Londres, en Nueva York, en Zurich, ha habido reuniones públicas y se han establecido periódicos redactados por señoras con sólo ese objetivo. Nosotras creemos que aunque esto es justo y lo dictamina un sentimiento de igualdad y fraternidad que nos dice: que formando el bello sexo la mitad de la humanidad, debe participar de todos los derechos que goza la otra mitad; sin embargo, no creemos que la cuestión es de gran importancia para la mujer." Quoted in Villavicencio and Zegarra, *Del Silencio a la Palabra,* 96.

14. Mercedes Cabello de Carbonera, "Influencia de la mujer en la civilización," in Villavicencio and Zegarra, *Del Silencio a la Palabra,* 98.

15. Clorinda Matto de Turner, "Luz entre sombras. Estudio filosófico-moral para las madres de familia," in Villavicencio and Zegarra, *Del Silencio a la Palabra,* 95.

16. Villavicencio and Zegarra, *Del Silencio a la Palabra,* 98.

17. Nicolás de Piérola entered government following a civil war between representatives of the government of the Partido Constitucional and the Coalición Nacional (an alliance between the Partido Civil and the Partido Democrático).

18. Basadre, *Elecciones y centralismo en el Perú,* Vols. 12–13.

19. Burga and Flores Galindo, *Apogeo y crisis.*
20. By Law 2851 of November 25, 1918. Sulmont, *El Movimiento Obrero Peruano.*
21. In 1908, before her feminist speech, she published the following articles in *Álbún* 1: "El objetivo de la escuela fiscal" and "Vida escolar."
22. Alvarado's article was titled "Feminismo," but in the congressional record it appeared as "Educación y Derechos de la Mujer." Zegarra Florez, "María Jesús Alvarado y el rol," 389, 503.
23. Zegarra Florez, 389, 503.
24. This assertion from Alvarado regarding the equality of women's political rights was an advance from an earlier posture expressed in a study she sent to the Argentine Congress in 1910, in which she remarked, "No sostengo yo que la mujer debe aspirar a una igualdad absoluta con el hombre, ejerciendo por consiguiente todos los derechos políticos y cumpliendo los deberes del ciudadano, no porque reconozca en ella inferioridad moral ni intelectual . . . si no . . . porque la naturaleza ha señalado a la mujer una misión que no tiene el varón: la de la maternidad, santa, nobilísima misión, cuyo cumplimiento es incompatible con ciertos deberes cívicos." María Jesús Alvarado, "Feminismo," in Zegarra Florez, "María Jesús Alvarado: la construcción," 148.
25. Cited in Zegarra Florez, "María Jesús Alvarado y el rol," 506.
26. On Carrie Chapman Catt's struggle for women's suffrage, see Booth and Jones, "Carrie Chapman Catt," 130–42.
27. The first president of the Consejo Nacional de Mujeres en el Perú was Juana Alarco de Dammert, who belonged to the Cuerpo Consultivo de Evolución Femenina, whose first elected secretary was María Jesús Alvarado. It was said that María Jesús Alvarado refused the presidency. *La Prensa,* Lima, March 1923, Biblioteca Nacional del Perú, Hemeroteca.
28. Miller, *Suffrage Movement in Latin America,* 80–81.
29. Miller, 81.
30. Cited in Zegarra Florez, "María Jesús Alvarado: la construcción," 185. See *Institución "Evolución Femenina." Exposición de Principios y Estatutos* (Lima: Imprenta Peruana, 1914).
31. Delegations attended from Argentina, Bolivia, Brasil, Colombia, Costa Rica, Cuba, the United States, Panama, Paraguay, Peru, Uruguay, and Venezuela. The event took place under the auspices of the Third Scientific Panamerican Congress, which occurred alongside the women's event. "Segunda Conferencia Panamericana de Mujeres. Lima, 21 de Diciembre, 1924-6 de Enero, 1925," Derecho International, January 26, 2014, http://www.dipublico.org/101313/segunda-conferencia-panamericana-de-mujeres-lima-21-de-diciembre-1924–6-de-enero-1925; Weaver, *Peruvian Rebel,* 104.
32. Some national and international newspapers said that Alvarado had been imprisoned for fighting for a "new social system" founded on the doctrine of "liberty and justice." *El Comercio,* Lima, December 25, 1924, CEDOC, Colección

María Jesús Alvarado; *El Diario Buenos Aires*, June 6, 1925; *La Razón*, Buenos Aires, December 1, 1925.

33. Aguilar, "Vía crucis de las mujeres peruanas."

34. Constitution of 1860, Article 38.

35. Constitution of 1933, Article 84.

36. Zoila Aurora Cáceres, a well-known author in Spain and Latin America, was born in Lima in 1872. Her father was Andrés A. Cáceres, hero of La Breña in the War of the Pacific, founder of the Partido Constitucional (1882), and ex-president of Perú (1886–1890 and 1884–1885). Her mother was Antonia Moreno. She studied in Lima at the Colegio de los Sagrados Corazones de Belén and later in England, Germany, and France, in addition to traveling to Switzerland, Italy, and Belgium. In Paris she was a student at the School of Advanced Social Studies at the Sorbonne, where she earned a diploma in social studies with the thesis "Feminism in Berlin." She was the first woman to obtain such a degree. During the 1940s, she was twice the Peruvian delegate to the Interamerican Commission of Women, whose seat was in Washington, DC. Cáceres, *Labor de armonía interamericana* 1946.

37. The feared writer and journalist Luis Bonafoux called her a "socialist Catholic" because of her 1909 book *Mujeres de ayer y de hoy*—which denounced long and intense working hours endured by the most vulnerable women in Lima—and because she was Catholic. Cáceres, *Labor de armonía interamericana*; Aguilar, "La 'aurora' del sufragio femenino en el Perú."

38. Aguilar, "La 'aurora' del sufragio femenino en el Perú."

39. *La Prensa*, Lima, October 1924, Biblioteca Nacional del Perú, Colección Zoila A. Cáceres.

40. *La Sanción*, Lima, January 1, 1932, Biblioteca Nacional del Perú, Colección Zoila A. Cáceres.

41. García-Bryce, "Transnational Activist."

42. Lavrin, "Ciudadanía y acción política femenina," 593.

43. Boesten, *Intersecting Inequalities*.

44. *La Crónica*, Lima, January 7, 1932, Biblioteca Nacional del Perú, Colección Zoila A. Cáceres.

45. *El Pueblo*, Lima, December 4, 1930, *La Crónica*, Lima, January 7, 1932, Biblioteca Nacional del Perú, Colección Zoila A. Cáceres.

46. Electoral Statute 7177, Article 6, May 26, 1931.

47. Basadre, *Elecciones y centralismo en el Perú*, 148.

48. *La Crónica*, Lima, April 28, 1931, Biblioteca Nacional del Perú, Colección Zoila A. Cáceres.

49. Villavicencio and Zegarra, *Del Silencio a la Palabra*, 180; Aguilar, "El sufragio de la mujer."

50. Miguelina Acosta Cárdenas (a lawyer specializing in women's civil rights) wrote about the necessity of preparing women to understand their legal

rights. Samuel Guy Inman, a professor at Columbia University in the United States, wrote about the feminist movement. *La Crónica*, Lima, June 21, 1931, *La Prensa*. Lima, April 2, 1931, Biblioteca Nacional del Perú, Colección Zoila A. Cáceres.

51. The organized women went to the palace on multiple occasions to lobby the presidents of the Juntas de Gobierno, José Luis Sánchez Cerro and David Samanez Ocampo, in 1930 and 1931, respectively, to recognize women's suffrage.

52. Biblioteca Nacional del Perú, Colección Zoila A. Cáceres.

53. Aguilar, "El sufragio de la mujer," 123–64.

54. *Diario de los Debates*, 568.

55. *Diario de los Debates*, 604.

56. *Diario de los Debates*, 615.

57. *Diario de los Debates*, 491.

58. *Diario de los Debates*, 491.

59. *Diario de los Debates*, 584.

60. *Diario de los Debates*, 611.

61. *Diario de los Debates*, 616.

62. *Diario de los Debates*, 612.

63. *Diario de los Debates*, 400.

64. *Diario de los Debates*, 400.

65. *Diario de los Debates*, 420.

66. *Diario de los Debates*, 501–2.

67. *Diario de los Debates*, 501.

68. *Diario de los Debates*, 501.

69. *Primer Manifiesto y Programa de Reivindicaciones Inmediatas, Aprobadas por la Primera Conferencia Nacional del Partido* (Lima: Partido Socialista del Perú, 1933), 12–13.

70. *Diario de los Debates*, 405.

71. *Diario de los Debates*, 405.

72. Congress approved it by sixty-nine to thirty-six votes. The Decentralized representatives supported the proposal, understanding that the municipal vote and the political vote were two different things. As municipal government is closer to the life of the community, the unrestricted women's vote was applicable. The Unión Revolucionaria agreed that "even the municipal vote is granted." The APRA, on the understanding that municipalities should be the cells making up the Peruvian state, continued to support the restricted vote because it thought municipal activities should not be confined the local level. *Diario de los Debates*, 731–36

73. Constitution of 1933 in García Belaunde, *Las Constituciones del Perú*, 386. In other countries in the region, the municipal vote was similarly granted in advance of the national vote. This was the case in Argentina, where in 1864 San

Juan permitted women to vote in municipal elections. In Chile as well, women participated at the municipal level from 1935, since the issues at that level were not considered to be political.

74. It was registered thus in Article 84 of the constitution of 1933: "All male Peruvians having achieved the age of majority, those who are married who are older than eighteen, and those who are emancipated." As can be seen, the addition of the word *varones* (male) makes clear that women were not included.

75. Zoila A. Cáceres's correspondence can be seen in the different Lima newspapers as she supported women's suffrage.

76. Mannarelli, "Mujeres, cultura y controversia pública en el Perú," 922.

77. Dahl, *Polyarchy*.

78. Cáceres, *Labor de armonía interamericana*, 14.

79. In the same fashion, she took advantage of the opportunity to request that women be considered for high state office and the judiciary, as well as the diplomatic service, the police, and municipal posts. Finally, she demanded wage equality, among other rights. These were progressive demands for the 1930s, asking for women to be able to participate in every public space with equal rights. Cáceres, *Labor de armonía interamericana*, 14.

80. "El memorial de la Mujer Peruana a la Octava Conferencia Panamericana," *La Crónica*, Lima, December 19, 1938, *Universal*, Lima, December 18, 1938, *El Comercio*, Lima, December, 1938. Biblioteca Nacional del Perú, Hemeroteca.

81. *Universal*, Lima, December 19, 1938, Biblioteca Nacional del Perú, Hemeroteca.

82. Elvira García García, "Campaña por el voto femenino," *La Crónica*, Lima, December 23, 1938, Biblioteca Nacional del Perú, Hemeroteca.

83. *La Crónica*, Lima, December 9, 1938, Biblioteca Nacional del Perú, Hemeroteca.

84. Aprista leader Magda Portal, who had confronted Cáceres's Feminismo Peruano from 1931–1933, was exiled in Chile under the repressive military government of Oscar R. Benavides (1933–1939). García-Bryce, "Transnational Activist," 197.

85. *El Comercio*, Lima, December 23, 1938, *Universal*, Lima, December 23, 1938, Biblioteca Nacional del Perú, Hemeroteca.

86. *El Comercio*, Lima, December 23, 1938, Biblioteca Nacional del Perú, Hemeroteca.

87. *El Comercio*, Lima, December 23, 1938, Biblioteca Nacional del Perú, Hemeroteca.

88. *Universal*, Lima, December 23, 1938. Biblioteca Nacional del Perú, Hemeroteca.

89. *Universal*. Lima, 23 December 1938. Biblioteca Nacional del Perú, Hemeroteca.

90. Cáceres, *Labor de armonía interamericana*, 15.

91. "Declaración de Lima a favor de los derechos de la mujer," Derecho Internacional, http://www.dipublico.com.ar/15179/declaracion-de-lima-a-favor-de-los-derechos-de-la-mujer-octava-conferencia-internacional-americana-lima-1938, accessed October 30, 2023.

92. *La Crónica*, Lima, December 19, 1938. Biblioteca Nacional del Perú, Hemeroteca.

93. The association was led by Mercedes C. de Ramos, who in addition to motivating her fellow representatives reminded conference delegates of the recognition of American women's political rights. *Universal*, Lima, December 20, 1938. Biblioteca Nacional del Perú, Hemeroteca.

94. This is the name given to the period under the regime of General Manuel A. Odría Amoretti (1948–1956).

95. Article 2 of the American Declaration of the Rights and Duties of Man.

96. Artices 1 and 21 of the Universal Declaration of Human Rights.

97. For more on this subject, see Matos Mar, *Las migraciones campesinas*, and Flores Galindo, *Movimientos campesinos en el Perú*.

98. By Decree Law 10890, November 1, 1948.

99. As mentioned previously, Article 84 defined citizens as "male Peruvians." Article 86 reads: "Citizens who know how to read and write shall enjoy suffrage rights; and, in municipal elections, Peruvian women having obtained the age of majority, those who or married or have been married, and mothers, regardless of whether they have reached the age of majority." Article 88 mentions that voter registration is obligatory and that men may vote until the age of sixty. Constitution of 1933.

100. In this case, the Commission on the Constitution. Roca de Salonen, "La mujer obtuvo el voto."

101. Archive of María Jesús Alvarado, CENDOC—Mujer. The archive is currently in the custody of the Centro de la Mujer Peruana Flora Tristán.

102. García-Bryce, "Transnational Activist," 702–3.

103. *La Nación*, Lima, October 28, 1954.

104. *Diario de Debates de la Cámara de Diputados, Legislatura Ordinaria de 1954* (Lima: Imprenta Torres Aguirre), 379–80.

105. *El Comercio*, Lima, November 6, 1954.

106. El Comercio, Lima, November 3, 1954.

107. *Diario de Debates de la Cámara de Diputados*, 447.

108. Less than two months after recognizing women's political rights, Congress signed the accords of the Inter-American Convention on the Granting of Political Rights to Women, approved at the Ninth International American Conference in 1948. The signing was ratified by Act 12409 on November 5, 1955.

109. *El Comercio*, Lima, September 2, 1855.

110. Macera and Souza Ferreira, *El Proceso Electoral de 1956*.

111. APRA tried to register its members on different political lists, without much success; they were soon detected. Nevertheless, aprista María Mercedes Colina Lozano de Gotuzzo managed to camouflage her registry under the party Frente Parlamentario de La Libertad, as she later admitted. Aguilar, "La ampliación del cuerpo electoral," 161–62.

112. For the 1962 elections, the party was renamed the Unión Nacional Odriísta, confirming the relationship between Odría and the party.

113. María Luisa Montori served as president on the first executive council. Francisca Benavides de Peña Prado was vice president, Matilde Pérez Palacio Carranza treasurer, and Lola de Idiaquez secretary. *El Comercio*, Lima, August 31, 1955.

114. *El Comercio*, Lima, September 6, 1955.

115. *El Comercio*, Lima, September 6, 1955.

116. *El Comercio*, Lima, September 6, 1955.

117. Chaney, *Supermadre*, 93.

118. Odría may have tried to win the support of poorer literate women as well. Similar to Argentina's Eva Perón, his wife, María Delgado Romero de Odría, had engaged in highly visible government assistance programs for the poor. She led the Central de Asistencia Social, which, in addition to symbolic gestures like food distribution at Christmas, included concrete efforts such as a vaccination campaign.

119. Weaver, *Peruvian Rebel*, 147.

120. *La Nación*, Lima, November 3, 1954.

121. For the number of women elected to Congress through the general elections of 2016, see Oficina Nacional De Procesos Electorales, *60 Años del Voto*; Aguilar, "La ampliación del cuerpo electoral," 154.

122. *El Comercio*, Lima, June 7, 1956.

IMPERIALIST SCENARIO

Examples: Puerto Rico, The Philippines

This scenario examines how women obtained the suffrage in countries that were not sovereign at the time of the suffrage extension. The year 1898 was a significant point of change for much of the Western Hemisphere. It signaled a definitive end to Spanish imperialism in the Americas and an inauspicious beginning to US attempts at political and military hegemony. Before 1898, independence leaders across the Americas saw themselves as acting together in a great historical shift: they had moved from being colonial subjects of European monarchies to being independent citizens of self-governing American republics. President James Monroe captured this shared feeling in 1823 in what came to be known as the Monroe Doctrine.

Monroe asserted that the United States would not intervene where Europeans still held colonies in the Americas. However, if a nation had successfully won its independence from a European metropolis, the United States could not see any attempt at recolonization "in any other light than as the manifestation of an unfriendly disposition toward the United States." Monroe shared with other American independence leaders a belief that the Americas were and should be fundamentally different from the European imperial states. America, they thought, was a new hemisphere, and it was destined for liberty. Within a few decades of independence, the hemisphere filled with constitutional republics.

When the United States invaded the few remaining territories left in the Spanish Empire in 1898, it was not only violating Monroe's doctrine; it was also repositioning itself as a new hegemon. Theodore Roosevelt, who famously fought in Cuba, soon refashioned the Monroe Doctrine to articulate and justify the conditions under which the United States would, "however reluctantly," be forced into "the exercise of an international police power." Countries that "obey the primary laws of civilized society" had nothing to fear, but others might "ultimately require intervention by some civilized nation." Roosevelt argued, nonsensically, that "adherence of the United States to the Monroe Doctrine" meant that his should be the "civilized nation" to intervene. The newly strengthened US Navy and US Marines began a series of merciless military invasions, and the slogan "America for the Americans" took on a new, sinister meaning. Pan-Hispanism developed into a popular intellectual current as the same Spanish-speaking leaders who had once looked to the United States as a beacon of liberty became nostalgic for Spain.

Suffragists in nations under neocolonial regimes faced the same sorts of challenges to their demands for political inclusion as those in countries with greater autonomy. The special conditions of a political system that was not itself sovereign, however, created a more complex geography of power, especially after 1920, when the United States passed the Nineteenth Amendment, which removed sex as a legal reason to deny someone the vote. Suffragists in these countries were locked between competing claims for liberation. National legislators, who chafed at their own colonial status and consequent lack of authority, were often nonetheless resistant to demands for the women's vote. Better allies might be found in the halls of power of the metropolis, but it was impossible to make use of them without further undermining local sovereignty. Suffragists were faced with an impossible choice: they could advocate for liberty either for their nation or their sex, but not both.

A special note is required to explain why this section has deliberately included the Philippines in a book about the Americas. Geographically speaking, the Philippines is clearly in Asia. However, a shared imperial history, first under Spain and then, after 1898, under the United States, has placed it culturally, linguistically, and historically in the Americas.

CHAPTER TWELVE

Filipina Women's Political Alterity Under US Empire, 1912–1937

CHRISTINE PERALTA

AMERICAN SUFFRAGISTS' RELATIONSHIP WITH US empire was contradictory. For many American suffragists, the opportunities of extending women's sphere of power globally proved too appealing to pierce through any cognitive dissonance from endorsing the imperial enterprise. As gender and US empire historians have pointed out, American suffragists argued for women's right to vote during the height of overseas imperial expansion, and therefore the imperial ascendance of the United States informed their views of its relationship to both the Pacific and Atlantic, as well as their own rightful role as white women civilizers of new populations that became wards of the US imperial state. While suffragists are often seen as champions of democracy and the purity of American values, they consistently endorsed imperial designs within the continental United States and overseas colonial expansionist projects because it meant widening (specifically white) women's sphere of authority. This included expansionist projects across the present-day continental United States and acquired overseas territory from Spain, such as Puerto Rico, Guam, and the Philippines. Because of this shared history of colonialism, these particular geographies were informed by empire but often are contained within different subdisciplinary conversations based on the transatlantic, transpacific, and Caribbean regions. Shared experiences from vastly different groups' encounters with US empire resonate differently when placed in conversation under the intellectual heuristic of the Americas, highlighting how women of color across empire were used as means to establish gains for white women and their ability to vote.

The approval of the Philippines constitution marked a critical step for women's suffragism in the Philippines. Article 5 of the constitution stated that the Philippine government would extend the right of suffrage to women on the condition that three hundred thousand women voted in support of the referendum. In 1937 women overwhelming approved the right to vote. This piece of legislation was not merely the product of government leaders or elites, particularly not elite US women. Rather it was the product of nearly three decades of grassroots Filipina organizing that led to women gaining more access to political representation independent from their husbands and fathers.

Despite the critical role that Filipina women played in securing the vote, the literature on suffragism in the Philippines often centers one specific event as a catalyst for suffragism in the American colony: a meeting initiated by suffragist Carrie Chapman Catt that led to the creation of a suffragist club called the Society for the Advancement of Women.[1] Despite this moment being well covered in the literature, when describing white American suffragist encounters with Filipina women, oftentimes the literature does not consider the perspective of Filipina women. The meaning of Catt speaking to Filipina women about democracy raises a few questions. What would the value of suffrage mean for women who were stateless? And what would it mean for Filipina women to hear about the concept of Filipina women's rights from women who represented the very same country that continued to oppress and colonize the Philippines? The very pretext of the encounter is inflected with hypocrisy. The seismic preposterousness of Americans teaching Filipinos the value of self-governance while stripping them of inherent human rights has to be considered within the history of suffragism in the Philippines.

Gender historian Allison L. Sneider characterizes American suffragists' relationship to US empire within these terms: "By the end of the nineteenth century, many suffragists were increasingly well-versed in the language of empire. In this imperial frame of reference, voting was less a right of citizenship than of civilization, and less defined by universal inclusion than by a shared capacity to exercise the privileges of democracy based on a combination of racial traits and religious commitments."[2] White US women were bearers of domesticity who could demonstrate their capacity to vote by taking on the job of civilizing the peoples of newly acquired territories that stretched across the Atlantic and Pacific. Suffragists' fraught relationship with abolition was similar to their relationship to US imperialism. White suffragists were in support of the inherent values of antislavery until black men gained the vote. The right to vote shifted from being understood as an inherent right of a member of a nation to a question of who exhibited capacity for self-governance and civility, and these evaluations imposed not only a gender but also a racial and imperial hierarchy.

As Stephanie Mitchell astutely argues in the conclusion of this anthology, suffrage rights for women were often framed as binary choices between gender or another mark of power difference. Therefore Filipina women found themselves caught between two narrow spaces: American colonial power and elite male Filipina nationalism. When it came to the specific interests of women and their families, they "were left to fend for their rights alone, rejected both by men who shared their class status and/or racialization and by women who did not." In the case of the history of suffragism in the Philippines, these power dynamics produced an end result centering white woman as the primary actors of suffragism. However, the Filipina women American suffragists encountered also had perspectives on voting rights and were actors in political history. Despite this fact, only limited scholarship places Filipina women as actors within the context of political history and US empire, and, in a larger sense, in conversation with other women of color.[3] Due to the ways that white women were informed by empire, slavery, and capitalism, it is only reasonable to assume that the women they encountered also had collective experiences in relation to political histories of US empire. These informed their perspectives on voting and how they decided to engage politically within their nation as well as globally.

The problem is that the history of US suffragism has integrated only the history of the mainland. When it has expanded to a US imperial framework, the tendency has still been to highlight white women as the only intellectual actors and the political spark of the suffragist movement in the Philippines. Furthermore, it wrongly assumes that enfranchising Filipina women was suffragists' only concern rather than one of many concerns within a US imperial context. In other words, the historiography has mostly focused on the unilateral transmission of American forms of democracy from US suffragists to Filipina women, despite the fact that the archive on suffragism in the Philippines reflects otherwise. US suffragists were equally concerned with the relationship between Filipino men and women and with US colonial government's impact on Filipina women and their families, as well as the role that white women who resided permanently in the Philippines would play in the suffragist movement of the islands. Therefore this chapter applies an intersectional approach that considers the multivalent ways that suffragists understood the American territory rather than lingering on an oversimplified stereotypical narrative of white women saving brown women. I argue that this narrative has been centered due to underlying bias in the literature, which presumes that American suffragist history is primarily a history of white women. Existing scholarship imagines the histories of women of color as merely marginal stories, not canon. Finally, US scholars writing on US empire and suffragism do not position Filipino sources correctly within the Filipino political context in which they were created.

To integrate more fully the perspectives of Filipina women and look at their history of suffragism on their own terms, this essay first reads two documents in conversation with one another: *How the Filipina Got the Vote*, written by Filipina suffragist Pura Villanueva Kalaw, and Carrie Chapman Catt's diary during her visit to the Philippines in 1912, when she gathered women to talk about the vote.[4] Examining these two sources serves two purposes. First it shows how Catt was primarily concerned with Filipino men's relationship to Filipina women while also radicalizing both American and Filipina women to advocate for the vote, which shifts what the encounter with Catt and Filipina women means. It also demonstrates a historiographical problem evident in the literature in that it does not position Filipina women's political writings within the context of Filipino nationalist writing because Filipina women are not seen as producers of Filipino political culture. I then examine how a collective critique of Filipino elite male nationalists created a strange political alliance between American women progressives, Filipina women, and American colonial officials, who all critiqued the incompetence of Filipino (male) leadership. I argue that the two American groups were motivated by both racism and self-serving political aspirations, while Filipina women, especially from the provinces, felt truly neglected by new Filipino leadership that had proved ineffective in improving the health and well-being of marginalized ethnic communities. Therefore these strange political allies forged common ground in the need for extended American colonial presence in the Philippines to fund and establish nursing education opportunities, where women would receive vital training to improve the health outcomes of non-elite and provincial communities in the Philippines. After establishing the political legacy of nursing in the Philippines, I end the chapter by analyzing Filipino women's speeches on health, and I argue that one of the most effective venues that Filipina women used to express political critique was through the authority they gained by advocating for the improvement of Filipino people's health.

While touring public schools established by the American colonial regime in the Philippines during July and August 1912, Carrie Chapman Catt spoke approvingly of the curriculum set forth for the young women of the Philippines. A US suffragist in the midst of a global tour to speak about women's rights, she was particularly interested in the conditions of the young women in the school. In her diary that evening, Catt described how young women in American public schools of the Philippines were taught cooking, embroidery, sanitation, nursing, and also the sewing of clothes. The school even acquired a trained nurse to teach the young women skills on caring for children, about which Catt noted, "Nothing is more needed than this training for the race is prolific, but 50% of the babies die under one year of age."[5]

Despite representing the critical edge of white radical feminist politics, Catt believed in the false premise of colonial medicine: since the infant mortality rate was high, it was important that women learn nursing skills to ensure that children would have better chances of survival. This idea neglected larger structural problems that the Filipino population faced, such as the impact of two wars with two Western powers, which caused the disruption of food and crops, and the unfortunate occurrence of both natural disasters and the spread of diseases, which further exacerbated health conditions for the Philippines. She endorsed statistics circulated by the American colonial regime that rationalized the presence of the United States in the Philippines, and she bought into a false premise of the racial inferiority of Filipino subjects. In the logic of this colonial mythology, the US imperialist presence was the solution to, not the cause of, poor health.

Of course, she was also critical of some American colonial policies that were premised on false gender ideals that she had devoted her life to critique. Catt was able to form a critique of the girls' curriculum because rather than teaching women to be financially independent, it was merely teaching them how to support the home. For instance, Catt surmised that sewing skills might create financial gains for women, "but all the rest is to make a happy home and keep them economically dependent."[6] It was obvious that the American suffragist did not agree with the type of gender roles the American public school system was creating abroad. Perhaps one way to consider Catt's concerns is in relation to idealized gender notions from the US mainland, notions that were not rooted in reality, and had the potential to end up limiting the futures of Filipina women under the American flag. Because she was used to critiquing idealized gender roles at home, she was able to identify and critique attempts to implant those same values abroad.

Throughout her travels, Catt was fascinated with Asian women laborers while at the same time casting elite Asian women as deserving of pity. This meant that Catt admired women who had the capacity to be financially independent. Ironically, just like the American public school that was importing a gender fantasy, Catt was also upholding values that few American women at the time were able to uphold—the ability to be completely economically independent from men. Therefore, her critiques of the American public school system reflect larger questions that Catt undoubtedly considered on her tour through the Philippines: What role would the United States have in the Philippines? How would Americans enrich the lives of Filipinos? And what aspirational form of womanhood would take root in the country?

Despite critiquing a rigid gender hierarchy that limited the economic advancement of women, Catt's viewpoints were equally informed by the rigid US racial and class hierarchy. Her investment in that hierarchy was as

strong as her investment in equal opportunities for women. Catt's position-
ality shows how empire's work was insidious and tempted the perceptions
of all who circulated in its sphere.[7] This involved the acceptance of certain
ideas, such as the racial inferiority of Filipina women who were inadequate
caregivers to their children. Racialized, imperialist logic also informed the
types of encounters that Catt and other suffragists had with Filipina women.

Catt, like other suffragists, romanticized women of color who were part of
the working class and was leery of women of color who were part of the elite
classes, despite their having commonalities with Catt and other suffragists,
such as access to education. Catt admired laboring women during her travels
in Asia—women who worked as boat dockers in Hong Kong, for example. She
watched the women in awe, stating, "We were surprised to see many boats
manned by women push up to our boat to get some of our passengers . . . and
they were strong minded and strong limbed, and so dexterous with their curious oar and tiller that one could not think of them as the 'weaker sex.'"[8] She
contrasted that with the Chinese ladies whose bound feet hobbled their gait.
This was a common theme for many suffragists. They romanticized women
from the working class and also endorsed colonial education, which emphasized vocational training rather than the type of education that had given Catt
the capacity to speak on behalf of women.[9] This viewpoint shows the trenchant
belief that women of color were best as beasts of burden or reproducers of the
labor force rather than those who could hold a station in life that would give
them the right to be seen as ladies and mothers.

White women's admiration for women of color was maternalistic. It was
the 1920s equivalent of saying, "That's cute . . . for you." Toiling was the noble
social position that women of color should aspire to but that white elite
women should not. The Chinese dock woman was not someone Catt personally wanted to emulate but rather was a model of who women of color should
be. This means that advancements for women of color were valued but only
in comparison to men of color, not to white women. In other words, Catt and
others like her believed in equal rights for women in relation to their racial
communities, not across racial lines. Catt's comments were part of a larger
strategy of white progressives across the US Empire who upheld the belief
that women of color would be the portal into civilizing people who resided
in new territorial acquisitions.

Similarly, Catt's endorsement of extensive training on maternal care and sanitation seems contradictory for a suffragist who wanted women to advance outside of traditional roles—unless she believed that establishing traditional white maternal roles was an advancement for a racially inferior colony with poor maternal practices. She also accepted data promoted by the US colonial government as objective truth. This is reflected in her citation of the statistics on infant mortality, which became the main talking point for both American colonial officials and progressive reformers, who rationalized their presence in the Philippines by arguing that the colony's health system needed American interventions. The high mortality statistics she cited were a main talking point for both American colonial officials and progressive reformers, who rationalized their presence in the Philippines by arguing that the colony's health system needed American health interventions. Even Catt's framing of the infant mortality statistics shows how the lens she applied to Filipinos was shaped by an imperial framework that connected the increased death rate to inherent racial flaws. Racial flaws explained the overproduction of Filipino bodies, and cultural flaws explained the need for health education. (Catt's acceptance of the need for health education meant she believed there was an absence of motherly care in Filipino homes.) This framing of course ignored the long impact of both the Spanish Philippine War and the Philippine American War, which created instability in civilian life, imposed brutal military policies that kept civilians away from water and food, and also increased levels of disease due to unsanitary living conditions during these times of precarity.[10] None of these factors was considered when assessing the needs and welfare of Filipinos. Instead, poor health was attributed to Filipinos' cultural and racial inferiorities.

What would it mean to think about Filipino suffragism in terms of Filipina women themselves? To do this, first I demonstrate how the literature on American suffragists in the Philippines is in friction with itself to show what we lose as historians when we center white women as actors in the narrative about suffragism within US empire. The history of Filipina suffragism within US imperial history often highlights white women suffragists as the main actors of the history, which the treatment of Carrie Chapman Catt's visit to the Philippines exemplifies. Hoganson states, "US suffragists were not oblivious to struggles for women's rights on the islands. In 1912, Carrie Chapman Catt traveled to the Philippines as part of a worldwide suffrage tour. During her six-week stay in Manila, Catt called a suffrage meeting of Filipina and American activists. Pura Villanueva Kalaw, one of the Filipinas present at the meeting, recalled that Catt spoke eloquently in English, but 'as most of the ladies present only understood Spanish, we did not get all the points she stressed in urging us to form an organization to launch the movement for woman suffrage here.'"[11] Hoganson does not use Kalaw's words to show the perspective of Filipina women. Kalaw merely co-signs Catt's efforts to create a suffragist movement in the Philippines. In other words, the historian uses the Filipina woman's narrative to amplify Catt's impact on the movement in the Philippines by basically staging Kalaw as the vessel that was filled by Catt's knowledge. Despite Kalaw's generous packaging, framing the incident as an inadequacy on the part of American colonials, it is ridiculous that Catt spoke to a group of Filipina women and did not bring an interpreter. When Filipinos went to the United States, they often used interpreters and were able to do this without too much trouble because they were fluent in Spanish. We could therefore view the same incident as an inadequate or inferior form of solidarity. Whom did Catt wish to address if she did not convey her ideas in Spanish? Furthermore, the way that Hoganson uses Kalaw's history contradicts the very nature of the source material. The main reason Kalaw wrote this history of voting was to center Filipina efforts to gain the vote rather than leaving Filipinas in the position of grateful side characters in need of US women's enlightenment. Positioning this encounter within the larger history of the Americas highlights the importance of being able to communicate with colonized populations rather than an intellectual inferiority of one of the groups. This becomes clear when we see that Kalaw organized the Asociación Feminista Ilonga in October 1906, six years before Catt came to the islands and embarked on a world tour to extend suffrage globally.[12]

Gender and empire historian Mina Roces questions the veracity of Kalaw's claim that she began a suffragist association before Catt. Roces rightfully does this to contest the uncritical nature of elite Filipino family histories.[13] However, for the purposes of this essay, I am less interested in when the first suffrage meeting occurred and more interested in thinking about intent. If Kalaw's position is incorrect, why would she aspire to remember it otherwise? And furthermore, what purpose does gender historians' casting of Kalaw as merely a recipient of white women's goodwill serve? What does her self-fashioning as a key figure of the suffragist movement mean? Roces described the encounter with Catt in these terms: "A meeting was arranged between Mrs. Catt and a number of prominent women. But the women who attended the meeting were reluctant to become suffragists."[14] Roces then lists the names of Filipina women who were present: Pura Villanueva Kalaw, María Villamor, Gorgina Mapa, Amparo Lichauco, Sofía de Veyra, and Concepción Felix (Calderón) Rodriguez. This list of names may have come from Kalaw's history, since the same names were listed on page 9 of the text, where Kalaw describes the suffrage meeting that Catt held.[15] To Roces's credit, she thickens the description of Filipina actors at play. Rather than focusing singularly on one Filipina woman, typically Kalaw or Clemencia López, as many US gender historians do, Roces fills the room with named Filipina actors. It is significant to think about why a fissure in the recounting of this moment exists in the historical record, why only Filipina feminist histories choose to acknowledge the possibility that Filipina women may have interpreted these encounters with white women differently, and also that Filipina women would have wanted to center themselves in their own liberation.

Catt's diary reveals a holistic approach to understanding the conditions of women in the Philippines. For instance, she held meetings with any women in the country who were interested in the education of women. She also used her spare time to study colonial reports and any popular and scholarly writings on the Philippines, and she examined a whole spectrum of conditions that impacted women in the Philippines. Catt's diary describe the day she started the woman's club. A fastidious documenter, she also preserved various newspaper clippings that covered her suffragism in the Philippines. She saved the *Manila Times* coverage of the meeting, which described "prominent American and Filipina women," including the Filipina women mentioned by Roces in her essay and also a Mrs. Goodale, a white US woman who was likely married to Francis Goodale, a mechanical engineer who helped construct the large machinery that processed sugar throughout empire, which meant that the family was exposed to many US territories.[16]

The *Manila Times* also mentioned Elizabeth Gibson, a white US woman who was a nurse and teacher from Texas and was married to an Arab doctor from Lebanon, and Ellen Ballon Lobinger, a schoolteacher and wife of a judge from Omaha, Nebraska.[17] Lobinger was also the only US woman who left any impression on Catt: she mentioned her by name and said she had a solid head on her shoulders. Gibson, part of an interracial family whose husband and children had mostly lived only within US territories, may have been different compared to women whose families could claim continental whiteness and American citizenship more clearly.[18]

Rather than Catt sweeping in to impress unenlightened Native women with the women's movement, she worked equally hard to persuade US women of the importance of fighting for equal representation. For instance, she described the meeting in these terms: "It is plain that the American women are afraid of the men and the Filipinos are afraid of ridicule of men both rather of weak fiber."[19] In the context of the Philippines, the presence of US women did not inherently equate to a more liberal notion of politics. Both Filipina and American women collectively struggled with what their activism would mean for their personal relationships with people in the colony. Therefore who stands as the white woman in these incomplete histories of American suffragism in the Philippines is important. By erasing the US women who also demonstrated hesitancy in embracing the suffrage movement, it is easier to render the historical narrative within stereotypical tropes of the colonial tutelary, with the Filipina woman as pupil being taught American values of democracy. This inevitably demonstrates US historians perpetuating rather than disrupting colonial racial hierarchies in their erasures of these nuanced relationships.

In reality, suffragists were more concerned with how their aspirations would be limited by both US and Filipino men. The critique of Filipino men was present in mainstream publications like the *Manila Times*, as well as in Catt's own writing. However, the strategies US women used to stage Filipino men as inadequate in comparison to Filipina women have not been fully explored in the literature. Most work on US suffragists in the Philippines has focused on their relationships with Filipina women rather than on their perceptions of Filipino men and other US women in the Philippines. But arguably it is important to disaggregate the perspectives suffragists had across gender and racial lines to fully comprehend key objectives that the women had, particularly when they reinforced or shaped projects and programs for women in the Philippines, a point that I develop in the latter half of this chapter.

To understand why US women in the Philippines were erased from this story, first we must return to Kalaw's narrative about how Filipina women got the vote. She does emphasize the roles of Filipina women who resided in the Philippines and does not mention by name any of the US women who participated in the meeting. She only mentions them in this line: "Mrs. Catt contacted several *American* and Filipina ladies to carry out her project" (my emphasis).[20] This was no innocent omission considering how important US officials' wives were to Filipina elite women as entry points into traditional forms of American power, but also there was ample media coverage of Catt's visit to the Philippines. Kalaw's omission was intentional, which is evident when you place Kalaw's history in conversation with the writing of other Filipino elite nationalists. Kalaw's writing is engaged in narrative tropes similar to those of other Filipino elite nationalists, who attempted to rectify a colonial archive that relegated them to the background by highlighting Filipino contributions. Americans insisted that it was their work civilizing Filipinos that created modern progress in the realms of childbirth, reproductive health, and maternal health. At the same time, they relied heavily on Filipinos to navigate a world they did not know or understand on a fundamental level, including its geography, language, and multiple ethnic subcultures. To maintain these relationships, they needed Filipinos. Americans often poured funding into projects Filipinos spearheaded, such as reducing infant mortality, expansion of reproductive health access, and education. Even more so, Filipinos were conscious of this relationship with US officials and therefore worked to domesticate tutelage, which essentially meant that Filipinos engaged with US political culture by integrating these values within their own Native stakes and virtues. This meant that Filipinos were able to get their interests funded and supported by merely embedding them to align with US values. The concept of domesticated tutelage was coined by Julian Go, who framed this practice as a strategy that only elite American colonials had the capacity to enact.[21] However, as this chapter demonstrates, since gender was an issue that reflected the future of the Philippine nation,

Filipina women also had opportunities to domesticate tutelage, and in this case they particularly used this strategy to extend educational and political opportunities for women.

In examining the political writing of both Pura Kalaw and her husband, Teodorio Kalaw, it is evident that both Filipino men and women strategically used domestic tutelage. Teodorio Kalaw was a statesman, litigator, and editor of the doomed *Renacimiento*. Dean Worcester, the secretary of the interior, sued Kalaw for libel, which led to him being charged with a criminal sentence and having to shutter the paper.[22] The strategy of demanding recognition for Filipino initiatives is evident in Teodorio Kalaw's speech on infant mortality, which was presented in front of the highest Filipino and American government officials: "The Government has, from the outset, displayed a constantly growing enthusiasm [in regard to infant mortality] and has made ever increasing efforts in this respect. In 1912, it created the first committee on infant mortality, which made the first remarkable investigations on the subject."[23] Seeing themselves cast to the margins, Filipinos used their writing, such as academic papers and public speeches, to assert a longer history of Filipino-initiated social programming. Reinterpreting Pura Kalaw's history within the genre of elite nationalists' writing (rather than seeing her as a minor actor) was a way to amplify the legacy of Filipina women. The practice of focusing on US white women's perspectives on the encounter with their Native counterparts reflects an enduring desire of white women to see women of color only as a mirror for their own self-actualization and growth.

Americans complimented Filipina women, casting them as virtuous, industrious, and invested in self-improvement. These compliments were often connected to disapproving assessments of Filipino men as lazy and indulgent in vices. For example, Catt's diary is filled with examples of American-produced media about the Philippines, which compliments Filipina women at the expense of Filipino men. Catt wrote in her diary, "Every person with whom I have spoken declares the women to be superior to the men in all business affairs."[24] Even more mainstream venues, such as the *Manila Times* article that announced Catt's visit, shared American suffragists' viewpoint that Filipina women were far more civilized than Filipino men: "They will quickly discern that they are whole lot better than the men, and the advantage by no means limited to mere morals. They excel their men in business, in energy and industry, in thrift. They do more for their homes and their families than do their men." The article also mentioned that Filipina women took the lead in progress and excelled in the professions of medicine and nursing.[25] Additionally, in her diary Catt cites a paragraph from a guidebook by George Miller entitled *Interesting Manila*. It argued that Filipina women were more liberated than other "Oriental" women:

> The Filipino woman is the equal of the Filipino man. . . . Her Chinese sister limps in small footed helplessness; her Hindoo cousin creeps about behind a veil; her Mohammedan relative is a harem slave, and even her Japanese neighbor is a doll to look at, but the Filipino stands up straight and with bare shoulder and sturdy carriage looks you squarely in the eye and is abundantly able to take care of herself. She is unbound in arm and waist, and not having the responsibilities of the social swim is free to go to market and to carry her end of the industrial load.[26]

Catt must have admired the thought that Filipino women were liberated to the degree that they were able to carry "the industrial load," because this meant they would be able to engage in the workforce and be financially independent. However, elite Filipina women did not participate in these forms of work and commerce; Miller cherry-picked middle- and working-class women to position Filipina women as racially more superior than other women on the continent of Asia. At the same time, Catt made Filipina women more familiar to the women of color who out of necessity engaged in the working-class sector in the continental United States. In this way she made Filipina women and therefore the new colony a more familiar space for Miller's American audience. Again, similar to the other comments embedded in critiques of Filipino men, this one relegated Indian, Japanese, and Chinese women—women who were encountered by British empire—to being vastly inferior to Filipina women. This shows how acknowledging the humanity of one Filipino social group always came at the expense of othering or dehumanizing another marginalized group. In this case, Catt compared the US Empire's acquisitions in Asia to Britain's for that purpose.

Catt did not limit her admiration to merely Filipina women's personal characteristics; she also commented on their physical beauty and desirability. Appraising them from the perspective of US men after a ball, she wrote with admiration, "Had I been a young man, I should have gone home bewildered as to which girl I was in love with—they were so pretty and sweet and had I been a white young man, I should have certainly have dreamed of brown beauties.[27] This diary entry makes it easy to imagine Catt, a queer woman who had intimate relationships with men and women, in a white nightgown under a mosquito net lulled to sleep with visions of Filipina beauties fluttering above her head. It is interesting that in her musings, she imagined her engagement in terms of a white man. What did it mean that Catt imagined Filipina women inspiring admiration in white men, which suggested an impulse of interracial marriage at a time when it was considered taboo? Perhaps she was so invested in the racial hierarchy that her imagination limited itself to mentally cross-dressing as a white man, or was it more of a compliment to say that US men would value these Filipina women rather than their male compatriots? I dwell on this comment to point out that even in her fantasies and dreams, Catt reflected the ways that progressive white women activists attempted to alienate their identification with Filipino men.[28]

The suffragists' ability to decenter the importance of US white masculinity in the US imperial project provides an important context for how we interpret US suffragists' critiques of Filipino men. Comments about their ineptitude and indulgences operated as a proxy to critique US white masculinity. Therefore white suffragists and white male imperialists overlapped in their belief that Filipino women needed to be saved from Filipino men. The only question was who was worthy of doing the saving: white men or white women? The discourse that these white women promulgated overlapped with US colonial officials' own reasoning for continuing their presence in the Philippines: saving Filipina women from Filipino men became one reason for the US presence in the Philippines. Just as white suffragists questioned the right of Black men to gain the right to vote over white women, white suffragists used their critiques of Filipino men and their backwardness and neglect of Filipina women as evidence of their own modernity over a class of men who were within the US Empire and therefore were symbolically juvenile inheritors of normative white US masculinity.

After traveling in the provinces of the Philippines, Catt wondered in her diary what the permanent US impact on the nation would be: "When the Spaniard departed, they left a Church or a Cathedral in every town. When the Americans leave, there will be a school house on every hill top, and we hope no cockpit, opium den, dance hall, or saloon."[29] The structures of the "cockpit, opium den, dance hall, and saloon," are all infrastructures of vice—the cockpit instigating gambling; opium, passivity and drug use; the dance hall, interracial sex outside of marriage; the saloon, drinking. These were sites that both Filipino and US men enjoyed. The opium den, dance hall, and saloon, however, were particularly facilitated by Anglo technologies of empire. For example, the dance hall and the saloon were spaces established in the outposts of US empire because they fostered intimate relationships between men and women but through a commercial industry that converted desire into dollars. In these homogenous male-dominated bachelor societies, they were spaces for sexual relief and facilitation of (or respites from) queer dalliances. The saloon, a centerpiece for female progressive ire, was seen as a space where the male head of the house could escape from his familial duties. The opium den was a vice industry furthered by both British and American commercial interests to ensure that the Anglo-speaking world maintained a commercial advantage over China, despite British citizens' demands for Chinese tea.[30] By contemplating the legacy of the United States in the Philippines in examining these spaces of deviance and vice that had cropped up after American occupation—spaces that both Filipino and American men indulged in and that were created to mollify the working classes of many races, spaces, and creeds to continue the engine of empire—Catt was able to make a domestic critique of masculine cheap amusements while at the same time questioning unchallenged male superiority and positioning it on a global scale. In doing so, she challenged the idea that Filipino men should be the key actors to shape a future nation and the presumption that US men would be the key people to civilize Filipino men.

Catt's underlying critique of Filipino men and American masculinity was best revealed when she was asked whether or not the Philippines was ready for independence. She described how local politicians were too susceptible to the influences of corruption and then stated, "For this reason, I think it would be a wise step if the women of the country were given the right to vote for all agree that the women of the islands are more upright and honorable then the men and they would make the men be honest too."[31] We know from her diary that Catt believed men were susceptible to corruption and therefore women needed to hold them accountable. We also learn how she saw Filipino male politicians as a proxy for the concerns US suffragists had about American masculinity.

American colonial gender constructions of women and men in the Philippines informed sources of funding and also how the United States attempted to govern its new colony. Alternatively, Filipina women were aware of these discourses and attempted to use them to forge their own power. However, due to the contradictory nature of these women attempting to harness colonial projects to enrich the lives of their own communities, female liberation resulted in mixed effects. If women were gaining more opportunities to enter the public sphere and to be seen as intellectual beings at the expense of Filipino men, as well as through discourses of empire, the power and advancement that they would gain from such discourses would be vexed and have a contradictory impact.

Filipina women were very aware that they were perceived as nonthreatening and that men in their communities were being cast as violent savages. They attempted to use this dynamic to advocate for the interests of their communities on a global platform. From 1901 to 1903, Clemencia López worked to push for her three brothers' release from prison after they were arrested for suspicion of Philippine insurgency against the Americans. López garnered a lot of attention on her public speaking tour advocating for Philippine independence. Her effectiveness to speak for her brothers emulates the pattern seen for other women of color who occupied the status of wards of the United States, which glorified women as civilized while vilifying men as revolutionaries and criminals. This is reflected in the words of Charles Edward Magoon, who worked as a US official for the Philippines at the time López went on her tour. When commenting on the tour, Magoon bluntly stated that López "was ready to become the tool . . . seeking the sympathy Americans naturally feel for a woman in distress, whatever the cause."[32] Magoon's comment reveals how Filipina women were seen as effective messengers for the Philippines as modern and civilized due to their gender, which was perceived as more effective because it was less threating due to the false perception that Filipino insurgency that was solely a masculine movement conducted by lawless and barbaric Filipino men.

Published in 1952, Pura Villanueva Kalaw's *How the Filipina Got the Vote* was written to disentangle white women's suffrage from Filipina women's political activism, which for both the historian and the historical actor has often been embedded within a legacy of white women's politics. What did it mean to define a critical act that all citizens regardless of class and race had the aspirations to engage in at the most fundamental level of politics, only to see it as an extension of white women's own ambitions? Could they even broach how it was connected to empire? What did this amount to? To understand what voting meant to Filipina women on their own terms, it is important to consider how the question of suffragism became a catalyst for Filipina women to begin to sort out competing influences that defined what it meant to be Filipina. As Mina Roces argues, "The colonizer's cultural constructions of the feminine were products of their own gendered views and agendas for the social engineering of the colony. The shift from Spanish to American colonial rule had profound consequences for redefining 'the Filipino woman' in the space of two decades. The Spanish colonizers defined the 'feminine' as convent-bred, religious, charitable, demure, chaste and strictly located in the domestic sphere."[33]

Of course, constructions of the ideal Filipina woman did not consider lower-class women at all. As Mina Roces established, Filipina women prioritized the realm of education and professionalization over suffrage because it was an extension of Filipina women's own investments. Extending Roces's argument, I posit that Filipina women's social activism centered on health, education, and enriching community opportunities posed an opportunity for Filipina women to express forms of alterity that were distinctive from both the colonial project and elite male nationalists' politics because it framed investment in health and sanitation within a radical feminist belief in the politics of local woman of color. Therefore Filipina feminists worked to strategically extend Filipina women's spheres of authority that were already culturally and socially ascribed to women, such as the realms of fashion, beauty pageantry, motherhood, and nursing.

Filipina women first harnessed power by cultivating ascribed traditional gender roles, such as beauty pageant queens. They used the ensuing public adoration to move into more political roles. Thus many Filipina women, particularly in the elite and middle class, expanded their sphere of influence from a starting place in the traditional roles of beauty, care, and motherhood. They cultivated power behind the scenes rather than overtly.[34] As the previous section showed, US economic and political colonialism and cultural differences combined to make Filipina women's stakes in politics different from those of white women in the United States. As Roces established with her seminal work that centers Filipina women as political actors while at the same time writing against uncritical biographies of elite Filipina women, women entered the world of politics through the established gender roles they were assigned. Thus many women who later became politicians and suffragists were first pageant queens. They also were invested in education as a means to create legitimacy for women to then participate in voting.[35]

The American colonial regime gave Filipina women opportunities to become politically active, especially through education that professionalized women's roles in health, family, and nutrition. That professionalization garnered legitimacy for Filipina women's roles. Their ability to talk about health through traditional roles gave them the capacity to then challenge these same roles to talk about medicine and health generally. They used conversations about the Philippines and medicine to define the type of country they wanted to build, which meant often challenging elite male nationalists' visions as well as divisions based on class and subethnic categories. For example, by focusing specifically on education, some Filipina women became deans and presidents of universities; Julita Sotejo established and became the first dean of a university-level nursing program in the Philippines in 1948. Ultimately, this foresight gave Filipina women access to professional credentials so they could obtain visas to work abroad—before those in many other countries had similar educational opportunities.[36] Thus nursing became a site for women to strategically nation-build.

Despite public critiques, Filipino men were guaranteed to inherit both political and social authority in the Philippines. There was no assurance that women would have the same opportunities. Therefore, using the same strategies of building from sanctioned public roles for women that had been operationalized since the early decades of the Philippine American War,

Filipina women used new roles that opened up under the colonial regime to express their political concerns even if they directly contradicted elite masculine Philippine politics. The last section of this essay specifically examines how women used nursing to critique Filipino elite male nationalism. They strategically built on critiques of Filipino men's competence lodged by American colonial officials. In this section, I argue that only through reclaiming the distinctive political alterity of Filipina women can we clearly see how Filipina women's critiques are a unique thread, which challenges both the inability of Filipino elites to value the health work of women as well as their concerns for their communities.

One year after Carrie Chapman Catt traveled to the Philippines, Woodrow Wilson ascended into power. His approach to the Philippines was incremental preparation for the colony's independence under a policy that replaced US leadership with Native authority. In 1921 the White House shifted from Democratic to the more pro-imperialist Republican leadership, which meant that all the progress Filipinos had made to finally exercise self-governance diminished. As wards of the state, Filipinos had elected neither party into office.

With the blessing of President Warren G. Harding, US officials moved to undermine Filipino leadership by making claims that health programs in the colony had eroded under the direction of Filipino politicians, physicians, and scientists. In an odd exception, the only trained health workers that two American officials cited as being effective were Filipino nurses. They stated, "Wherever you find good nurses you find lowered infant mortality and improved sanitary conditions."[37] Focusing on nurse labor was not an entirely altruistic endeavor but was enfolded in a critique that justified US colonialism in the Philippines. A decade after suffragist and popular US American discourse celebrated the effectiveness of Filipina women in subordinate roles while demonizing Filipino men who claimed roles of authority, American officials reused the same narrative.

Many working-class Filipina women shared American officials' opinions about the ineffectiveness of national Filipino leadership and also thought that Filipina women would do a better job at serving the health needs of their communities. One Ilocana woman, "Miss Morales," went so far as to blame the "number of untimely deaths in the provinces" not on

Native midwives but rather on health officers' neglect of the provinces. Related to the idea of improving the training of health officers, Anatolla Galano, a member of a women's club from Ilocos Norte, asked for more trained nurses to replace sanitary officers in the provinces.[38] This meant that Ilocana women shared the same idea as US officials who believed the Philippines required more nurses. Ilocana women's demands for an increase in trained nurses in every municipality overlapped with US interests, which led to increased training in nursing in the Philippines. This also indicates that nursing education is the product of multiple legacies, all of which stem from a question: What sort of political authority would Filipina women have under the US colonial regime? For Filipina women who attempted to claim power through first increasing their access to education in traditionally feminized roles, this shift to more trust in not only Filipina women but specifically Filipina nurses represented a means for Filipina women to gain more political authority. The new political authority was not clearly linked to Filipino men but to a fraught political legacy that saw empowered, radicalized Native men as a dangerous racial threat and saw subservient women performing bodily care as a clear path forward for the nation.

Conclusion

Many women of color under US empire shared the experiences of being compared favorably to Native men. This binary logic that placed women of color on a moral high ground led to a natural interrogation of the humanity of men of color and at the same time questioned the inferiority of any community or civilization where women were more advanced than men. For example, white suffragists from the United States cited race-based biology theorists like Otis Mason, whose work promoted the idea that colonized territories with backward racialized subjects could only be "elevated chiefly through their women."[39] The focus on women as more passive and civil also was connected to the idea of vilifying Filipino male leaders of the revolution. Positioning women as the potential port of entry for Americanization meant that Americans would be able to disempower Filipino men. In other words, the desire to elevate Filipina women in direct opposition to the value of Filipino men had to do with choking insurgency in an unstable colony.

This pattern of playing women of color against men of color in specific communities was replicated throughout US empire. George Sanchez's seminal essay "Go After the Women" indicates that this strategy of targeting women to manage insurgency was used not only in the Philippines but in territorial acquisitions from Mexico, such as California. Sanchez examines Pearl Ellis, who educated Mexican girls in Southern California. Teaching Mexican women to create a stable and Anglicized home meant creating workers who were "more dependable and less revolutionary in [their] tendencies. . . . The homekeeper creates the atmosphere, whether it be one of harmony and cooperation or of dissatisfaction and revolt."[40]

Just as white US suffragists migrated to the Philippines, they also descended upon the American South to enlist African American women into the movement. Similar to Catt, white women tried to form bonds with Black women in the South by validating their worthiness for enfranchisement by belittling African American men's capacity to engage in politics. Elizabeth Bothume, a white northern schoolteacher working in South Carolina, believed African American women had a stronger work ethic and would be more well-informed voters than African American men, whom she criticized for gathering in public spaces to discuss politics rather than going back to work after voting. Bothume's comments ignore the fact that African American women engaged in Black political social life in the same manner. Reflecting on Bothume's critiques of Black political life, Elsa Barkley Brown, an African American gender historian, argued, "Central to [Bothume's] complaint about African American women's disenfranchisement is her exasperation at African American men's assumption that political rights included the right to participate in political discussions (and thereby political decision making)."[41] In these parallel discourses of white American suffragists in multiple regions across US empire, suffragists effectively worked to hold women to an almost mythological ideal at the expense of critiquing men.

Again, this shows how political and revolutionary practices in Filipino, Mexican, and Black communities had to be gendered as fully masculine in order to frame women as docile and more civilized. In all three examples, compliments paid to women actually were a means to create a malleable workforce that would not question its position in the racial hierarchy of US empire. Also, white women progressives used their social uplift work to demonstrate their own modernity as well as to reinforce the incompetence of men of color. The result was a comparative framework that signifies patterns of white first wave feminist dominance unfurled on women of color. Asian, Latina, and Black women experienced white feminist designs to prove the modernity of their communities as an expressed limitation on men in the same communities. This informed both the expectations of women of color and how white women attempted to intervene in those communities.

Writing about US and British empire in the West Indies, Christopher Taylor described the double bind West Indians found themselves in when the high-minded ideas of well-intentioned white people ended up having concrete and physical consequences for colonial Natives on the ground: "West Indians lived not in the warm glow of abolitionists and political economists' hearts but the effects induced by the institutional structures induced by those intentions."[42] Filipina women found themselves in a similar state of having to live the consequences of somebody else's ideals. Thus the ideas about Filipina women and men that white suffragists used in the Philippines to demonstrate their own agency, without really considering the real-world implications, had clear consequences for the Philippines, particularly for Filipina women, whom US suffragists deluded themselves into thinking they could speak for and represent.

Notes

1. Hoganson, "As Badly Off as the Filipinos"; Holt, *Colonizing Filipinas*; Prieto, "A Delicate Subject"; Roces, "Orienting the Global Women's Suffrage Movement"; Roces, "Women in Philippine Politics and Society."
2. Sneider, *Suffragists in an Imperial Age*, 6.
3. Edwards and Roces, *Women's Suffrage in Asia*; Prieto, "A Delicate Subject"; Roces, "Women in Philippine Politics and Society"; Tiongson, *Women of Malolos*.
4. Carrie Chapman Catt Papers; Villanueva Kalaw, *How the Filipina Got the Vote*.
5. Carrie Chapman Catt Papers, 7.
6. Carrie Chapman Catt Papers, 7.

7. Hoganson, *Consumers' Imperium*; Ngô, *Imperial Blues*.

8. Carrie Chapman Catt Papers, 4.

9. Carrie Chapman Catt Papers, 4. Ware, "Carrie and Mollie and Anna and Lucy."

10. De Bevoise, *Agents of the Apocalypse*; Daniel Doeppers, *Feeding Manila: In Peace and War, 1850–1945* (Quezon City: Ateneo De Manila University Press 2016); Ventura, "Medicalizing Gutom."

11. Hoganson, "As Badly Off as the Filipinos"; Holt, *Colonizing Filipinas*, 26.

12. Villanueva Kalaw, *How the Filipina Got the Vote*, 7.

13. Roces, "Women in Philippine Politics and Society," 162–63.

14. Roces, 175.

15. Villanueva Kalaw, *How the Filipina Got the Vote*, 9.

16. Francis Goodale Papers, MC 158, Department of Distinctive Collections, Massachusetts Institute of Technology, Cambridge Massachusetts.

17. "Suffragettes For Islands: Mrs. Catt Organizes Local Women for Work," *Manila Times*, August, 16, 1912, in Carrie Chapman Catt Papers.

18. Marr, "Diasporic Intelligences."

19. Carrie Chapman Catt Papers, 36.

20. Pura Villanueva Kalaw, *How the Filipina Got the Vote*, 9.

21. Go, *American Empire and the Politics of Meaning*.

22. For more on the libel suit against *Renacimiento*, see Kramer, *Blood of Government*, 342.

23. Kalaw, "Address of the Hon. Teodoro M. Kalaw."

24. Carrie Chapman Catt Papers, 11.

25. "The Women of the Philippines," *Manila Times*, July 13, 1912, Carrie Chapman Catt Papers. Catt transcribed this article by hand in her diary.

26. Miller, *Interesting Manila*, Carrie Chapman Catt Papers, 12. Catt transcribed Miller's text by hand in her diary.

27. Carrie Chapman Catt Papers.

28. Ware, "Carrie and Mollie and Anna and Lucy."

29. Carrie Chapman Catt Papers, 29.5

30. For more on British and American strategies to import opium into China to curb Asian countries, economic dominance, see Lowe, *The Intimacies of Four Continents*.

31. "Suffragettes for Islands: Mrs. Catt Organizes Local Women for Work," *Manila Times*, August, 1912, Carrie Chapman Catt Papers. Catt clipped this article out of the newspaper and fixed in her diary.

32. Eyot, *Story of the Lopez Family*. I want to thank Gabrielle Avena, one of my students at Amherst College, who shared this quote and source with me.

33. Roces, "Orienting the Global Women's Suffrage Movement," 25.

34. Roces, 28.

35. Mina Roces, "Women in Philippine Politics and Society," 160.

36. Peralta, "Nursing the Nation."

37. Woods and Forbes, *Report of the Special Mission.*
38. Intengen, "The Function and Duties of a Health Officer."
39. Holt, *Colonizing Filipinas*, 62.
40. Sanchez, "Go After the Women," 481
41. Barkley Brown, "To Catch the Vision of Freedom."
42. Taylor, *Empire of Neglect*, 4.

CHAPTER THIRTEEN

A Look at the Struggle for Universal Suffrage in Puerto Rico through the Endeavors of Two Unusual Women, Genara Pagán and Ricarda López de Ramos Casellas

ROXANNA DOMENECH CRUZ

"La historia [de las mujeres] es necesaria para el conocer, para la comprensión del mundo en el cual vivimos."[1]

"Women are often depicted as passive recipients of rights."[2]

"Pidamos a la mujer un poco de calma."[3]

MUCH OF THE US POPULATION (as well as those in other countries in the Americas) does not fully understand the territorial relationship between the United States and Puerto Rico. Many do not even know that Puerto Ricans who reside in the Puerto Rican archipelago may not vote in US presidential elections and that even though a woman serves as our commissioner in Washington, DC, she has neither voice nor vote in our governing bodies. In summary, there is a generalized ignorance regarding the territorial relationships (colonial, in the case of Puerto Rico) between much of the Antilles (especially the Lower Antilles) and their European and US metropoles.[4]

Following the invasion in 1898, Puerto Rico immediately became an unincorporated territory of the US Empire. A few years later, while Puerto Rico was still under military occupation, the Jones Law of 1917 was passed. It included the cabotage laws that continue to control the Puerto Rican economy and imposed US citizenship.[5] The law also extended the vote to men while excluding all women. Although Puerto Rico was the third country in the Americas where women voted (the United States in 1920, Ecuador in 1924, and Puerto Rico in 1929, with restricted suffrage), this achievement was the result of various complex and contentious struggles during a moment in history when many Puerto Ricans saw the United States as a country that promoted democracy, liberty, and equality. Surely, they thought, the United States would grant those same rights to Puerto Rico. In part because that did not happen, this period in Puerto Rican history is complicated and contradictory.

This chapter shares ongoing research on women's suffrage, with a particular look at citizenship and women's demands for equality and decolonization in Puerto Rico. Over the course of this research, I encountered several important women representing different strata of that period's society. Those who most stood out to me were Genara Pagán and Ricarda López de Ramos Casellas. In 1920 Pagán demanded her right to vote as a citizen who had achieved the age of majority. She approached Puerto Rico's Junta de Inscripción to register to vote, noting that the nineteenth amendment to the US Constitution had given her that right. López de Ramos Casellas made similar demands using her different positions in the Suffragist Social League (and other organizations) via speeches, articles, and letters. Both women's demands went beyond the struggle for universal suffrage to include improving living conditions for women and society.

Henrice Altink has observed that citizenship, in the context of feminist studies, "is generally defined as both *status* and *practice*; that is, to be a citizen is to have a set of legal rights and duties endowed by the state . . . and also to possess the ability to exercise these rights and duties and assert agency in civil society organisations."[6] Gladys M. Jiménez-Muñoz, writing on the 1928 hearings in the US Congress on Puerto Rico women's suffrage, adds an important analysis regarding the tension between suffragist demands and US citizenship: "This hearing anticipated in a condensed manner many of the textual practices and themes prevailing in the debate on women's suffrage: the persistent question of colonial ambivalence in general, particularly the tensions within Puerto Rico's suffrage movement over the impact and onus of having 'natives' appeal to the highest colonialist authorities; the looming barbarism of the 'native' uneducated classes; the citizenship controversies among the colonized and within colonizer circles themselves; the contradictory codifications of patriotism; the blatant heteronormativity of positioning Puerto Rican 'women' as devout partners of 'their' men; and, in turn, the multifaceted issue of 'woman's proper place.'"[7] In other words, Puerto Rican women were always subject to more than one kind of subjugation, and the tensions between competing structures of domination layer the history in sheets of complexity like an especially thick onion—every time we peel some of it away, we find more underneath.

Historian Martín Cruz Santos invites us to ask ourselves how it must have been to experience the imposition of US citizenship by examining individuals from the period, including those who decided to renounce US citizenship. "What did it mean to be a citizen for Calixto Pérez, a peasant from Las Marías," he writes, "and for his wife, Amalia Rodríguez; for Jovita Flores, a housewife and ironer from the Toíta de Cayey neighborhood; for Lorenzo Babilonia, a rancher from Hatillo; for Juana Colón, a tobacco labor leader from Comerío; for María Negrón, a rural teacher from Naguabo; for Pedro Cortijo, a railroad brakeman and resident of Puerta de Tierra; for Ramón Lagares, a small business owner from Juana Díaz, etc."[8] The consequences of the Jones Act and subsequent struggles over both the possession and meaning of citizenship are ongoing. I write this chapter in Puerto Rico, in an atmosphere of precariousness and during the process of recovery from two hurricanes, Irma and María (September 2017 to the present), followed by a coup (summer of 2019) that demanded and resulted in the resignation of Governor Ricardo Rosselló, under the framework of the PROMESA law and a Fiscal Control Board imposed by the US Congress to control Puerto Rican finances under crushing austerity policies.[9] These policies have included the sale and privatization of our energy authority, Autoridad de Energía Eléctrica, to Luma Energy, which has resulted in recurrent blackouts.[10] The pandemic that affected the entire planet in many ways resulted in salary reductions, job cuts, and population loss. Finally, Hurricane Fiona (2022) left Puerto Rico (along with other parts of the Caribbean) in devastation. Thus I share what I write here also as an act of resistance and from a place of fury, love, and sense of responsibility that I feel toward my homeland, with all of its charms, challenges, and contradictions.

At the same time, and as Lizandra Torres notes in one of her essays about women's history, this chapter aims to go beyond "[merely seeking] out the feminine presence in those times and places where their own social issues occurred; they have a basic importance regarding actions, masculine interests. Rather, the women's 'doings' in their daily lives must become relevant. . . . For this reason, we should study the multiplicity of unusual events they experienced every day. This analysis should consider a wide range of complex and unexpected variations and dynamics."[11] Puerto Rican scholars and researchers have produced work that meets this standard. They hail from the Centro de Estudios, Recursos y Servicios a la Mujer (CERES) in the Universidad de Puerto Rico (UPR), Recinto de Río Piedras; the research center PRO MUJER de la UPR, Recinto Cayey; and the Universidad Interamericana, Recinto Metropolitano, as well as from the Universidad del Sagrado Corazón and at the Centro de Estudios de la Realidad Puertorriqueña. In the same vein, for more than a decade, the Asociación Puertorriqueña de Investigación de Historia de las Mujeres has yielded abundant research, presented annually at its Coloquio de Historia de las Mujeres at the Universidad de Puerto Rico, Recinto de Utuado, where I have contributed since 2011.

Genara Pagán and Ricarda López de Ramos Casellas: Puerto Rico, Women's Suffrage, and US Citizenship

Genara Pagán was born at the end of the nineteenth century in Puerta de Tierra, San Juan.[12] As a result of the US invasion of Puerto Rico in 1898, Pagán grew up during a period that gave rise to economic development on the island in the mode of capitalist production.[13] This accelerated the incorporation of thousands of women like Pagán into salaried work, especially in the tobacco and needlework industries. It is thought that she left school in the fifth grade and in her youth became a tobacco leaf de-stemmer. Shortly afterward, she joined unions that, by 1904, included about five hundred unionized working women: tobacco workers, seamstresses, and embroiderers, according to the Federación Libre de Trabajadores.[14]

Norma Valle suggests that "there is historical evidence indicating that Puerto Rico felt the influence of the Workers International, held in Europe in 1866. . . . Puerto Rican workers leaned towards the libertarian socialism of Mikhail Bakunin."[15] According to Valle, "In the ideological framework of anarchism is found the most ferocious defence of women's liberation . . . anarchism is conceived as a 'way of life.' And considering it a way of life and demanding that its followers 'live' according to its ideology, they are obliged to grapple with women's conditions, that she is the natural partner together with men in raising children, which are the 'natural' fruit of men and women in their 'natural' state."[16] Valle adds that during the last decades of the nineteenth century, workers' quality of life deteriorated with "the agricultural economic transformation of the Puerto Rican colonia, the rise of cost of living, the hike in taxes, monetary crises; the pluralist relationship between workers and owners also transformed, and workers developed a new proletaritized mentality, similar to industrial laborers."[17]

She notes that in the last decade of that century, "spontaneous strikes took place among sugarcane agricultural laborers, and tobacco workers organized and directed by leaders like José Ferrer y Ferrer, Angel María Dieappa, Santiago Iglesias Pantín, Alonso Torres, Ramón Romero Rosa, among others."[18] She also mentions that "in their theoretical work, these same enlightened laborers theorized on the condition of women, fomented women's organizing into unions, uniting their voices in solidarity with liberals on women's rights to education . . . for all women, especial working class women and their daughters." Other labor leaders included Luisa Capetillo, Franca de Armiño, and Concha Torres.[19] Liberals also began forming organizations that eventually worked on issues such as suffrage and education, a cause that united socialists and liberals. Liberal leaders included Ana Roqué de Duprey, María Luisa de Argelis, and Isabel Andreu de Aguilar.[20]

According to research on gender and the struggles of working women from Yvette Rivera-Giusti, working together on labor issues and politics also impacted everyday life. For workers, it was not possible to separate out issues like unemployment and other economic challenges from daily living.[21] Among the women who fought for better living conditions, equity, and liberty, we find the renowned feminist labor leader Luisa Capetillo, as well as Juana Colón and others.[22] In 1914 Genara Pagán was one of these unionized women who organized strikes and demanded improved working conditions, while others sought equality, including universal suffrage.[23]

Various pieces of legislation proposing women's suffrage were presented to the Puerto Rican legislature starting in 1900. This legislation sought "the legal emancipation of the woman" and proposed universal suffrage as well as "equalizing the position of men and women in other aspects of juridical norms."[24] (Neither this nor any other law was approved over the next twenty years.) The Socialist Party was the first to show support for universal suffrage. Lizandra Torres Martínez warns against ignoring intersectional complexities. "Many," she observes, "take up themes from historical materialism and others that place a greater economic emphasis on social relationships."[25] Gender-specific forms of oppression should not be subsumed under class-based arguments; women experienced simultaneous, overlapping systems of domination and subordination. Torres Martínez writes, "We have examples of the opposition some male workers had towards the participation of women from the tobacco industry that cannot be reduced to a question of class."[26] We can see this clearly in the speeches and approaches taken by women's labor leaders as well as in the political speeches of Ricarda López de Ramos Casellas, even though she was not a member of the labor movement. She was a republican who also belonged to the coalition, together with socialists who supported universal suffrage with a secret ballot for women and men.[27] According to Sandra Enríquez Seiders, López de R. Casellas always felt supported "as much by Rafael Martínez Nadal as by Santiago Iglesias Pantín."[28] On this point, María Fátima Barceló Miller aptly notes that Enríquez Seiders "studies this figure as a woman who was committed to various causes: obtaining women's suffrage, teachers' rights, and a reform of Puerto Rico's educational system."[29]

López was the object of harsh attacks not only during her time but within feminist historiography. Her annexationist ideology has served as an incentive for distorting who she was and marking her as a conservative. To perpetuate this twisted vision is to fail to understand fully early twentieth-century politics. Additionally, we should not forget that at the time in which she lived, the relationship between Puerto Rico and the United States had just begun. There was still enthusiasm that the new metropolis might bring forth on the island an exported vision of a democratic nation that defended justice and equality.[30]

For López de Ramos Casellas, the suffragist struggle was tied to the annexationist cause; she saw US citizenship as "synonymous with democracy and liberty, and for that reason, she associated their ideas with her struggle on behalf of women's rights." Barceló Miller points out that these strategies "to tie the political struggle to feminist demands" occurred elsewhere in the world, mentioning work by Asunción Lavrin and Barbara Southad. She underscores the importance of remembering that López de Ramos Casellas was a "good example of the feminist struggle in a colonial context," where we see "the compatibility of [feminist] demands with those of greater powers for all citizens, including women."[31]

López was born on May 13, 1879, in the town of Manatí to a "comfortable, politically powerful" family with "liberal sympathies."[32] She graduated with a pedagogy degree in 1896 at the age of sixteen; four years later she married Juan Ramon Ramos Casellas. She taught at an elementary school in Manatí from 1898 to 1907 and in Cataño until 1912, when she obtained her license to teach English. She became an English teacher in San Juan, where she stayed until her retirement in 1922.[33] Shortly after, she became director of a Catholic school in Barrio Obrero de Santurce. Sandra Enríquez uses López to show the importance of education for women: "As a feminist, she said of the school, 'it is the evidence of what feminine will and charity can accomplish.'"[34]

It is worth pointing out, as Norma Valle says, that women's education and women's dominance in the field unified women and "motivated women's emancipatory struggles because the people who were brought together crossed class and social barriers and created, albeit fleetingly, solidarity between liberals from the proletarian classes and the most alert members of the incipient labor movement."[35] López de Ramos Casellas was clearly a part of first wave feminism. She was a member of the first suffragist organization—the Puerto Rican Feminine League—created in 1917 by Ana Roqué de Duprey. Eventually she held many posts in the league, even after it changed its name to the Suffragist Social League, including president.[36] Enríquez describes López's participation in the struggle for the vote as "pioneering, brave, constant, and defiant."[37] She can be credited with transforming the league into a suffragist organization. In addition to being the mother of seven children, she was vice president of the Island Teachers' Association, president of the Suffragist Social League, and president of the Women's Bloc of the Republican Union (previously named the Bloc of Pure Republican Women).[38] She debated extensively in the press on feminism, suffrage, politics, education, birth control, and other topics.

As stated above, when the Jones Law extended US citizenship to all Puerto Rican residents in 1917, Ana Roqué de Duprey and Mercedes Solá (both members of the Puerto Rican elite) founded the Puerto Rican Feminine League (the first suffrage league, which advocated for the vote for literate women). That same year, Genara Pagán moved to New York with her son after her husband was killed in the First World War. In New York she found salaried work at a shirt factory. There she participated in unions and became involved in the US suffrage movement.[39] According to Rivera-Giusti, Pagán represented Union 453 at the First Workers Congress in 1920, along with Carmen Puente and Emilia Hernández. She already had leadership experience in union organizing. In 1919 she had led the First Women Workers' Congress in Puerto Rico. According to Azize, at that congress, tobacco workers, de-stemmers, needleworkers, domestic workers, washerwomen, coffee pickers, and seamstresses demanded "The enlargement and moral and cultural elevation of the woman, as a mother, wife, and daughter, recognizing all civil rights on the same scale that men enjoy; the woman should be a free citizen."[40]

Rivera-Giusti used union documents, including a report that reads, "Working women in Puerto Rico should be granted the right of suffrage . . . because they were American citizens."[41] It is clear that female Puerto Rican tobacco workers (Pagán's coworkers and co-militants) were prominent feminist leaders, but they also confronted "homelessness, hunger, and disease" due to the practices of the Tobacco Trust, "whose labor practices and commanding position in Puerta des Tierra, overpowered workers' daily lives."[42]

In 1920, when the Nineteenth Amendment to the US Constitution was approved, removing sex as a barrier to the suffrage, Pagán was living in New York and working in a clothing factory. That same year, she traveled to Puerto Rico and demanded that the registration board register her to vote. Despite having achieved the age of majority and holding US citizenship, she was denied that right. Pagán presented a legal complaint that forced the governor of Puerto Rico, Arthur Yager, to consult with the Office of Insular Affairs in Washington, DC, which determined that the constitutional amendment was not valid for women in Puerto Rico. As a representative of the AFL, Pagán brought forward a legal complaint before the local board of registration, demanding the right to vote. She lost the case and was criticized by some elite suffragists in Puerto Rico. Nevertheless, as Yamila Azize points out, Pagán's actions "shocked the juridical structures in Puerto Rico."[43]

Four years later, Milagros Benet de Mewton (an upper-class Puerto Rican woman who belonged to the Pan American Association of Women) repeated Pagán's experiment and tried to register to vote. According to María Fátima Barceló Miller, women like Milagros Benet failed to include working-class women in a consistent way in the campaigns they organized after 1924. Instead they focused on recruiting new members for their associations and on seeking support from other feminist groups in the United States and Latin America. In 1925 the league divided along party lines. By November, Ana Roqué, Isabel Andreu, and Beatriz Lasalle had founded the Puerto Rican Association of Suffragist Women. Marta Robert's Suffragist Social League was comprised of women from the Pure Republican Party and the Republican–Socialist Coalition. In 1925 López was elected vice president of the league. It is worth noting that Marta Robert represented Puerto Rican women at the Pan American Congress in Washington, where the US National Women's Party, the International League of Women Voters, and the National League of Women Voters also participated. According to Enríquez and other researchers, "The affiliation of these organizations is what permitted the lobbying in the US Congress to achieve [success]."[44]

In February 1926, López was elected president of the Suffragist Social

League. She consistently published letters, editorials, and articles in the national newspapers, such as *El Mundo*, *El Tiempo*, and *La Correspondencia*, arguing for suffrage for all women. She also gave and wrote numerous speeches, including that given by Muna Lee de Muñoz Marín on February 7, 1928, at the Pan American Congress in Havana, Cuba, which was published in *El Mundo* on February 22.[45] In a letter to Edgar R. Kiess, chairman of the Insular Affairs Committee of the US House of Representatives, López stated clearly that the suffragists felt mocked and offended. She reminded him that they were US citizens: "Please remember, Mr. Kiess, that we are American citizens, and that our own country under the folds of the stars and stripes we are denied a right which we enjoy and can exercise as soon as we take up residence in one of the states of the Union, where, if domiciled there, we can participate in the presidential elections; whereas here we cannot even vote for the election of a second-class municipal officer. We hope, Mr. Kiess, that you will aid us and cooperate with other national leaders in order that full justice may be done to us."[46]

Her writing balanced forcefulness with poise. She leaned into the demands suffragists had been making since the turn of the century, in Puerto Rico, in other international arenas, and especially while lobbying members of the US Congress:

My dear Mr. Kiess:

You no doubt remember our interview at the Condado Vanderbuilt Hotel when you visited our Island recently. You may recall that I told you then, that the Insular Legislature would not enact the Suffrage Bill because the majority party feared losing its power if the women secured the electoral franchise, and it still fears the intervention of a new wholesome and unfettered element in the political life of the Island.

You may likewise remember that I told you we were tired of offers and promises, that in all previous legislatures they had offered us much at the beginning but that afterwards, sometimes due to the action of the House and others because of the attitude of the Senate, they would not approve the bill; thus giving us the impression of a well rehearsed comedy performed for our benefit.

She then underscored the lack of support they were receiving from both the legislature and the Puerto Rican political leadership:

You may also remember that you assured us relying on the assurances conveyed to you by Messrs. Towner, Barceló and Tous Soto, that in case these gentlemen would not fulfill their promise you would then be willing to support any bill that might be introduced in Congress granting the vote to the Porto Rican women.

Everything happened here as I predicted. The Legislature adjourned, without the House even passing a ridiculous and discriminating Suffrage Bill, which the Senate had approved, it seems only to make us believe that it favored Women Suffrage; when we all know that this was just a trick which they conceived and played at the last moment. At the next session of Congress, it is very likely that appropriate legislation which will enable us to secure the electoral franchise, will be introduced, and we desire now to remind you of your kind offer to aid and support this legislation.

In response to their international lobbying efforts, specifically those directed at the US Congress, Puerto Rican legislators began publicly criticizing the suffragists, accusing them of being ignorant, desperate, and antipatriotic. López responded with fury and astuteness, pointing to the fact that women had been making the same demands for many years: "We can do no less than counter the statements by our distinguished friend Mr. Tous y Soto because he has made us out to be impatient, even ignorant."[47] Women, she continued, had been fighting for the right to vote since 1909. She defended the decision (and strategy) of turning to the US Congress in search of allies. Tous y Soto had once aligned himself with López and her colleagues, but he had recently switched his support in favor of only a restricted women's suffrage. To this, López responded,

Our illustrious friend affirms his support for the feminine vote, but with restrictions, and the only restriction that he mentions is literary.

Of course, we do not intend to enter into a polemic over this point, but we would like to refresh the memory of the illustrious President of the House of Representatives.

Eleven years ago, in 1917, Mr. Tous y Soto introduced a law to recognize women's electoral rights, without literacy restrictions; now in 1928, he presents himself as the friend of women's suffrage, but only for literate women.

Eleven years ago, Tous supported us in our efforts to obtain recognition of our rights without any kind of restrictions, in the same way that men enjoy them, but now, 'He doesn't think that any illiterate, whatever their sex, should enjoy the right to vote.'[48]

. . . When Mr. Tous Soto was elected for the first time to hold a position in our parliament, and when he was re-elected, and during the entire time that he has occupied a post in our highest representative body, he has done so because the votes from illiterates have helped him climb to such heights.

If we women were to think the same way as our friend, we never would have occupied by votes a post elected by persons who should not enjoy the right to vote.

López named proposals suffragists had brought forth, as well as mockeries and lack of support they had endured. In response to the accusations of having turned to the US Congress, she stated the following:

In no way are we the ones who have been trying to make trouble between the metropolis and its possession, friend Tous Soto; in which case it is the legislators who are causing the difficulties without any reason except the caprice of a few, and without any more motivation than really personal convenience. This is what has obliged us to turn to national powers to demand our rights. They want us to continue to endure a humiliating and depressing situation out of patriotism, a situation made even more humiliating because it is our own legislators who uphold it, those who have in their hands the opportunity to do us justice and nothing more than justice, but obstinately maintain an attitude that has no explanation other than personal egotism and the fear of losing their positions.

López's complaints explain why the women chose to seek support for universal suffrage from the US Congress, emphasizing how many years women had been presenting Tous y Soto and other Puerto Rican legislators all the reasons why women in Puerto Rico should be able to vote:

> Reading the protestations of Mr. Tous Soto, anyone would think that we had never made our demands known to the Insular Legislature when he knows that we presented the first legislative proposal for the legal emancipation of the woman in 1909 via our unforgettable friend Mr. Canales, the proposal carries the number 39; and that since that time, we have proposed the same thing in every legislative session, without tiring or becoming impatient, to achieve the same end. We have been working for 19 years asking for the same thing, so it is not that we lack patience, that we just need to bide our time until the next legislative session in order to be able to make our desires known through the governmental agencies constituted in Puerto Rico; no, no it is not like that; let it be known once more, esteemed friend Mr. Tous Soto and let the country know it once and for all.[49]

In 1928 the US House of Representatives approved a proposal to extend the Nineteenth Amendment of the US Constitution to Puerto Rico. The Bingham Proposal "proposed to modify Article 35 of the Jones Law, adding that the right to vote could not be denied on account of sex." In 1929 the Committee on Territories and Island Possessions supported women's suffrage in Puerto Rico and "sent an ultimatum to the insular legislature, a report to the Suffragist Social League: 'if in February your Congress has not conceded the right that justly belongs to you, we will concede it ourselves.'" According to Barceló Miller, and as we have seen in López's 1928 letter, the unionist senators "criticized the suffragists severely . . . for having turned to the North American government to solicit the franchise, which concession was the prerogative of the Puerto Rican Legislative Assembly. They called them unpatriotic for having discredited their own legislators before the federal government, and having made it seem as though they were denying women the suffrage capriciously."[50] The president of the Senate, Antonio R. Barceló, defended the most recent legislative proposal, submitted on April 11, 1929, in Puerto Rico, focusing "not on the vindication of women's right to vote and be elected to office, but rather on the urgency to pass restricted suffrage before the Bingham Proposal became law." In his speech, he pitted women's rights directly against the interests of Puerto Rico's self-determination: "Before it is imposed on us as an arbitrary and despotic act, and as an indictment of our incapacity, we should go through with this measure, whether or not the women want it, because ahead of them, ahead of ourselves, we must place the Right, the Liberty, and the Dignity of Puerto Rico."[51]

The Puerto Rican legislature conceded restricted suffrage to literate Puerto Rican women above the age of twenty-one. The governor, Horace Mann Towner, signed the law on April 18, 1929. The new law discriminated against thousands of working-class women, resulting in a generalized outcry from the Suffragist Social League, the Socialist Party, and the Free Federation of Workers.[52] Women workers in tobacco and sewing parts of the economy continued laboring under terrible conditions, giving rise to increased strike activity. Finally, in 1935, Bolívar Pagán, representing the Socialist Party, presented a successful petition to eliminate the literacy requirement.[53]

According to Gladys Jimenez, in February 1927 readers of *La Democracia* saw the whole text of a long message delivered by Horace Mann Towner to the Eleventh Legislative Assembly of Puerto Rico. It stated, "Since the women of Puerto Rico are American citizens, suffrage should be granted to them as soon as possible so as to in this way harmonize our political conditions with the 19th Amendment to the Constitution of the US. This right should also be granted to women because the government of Puerto Rico is obligated to them for the cooperation and help they provide in the fields of education, hygiene and public health, compliance with the law, and in all those measures promoting good morals, social betterment, and the general welfare of the people."[54] Jimenez argues that the governor's speech is evidence of a hegemonic ideology: "The colonialist identity being enacted through the colonial government's practices and pronouncements evidently desired a colonized subject."[55] Antonio R. Barceló presided over the Senate and stated that the vote should only go to educated women. He admitted to the mistake of having granted universal male suffrage in 1904. On this point, Jimenez comments, "Barceló wants to participate in US colonialist dream of a 'class of interpreters between us and the millions whom we govern—a class of persons,' Puerto Rican in blood and color, but North American in tastes, in opinions, in morals and in intellect."[56] She describes Barceló as having participated in "colonial mimicry," in which "the leader of the 'naïve' elites's attempts to transcend the mistakes of the colonizers by improving on the latter's methods of colonialist governance. . . . Some colonized subjects were more equal than others."[57]

It is worth noting, as María Fátima Barceló Miller reminds us, that the Jones Law simultaneously gave Puerto Ricans citizenship rights and "ratified the colonial condition of the island." It affirmed "the primordial objective of the North American colonialist policy toward Puerto Rico: the permanent retention of the Island."[58] Article 35 of the Jones Law allowed the Puerto Rican legislature to restrict the suffrage for any noneconomic reason. Thus one of the ironies of this history is that the approval of the Nineteenth Amendment to the US Constitution in 1920 demarcated the colonial condition of Puerto Rico.

Genara Pagán's failure to register to vote was the test case that confirmed her country's colonial status. As a result of Pagán's request, the governor, Arthur Yager, brought in the Insular Affairs Office on the question of the applicability of the Nineteenth Amendment in Puerto Rico. According to Barceló Miller, Attorney General E. H. Crowder reported to the office his conclusion that it was not applicable. The amendment, according to his reasoning, applied only to states and the US federal government. Puerto Rico belonged to the United States, but it was not part of the United States.[59] When a US suffragist asked the secretary of state to clarify the difference between Puerto Rico and other territories, such as Alaska and Hawaii, the head of the Office of Insular Affairs responded that Alaska and Hawaii were organized territories and that Puerto Rico was neither an organized territory nor an incorporated one.[60]

In her book on Puerto Rican women's suffrage, Barceló Miller cites at least three legal studies that look at the Jones Law and universal suffrage. They classify it as a colonialist, antidemocratic, and antifeminist law. Bolívar Pagán believed that the Jones Law "did not expressly confer suffrage on women, but neither did it deny it. Congress delegated to the local Assembly the power to impose restrictions on account of sex or other reasons unrelated to economics. Nevertheless, they lost that power as soon as the 19th Amendment was passed . . . [which] prohibited restrictions on the suffrage on account of sex."[61] She argued that "by denying the vote on account of sex, from 26 August 1920, the date on which the 19th Amendment passed, it was unconstitutional." For that reason, the assembly had to modify voting legislation, removing language referring to "all citizens" and replacing it with "male citizens." Otherwise, all Puerto Rican women would be included as becoming citizens in 1917, despite the fact that they resided in an unincorporated territory.[62]

In 1936, more than two hundred thousand women achieved the right to vote, and some of them held various political offices. Nevertheless, throughout the twentieth century, women on the island realized that the vote had failed to engender equality either in local politics or in society. For example, the slogan of the Pro-Statehood Civic Education Association included the words "We love and defend our American citizenship because it symbolizes the liberty we seek for Puerto Rico."[63]

Ricarda López de Ramos Casellas was president of this association. The Centro de Investigaciones Históricas holds documents that show the role women played in the associations of the Republican Union in 1943, when they requested representation in the territorial committee of the party along with other administrative posts.[64]

Document 7 contains the letterhead of the Progressive Republican Union Party (it is the only document in the collection with this letterhead), which added the word *progresista* to the association name on August 14, 1944. The document details party visits to different towns, in this case in the district of Aguadilla, affirming that members met with various women, recruiting them for the ladies' committees. Several towns are mentioned, distinguishing between those that have women's committees and those that do not, as well as those that have men's committees and those that lack them. Some towns proved more challenging than others for the organizers; one was Rincón.[65] The same document reveals they had a $900 car at their disposal. On this subject, the notes maintain,

The Madam president would like to make known that the automobile that has been purchased is not for Mrs. Ramos Casellas, but for the Women's Association of the Progressive Republican Union. [It is for] the activities of the Association in benefit of the Party, and additionally, that the Association has had great difficulty acquiring a car in order for the president to travel to the different locations where she was invited to attend meetings and other Association and Party activities, seeing as how the Association on innumerable occasions has been unable to respond to such request for lack of adequate transportation.[66]

The minutes also explain that the president maintained during the meeting that it was not the moment to petition the party for women's participation in administrative posts or political seats. On this point, they note, "The Madam President explains that since it is not the moment to present the party with problems that demonstrate personal ambitions, we will not ask anything of the party if we are offered nothing, since what we all desire is to win the elections. As such, there is no need, informs the president, to hold our assembly at the same time as the ordinary one for the Party, but rather it can take place later. If we are able to achieve 'a good act, this will help raise up women in the next elections.'" A woman named Caldas opposed Ramos's position:

Mrs. Caldas maintains that she does not agree with not placing women on the electoral "ticket," and that she wants to send a letter to the address of the Party saying that the woman is an important factor and should take part in everything. She is not content for women to play no part in any of the organizations of the party. The president explained that she spoke of legislative posts, not administrative posts. Mrs. Caldas says that she wants the President to continue as a member of the Board of Commissioners in the Capital. The president insists they should not present the party with problems. Mrs. Caldas says that we must communicate to the party that we have rights and that they must be recognized. Mrs. Gaetán adds that, at the same time as lending our determined support to the cause of the party, our personality corresponding to the entire people, being a much large feminine group, should not be eclipsed. It is agreed that we should send a letter to the

President of the Party concerning what was discussed. Doña Sara agrees with the President that we shouldn't put the Party in even greater difficulty.[67]

Another document shows the association's concerns about suffrage and members' displeasure at the lack of support they were receiving from the party regarding even administrative positions, never mind elected posts. Among their demands were the following:

In order to express to the Territorial Central Committee of the Progressive Republican Union the intense displeasure that we women feel in the 'Women's Association of the P.R.U.' for our Party having failed to give women representation in the popularly elected posts during these elections. . . . As to how many: in the 1932 elections, the first in which women had the use of the vote, that citizen's right, we have confirmed that 35,000 more women cast ballots than men.[68]

They declare that they feel "disappointed and discouraged with that same enthusiasm, the struggle with which so much patriotism they began." They ask for "justice for those who have a perfect right to it, for their numeric, intellectual, and moral force, within the ranks of this great P.R.U. Party."[69] They ask that their resolution be sent to the territorial central committee by way of President Celestino Iriarte and that it be read at their first meeting following the resolution's creation in San Juan, Puerto Rico, on October 15, 1944.

According to the editors of the special edition of *Identidades*, dedicated to the seventy-five years since the first women voted in Puerto Rico, the 1932 elections were "transcendent":

"The first woman was elected to the Legislature, María Luis Arcelay, whose contributions in defense of women at the legislative level were significant. Hundreds of women joined party organizations during the decades of the 1930s and 1940s, among them, the Puerto Rican Union Party, the Republican Party, the Liberal Party, the Workers' Socialist Party, the Popular Democratic Party, and the Nationalist Party."[70] They highlight the fact that women "distinguished themselves as organizers at every level, as orators and theorists in their parties, generally without receiving much public intellectual recognition. Some excelled as mayors of towns, others as municipal council members. Nevertheless, most of their contributions have been ignored for decades, which has made it very difficult for them to climb to positions of leadership within their own political parties."[71] The editors observe that the "ferocious, aggressive, and contentious" nature of the political-electoral processes "discourages women from participating." They continue, "Party politics is not just a world of men, but of *machos*, given their styles of leadership and behavior. Women, who make up more than half the population . . . are not equitably represented in the country's spheres of power, in the executive, judicial, or legislative branches."[72]

In recent years, Luz del Alba Acevedo Gaud, María Dolores Fernós, and other feminists have written and commented on women's political participation.[73] Fernós writes, "In general, what is involved is the broader issue of the presence—or absence—of women in politics. Personally, I consider this topic an area in which Puerto Rican women have still not achieved the full rights of citizenship."[74]

Conclusions

The strategies, work, and accomplishments of Genera Pagán, Ricarda López, and the Puerto Rican suffragist movement illustrate interconnections and intersections, not only between different sociopolitical movements but also with the transnational support networks that nourished them (sindicalism, suffragism, Antillianism, pan-Americanism, and others). They sought equality, recognition of their human and civil rights, sovereignty, and national and political identity, among other claims framed within a historical context of aspiration toward progress and modernity. At the end of the nineteenth century and the beginning of the twentieth, Puerto Rico saw the United States as a country of liberty and justice.[75] In Puerto Rico (an practically the entire hemisphere), the discourse of propagating democracy and modernity permitted the United States to intervene in an aggressive and expansive manner. Women made use of some expansionist processes to question and challenge civil codes and citizenship. Ellen Carol Dubois posited in 1994 that women's international cooperation provided them resources to combat the political marginalization women experienced in their own countries.[76]

Part of the intention of this chapter and its brief studies of Genara Pagán and Ricarda López de Ramos Casellas is what Virginia Vargas calls "the importance of tracing collective strategies, forms of articulating the local [Puerto Rico] within the regional-global [the United States, the Caribbean, and Latin America], the effects on transforming the ideology of the national-states, and the effectiveness in producing a regional discourse based on the nuances and diversities that existed within the countries and movements." In particular, I focus on Puerto Rico and its colonial status as an unincorporated territory of the United States in the postcolonial period.[77] Vargas also sustains that "the feminist agenda is both an historical and contextual [coyuntural] construction. Its radicalism [exists] in a particular historical moment." I would add that it also exists in a particular place.[78]

In sum, this is a critical reflection framed within a context that does not pretend to encompass everything or to recount all that occurred before, during, and after universal suffrage was achieved in Puerto Rico—never mind the complex processes and implications of US citizenship for those born in the archipelago and their demands for decolonization (be it through independence or statehood). According to Gervasio Garcia, "The historian's goal is to establish the links between two essential correlations, between what we do and the complex factors, often imperceptible, that cause us to act."[79] This is precisely what we are compelled to historicize: the experiences, events, and mentalities that drove Genara Pagán and Ricarda López to act. As women, we make history from diverse critical and transnational perspectives, weaving together all these strands. In García's case, labor historians may find archival evidence of "proclamations and programs, meetings and marches, strikes and insurrections," but the historians look past the documents to "go beyond them and pick up the rest."[80]

To this view we must add that to "pick up the rest" there must be a critical analysis of gender and, in the case of Puerto Rico, of its colonial history, first under Spain and then (continuing into the present) under the United States. As presented here, the process of understanding the time and place in which Genara Pagán and Ricarda López were born and developed into a female worker–labor leader and an educator–political leader, respectively, involves understanding Puerto Rico, not only in terms of key political, economic, or cultural events but also from intersectional perspectives. Only this view will be able to encompass the realities that circumscribed the lives of women with little formal education and restricted juridical, social, labor, and political rights.[81]

It is also important to take into account influential mentalities from the period just before and during the decades that followed the US invasion of Puerto Rico. We are still confronting some of the repercussions and implications of that period 123 years later. A hundred years after women like Genara Pagán and Ricarda López de Ramos Casellas took on both local and colonial governments to demand the right to vote (along with other rights), other Puerto Rican women continue to challenge US hegemony through political, environmental, and social activism. They continue to confront both the patriarchy and the state to demand full voting rights and to be recognized as citizens of a sovereign nation.

Notes

1. Mergal, "Puerto Rican Feminism at a Crossroads," 1.
2. Teele, *Forging the Franchise*, 182.
3. Senator Francisco M. Zeno, quoted in *El Mundo*, 1927, in Barceló Miller, *La lucha por el sufragio femenino en Puerto Rico*, 182.
4. For more information about these relationships and topics, see Aarón Gamaliel Ramos, *Islas migajas: los países no independientes del Caribe contemporáneo* (San Juan: Travesier & Leduc, 2016).
5. The Puerto Rican historian Martín Cruz Santos comments on (and questions) US citizenship (its imposition, acceptance, and renunciation) in a 2018 essay he wrote for the Jornada de Puerto Rico y el Caribe de la Universidad Ana G. Méndez: "On 2 March 1917, Woodrow Wilson signed the Jones Act, legislated by the US Congress, which included, among other provisions, US citizenship for the residents of Puerto Rico. This political and juridical decision opened an interminable debate. . . . What happened to the people on a Caribbean island named Puerto Rico from the moment we became citizens of another country, one that we entered as members of a territory won during a war, the Spanish American? How was it experienced by ordinary citizens? What happened to the 288 individuals who refused to being citizens of the United States? This is another face of the history."

6. De Haan et al., *Women's Activism*, 77. In her essay, Altink makes some interesting observations, which are sometimes contradictory, regarding the case of Jamaica during the last decades of the nineteenth century and the first of the twentieth. Citizenship as manifested by women in their struggles under British rule is worth exploring in more depth.

7. Jiménez-Muñoz, "So We Decided to Come and Ask You Ourselves," 140–41.

8. Cruz Santos, "Identidades culturales y ciudadanías," 3.

9. For an analysis of the PROMESA Law and austerity policies, see Ariadna Godreau Aubert, *Las propias: Apuntes para una pedagogía de las endeudadas* (Cabo Rojo: Editora Educación Emergente 2018). Mabel Rodríguez Centeno praised Godreau's work. In a blurb for the book she wrote, "[She] proposes a radical pedagogy for speaking about the crisis/crises that have invaded us and displaced us . . . indebtedness, criminalization, the right to protest, and the ways in which we reclaim our bodies before the state . . . about human rights, labor reform issues, the meaning of poverty, the ashes that kill us, austerity measures, colonialism, and machista violence."

10. Luma is a joint venture between Houston-based Quanta Services, Inc. and ATCO, a company from Alberta, Canada. For a view on this situation from pop culture, see "Bad Bunny—El Apagón—Aquí Vive Gente, YouTube, 2022, https://www.youtube.com/watch?v=1TCX_Aqz0o4.

11. Torres Martínez, "Procesos sociales, política, poder y género," 142.

12. For a description and historical recounting of Puerta de Tierra, see Aníbal Sepúlveda Rivera and Sylvia Álvarez Curbelo, "Puerta de Tierra, un espacio urbano," Enciclopedia de Puerto Rico of the Fundación Puertorriqueña de las Humanidades, https://enciclopediapr.org/puerta-de-tierra-un-espacio-urbano, accessed October 30, 2023.

13. "Immersed as a US colony in capitalist production strategies for export and related modernizing social programs, the predominance of wage relations throughout the 20th century in Puerto Rico reduced family production and made monetary remuneration more necessary to acquire goods and services in a commodified society" (Colón Warren et al., *Estirando el peso*, 10). Capitalist economic modernization created new employment opportunities for women, including tobacco work and needlework for poorer women and state-sponsored programs in health, education, and welfare for middle- and upper-class women. Those new opportunities did not translate into a significant challenge to male dominance at home, however, or to the view that women were uniquely suited to domestic labor. Instead, women's entry into the workforce was viewed as a sad but necessary reality when a man was not available to provide for the family.

14. Azize, *La Mujer En Puerto Rico*, 41.

15. Azize, 34.

16. Azize, 34–35.

17. Azize, 36.
18. Azize, 36.
19. Azize, 37.
20. Azize, 37.
21. Rivera-Giusti, *Gender, Labor, and Working-Class Activism*.
22. Norma Valle presents Luisa Capetillo as the "first Puerto Rican to organize her feminist ideas and publish them as a theoretical thesis" (Norma Valle, *Luisa Capetillo: Historia de una mujer proscrita* [San Juan: Editorial cultural, 1998], 81). According to Comerío police reports, López de Ramos Casellas shared a platform with Colón for the coalition during the election month of 1936 in Comerío. From these reports, it is clear that these two feminist leaders were campaigning for the coalition in Comerío. Two women whose origins and education were totally different shared a platform.
23. As related in the blog *Anarquismo en Puerto Rico*, Igualdad Iglesias vda. de Pagán described the workers' strike at the *colectiva* in San Juan: "They abandoned their workplace because of the employer's mistreatment, according to this strike of 1918. . . . Large US corporations see in Puerto Rico a fertile field in the tobacco industry, and women as cheap labor." Iglesias added that working women "were different from feminist women in that they only owned their own labor (their two hands) and were not economically well off." In worker feminism, women were organized, and their petitions and demands were raised, with the union's understanding that their gender should be respected and their demands should be listened to. In another post in the same blog, Evelyn Solá Maldonado notes, "The uprising of the despalilladoras of La Colectiva was in August 1918, the Free Federation had agreed to a general strike for September in the Workers Congress held in the city of Bayamón. Before the agricultural strike of 1918, there were great debates [over issues] such as the women's vote, with the Free Federation demanding women's participation in the elections." In this strike, Genera Pagán participated on behalf of the colectiva's de-stemmers. Luisa Capetillo was a leader in the Fajardo strike, Juana Colón was a leader in Comerio, and Isabel Villanueva was a delegate for San Lorenzo. The blog continues, "According to the telegrams in the SIP Documentary Fund, women and children received less money than men. The uprising of de-stemmers from the Colectiva in 1918 is a call to reflection on the constant abuses these Puerto Rican women workers received and their participation for labor justice, united by the unresolved struggles of the 19th century." "Huelga Agrícola 1918, participación femenina," *Anarquismo en Puerto Rico*, 2012, https://anarquismoenpuertorico.blogspot.com/2012/10/huelga-agricola-1918-participacion.html.
24. Azize, *La Mujer En Puerto Rico*, 40–41.
25. Torres Martínez, "Procesos sociales, política, poder y género," 140.
26. Torres Martínez, 141.

27. Enríquez, *Ricarda López de Ramos Casellas*, 153.

28. Enríquez, 154–55.

29. Enríquez, 14.

30. Enríquez, 14–15.

31. Enríquez, 15.

32. Enríquez, 73–74.

33. Enríquez, 74.

34. Enríquez, 84.

35. Valle, *Luisa Capetillo*, 25. According to Valle, women's education was funda-mental "for a progressive society" (29). She adds that during Capetillo's time (as well as that of Genera Pagán, Ricarda López de Ramos Casellas, and other feminist leaders of the era), in England, France, and the United States, femi-nist pioneers embraced the defense of women's education as "one of the first symbols of struggle" (31). Among the writers who took up the cause of women's education in Puerto Rico was Eugenio María de Hostos, who argued that "the most effective way to change attitudes and form a new generation is to edu-cate women so that they, as mothers, can transmit respect for the truth to their children" (33). Valle affirms (as was the case with Ricarda), "To this liberal current also belong some of the first Puerto Rican feminists, almost all were educated at home or in the small private schools that were formed around a teacher" (33). She presents as examples Josefina Moll (Flor Daliza), María Luisa de Argelis, and Ana Roque de Duprey, remarking that Argelis and Duprey "excelled at organizing and at producing important publications in defense of the cause of women's education" (33). They published numerous books and edited newspapers.

36. Enríquez, *Ricarda López de Ramos Casellas*, 152.

37. Enríquez, 153.

38. Enríquez, 239.

39. Luisa Capetillo lived in New York City at the same time as Genara Pagán. In 1919 she had a room in a boarding house in New York, where she worked as a reader in a cigar factory "and took part in public controversies about the class struggle." (Valle, *Luisa Capetillo*, 89). In 1920 she campaigned for the Partido Socialista Obrero, attending "rallies in support of the candidacy of Santiago Iglesias Pantín, whom she admired and considered her comrade" (95).

40. Azize, *La Mujer En Puerto Rico*, 41.

41. Rivera-Giusti, *Gender, Labor, and Working-Class Activism*.

42. Rivera-Giusti.

43. Azize, *La Mujer en Puerto Rico*, 41.

44. Enríquez, *Ricarda López de Ramos Casellas*, 158.

45. Enríquez, 167, 263–64. Enriquez details the activities of the league in Havana, including its interactions with Bingham and Edgar Kiess (161–66). Evidence for this is contained in documents of the Colección de Ricarda López de

Ramos Casellas (RLRC), Centro de Investigaciones Históricas (CIH), Universidad de Puerto Rico, Recinto de Río Piedras (Caja 3, Cartapacios 1–5).

46. RLRC, CIH, Cartapacio 1, Document 6.

47. RLRC, CIH, Cartapacio 1, Document 7, p. 1, 1928.

48. Quotes from RLRC, CIH, Caja 3. All text, including underlined words, is from Ricarda López de Ramos Casellas.

49. RLRC, CIH, Caja 3, pp. 3–4.

50. All quotes from Barceló Miller, *La lucha por el sufragio femenino en Puerto Rico*, 175, 177.

51. Barceló Miller, 184.

52. Azize, *La Mujer en Puerto Rico*, 43. Documents from the president of the league and other labor leaders confirm this.

53. Azize, *La Mujer En Puerto Rico*, 43.

54. Jimenez-Muñoz (quoting Mann), "So We Decided to Come and Ask You Ourselves," 147.

55. Jimenez-Muñoz, 148.

56. Jimenez-Muñoz (quoting Babington Macaulays), 149.

57. Jimenez-Muñoz, 149.

58. Barceló Miller (using José Trías Monge's work), *La lucha por el sufragio femenino en Puerto Rico*, 158–59.

59. Barceló Miller, 160.

60. Barceló Miller (citing Clark), 161. For a more extensive analysis, refer to the work of Gladys Jimenez-Muñoz, especially "So We Decided to Come and Ask for Ourselves."

61. Barceló Miller (citing Bolívar Pagán), *La lucha por el sufragio femenino en Puerto Rico*, 168–69.

62. Quotes from Barceló Miller, 169.

63. Document 1 of the Congreso Pro-Estadidad agenda of 1943; Document 2: Reglamento de la Asociación Puertorriqueña de Mujeres Estadistas de Puerto Rico 1944; RLRC, CIH, Caja 3, Cartapacio 2, nos. 1–6.

64. Document 5: Certificate of registration of the Asociación de mujeres de la Unión Republicana Progresista (May 29, 1944). In Cartapacio 3, Documents 1–7, we found Document 2: Acta 1 de la Asociación de mujeres del a Unión Republicana (San Juan, July 17, 1943). RLRC, CIH, Caja 3 contains meeting minutes from the general assembly of the board of commissioners. It requests women's representation on the party's territorial committee.

65. "In Rincón, it is difficult to organize a committee, since this town has been mostly socialists, and they are now popular." RLRC, CIH, Caja 3, Acta 5, p. 1.

66. RLRC, CIH, Caja 3, Acta 5, p. 2.

67. RLRC, CIH, Caja 3, Acta 5, p. 3.

68. Colonel Ricarda López de Ramos Casellas is number 3 from Cartapacio 4. RLRC, CIH, Caja 3.

69. RLRC, CIH, Caja 3, p. 2.

70. *75 años del primer voto*, special edition of *Identidades: Revista Interdisciplinaria de Estudios de las Mujeres y el Género* 5 (2007): 7.

71. *75 años del primer voto*, 7.

72. *75 años del primer voto*, 8.

73. See Luz del Alba Acevedo Gaud, "Un senado para la historia: género, poder y elecciones 2020 en Puerto Rico," *Revista Cruce*, March 2021, https://issuu.com/revistacruce/docs/asunto_1.

74. Fernós, "Las mujeres en la política," 11.

75. This is seen in López's own speeches and in work from researchers like Sandra Enríquez and Maria Fátima Barceló Miller.

76. DuBois, "Woman Suffrage around the World," 254.

77. Vargas, "Los nuevos derroteros a fin de milenio: derechos y autonomía."

78. Vargas.

79. Gervasio García, *Armar la Historia: la tesis en la región menos transparente y otros ensayos* (Río Piedras: Ediciones Huracán, 1989), 88.

80. García, 88.

81. For further examples of women who belonged to and held relevant positions within the Puerto Rican Nationalist Party, see Olga Jiménez de Wagenheim, *Nationalist Heroines: Puerto Rican Women History Forgot 1930s–1950s* (Princeton, NJ: Markus Wiener, 2017), as well as Asociación Puertorriquena de investigación de historia de las mujeres, http://senriquezseiders.blogspot.com/p/blog-page_17.html.

Conclusion

STEPHANIE MITCHELL

THE FIVE SCENARIOS DESCRIBED IN this book, in which some women received some political rights in some of the countries that make up the Americas, are at best a partial effort to understand an enormously complicated history. Additionally, we should remember that any categorization scheme becomes arbitrary when the details of the landscape are magnified enough to reveal the unique characteristics of each story. Categories are useful only from a vantage point of height. We hope these chapters have made the three commonalities (shared historical trajectory, shared assumptions, and similar experiences of divided sisterhood) and three differences (transnational and international context, political environment, and efficacy of the movement) identified in the introduction clearer. What other things can we learn from this kind of comparative approach?

Aspects of a particular national history can take on a different meaning when held up next to others. In Canadian suffrage history, for example, Quebec is an outlier. It enfranchised women later than the other provinces and the political dynamic of the movement was distinct from that in English-speaking regions. Catholic women's roles in Quebec begin to look familiar, however, when we compare them to other places where Catholicism figured strongly in national politics. The cases in both the Delayed Liberal and Conservative Strategic Advantage Scenarios share similarities with the story in Quebec, making it seem less exceptional. In the same way, literacy requirements might seem peculiar to the Jim Crow South until we realize how often the same strategy was employed as a proxy to exclude subaltern races and classes in other places with high illiteracy. Highly literate and more racially homogenous Argentina, where there were no literacy requirements, may have had more in common with northern states in the United States than the former Confederate states, at least with regard to the struggle for voting rights.

Nearly all our authors made it a point to mention that early national constitutions were vague on gender. In other words, it was usually not clear from the language whether women were included as citizens or not. Seeing this pattern repeated over and again strengthens our understanding of the profound accomplishment nineteenth-century intellectuals achieved in placing the normative quality of masculine citizenship into question. Before their work, legislators felt no need to specify women's exclusion from politics because they took that exclusion for granted. Laws that subsequently restricted the vote by sex and frequently by race or property ownership might otherwise look like setbacks. From a distance, however, we can see these restrictions as evidence of remarkable success on the part of the earliest suffragists.

Prior to our collaboration, many of us had observed in our own areas of expertise how activists and politicians alike often framed suffrage rights as a binary choice between gender and some other mark of power difference. In other words, either legislators could extend the franchise to a group that belonged to the dominant gender but subordinate race, ethnicity, or class *or* they could extend it to a group that belonged to the dominant race, ethnicity, or class but subordinate gender. For example, in Ecuador, politicians, newspaper columnists, and activists all engaged in conversations about whether Indigenous men or European-descended women were more qualified to vote. Nearly the same conversation took place in the United States over the qualifications of Black men versus white women. Suffragists from the dominant race, ethnicity, or class played into this binary construction by arguing that they were better qualified than the male members of the opposite group to exercise political rights. This pattern had a tendency to reinforce the intersectional subjugation that poor women and women from racialized groups experienced. They were left to fend for their rights alone, rejected both by men who shared their class status and/or racialization and by women who did not. Yet this same tendency led many of them to more capacious demands for justice. They were not content with agitating for the vote but pressed on for racial equality, respect for Indigenous culture, and economic and social rights. The most comprehensive critiques, the most radical demands, have usually come from groups that experienced double or triple exploitation, and this has been true from the southern Andes to the western Canadian plains.

All the people who worked on this project found that the endeavor served to highlight the mountain of work historians still need to do if we really want to understand suffrage history. If anyone reading these words is looking for a thesis topic, our collaborators would like to help. We suggest three areas where more research is badly needed.

The first area is not new, and it involves our ongoing efforts to fill in gaps in this history. There is still so much we do not know. There is wide variation among the countries that make up the Americas in terms of how well developed the historiography is on suffrage. In 2018, when forty of fifty of us sat in a room together, we did an informal ranking in which 1 signified a highly developed historiography, 2 meant there were still significant gaps, and 3 meant that very little was known. Of the countries studied by the researchers in the room, none merited a 1 and there were plenty of 3s. There are biographies to be written, anti-suffragists to be understood, political machinations to be uncovered. Please consider telling one of these untold stories.

The second area of badly need research is intersectionality. Most countries' historiographies have barely scratched the surface in understanding the role of nondominant groups in suffrage history. In 1981 bell hooks perfectly explained why black women faced exclusion and silencing from both other feminists and other black antiracists: "The labeling of black women who engage feminist thinking as race traitors is meant to prevent us from embracing feminist politics as surely as white-power feminism acts to exclude our voices and silence our critiques."[1] A similar dynamic has ensured the erasure of women belonging to racialized groups from suffrage historiography and indeed from women's history more broadly. Historians interested in writing these women back into the history will need to abandon notions of purity so that women resisting multiple sources of oppression simultaneously can be heard. In other words, a "suffrage" historian may need to forget about trying to find Indigenous women who cared only or even mostly about voting rights because their lived experiences may have made such luxuries absurd in the face of multiple and competing structures of oppression that conspired to extinguish their entire existence. In the same way that people affected by "intersecting structures of oppression" were forced to engage in broad strategies of resistance, historians must be able to look beyond the narrower kinds of questions we have asked to reveal more complicated histories.[2]

Finally, we need to learn what happened next. We invite researchers to help us understand what happened after suffrage extensions occurred. If one group was enfranchised and another excluded, how did both groups act politically in the interim, when one group could vote and the other could not? Did enfranchised women use their votes to expand the electorate to their sisters? Did they do the opposite, preferring to keep power to themselves? What did suffrage movements look like during these sometimes extensive in between periods? More broadly speaking, what did it matter when women began to participate in electoral politics? Of the countries presented in this volume, we know only about Argentina, where women were either blamed or credited (depending on your politics) for having reelected Juan Perón, despite the fact that male voters overwhelmingly cast their ballots for him.[3] Most of the time, we simply do not know the impact newly enfranchised groups of women had on elections.

In addition to these thematic areas, we could expand on the work of looking at the history through the lens of scenarios. What other scenarios would highlight different elements of the history we are not yet seeing? For example, a number of countries not covered in this volume might fit into a Revolutionary Scenario, in which women gained the suffrage by virtue of their participation in a successful revolutionary movement. Cuba, Belize, Venezuela, and Guatemala all had suffrage extensions, acting on demands from women whose work had been essential to winning victory for revolutionaries. How many other scenarios would help us see patterns like this?

As this researcher approaches the conclusion of a project many years in the making, I feel called to reflect on the protracted struggle for democratic inclusion in our hemisphere. It must have been an extraordinary thing to have lived as a member of any of the settler societies in the

Americas during the first few decades of the nineteenth century. While the causes of revolution were complex and varied, its scale and pace were immense. The stakes were similar across vast geographies: monarchy or self-government? Empire or independence? With few exceptions, Europe chose one path and the Americas another. Within the span of a few years, America became a hemisphere of self-governing independent republics, each struggling to put into practice ideas that had, until recently, been little more than words on paper. Liberty and equality before the law for citizens became enshrined in constitutions that extend over two continents, displacing three centuries of colonial monarchical rule, in which different sets of laws had applied to different groups of subjects according to rank and caste. Enlightened thought had given way to revolutionary action, which had in turn birthed a prodigious new republican reality.

Not everyone was pleased. Many argued that democracy would be the ruin of the West—it would level out society, obliterating anything fine or beautiful, elevating only mediocrity. Others worried that the passions of the rabble had only barely been constrained by the imperial structures liberals were now rushing to dismantle, including a forceful state religion. While few mourned the passing of foreign taxes or restrictions on trade, would it not be wiser to preserve centralized systems of government with enough authority to maintain order? Was it not sensible to restrict the exercise of power to those whose birth and education had equipped them to wield it well? When we say "self-governing," whom do we mean by "self"? When we say "equality before the law for all citizens," whom do we mean by "citizen"? The constitutions did not specify. We have been arguing about it ever since.

Most of us carry in our heads a vague notion of an arc of history bending toward progress, in which ever greater numbers of Americans, South and North, have claimed inclusion in the rights of citizenship. This book has tried to disrupt that narrative to an extent. While it is true that slavery is no longer legal and there are no longer voting restrictions based on sex, race, or other broad categories of difference, none of us has achieved true universal suffrage and none can boast that our citizens enjoy true equality before the law. In no country are the descendants of those who were enslaved or colonized equal to the descendants of those who colonized and enslaved. In all of our nations, power or weakness is still largely conferred at birth.

Some countries have made greater strides than others in promoting gender equity. While no country in the world has attained gender equality (which would be measured by a United Nations Gender Inequality Index of 0), only one American nation, Canada, even ranks among the top twenty. Only Barbados, Chile, Costa Rica, the United States, and Uruguay have managed to get their index under 0.3 (on a scale in which 1 is the worst), with most falling between 0.3 and 0.5 and with Haiti, one of the first American republics to have obtained independence and abolished slavery, at a dismal 0.636.[4] Some countries, notably Mexico, Argentina, and Chile, have had remarkable success in increasing gender parity with respect to political representation by employing quota systems.[5] At the same time, intolerable levels of violence toward women, including femicides, have led to increasing calls for *despatriarcalización* of both the state and civil society.[6] Since sex and gender intersect and cut across race, caste, and class in all our American republics, patriarchy multiplies the burdens for those whose ancestors survived enslavement and colonization. I struggle with how to balance my sense of despair at these truths with my historian's conviction that almost all women are better off now than they were on the eve of independence. One moment, my cynical mind decides that de-patriarchalization is an unattainable fantasy, but then I remember that the freedoms I enjoy now would not have been possible if someone in the past had not first imagined them and then fought to achieve them.

At the conclusion of the 2018 NEH Summer Institute that made possible much of the work that went into writing this book, the incomparable Asunción Lavrin gave a public lecture. We expected her to speak mostly about the history of women's suffrage, the ostensible topic of the institute. She chose, however, to focus on the future. She fixed her gaze on the room full of researchers and asked us what our foremothers had fought so hard to achieve. Was suffrage an end unto itself? Did they intend for us to achieve citizenship for no other purpose than to have it? Or was the vote always a means to another end? She suggested that the generations of activists who fought so hard for political rights did so that we might use them to achieve just societies, and that in this respect we have largely failed to live up to the dreams they had for us. They did not give us a voice that we should remain silent. In this sense, dear reader, we ask that you not only reflect on how you might contribute to understanding history but that you also consider how you might make the struggles of the past meaningful in the present. You are not obligated to complete the work but neither are you free to abandon it.[7]

Notes

1. hooks, *Ain't I a Woman?*, cited in Susan Shaw and Janet Lee, *Women's Voices, Feminist Visions* (Mountain View, CA: Mayfield Publishing Company, 2001), 34.
2. Crenshaw, "Mapping the Margins."
3. See Adriana Valobra's chapter, this volume.
4. "Human Development Insights," United Nations Development Programme, 2023, http://hdr.undp.org/en/indicators/68606#.
5. Chile, for example, used a quota system to ensure that its new constitutional process maintained equal representation.
6. Sandoval Sánchez, "Sin despatriarcalización no habrá transformación."
7. From the Talmud; Pirkei Avot (Ethics/Chapters of the Fathers) 2:16.

Bibliography

Aboy Carlés, G. "Las dos caras de Jano: acerca de la compleja relación entre populismo e instituciones políticas." *Pensamento Plural* 7 (2014): 21–40. https://doi.org/10.15210/pp.v0i7.3642.

Acevedo Gaud, L. del Alba. "Un senado para la historia: género, poder y elecciones 2020 en Puerto Rico." *Revista Cruce*, March 2021. https://issuu.com/revistacruce/docs/asunto_1.

Acha, Omar. "Género y política ante el voto femenino en el catolicismo argentino, 1912–1955." In *El sufragio femenino en América Latina*, edited by Carolina Barry, pp. 63–89. Buenos Aires: UNTREF, 2011.

Acosta, María Teresa. "Políticas de maternidad durante el período peronista: Quiebres y continuidades en las relaciones de género." *Trabajos y Comunicaciones*, no. 40 (2014). http://www.memoria.fahce.unlp.edu.ar/art_revistas/pr.6648/pr.6648.pdf.

Acosta de Samper, Soledad. *La mujer. Lecturas. Revista quincenal redactada exclusivamente para señoras y señoritas, bajo la dirección de la Señora Soledad Acosta de Samper.* Bogotá: Imprenta de Silvestre y Compañía, 1880.

Acuña, Ángela. *La Mujer Costarricense a través de Cuatro Siglos*, Vols. 1 and 2. San José: Imprenta Nacional, 1969.

———. "'Nuestros derechos' nos interesan a las feministas." *La Nación*, August 10, 1954.

Aguilar Gil, Roisida. "El sufragio de la mujer: debate en el Congreso Constituyente de 1931–1932." *Elecciones* 1 (2002).

———. "La 'aurora' del sufragio femenino en el Perú: Zoila A. Cáceres, 1924–1933." In *Mujeres, Familia y Sociedad en la Historia de América Latina, Siglos XVIII–XXI.* Lima: CENDOC-Mujer, IRA-PUCP, and IFEA, 2006.

———. "La ampliación del cuerpo electoral. Ciudadanía, sufragio femenino y experiencia parlamentaria 1956–1962." *Elecciones* 2 (2003).

———. "Vía crucis de las mujeres peruanas para salir de la marginación política, 1924–1956." In *La marginación en el Perú*, edited by Claudia Rosas Lauro. Lima: PUCP, 2011.

Aidt, Toke S., and Bianca Dallal. "Female Voting Power: The Contribution of

Women's Suffrage to the Growth of Social Spending in Western Europe (1869–1960)." *Public Choice* 134 (2008): 391–417.

Alencar, J. M. *O sistema representativo*. Rio de Janeiro: Garnier, 1868.

Alfaro, Eloy. "Mensaje del Presidente de la República solicitando la protección especial a la mujer y la participación a los empleos públicos." In *Recopilación de Mensajes Dirijidos por los Presidentes y Vicepresidentes de la República, Jefes Supremos y Gobiernos Provisorios a las Convenciones y Congresos Nacionales Desde el año 1819 hasta nuestros días*, Vol. 4, edited by Alejandro Noboa. Guayaquil: Imp. El Tiempo, 1907.

Alianza Femenina Ecuatoriana. *Estatutos de Alianza Femenina Ecuatoriana*. Quito: Talleres Gráficos de Educación, 1938.

Almeida, Prisciliana D. "Com ares de crónica." *A Mensageira: Revista literaria dedicada a mulher brasileira* 2, no. 33 (October 15, 1899).

Alonso, A. *Ideias em Movimento: A Geração de 1870 na crise do Brasil-Império*. São Paulo: Paz e Terra, 2002.

———. *The Last Abolition: The Brazilian Antislavery Movement, 1868–1888*. New York: Cambridge University Press, 2022.

Alonso, Paula. "Politics and Election in Buenos Aires, 1890–1898: The Performance of the Radical Party." *Journal of Latin American Studies* 25, no. 3 (1993): 465–87.

Amaral, Samuel, and Carolina Barry. *Diccionario histórico del peronismo, 1943–1955*. Sáenz Peña: Eduntref, 2022.

Amoros, Cecilia. "Espacio de los iguales, uespacio de las idénticas. Notas sobre poder y principio de individuación." *Arbor*, November–December 1987.

Anderson, Carol. *One Person, No Vote: How Voter Suppression Is Destroying Our Democracy*. New York: Bloomsbury Publishing, 2018.

Arendt, Hannah. *La condición humana*. Barcelona: Paidos, 1998.

Arrom, Silvia. "Changes in Mexican Family Law in the Nineteenth Century: The Civil Codes of 1870 and 1884." *Journal of Family History* 10, no. 3 (September 1985): 305–17.

Aylwin, Mariana, and Ricardo Krebs Wilckens. *Chile en el Siglo XX*. 13. ed. Santiago, Chile: Editorial Planeta Chilena, 2008.

Azevedo, Josephina. *A Família*. http://memoria.bn.br/docreader/DocReader.aspx?bib=379034&pagfis=1.

Azize, Yamila. *La Mujer En Puerto Rico: Ensayos de Investigación*. Colección Huracán Academia. Río Piedras: Ediciones Huracán, 1987.

Bacchi, Carol Lee. *Liberation Deferred? The Ideas of the English-Canadian Suffragists*. Toronto: University of Toronto Press, 1983.

Baillargeon, Denyse. *To Be Equals in Our Own Country: Women and the Vote in Quebec*. Vancouver: UBC Press, 2019.

Baker, Jean H., ed. *Votes for Women. The Struggle for Suffrage Revisited*. Oxford: Oxford University Press, 2002.

Baltodano Marcenaro, Ricardo. "Ciudadanas por y para la dictadura: el Ala

Femenina Liberal de Juventud Liberal Nicaragüense, 1954–1961." *Boletín AFEHC* 34 (February 2008). http://afehc-historiacentroamericana.org/index.php ? action=fi_aff&id=1826.

Banaszak, Lee Ann. *Why Movements Succeed or Fail? Opportunity, Culture, and the Struggle for Woman Suffrage.* Princeton, NJ: Princeton University Press, 1996.

Barahona, Macarena. *Las Sufragistas de Costa Rica.* San José: Editorial Universidad de Costa Rica, 1994.

Barceló Miller, M. de F. *La lucha por el sufragio femenino en Puerto Rico, 1896–1935.* San Juan: Centro de Investigaciones Sociales; Río Piedras: Ediciones Huracán, 1997.

Barkley Brown, Elsa. "To Catch the Vision of Freedom: Reconstructing Southern Black Women's Political History, 1865–1880." In *Unequal Sisters: A Multicultural Reader in U.S. Women's History,* edited by Vicki L. Ruiz and Ellen Carol DuBois. New York: Routledge, 2000.

Barragán, Leticia, and Amanda Rosales. "Congresos Nacionales de Obreras y Campesinas." *Historia Obrera* 5 (June 1975).

Barrancos, Dora. "Ciudadanía femenina en la Argentina. Debates e iniciativas en las primeras décadas del Siglo XX." In *El pensamiento alternativo en la Argentina del siglo XX: identidad, utopía, integración (1900–1930),* edited by Hugo Biagini and Arturo Roig, pp. 153–76. Buenos Aires: Biblos, 2004.

———. "Derivaciones de la ley 13.010: los derechos políticos de la mujer en las provincias." *Estudios,* no. 35 (January–June 2016): 145–61. https://doi.org/10.31050/re.v0i35.15665.

———. "Evita capitana: El Partido Peronista Femenino 1949–1955." *Trabajos y Comunicaciones,* no. 36 (2009): 352–56. http://www.memoria.fahce.unlp.edu.ar/art_revistas/pr.5072/pr.5072.pdf.

———. *Historia mínima de los feminismos en América Latina.* Mexico City: El Colegio de México, 2020.

———. *Inclusión/Exclusión: Historia con Mujeres.* Buenos Aires: Fondo de Cultura Económica, 2002.

———. *Mujeres en la sociedad argentina. Una historia de cinco siglos.* Buenos Aires: Sudamericana, 2007.

———. *Mujeres, entre la casa y la plaza.* Buenos Aires: Sudamericana, 2008.

———. *Primer Congreso Femenino, Buenos Aires 1910. Historia, Actas y Trabajos,* 7–19. Córdoba: Universidad Nacional de Córdoba, 2007.

———. "Reflexiones sobre la saga de los derechos políticos femeninos." *Estudios Sociales* 43 (2012): 147–60. https://bibliotecavirtual.unl.edu.ar/ojs/index.php/EstudiosSociales/article/viewFile/2706/3885.

———. "Socialismo y sufragio femenino. Notas para su historia (1890–1947)." In *El Partido Socialista en Argentina. Sociedad, política e ideas a través de un siglo,* edited by Hernán Camarero and Carlos M. Herrera, pp. 139–83. Buenos Aires: Prometeo, 2005.

———. "Sociedad y género. Debates sobre el sufragio femenino en la Argentina (1870–1920)." *Debate Feminista* 29 (April 2004): 293–329.

Barros, Martina. *Prólogo a la esclavitud de la mujer.* Santiago: Palinodia: 2009.

Barry, Carolina. "Evita, la política y las peronistas bonaerenses." In *Mujeres en escenarios bonaerense,* edited by Adriana Valobra, pp. 153–65. La Plata: Edulp-Archivo Histórico de la Provincia de Buenos Aires, 2009.

Barry, Carolina, ed. *Sufragio Femenino: Prácticas y Debates Políticos, Religiosos y Culturales en Argentina y América Latina.* Buenos Aires: Editorial de la Universidad de Tres de Febrero, 2011.

Basadre Ghoman, Jorge. *Elecciones y centralismo en el Perú (Apuntes para un esquema histórico).* Lima: Centro de Investigación de la Universidad del Pacífico, 1980.

———. *Historia de la República del Perú, 1822–1933,* Vols. 11–17. Lima: Cantabria, 2015.

Bashevkin, Sylvia, ed. *Doing Politics Differently? Women Premiers in Canada's Provinces and Territories.* Vancouver: UBC Press, 2019.

Becerra, Marina "Herminia Brumana y Angélica Mendoza en los años 20': entre la emancipación femenina y la revolución social." *Descentrada* 7, no. 1 (2023): e195. https://doi.org/10.24215/25457284e195.

———. "Políticas de resistencia: género y escritura en la Argentina de 1920 y 1930 a través de Herminia Brumana, Angélica Mendoza, María Rosa Oliver y Anais Vialá." In *Alzar la voz. Archivos, derechos y géneros,* edited by Tania Diz and Florencia Angilletta. Córdoba, Argentina: Eduvim, T. III, en prensa.

———. "Soy comunista y maestra: resistencias a la maternalización de las mujeres a través de la obra de Angélica Mendoza en la Argentina de los años 20' y 30'." *Izquierdas,* no. 49 (2020): 385–411. http://www.izquierdas.cl/images/pdf/2020/n49/art23_385_411.pdf.

———. "Un cuarto propio: relaciones de género, amor y magisterio en la Argentina de inicios del siglo XX." *Propuesta Educativa* 1, no. 51 (June 2019): 42–60. https://www.redalyc.org/journal/4030/403061372005/html.

Becker, Marc. *Indians and Leftists in the Making of Ecuador's Modern Indigenous Movements.* Durham, NC: Duke University Press, 2008.

Bellota, Araceli. *Julieta Lanteri. La pasión de una mujer.* Buenos Aires: Planeta, 2001.

Beltrão, K., and M. S. Novellino. *Alfabetização por raça e sexo no Brasil: evolução no período 1940–2000.* Rio de Janeiro: Escola Nacional de Ciências Estatísticas, 2002.

Besse, S. K. *Restructuring Patriarchy: The Modernization of Gender Inequality in Brazil, 1914–1940.* Chapel Hill: University of North Carolina Press, 1996.

Bianchi, S. "Peronismo y sufragio femenino: la ley electoral de 1947." *Anuario IEHS* 1, no. 1 (1986): 255–96.

Bianchi, Susana, and Norma Sanchís. *El partido peronista femenino (1949–1955).* Buenos Aires: CEAL, 1988.

Biernat, Carolina, and Karina Ramacciotti. *Crecer y multiplicarse. La política sanitaria materno-infantil. Argentina 1900–1960.* Buenos Aires: Biblos, 2013.

Blee, Kathleen M. *Women of the Klan: Racism and Gender in the 1920s*. Berkeley: University of California Press, 1991.

Boesten, Jelke. *Intersecting Inequalities: Women and Social Policy in Peru, 1990-2000*. University Park, Pa.: Pennsylvania State University Press, 2010.

———. "Los débiles de la sociedad: mujeres e indios." *Skript: Historisch Tijdschrift* 20 (Winter 1998).

Bonald, L. G. *Oeuvres de M. de Bonald: Mélanges Literaires Politiques et Philosophiques*. Paris: A. Le Clere, 1858.

Booth, Robert, and Spencer Jones. "Carrie Chapman Catt and the Last Years of the Struggle for Woman Suffrage." In *Votes for Women. The Struggle for Suffrage Revisited*, edited by Jean H. Baker. New York: Oxford University Press, 2002.

Bordagaray, M. E. "Controversias libertarias: la interpelación anarquista en tiempos del peronismo." PhD thesis, Department of History, Universidad Nacional de La Plata, 2014.

Borge de Sotomayor, Amelia. *La mujer y el derecho*. León: Editorial San José, 1953.

Borrayo, Ana Patricia. *Por la equidad de género en la educación superior. Tras las huellas de las precursoras en la educación superior: Universidad de San Carlos de Guatemala 1897-2005*. Guatemala City: UMUSAC, 2006.

Bowman, Kirk S. "¿Fue el Compromiso y Consenso de las Elites lo que Llevó a la Consolidación Democrática en Costa Rica? Evidencias de la década de 1950." *Revista de Historia* 41, no. 1 (2000): 91–127.

Boylan, Anne. "Benevolence and Anti-Slavery Activity." In *The Abolitionist Sisterhood: Women's Political Culture in Antebellum America*, edited by Jean Fagan Yellin and John C. Van Horne. Ithaca, NY: Cornell University Press.

———. *The Origins of Women's Activism: New York and Boston, 1797–1840*. Chapel Hill: University of North Carolina Press, 2002.

Branco, M. A., and Silva, J. B. Andrada. Projeto de Lei de Eleições, Bill 154/1831, July 28, 1831, House of Representatives Archives, Brasília.

Brasil. *Annaes do Congresso Constituinte da República*. 3 vols. Rio de Janeiro: Imprensa Nacional, 1926.

———. *Anais da Assembleia Nacional Constituinte, 1890–1891*. Rio de Janeiro: Imprensa Nacional, 1891.

———. *Anais do Parlamento Brasileiro*. Rio de Janeiro: Tipografia Nacional, 1879.

———. *Anais do Senado Federal, 1899*. Rio de Janeiro: Tipografia Nacional, 1900.

———. *Synopses dos Trabalhos Parlamentares da Câmara dos Deputados, 1869–1873*. Rio de Janeiro: Tipografia da Câmara dos Deputados, 1873.

Brasil, J. F. Assis. *Democracia representativa: do voto e do modo de votar*. Buenos Aires: Argos Imprenta y Casa Editora, 1894.

Briones, Ignacio "Las mujeres nicaragüenses ayer y hoy." *Bolsa de noticias*, March 20, 2007.

Brookfield, Tarah. *Our Voices Must Be Heard: Women and the Vote in Ontario*. Vancouver: UBC Press, 2018.

Brown Scott, James. *La Séptima Conferencia de la Naciones Americanas*. Havana: Molina y Cia, 1935.

Buechler, Steven M. *Women's Movements in the United States: Woman Suffrage, Equal Rights, and Beyond*. New Brunswick, NJ: Rutgers University Press, 1990.

Burga, Manuel, and Alberto Flores Galindo. *Apogeo y crisis de la república aristocrática*. Lima: Rikchay Perú, 1991.

Bushnell, David. *The Making of Modern Colombia: A Nation in Spite of Itself*. Berkeley: University of California Press, 1993.

Butler, Matthew. *Popular Piety and Political Identity in Mexico's Cristero Rebellion: Michoacán, 1927–29*. Oxford: Oxford University Press, 2004.

Cáceres, Zoila Aurora. *Labor de armonía interamericana en los Estados Unidos de Norte América 1940–1945*. Washington, DC: Comisión Interamericana de Mujeres, 1946.

———. *Mi vida con Enrique Gómez Carrillo*. Madrid, Buenos Aires: Renacimiento, 1929.

———. *Mujeres de Ayer y Hoy*. Paris: Gernier Hnos, 1909.

Cahill, Cathleen D. *Recasting the Vote: How Women of Color Transformed the Suffrage Movement*. Chapel Hill: University of North Carolina Press, 2020.

Cammarota, Adrián. *Malas maestras. Educación, género y conflicto en el sistema escolar argentino*. CABA: Grupo Editor Universitario, 2021.

Campbell, Lara. *A Great Revolutionary Wave: Women and the Vote in British Columbia*. Vancouver: UBC Press, 2020.

Campos, Myrthes. "Comentario jurídico sobre o voto femenino." *Arquivo Judiciario* 9 (January–March 1920): 67–71, 141–45.

———. "O Voto Feminino. A propósito da decisao da Junta de Recursos Eleitorais do Estado do Rio de Janeiro." *Arquivo Judiciario* 9 (January–March 1929): 71.

———. "Podera haver perfeita igualdade nos direitos civis e de familia entre conjuges?" In *Relatorio do Primeiro Congresso Jurídico Brasileiro*, pp. 379–94. Rio de Janeiro: Imprensa Nacional, 1909.

Cano, Gabriela. "Debates en torno al sufragio y la ciudadanía de las mujeres en México." *Estudios Sociológicos* 31 (2013): 7–20.

———. "Feminism," In *Encyclopedia of Mexico*, edited by Michael S. Werner. Chicago: Fitzroy Dearborn, 1997.

———. "Sufragio femenino en el México posrevolucionario." In *La revolución de las mujeres en México*, edited by Patricia Galeana de Valadés, pp. 33–46. Mexico City: Instituto Nacional de Estudios Históricos de las Revoluciones de México, 2014.

Caraway, Teri L. "Inclusion and Democratization: Class, Gender, Race, and the Extension of Suffrage." *Comparative Politics* 36 (2004): 443–60.

Cárdenas de Bustamante, Hipatia. *Oro, rojo, azul*, 1944 Quito: Abya-Yala, 2002.

Carlés, G. A. Las dos caras de Jano: acerca de la compleja relación entre populismo e instituciones políticas. *Pensamento Plural* 7 (2014): 21–40. https://doi.org/10.15210/pp.v0i7.3642.

Carlson, Marifran. *¡Feminismo!: The Woman's Movement in Argentina from Its Beginnings to Eva Perón.* Chicago: Academy Chicago Publisher, 1988.

Carr, Barry. *Marxism and Communism in Twentieth-Century Mexico.* Lincoln: University of Nebraska Press, 1992.

Carrie Chapman Catt Papers: Diaries, 1911–1923; Philippines, 1912, July 19–Aug. 20. Library of Congress. https://www.loc.gov/item/mss154040012.

Carrillo, Lorena. *Las luchas de las guatemaltecas del siglo XX. Mirada al trabajo y la participación política de las mujeres.* Antigua Guatemala: Ediciones del Pensativo, 2004.

Carter, Sarah. *Ours by Every Law of Right and Justice: Women and the Vote in the Prairie Provinces.* Vancouver: UBC Press, 2020.

Casal v. de Quirós, Sara. *El voto femenino.* San José: Imprenta Nacional, 1925.

———. "El feminismo y la Mujer Costarricense." *La Tribuna,* January 23, 1924, 7.

Casola, Natalia. "Con 'm' de 'mamá': las militantes comunistas y la Unión de Mujeres Argentinas durante la segunda mitad del siglo XX." *Amnis, Revue de civilisation contemporaine Europes/Amériques,* no. 13 (2014). https://doi.org/10.4000/amnis.2097.

Castillo, Alejandra. *El desorden de la democracia: partidos políticos de mujeres en Chile,* Santiago: Palinodia, 2014.

Castillo Ramírez, Guillermo. *El debate sobre el sufragio femenino en la prensa tapatía (1946–1955).* Colección del Centro de Estudios de Género 4. Guadalajara: Universidad de Guadalajara, 2013.

Castro Ricalde, Maricruz. "El feminismo y el derecho al sufragio en la prensa mexicana. Los cartones (1939–1940) de Ernesto 'El Chango' García Cabral." *Hispanófila* 186, no. 1 (2019): 3–22.

Cavalcanti, J. B. U. *Constituição Federal Brasileira: Comentarios.* Rio de Janeiro: Tipografia da Companhia Litho-Typographia, 1901.

Cavarozzi, M. "El 'Desarrollismo' y las relaciones entre democracia y capitalismo dependiente en 'Dependencia y Desarrollo en América Latina.'" *Latin American Research Review* 17, no. 1 (1982): 152–65. https://www.jstor.org/stable/pdf/2502946.pdf.

Cawen, Ines C. *Feminismos y política en el Uruguay del Novecientos (1906–1932), Internacionalismo, culturas políticas e identidades de género.* Montevideo: Ediciones de la Banda Oriental, Asociación Uruguaya de Historiadores, 2018.

Cejas, Mónica I., and Ana Lau J. *En la encrucijada de género y ciudadanía sujetos políticos, derechos, gobierno, nación y acción política.* Mexico City: Universidad Autónoma Metropolitana, Unidad Xochimilco, 2011.

Chacón, María Cecilia. "Las Mujeres del 2 de Agosto de 1947 en la Vida Política del País." *Licenciatura* dissertation, University of Costa Rica, 1984.

Chaney, Elsa. *Significado de la obra de María Jesús Alvarado.* Lima: Centro de Documentación sobre la Mujer, 1988.

———. *Supermadre: Women in Politics in Latin America.* University of Texas Press, 2014.

———. *Women in Latin American Politics: The Case of Peru and Chile*. Madison: University of Wisconsin Press, 1971.

Chapa, María E., and Mercedes Barquet Montané. *La conquista del voto femenino*. San Nicolás de los Garza: UANL, 2004.

Chapman, Mary, and Angela Mills, eds. *Treacherous Texts: US Suffrage Literature, 1846–1946*. New Brunswick, NJ: Rutgers University Press, 2011.

Chartier, R., and G. Cavallo, eds. *História da leitura no mundo occidental*. São Paulo: Ática, 1999.

Cichero, Marta. *Alicia Moreau de Justo. La historia privada y pública de una legendaria y auténtica militante*. Buenos Aires: Planeta, 1994.

Cifuentes, Abdón. "Acerca del derecho electoral de la mujer, leído en la Sociedad de San Luis, el 16 de agosto de 1865." In *Colección de Discursos de Don Abdón Cifuentes*, Vol. 1, p. 241. Santiago: Escuela tipográfica La Gratitud Nacional, 1916.

Clark, Kim. "Feminismos estéticos y antiestéticos en el Ecuador de principios del siglo XX: Un análisis de género y generaciones." *Procesos* (Quito), no. 22 (2005): 85–105.

Clark, A. Kim, and Marc Becker. "Indigenous Peoples and State Formation in Modern Ecuador." In *Highland Indians and the State in Modern Ecuador*, edited by A. Kim Clark and Marc Becker, pp. 1–21. Pittsburgh: Pittsburgh University Press, 2007.

Cleverdon, Catharine Lyle. *The Woman Suffrage Movement in Canada*. Toronto: University of Toronto Press, 1950.

Cobo del Arco, Teresa. "Populismo, somocismo y el voto femenino: Nicaragua, 1936–1955." In *Poder local, poder global en América Latina*, edited by Gabriela Dalla Corte, Pilar García Jordán, Javier Laviña, Lola G. Luna, Ricardo Piqueras, José Luis Ruiz-Peinado Alonso, and Meritxell Tous. Barcelona: Universitat de Barcelona, 2008.

Cole Chamorro, Alejandro. *145 años de historia política: Nicaragua*. Managua: Editora nicaragüense, 1967.

Colón Warren, A., M. Mergal, and N. Torres. *Participacion de la mujer en la Historia de Puerto Rico (las primeras décadas del siglo veinte)*. San Juan: Centro de Investigaciones Sociales, Universidad de Puerto Rico, 1985.

Colón Warren, Alice, María Maité Mulero, Luis Santiago, and Nilsa Burgos. *Estirando el peso: Acciones de ajuste y relaciones de género ante el cierre de fábricas en Puerto Rico*. San Juan: Centro de Investigaciones Sociales, Universidad de Puerto Rico, 2008.

Comte, A. *Cours de Philosophie Positive*. 6 vols. Paris: Bachelier, 1830.

———. *Lettres d'Auguste Comte a John Stuart Mill, 1841–1846*. Paris: Ernest Leroux, 1877.

———. *Système de Politique Positive ou Traité de sociologie, instituant la religion de l´humanité*. Paris: Chateaudun, 1852.

Congreso Feminista de Yucatán. *El Primer Congreso Feminista de Yucatán*. Mérida: Ateneo Peninsular, 1916.

Contreras, Carlos. *Maestros, Mistis y campesinos en el Perú rural del siglo XX*. Lima: Instituto de Estudios Peruanos, 1996.

Cosse, Isabella. "La lucha por los derechos femeninos: Victoria Ocampo y la Unión Argentina de Mujeres (1936)." *Revista Humanitas* 26 (2008): 131–49. https://www. aacademica.org/isabella.cosse/11.pdf.

Costa, Jorge. *La Mujer. Su situación legal*. Santiago: Imprenta El Progreso, 1915.

Cother, Julio. *Clase Estado y Nación en el Perú*. Lima: IEP, 2009.

Crenshaw, Kimberlé. "Mapping the Margins: Intersectionality, Identity Politics, and Violence against Women of Color." *Stanford Law Review* 43, no. 6 (1991): 1241. doi:10.2307/1229039.

Cruz Santos, Martín. "Identidades culturales y ciudadanías." *Jornada de Puerto Rico y el Caribe*, November 6, 2018.

Cueva, Agustín. "El Ecuador de 1925 a 1960." In *Nueva Historia del Ecuador*. Vol. 10, *Época Republicana IV*, edited by Enrique Ayala Mora, pp. 91–121. Quito: Corporación Editora Nacional, 1990.

Dahl, Robert A. *Polyarchy: Participation and Opposition*. New Haven, CT: Yale University Press, 1971.

Dalla Corte, Pilar García Jordán, Lola G. Luna, Michael Izard, Javier Laviña, Ricardo Piqueras, José Luis Ruiz Peinado, and Meritxell Tous, eds. *Homogeneidad, Diferencia y Exclusión en América*. Barcelona: Ediciones Universidad de Barcelona, 2006.

Daltro, Leolinda F. *Da catechese dos indios no Brasil. Noticias e documentos para a historia, 1896–1911*. Rio de Janeiro: Tipografia da Escola Orsina da Fonseca, 1920.

———. *O inicio do feminismo: subsidios para a historia*. Brasilia: Edições Câmara, 2022.

Darnton, R. "History of Reading." In *New Perspectives on Historical Writing*, edited by Peter Burke, 157–86. Philadelphia: Pennsylvania State University, 1992.

De Bevoise, Ken. *Agents of the Apocalypse: World History of Human Disease*. Cambridge: Cambridge University Press, 1993.

De Haan, Francisca, Margaret Allen, June Purvis, and Krasimira Daskalova. *Women's Activism: Global Perspectives from the 1890s to the Present*. Hoboken, NJ: Taylor and Francis, 2012.

De Ípola, Emilio. *Ideología y discurso populista*. Buenos Aires: Folios Ediciones, 1983.

De Privitellio, Luciano. "Los límites de la abstracción: individuo, sociedad y sufragio femenino en la reforma constitucional de San Juan (1927)." *Polhis* 4, no. 7 (January–June 2011): 59–79. http://historiapolitica.com/datos/boletin/polhis7_privitellio.pdf.

Debayle, Luis Manuel. "The Status of Women in Nicaragua." *Mid Pacific Magazine* (Honolulu), no. 45 (1933).

Deleis, Mónica, Ricardo De Titto, and Diego L. Arguindeguy. *Mujeres de La Política Argentina*. Buenos Aires: Aguilar, 2001.

Demichelli, S. A. *Igualdad jurídica de la mujer. Alberdi, su precursor en América*. Buenos Aires: Depalma, 1973.

Denegri, Francesca. *El Abanico y la Cigarrera: La Primera Generación de Mujeres Ilustradas en el Perú*. Lima: Flora Tristán Centro de la Mujer Peruana, 1996.

Díaz, Estela, ed. *Feminismo y peronismo: reflexiones históricas y actuales de una articulación negada*. La Plata: EDULP, 2019.

Domenech, R. "La huella político-feminista de Margarita Mergal." *Revista Cruce*, March 19, 2013.

———. "Voces y hazañas de las mujeres." *Revista Cruce*, April 2017. http://revistcruce. com/new_revista/?q=voces-y-haza-de-las-mujeres-parte-i.

Dore, Elizabeth, and Maxine Molineaux, eds. *Hidden Histories of Gender and the State in Latin America*. Durham, NC: Duke University Press, 2000.

Drinot, Paulo, and Alan Knight. *The Great Depression in Latin America*. Durham, NC: Duke University Press, 2014.

Duarte, C. *Imprensa feminina e feminista no Brasil, século XIX*. Belo Horizonte: Editora Autêntica, 2016.

Dubois, Ellen C. *Feminism and Suffrage: The Emergence of an Independent Women's Movement in America, 1848–1869*. Ithaca, NY: Cornell University Press, 1978.

———. "Woman Suffrage around the World: Three Phases of Suffragist Internationalism." In *Suffrage and Beyond: International Feminist Perspectives*, edited by Caroline Daley and Melanie Nolan. New York: New York University Press, 1994.

Dunbar-Ortiz, Roxanne. *An Indigenous Peoples' History of the United States*. Boston: Beacon Press, 2014.

Eduardo Arellano, Jorge. *María Cristina Zapata: Escritora Liberal de Nicaragua*. Miami, 2020.

Edwards, Louise P., and Mina Roces. *Women's Suffrage in Asia: Gender, Nationalism and Democracy*. London: Routledge Curzon, 2004.

Enríquez Seiders, Sandra. *Ricarda López de Ramos Casellas: Tizas, conciencia y sufragio*. San Juan: Ediciones Callejón, 2006.

Errázuriz, Javiera. "Discursos en torno al sufragio femenino en Chile 1865–1949." *Historia* 38, no. 2 (2005): 257–86.

Estrada, Jenny. *Matilde Hidalgo de Procel: Una mujer total*, 1981. Quito: Grupo Santillana, 2006.

Eyot, Canning. *The Story of the Lopez Family*. Boston: J. H. West, 1904.

Faderman, Lillian. *To Believe in Women: What Lesbians Have Done for America*. Boston: Houghton Mifflin, 1999.

Faguet, E. *Le Libéralism*. Paris: Lecène, Oudin et Cie., 1903.

Faulkner, Carol. *Lucretia Mott's Heresy: Abolition and Women's Rights in Nineteenth-Century America*. Philadelphia: University of Pennsylvania Press, 2011.

Fernandes, J. B. "A Constituinte de 1891–1891. A institucionalização dos limites da cidadania." *Acervo* 19, no. 12 (2006).

Fernández, Felipe, *El voto femenino en Costa Rica: debates constituyentes 1917–1949 y la reforma constitucional de 1947*. San José: Asamblea Legislativa, 1985.

Fernández, M. Elisa. "Conformación de partidos políticos en Chile." In *Historia* política de Chile 1810–2010, Vol. 1, Prácticas Políticas, edited by Iván Jaksic and Juan Luis Ossa. Santiago: Fondo de Cultura Económica, 2017.

Fernández Aceves, María Teresa. "La lucha sobre el sufragio femenino en Jalisco, 1910–1958." Revista de Estudios de Género: La Ventana, no. 19 (2004): 132–51.

Fernández Poncela, Anna María. "Sufragio femenino, ciudadanía y elecciones." Géneros: Revista de Análisis y Divulgación Sobre los Estudios de Género 11, no. 32 (February 2004): 5–14.

Fernos, María Dolores. "Las mujeres en la política: María Libertad Gómez." Alborada: Revista Interdisciplinaria de la Universidad de Puerto Rico en Utuado 11, no. 1 (June 2015–May, 2016): 11–18.

Flores, Ana Lorena. "'Ni Histéricas, Ni Reinas . . . Ciudadanas' Mujeres y política en Costa Rica 1940–1949." Master's dissertation, Universidad de Costa Rica, 2001.

Flores Galindo, Alberto. Movimientos campesinos en el Perú: Balance y esquema. Lima: Taller de Investigación Rural, Programa de Ciencias Sociales, PUCP, 1976.

Gage, Matilda Joslyn. Woman Church and State. Edited by Sally Roesch Wagner. Aberdeen, SD: Sky Carrier Press, 1998.

Galeana de Valadés, Patricia, Gabriela Cano, Rosa M. Valles Ruiz, Enriqueta Tuñón, Lucía Melgar-Palacios, Delia S. de Dios, and María P. Del Hernández. La revolución de las mujeres en México. Mexico City: Secretaría de Educación Pública, 2014.

Gallo, Edit. Las mujeres en el radicalismo argentino. 1890–2020. Buenos Aires: Eudeba, 2022.

Galloway, Stuart. The American Equal Rights Association, 1866–1870: Gender, Race, and Universal Suffrage. Leicester, UK: University of Leicester, 2014.

García, Ana Isabel, and Enrique Gomariz. Mujeres centroamericanas ante la crisis: La guerra y el proceso de paz, Vol 1. San José: FLACSO, 1999.

García, Genaro. Apuntes sobre la Condición de la Mujer. Mexico City: Limit. de Tipografos, 1891.

García Belaúnde, Domingo. Las Constituciones del Perú. Lima: Ministerio de Justicia, 1993.

García Gervasio, L. Armar la historia: La tesis en la región menos transparente y otros ensayos. 3rd ed. San Juan: Ediciones Huracán, 2007.

García Guevara, Aldo Vladimir. "Military Justice and Social Control: El Salvador, 1931–1960." PhD dissertation, University of Texas, 2007.

García Olmedo, María del Rocío. Sesenta años de lucha por el sufragio femenino en México, 1953–2013 miradas regionales sobre el reconocimiento del voto de la mujer. Puebla: Benemérita Universidad Autónoma de Puebla, Dirección de Fomento Editorial, 2014.

García Sebastiani, Marcela. Los antiperonistas en la Argentina peronista. Radicales y socialistas en la política argentina entre 1943 y 1951. Buenos Aires: Prometeo, 2005.

García-Bryce, Iñigo. "Transnational Activist: Magda Portal and the American Popular Revolutionary Alliance (APRA), 1926–1950." Americas 70, no. 4 (April 2014): 677–706.

Garrigou, Alain. *Histoire Sociale du Suffrage Universel en France, 1848–2000*. Paris: Éditions du Seuil, 2002.

Gaviola, Edda. *"Queremos votar en las próximas elecciones": Historia del movimiento femenino chileno 1913–1952*, Santiago: Centro de Análisis y Difusión de la Condición de la Mujer, 1986.

Gayol, Sandra, and Laura Erhlich. "Las vidas post-mortem de Eva Perón: cuerpo, ausencia y biografías en las revistas de masas de la Argentina." *Historia Crítica* 1, no. 70 (2018): 111–31. https://doi.org/10.7440/histcrit70.2018.06.

Germani, G. *Política y sociedad en una época de transición*. Buenos Aires: Editorial Paidós, 1968.

Giordano, Verónica. *Ciudadanas Incapaces. La construcción de los derechos civiles de las mujeres en Argentina, Brasil, Chile y Uruguay en el siglo XX*. Buenos Aires: Teseo, 2012.

Go, Julian. *American Empire and the Politics of Meaning: Elite Political Cultures in the Philippines and Puerto Rico during US Colonialism*. Durham, NC: Duke University Press, 2008.

Goetschel, Ana María. "Estudio Introductorio." In *Orígenes del feminismo en el Ecuador: Antología*, edited by Ana María Goetschel, pp. 13–56. Quito: CONAMU, FLACSO, Secretaría de Desarrollo y Equidad Social, UNIFEM, 2006.

———. *Educación de las mujeres, maestras y esferas públicas: Quito en la primera mitad del siglo XX*. Quito: FLACSO, Abya Yala, 2007.

Goetschel, Ana María, ed. *Orígenes del feminismo en el Ecuador: Antología*. Quito: CONAMU, FLACSO, Secretaría de Desarrollo y Equidad Social, UNIFEM, 2006.

Gomes, Joaquim Barbosa. *La Cour Suprême dans le Système Politique Brésilien*. Paris: Librairie Générale de Droit et de Jurisprudence, 1994.

Gómez Molla, Rosario. "Universitarias argentinas. Desafíos para contarlas." *Anuario del Instituto de Historia Argentina* 18, no. 1 (2018), e064. https://doi.org/10.24215/2314257Xe064.

González Moral, Ireneo, and Internationale Soziale Studienvereinigung. *Códigos de Malinas: Social, Familiar, Moral Internacional, Moral Política*. Santander: Ed. Sal Terrae, 1959.

González Rey, Diana Crucelly. "La educación de las mujeres en Colombia a finales del siglo XIX." *Revista Historia de la Educación Latinoamericana* 17, no. 24 (2015).

González, Yolanda. "Movimientos de mujeres en los años 60 y 70." In *Las mujeres en la historia de Colombia*, Vol. 1. Bogotá: Grupo Editorial Norma, 1995.

González-Rivera, Victoria. *Before the Revolution: Women's Rights and Right-Wing Politics in Nicaragua, 1821–1979*. University Park: Penn State University Press, 2011.

González-Rivera, Victoria, and Karen Kampwirth. *Diversidad Sexual en el Pacifico y Centro de Nicaragua. 500 Años de Historia*. San Diego, 2021.

Gordon, Ann D., ed. *The Selected Papers of Elizabeth Cady Stanton and Susan B. Anthony: Against an Aristocracy of Sex, 1866–1873*, Vol. 2. New Brunswick, NJ: Rutgers University Press, 2000.

Gorza, Anabella. *Insurgentes, misioneras y políticas. Mujeres y género en la resistencia peronista (1955–1966)*. Buenos Aires: Biblos, 2022.

———. "Las mujeres peronistas en los años '80. Indagaciones a través del archivo personal de Beba Gil." *Revista Electrónica de Fuentes y Archivos*, no. 9 (2018): 182–206. https://revistas.unc.edu.ar/index.php/refa/article/view/33621

———. "Mujeres peronistas en el Congreso de la Nación (1965–1966)." In *Caleidoscopio del género. Nuevas miradas desde las ciencias sociales*, edited by Luisina Bolla, pp. 71–96. Temperley: Tren en movimiento, 2021. https://www.trenenmovimiento.com.ar/pdfs/Caleidoscopio_del_genero_web.pdf.

Gorza, Anabella, and Adriana Valobra. "¿Mujeres modernas para la modernización política? Prácticas y debates sobre la participación de las mujeres en la política, 1955–1966." *Avances del Cesor*, no. 19 (December 2018): 129–53. http://www.scielo.org.ar/pdf/avances/v15n19/v15n19a07.pdf.

Gradskova, Yulia. "La FDIM y los derechos de las mujeres en América Latina: expectativas y alianzas durante la Guerra Fría, 1950–1970." *Descentrada 5*, no. 2 (2021): e150. https://doi.org/10.24215/25457284e150.

Graham, Richard. *Patronage and Politics in Nineteenth-Century Brazil*. Stanford, CA: Stanford University Press, 1994.

Graham, Sara Hunter. *Woman Suffrage and the New Democracy*. New Haven, CT: Yale University Press, 1996.

Green, Joyce. "Canaries in the Mines of Citizenship: Indian Women in Canada." *Canadian Journal of Political Science* 24, no. 4 (2001): 715–38.

———. "Constitutionalizing the Patriarchy: Aboriginal Women and Aboriginal Government." *Constitutional Forum* 4, no. 4 (1993), 110–20.

———. "Sexual Equality and Indian Government: An Analysis of Bill C-31." *Native Studies Review* 1, no. 2 (1985): 81–95.

Green, Joyce, ed. *Making Space for Indigenous Feminism*. Halifax: Fernwood Publishing, 2017.

Guillin, V. P. E. *Auguste Comte and John Stuart Mill on Sexual Equality: Historical, Methodological and Philosophical Issues*. London: London School of Economics and Political Science, 2005.

Guy, Donna J. *Creating Charismatic Bonds in Argentina : Letters to Juan and Eva Perón*. Diálogos Series. Albuquerque: University of New Mexico Press, 2016.

———. "Suffrage in San Juan: The Test of Women's Rights in Argentina." *Bulletin of American Research*, no. 28 (2009), 1–18. https://doi.org/https://doi.org/10.1111/j.1470-9856.2008.00287.x.

———. *Women Build the Welfare State: Performing Charity and Creating Rights in Argentina, 1880–1955*. Durham, NC: Duke University Press, 2009.

Hahner, J. E. *Emancipating the Female Sex: The Struggle for Women's Rights in Brazil, 1850–1940*. Durham, NC: Duke University Press, 1990.

———. "Feminism, Women's Rights, and the Suffrage Movement in Brazil, 1850–1932." *Latin American Research Review* 15, no. 1 (1980): 65–111.

———. *A mulher brasileira e suas lutas sociais e políticas, 1850–1937*. São Paulo: Brasiliense, 1981.

———. *Poverty and Politics: The Urban Poor in Brazil, 1870–1920*. Albuquerque: University of New Mexico Press, 1986.Halperín Donghi, Tulio. *Historia Contemporánea de América Latina*. Madrid: Alianza, 1997.

Hammond, Gregory. "Suffrage in San Juan: The Test of Women's Rights in Argentina." *Bulletin of American Research* 28 (2009): 1–18.https://doi.org/10.1111/j.1470–9856.2008.00287.x.

———. *The Women's Suffrage Movement and Feminism in Argentina from Roca to Perón*. Albuquerque: University of New Mexico Press, 2011.

Harms, Patricia. *Ladina Social Activism in Guatemala City 1871–1954*. Albuquerque: University of New Mexico Press, 2020.

Henales, Lidia, and Josefina del Solar. *Mujer y política: participación y exclusión (1955–1966)*. Buenos Aires: CEAL, 1993.

Henault, Mirta. *Alicia Moreau de Justo*. Buenos Aires: CEAL, 1983.

Henderson, James D. *Modernization in Colombia: The Laureano Gómez Years, 1889–1965*. Gainsville: University Press of Florida, 2001.

Hernández Carballido, Elvira, and Josefina Hernández Téllez. *Mujeres independientes, mujeres revolucionarias*. Pachuca: Universidad Autónoma del Estado de Hidalgo, 2013.

Herrera, Carlos. "El frustrado accionar de un partido socialista nacional en la Argentina (1915–1922)." *Archivos de historia del movimiento obrero y la izquierda*, no. 13 (September 2018): 121–41. https://doi.org/10.46688/ahmoi.n13.51.

Higginbotham, Evelyn Brooks. "Clubwomen and Electoral Politics in the 1920s." In *African American Women and the Vote, 1837–1965*, edited by Ann D. Gordon, Bettye Collier-Thomas, John H. Bracey, Arlene Voski Avakian, and Joyce Avrech Berkman, pp. 147–50. Amherst: University of Massachusetts Press.

Hoganson, Kristin L. "'As Badly Off as the Filipinos': US Women's Suffragists and the Imperial Issue at the Turn of the Twentieth Century." *Journal of Women's History* 13, no. 2 (2001): 9–33. https://doi.org/10.1353/jowh.2001.0050.

———. *Consumers' Imperium: The Global Production of American Domesticity, 1865–1920*. Chapel Hill: University of North Carolina Press, 2010.

Holmes, S. *Benjamin Constant and the Making of Modern Liberalism*. New Haven, CT: Yale University Press, 1984.

Holt, E. M. *Colonizing Filipinas: Nineteenth-Century Representations of the Philippines in Western Historiography*. Quezon City: Ateneo de Manila University Press, 2002.

hooks, bell. *Ain't I a Woman?* London: Pluto Press, 1981.

Howard, Irene. *The Struggle for Social Justice in British Columbia: Helena Gutteridge, the Unknown Reformer*. Vancouver: UBC Press, 1992.

Hughes, Vivien. "Women in Public Life: The Canadian Persons Case of 1929." *British Journal of Canadian Studies* 19, no. 2 (September 2006): 257–70.

Illanes, María Angélica. "Maternalismo popular e hibridación cultural en Chile 1900–1920." *Nomadías* 1 (1999): 185–211.

Instituto Nacional de las Mujeres. *Las mujeres y el voto, 17 de octubre de 2001 48 aniversario del sufragio femenino en México.* Mexico City: Instituto Nacional de las Mujeres, 2001.

Intengan, Gabriel. "The Function and Duties of a Health Officer." In *Proceedings of the First National Conference on Infant Mortality and Public Welfare: Organized and Conducted by the Office of the Public Welfare Commissioner and Held Under the Patronage of His Excellency Leonard Wood. Manila, Philippine Islands, December 6, 7, 8, 9, 10, 1921.* Manila: Bureau of Printing, 1922.

Jacksic, Iván, and Sol Serrano. "El gobierno y las libertades. La ruta del liberalismo chileno en el siglo XIX." In *Liberalismo y poder. Latinoamérica en el siglo XIX,* edited by Iván Jaksic and Eduardo Posada. Santiago: Fondo de Cultura Económica, 2011.

Jaume, Lucien. *L'Individu Effacé, ou le paradoxe du libéralisme français.* Paris: Fayard, 1997.

Jimenez-Muñoz, Gladys M. "'So We Decided to Come and Ask You Ourselves': The 1928 U.S. Congressional Hearings on Women's Suffrage in Puerto Rico." In *Puerto Rican Jam: Essays on Culture and Politics,* edited by Frances Negrón-Muntaner and Ramón Grosfoguel, pp. 140–68. Minneapolis: University of Minnesota Press, 1997.

Jonguitud Aguilar, Leticia. *La mujer y el voto femenino en San Luis Potosí (1921–1926).* L. Jonguitud Aguilar, 2002.

Kalaw, Teodorio M. "Address of the Hon. Teodoro M. Kalaw." In *Proceedings of the First National Conference on Infant Mortality and Public Welfare: Organized and Conducted by the Office of the Public Welfare Commissioner and Held Under the Patronage of His Excellency Leonard Wood. Manila, Philippine Islands, December 6, 7, 8, 9, 10, 1921.* Manila: Bureau of Printing, 1922.

Keyssar, Alexander. *The Right to Vote: The Contested History of Democracy in the United States* New York: Basic Books, 2000.

Kirkwood, Julieta. *Ser política en Chile: Las feministas y los partidos, 1986.* Santiago: LOM, 2010.

Kramer, Paul. *The Blood of Government: Race, Empire, the United States and the Philippines.* Quezon City: Ateneo de Manila University Press, 2006.

La Capra, D. *Rethinking Intellectual History: Texts, Contexts, Language.* Ithaca, NY: Cornell University Press, 1983.

Lagarte, Marcela. *Género y feminismo. Desarrollo humano y democracia.* Madrid: Horas y Horas, 1996.

Lamas, Marta. *Miradas feministas sobre las mexicanas del siglo XX.* Mexico City: Fondo de Cultura Económica, 2007.

Lange, Allison K. *Picturing Political Power: Images in the Women's Suffrage Movement.* Chicago: University of Chicago Press, 2020.

LaRosa, Michael J., and Germán R. Mejía. *Colombia: A Concise Contemporary History.* Lanham, MD: Rowman & Littlefield, 2012.

Latorre Carabelli, Matías. "Entre la escuela y la prensa. Primeras experiencias de organización sindical docente en Mendoza (1919)." *Prohistoria*, no. 32 (2019): 97–126.

Lau Jaiven, Ana, and Roxana Rodríguez Bravo. "El sufragio femenino y la Constitución de 1917. Una revisión." *Política y cultura*, no. 48 (2017): 57–81.

Lau Jaiven, Ana, and Mercedes Zúñiga Elizalde. *El sufragio femenino en México voto en los estados (1917–1965).* Hermosillo: El Colegio de Sonora, 2013.

Lavigne, Marie, and Michèle Stanton. *Idola Saint-Jean. L'insoumise.* Montreal: Boréal, 2017.

———. *Joséphine Marchand et Raoul Dandurand. Amour, politique et féminism.* Montreal: Boréal, 2021.

Lavrin, Asunción. "Ciudadanía y acción política femenina en Chile y Perú hasta mediados del siglo XX." In *Historia de las mujeres en España y América Latina*, Vol. 4, edited by Isabel Morant. Madrid: Cátedra, 2006.

———. "Género e Historia: Una conjunción a finales del siglo XX." In *Memorias 49° Congreso Internacional de Americanistas*, pp. 57–90. Quito: Ediciones Abya-Yala, 1997.

———. "Recordando la Génesis del Sufragio Femenino en América Latina." In *Un Siglo de Luchas Femeninas en América Latina*, edited by Eugenia Rodríguez, pp. 3–22. San José: Editorial Universidad de Costa Rica, 2002.

———. *Women, Feminism, and Social Change in Argentina, Chile and Uruguay 1890–1940.* Lincoln: University of Nebraska Press, 1995.

Lecaro Pinto, María Luisa. "La mujer y sus derechos." In *Orígenes del feminismo en el Ecuador: Antología*, edited by Ana María Goetschel, pp. 161–62. Quito: CONAMU, FLACSO, Secretaría de Desarrollo y Equidad Social, UNIFEM, 2006.

Ledesma Prietto, Nadia. "Anarquismo(s) y feminismo(s): un estudio sobre las intervenciones de las mujeres anarquistas en la prensa. Buenos Aires (1896–1947)." *Izquierdas*, no. 34 (July 2017): 105–24. http://hdl.handle.net/11336/63217.

———. *La Revolución Sexual de nuestro tiempo. El discurso médico anarquista sobre el control de la natalidad, la maternidad y el placer sexual. Argentina, 1931–1951.* Buenos Aires: Biblos, 2016.

Lehoucq, Fabrice. "Political Competition and Electoral Fraud: A Latin American Case Study." *Journal of Interdisciplinary History* 30, no. 2 (1999): 199–234.

Lehoucq, Fabrice, and Iván Molina. *Stuffing the Ballot Box: Electoral Fraud in Costa Rica.* New York: Cambridge University Press, 2002.

Lerner, Gerda. *The Grimke Sisters from South Carolina: Pioneers for Women's Rights and Abolition.* Chapel Hill: University of North Carolina Press, 2004.

Lindo, Héctor. "Las salvadoreñas fueron las verdaderas pioneras del voto femenino en Latinoamérica," *El Faro*, June 26, 2020. https://elfaro.net/es/202006/

ef_academico/24586/Las-salvadore%C3%B1as-fueron-las-verdaderas-pion-eras-del-voto-femenino-en-Latinoam%C3%A9rica.htm.

Lobato, Mirta. *Eva Perón (1919–1952)*. Madrid: Ediciones del Orto, 2003.

Lopez, Elvira. *El movimiento feminista. Primeros trazos del feminismo en Argentina, 1901*. Buenos Aires: Ediciones Biblioteca Nacional, 2009.

López, Miguel, and Ricardo Gamboa. "Sufragio femenino en Chile: origen, brecha de género y estabilidad 1935–2009." *Revista de Estudios Sociales*, no. 53 (July–December 2015): 124–37.

López J., Sinesio. "Perú: mapas de una ciudadanía inconclusa." *Páginas* 22, no. 143 (1977): 22–23.

Lowe, Lisa. *The Intimacies of Four Continents*. Durham, NC: Duke University Press, 2015.

Luna, Lola G. "El logro del voto femenino en Colombia: la violencia y el maternalismo populista, 1949–1957." *Boletin Americanista* (Barcelona) 51, no. 51 (2001): 81–94.

Luna, Lola G., and Norma Villareal. *Historia, género y política. Movimiento de mujeres y participación política en Colombia 1930–1991*. Barcelona: Edición del Seminario Interdisciplinar Mujer y Sociedad, 1994.

———. "La feminidad y el sufragismo colombiano durante el período 1944–1948." *Anuario Colombiano de Historia Social y de la Cultura*, no. 29 (1999).

———. "SENDAS en el discurso populista del gobierno de Rojas Pinilla en Colombia 1953–1957." In *Poder local, poder global en América Latina*, edited by Gabriela Dalla Corte, Pilar García Jordán, Javier Laviña, Lola G. Luna, Ricardo Piqueras, José Luis Ruiz-Peinado Alonso, and Meritxell Tous. Barcelona: Publicaciones Universidad de Barcelona, 2008.

MacDonald, Heidi. *We Shall Persist: Women and the Vote in the Atlantic Provinces*. Vancouver: UBC Press, 2023.

Macera, César Francisco, and Alfonso de Souza Ferreira. *El Proceso Electoral de 1956: Cómputos finales y documentación oficial*. Lima: César Francisco Macera and Alfonso de Souza Ferreira, 1956.

Macías, Anna. *Against All Odds: The Feminist Movement in Mexico to 1940*. Westport, CT: Greenwood, 1982.

Macón, Cecilia. "La simulación como *performance* afectiva en los orígenes del feminismo." *Revista Estudios Feministas* 28, no. 2 (2020): e72434. https://doi.org/10.1590/1806-9584-2020v28n272434.

Mannarelli, María Emma. "Mujeres, cultura y controversia pública en el Perú." In *Historia de las mujeres en España y América Latina*, Vol. 3, edited by Isabel Morant. Madrid: Ediciones Cátedra, 2006.

Manzoni, Gisela. *Organizar la paz: Las mujeres y las luchas contra la guerra en América Latina (1910–1936)*. Buenos Aires: GEU, 2021.

Marco, Yolanda. *Clara González de Behringer. Biografía*. Panama City: Universidad de Panamá, Cooperación Española, and UNIFEM, 2007.

———. "El Movimiento Sufragista en Panamá y la Construcción de la Mujer Moderna." In *Historia de los Movimientos de Mujeres en Panamá en el Siglo XX*, edited by Yolanda Marco, Fernando Aparicio, Miriam Miranda, and Josefina Zurita, pp. 45–132. Panama City: Instituto de la Mujer de la Universidad de Panamá, Agenda del Centenario, 2002.

Marilley, Suzanne M. *Woman Suffrage and the Origins of Liberal Feminism in the United States, 1820–1920*. Cambridge, MA: Harvard University Press, 1996.

Marín Taboada, Jorge Iván. "María Cano. Su época, su historia. In *Las mujeres en la historia de Colombia*, Vol. 1, edited by Magdala Velásquez. Bogotá: Grupo Editorial Norma, 1995.

Marino, Katherine M. *Feminism for the Americas: The Making of an International Human Rights Movement*. Chapel Hill: University of North Carolina Press, 2019.

———. "Latin America and the Caribbean." In *The Routledge Global History of Feminism*, edited by Bonnie G. Smith and Nova Robinson, pp. 271–85. London: Routledge.

———. "Marta Vergara, Popular-Front Pan-American Feminism and the Transnational Struggle for Working Women's Rights in the 1930s." *Gender and History* 26, no. 3 (2014): 642–60. https://doi.org/10.1111/1468–0424.12093.

Marks, Lynne, Margaret Little, Megan Gaucher, and T. R. Roddings. "'A Job That Should Be Respected': Contested Visions of Motherhood and English Canada's Second Wave Women's Movements, 1970–1990." *Women's History Review* 25, no. 5 (2016): 771–90.

Marques, T. C. N. "A Correspondência, o Feminismo sufragista e o senador Adolpho Gordo." In *Bertha Lutz e o Voto Feminino no Acervo da CMU*, edited by J. Berto. Campinas: Centro de Memoria da Unicamp, 2021.

———. "Entre o igualitarismo e a reforma dos direitos das mulheres: Bertha Lutz na Conferencia Interamericana de Montevideu, 1933." *Revista Estudos Feministas* 21, no. 3 (September–December 2013).

———. "Federação Brasileira pelo Progresso Feminino." In *Diccionario Mulheres do Brasil—de 1500 ate a atualidade*, edited by Schuma Schumaher and Erico Brazil. Rio de Janeiro: Jorge Zahar, 2000.

———. *Perfil parlamentar: Bertha Lutz*. Brasília: Edições Câmara, 2016.

_____. "Women's Rights and Regional Politics under Cold War: Political and Civil Rights for Latin American Women, 1944–1954." *Topoi* 24, no. 52 (January–April 2023): 77–102.

———. *Women's Vote in Brazil*. Brasilia: Edições Câmara, 2021.

Marr, Timothy. "Diasporic Intelligences in the American Philippine Empire: The Transnational Career of Dr. Najeeb Mitry Saleeby." *Mashriq & Mahjar Journal of Middle East and North African Migration Studies* 2, no. 1 (2014). https://doi.org/10.24847/22i2014.27.

Martínez Assad, Carlos. *El laboratorio de la revolución: El Tabasco garridista*. Mexico City: Siglo Veintiuno Editores, 1991,

Martínez Macías, María Esther. "La mujer y el sufragio," In *Orígenes del feminismo en el Ecuador: Antología*, edited by Ana María Goetschel, pp. 173–80. Quito: CONAMU, FLACSO, Secretaría de Desarrollo y Equidad Social, UNIFEM, 2006.

Martínez, Nela. *Yo siempre he sido Nela Martínez Espinosa: Una autobiografía hablada.* Quito: CONAMU, UNIFEM, 2006.

Mata, Humberto. *Feminismo?* Quito: Talleres Gráficos Nacionales, 1935.

Matos Mar, José. *Las migraciones campesinas y el proceso de urbanización en el Perú.* Lima: UNESCO, 1990.

Maxwell, K. *Naked Tropics: Essays on Empire and Other Rogues.* New York: Routledge, 2003.

Maza Valenzuela, Erika. "Catolicismo, anticlericalismo y la extensión del sufragio a la mujer en Chile." *Estudios Públicos* (Santiago), no. 58 (1995).

——. "Las mujeres chilenas y la ciudadanía electoral de la exclusión al voto municipal, 1884–1884." In *Legitimidad, representación y alternativa en España y América Latina: Las reformas electorales (1880–1930)*, edited by Carlos Malamud. Mexico City: Colegio México/FCE, 2000.

——. "Liberales, radicales y la ciudadanía de la mujer en Chile (1872–1930)." *Estudios Públicos* 69 (Summer 1998): 319–56.

McAdam, Doug, Sidney Tarrow, and Charles Tilly. *Dinámica de la contienda política.* Barcelona: Edit. Hacer, 2005.

McConnaughy, Corrine M. *The Woman Suffrage Movement in America: A Reassessment.* New York: Cambridge University Press, 2013.

McGee Deutsch, Sandra. *Crossing Borders, Claiming a Nation: A History of Argentine Jewish Women, 1880–1955.* Durham, NC: Duke University Press, 2010.

——. *Gendering Antifascism: Women's Activism in Argentina and the World, 1918–1947.* Pittsburgh: University of Pittsburgh Press, 2023.

——. *Las derechas: La extrema derecha en la Argentina, el Brasil y Chile. 1890–1939.* Quilmes: Universidad Nacional de Quilmes, 2005.

——. "Mujeres, antifascismo y democracia: la Junta de la Victoria, 1941–1947." *Anuario IEHS*, no. 28 (2013): 157–75. http://anuarioiehs.unicen.edu.ar/2013.html.

McPherson, James M. *The Struggle for Equality: Abolitionists and the Negro in the Civil War and Reconstruction.* Princeton, NJ: Princeton University Press, 1992.

Mead, Rebecca. *How the Vote Was Won: Woman Suffrage in the Western United States, 1868–1914.* New York: New York University Press, 2004.

Mello, E. C. *A outra independência: o federalismo pernambucano de 1817 a 1824.* São Paulo: Editora 34, 2004.

Mergal, Margarita. "¿Por qué nos debe importar la historia?" Paper presented at the Second Coloquio de Investigación de Historia de Mujeres, Universidad de Puerto Rico, Utuado, March 8, 2013.

——. "Puerto Rican Feminism at a Crossroads: Challenges at the Turn of the Century." In *Colonial Dilemma: Critical Perspectives on Contemporary Puerto Rico,* edited by Edwin Meléndez and Edgardo Meléndez, pp. 131–42. Boston: South End Press, Boston, 1993.

Mérida, Cecilia, "Mujer y ciudadanía: un análisis desde la antropología de género." *Licenciatura* dissertation, Universidad de San Carlos de Guatemala, 2000.

Mikkola, M. "Kant on Moral Agency and Women's Nature." *Kantian Review* 16, no.1 (2001): 89–111.

Milk, Richard. *Movimiento obrero ecuatoriano: El desafío de la integración.* Quito: Abya Yala, 1997.

Mill, John Stuart. *The Subjection of Women.* London: Longmans, Green, Reader, and Dyer, 1869.

———. *On Liberty.* London: John W. Parker and Son, 1859.

———. *Considerations on Representative Government.* London: Parker, Son, and Bourn, 1861.

Millan, Verna C. "Mexico Reborn." *Books Abroad* 14, no. 4 (1940). https:// doi:10.2307/40082003.

Miller, Francesca. *Latin American Women and the Search for Social Justice.* Hanover, NH: New England University Press, 1991.

———. "The Suffrage Movement in Latin America." In *Confronting Change, Challenging Tradition: Women in Latin American History,* edited by Gertrude M. Yeager, pp. 157–76. Wilmington, DE: Scholarly Resources, 1994.

Mitchell, Stephanie. "Revolutionary Feminism, Revolutionary Politics: Suffrage Under Cardenismo." *Americas* 72, no. 3 (July 2015): 439–68.

———. "Death of a Revolution: Women's Suffrage and Mugiquismo in the 1940 Election in Mexico." *Descentrada* 7, no 1. (2023): e197. https://doi. org/10.24215/25457284e197.

Mitchell, Stephanie, and Patience Schell, eds. *The Women's Revolution.* Lanham, MD: Rowman and Littlefield, 2007.

Molina, Iván. *Anticomunismo Reformista, Competencia Electoral y Cuestión Social en Costa Rica (1931–1948).* San José: Editorial Costa Rica, 2007.

———. "Costa Rica." In *The Oxford Handbook of Central American History,* edited by Robert H. Holden, pp. 591–613. New York: Oxford University Press, 2022.

———. *Demoperfectocracia. La democracia pre-reformada en Costa Rica (1885–1948).* Heredia: Editorial Universidad Nacional, 2005.

———. "Desertores e invasoras. La feminización de la ocupación docente en Costa Rica en 1904." In *Educando a Costa Rica. Alfabetización popular, formación docente y género (1880–1950),* edited by Iván Molina and Steven Palmer, pp. 143–98. San José: Editorial Porvenir, Plumsock Mesoamerican Studies, 2000.

———. *La estela de la pluma. Cultura impresa e intelectuales en Centroamérica durante los siglos XIX y XX.* Heredia: Editorial Universidad Nacional, 2004.

———. *Moradas y Discursos. Cultura y Política en la Costa Rica de los Siglos XIX y XX.* Heredia: Editorial Universidad Nacional, 2010.

———. "Reforma educativa y resistencia ciudadana en la Costa Rica de finales del siglo XIX," *Secuencia* 90, no. 3 (2014): 57–75.

Molina, Iván, and Fabrice Lehoucq. *Urnas de lo Inesperado. Fraude Electoral y Lucha Política en Costa Rica (1901–1948)*. San José: Editorial Universidad de Costa Rica, 1999.

Molina, Iván, and Steven Palmer, eds. *The History of Costa Rica*. San José: Editorial Universidad de Costa Rica, 2018.

———. "Popular Literacy in a Tropical Democracy: Costa Rica 1850–1950," *Past and Present* 184 (2004): 169–207.

Molyneux, Maxine. *Women's Movements in International Perspective: Latin America and Beyond*. London: Institute of Latin American Studies, 2003.

Montenegro, Rosario. "El voto femenino en Nicaragua: una historia occulta." *Encuentro* 91 (2012): 91–115.

Monteón González, Humberto, and Gabriela M. Riquelme Alcántar. "El presidente Cárdenas y el sufragio femenino." *Espiral* (Guadalajara) 13, no. 38 (2007): 81–109.

Montero, Claudia. "Trocar agujas por la pluma: las pioneras de la prensa de y para mujeres en Chile 1860–1890." *Meridional Revista Chilena de Estudios Latinoamericanos*, no. 7 (October 2016): 55–81.

Mora, Virginia. "La mujer obrera en la educación y en el discurso periodístico en Costa Rica (1900–1930)." *Anuario de Estudios Centroamericanos* 19, no. 1 (1993): 67–77.

———. "Redefiniendo la política. La participación de las reformistas en la campaña electoral de 1923." In *Un siglo de luchas femeninas en América Latina*, edited by Eugenia Rodríguez, pp. 111–30. San José: Editorial Universidad de Costa Rica, 2002.

———. *Rompiendo Mitos y Forjando Historia. Mujeres Urbanas y Relaciones de Género en el San José de los Años Veinte*. Alajuela: Museo Histórico Cultural Juan Santamaría, 2003.

Morton, Ward M. *Woman Suffrage in Mexico*. Gainesville: University of Florida Press, 1962.

Moura, M. L. *A mulher é uma degenerada*. Rio de Janeiro: Civilização Brasileira, 1932.

Nállim, J. *Las raíces del antiperonismo: orígenes históricos e ideológicos*. Buenos Aires: Capital Intelectual, 2014.

Nari, Marcela. *Políticas de maternidad y maternalismo político, Buenos Aires, 1890–1940*. Buenos Aires: Biblos, 2004.

National American Woman Suffrage Association. *Victory: How Women Won It, a Centennial Symposium, 1840–1940*. New York: H. W. Wilson, 1940.

Navarro, Marysa. *Evita*. Buenos Aires: Planeta, 1994.

———. "Evita." In *Los Años Peronistas (1943–1955)*, edited by Juan Carlos Torre, pp. 313–55. Buenos Aires: Sudamericana, 2002.

———. *Evita. Mitos y representaciones*. Buenos Aires: FCE, 2002.

Ngô, Fiona I. B. *Imperial Blues: Geographies of Race and Sex in Jazz Age New York*. Durham, NC: Duke University Press, 2014.

Norando, Verónica. "Relaciones de género y militancia política: las obreras textiles y el comunismo entre 1936 y 1946." *Trabajos y comunicaciones*, no. 39 (2013). https://www.trabajosycomunicaciones.fahce.unlp.edu.ar/article/view/TyC2013n39a05.

Novick, Susana. *Mujer, Estado y Políticas Sociales*. Buenos Aires: CEAL, 1993.

O'Connor, Erin. *Gender, Indian, Nation: The Contradictions of Making Ecuador, 1830–1925*. Tucson: University of Arizona Press, 2007.

Obregón, Clotilde. *Las Constituciones de Costa Rica*, Vol. 4. San José: Editorial Universidad de Costa Rica, 2007.

Offen, Karen. "Defining Feminism: A Comparative Historical Approach." *Signs* 14, no. 1 (1986): 119–57.

Offen, Karen, and Marisa Ferrandis Garrayo. "Definir el feminismo: Un análisis histórico comparativo." *Historia Social* 9, no. 9 (1991): 103–35.

Oficina Nacional de Procesos Electorales. *60 Años del voto de las mujeres*. Lima: ONPE, 2016.

Oikión Solano, Verónica. *Cuca García (1889–1973): Por las causas de las mujeres y la revolución*. Mexico City: El Colegio de Michoacán; El Colegio de San Luis, 2018.

Osta Vazquez, M. L. "Brasil e Uruguai: pioneiros na discussão do voto das mulheres na America Latina." In *Cem anos da luta das mulheres pelo voto na Argentina, Brasil e Uruguai*, edited by Ana M. Prestes, pp. 168–95. Porto Alegre: Instituto EE Se Fosse Você, 2021.

Osten, Sarah. "The Implications and Legacies of Chiapas' 1925 Women's Suffrage Decree." *Revista pueblos y fronteras digital* 2, no. 3 (2007): 185–219. doi:10.22201/cimsur.18704115e.2007.3.236.

Palacios, Marco. *Between Legitimacy and Violence: A History of Colombia, 1875–2002*. Durham, NC: Duke University Press, 2006.

Palermo, Silvana. "El Sufragio Femenino en el Congreso Nacional: Ideologías de Género y Ciudadanía en la Argentina (1916–1955)." *Boletín del Instituto de Historia Agentina y Americana* 16–17 (1998): 151–78.

———. *Los derechos políticos de la mujer. Los proyectos y debates parlamentarios. 1916–1955*. Los Polvorines: Secretaría de Relaciones Parlamentarias-UNGS, 2012.

———. "Sufragio femenino y ciudadanía política en la Argentina, 1912–1947." In *Sufragio Femenino. Prácticas y debates políticos, religiosos y culturales en Argentina y América*, edited by Carolina Barry, pp. 29–62. Caseros: EDUNTREF, 2011.

Palm, Trineke. "Embedded in Social Cleavages: An Explanation of the Variation in Timing of Women's Suffrage." *Scandinavian Political Studies* 36, no. 1 (2013): 1–22.

Palmer, Steven, and Gladys Rojas. "Educando a las señoritas: formación docente, movilidad social y nacimiento del feminismo en Costa Rica (1885–1925)." In *Educando a Costa Rica. Alfabetización popular, formación docente y género*, edited by Iván Molina and Steven Palmer, pp. 67–141. San José: Editorial Universidad Estatal a Distancia, 2004.

———. "Educating Señorita: Teacher Training, Social Mobility and the Birth of

Costa Rican Feminism, 1885–1925." *Hispanic American Historical Review* 78, no. 1 (1998): 45–82.

Pateman, Carole. *The Disorder of Women: Democracy, Feminism and Political Theory.* Stanford, CA: Stanford University Press, 1989.

———. *The Sexual Contract.* 30th anniversary ed. Stanford, California: Stanford University Press, 2018.

Patrocínio, Jose, ed. *Cidade do Rio: Jornal da Tarde,* December, 29, 1899.

Peralta, Christine N. "Nursing the Nation: Examining the History of Early Migrant Nurses and the Origins of University Nursing Programs in the Philippines." In *Global Migration, Gender, and Health Professional Credentials. Transnational Value Transfers and Losses,* edited by Margaret Walton-Roberts. North York: University of Toronto Press, 2022.

Pérez Brignoli, Héctor. *A Brief History of Central America.* Berkeley: University of California Press, 1989.

Pérez Inés. *El hogar tecnificado. Familias, género y vida cotidiana: 1940–1970.* Buenos Aires: Biblos, 2012.

Pérez Inés, Romina Cutuli, and Débora Garazi. *Senderos que se bifurcan. Servicio doméstico y derechos laborales en la Argentina del siglo XX.* Mar del Plata, Argentina: EUDEM, 2018.

Perrig, Sara. *La mujer en el discurso peronista (1946–1952).* Villa María: EDUVIM, 2011.

Pieper Mooney, Jadwiga E. "El antifascismo como fuerza movilizadora: Fanny Edelman y la Federación Democrática Internacional de Mujeres." *Anuario IEHS* 28 (2013): 207–26.

Pineo, Ronn R. *Social and Economic Reform in Ecuador: Life and Work in Guayaquil.* Gainesville: University Press of Florida, 1996.

Pinzón de Lewin, Patricia. *Esmeralda Arboleda. La mujer y la política.* Bogotá: Taller de Edición Rocca, 2014.

Plotkin, Mariano. *Mañana es San Perón. Propaganda, rituales políticos y educación en el régimen peronista (1946–1955).* Buenos Aires: Ariel, 1994.

Pollard, John F. *The Unknown Pope Benedict XV (1912–1922) and the Pursuit of Peace.* London: Geoffrey Chapman, 2000.

Porter, Susie S. *From Angel to Office Worker: Middle-Class Identity and Female Consciousness in Mexico, 1890–1950.* Lincoln: University of Nebraska Press, 2018.

Posada Carbó, Eduardo. "Las prácticas electorales en Chile 1810–1970." In *Historia política de Chile 1810–2010,* Vol. 1, *Practicas Políticas,* edited by Iván Jaksic and Juan Luis Ossa, pp. 179–210. Santiago: Fondo de Cultura Económica, 2017.

Prieto, Laura R. "A Delicate Subject: Clemencia López, Civilized Womanhood, and the Politics of Anti-Imperialism." *Journal of the Gilded Age and Progressive Era* 12, no. 2 (2013): 199–233. https://doi.org/10.1017/s1537781413000066.

Prieto, Mercedes. "A Liberalism of Fear: Imagining Indigenous Subjects in Postcolonial Ecuador, 1895–1950." PhD dissertation, University of Florida, 2003.

Prieto, Mercedes, and Ana María Goetschel. "El sufragio femenino en Ecuador, 1884–1940." In *Mujeres y escenarios ciudadanos*, edited by Mercedes Prieto, pp. 299–330. Quito: FLACSO, Ministerio de Cultura, 2008.

Przeworski, Adam. "Conquered or Granted? A History of Suffrage Extensions." *British Journal of Political Science* 39 (2009): 291–321.

Puerta de Tierra. "Genara Pagán de Arce," 2018. http://www.puertadetierra.info/figuras/gente/genara/genara_pagan.htm.

Purnell, Jennie. *Popular State Movement and State Formation in Revolutionary Mexico: The Agraristas and Cristeros of Michoacán*. Durham, NC: Duke University Press, 1999.

Purvis, June, and Sandra Stanley Holton, eds. *Votes for Women*. London: Routledge, 2000.

Queirolo, Graciela. "'Igual salario por igual trabajo': La Organización Internacional del Trabajo y el Estado argentino frente al trabajo femenino (1919–1960)." In *Una historia regional de la OIT: Aportes sobre regulación y legislación del trabajo latinoamericano*, edited by by Laura Caruso and Andrés Stagnaro, pp. 87–196. La Plata: Universidad Nacional de La Plata, 2014. https://www.memoria.fahce.unlp.edu.ar/libros/pm.4763/pm.4763.pdf.

———. "La mujer en la sociedad moderna a través de los escritos de Victoria Ocampo (1935–1953)." *Revista Zona Franca*, no. 14 (2005): 144–54.

———. *Mujeres en las oficinas. Trabajo, género y clase en el sector administrativo (Buenos Aires, 1910–1950)*. Buenos Aires: Biblos, 2018.

———. *Mujeres que trabajan. Labores femeninas. Estado y sindicatos (Buenos Aires, 1910–1960)*. Buenos Aires: CABA, Eudem-Grupo Editor Universitario, 2020.

———. "Mujeres que trabajan: una revisión historiográfica del trabajo femenino en la ciudad de Buenos Aires (1890–1940)." *Nuevo Topo: Revista de historia y pensamiento crítico* 3 (2006): 29–49. https://nuevotopo.wordpress.com/nuevo-topo-n%c2%ba3/.

———. "Victoria Ocampo (1890–1979): cruces entre feminismo, clase y elite intelectual." *Clío y Asociados* 1, no. 13 (2009): 135–57. https://doi.org/10.14409/cya.v1i13.1665.

Quintero, Rafael. *El mito del populismo en el Ecuador*. Quito: FLACSO, 1980.

Rachum, Ilan. "Feminism, Woman Suffrage, and National Politics in Brazil: 1922–1937." *Luso-Brazilian Review* 14, no. 1 (1977): 118–34.

Rama, Ángel. *La ciudad letrada*. Hanover, NH: Ediciones del Norte, 2002.

Ramacciotti. Karina, and Adriana Valobra. "El dilema Nightingale: controversias sobre la profesionalización de la enfermería en Argentina 1949–1967." *Dynamis* 37, no. 2 (2017): 367–87.

———. *Generando el peronismo. Estudios de cultura, política y género*. Buenos Aires: Proyecto Editorial, 2004.

Ramella de Jefferies, Susana. *El radicalismo bloquista de San Juan*. San Juan: Gobernación de la provincia de San Juan, 1986.

———. "El régimen electoral de San Juan en la década de los años 1880." *Cuadernos de La Universidad Católica de Cuyo* 14, no. 15 (1982): 105–37.

Ramírez, Alejandre, Gloria Luz, and Eduardo Torres Alonso. "El Primer Congreso Feminista de Yucatán 1916. El camino a la legislación del sufragio y reconocimiento de ciudadanía a las mujeres. Construcción y tropiezos." *Estudios Políticos* 39 (2016): 59–89.

Ramirez, F. O., Y. Soysal, and S. Shanahan. "The Changing Logic of Political Citizenship: Cross-National Acquisition of Women's Suffrage Rights, 1890 to 1990." *American Sociological Review* 62, no. 5 (1997): 735–45.

Ramós Escandón, Carmen. "Women and Power in Mexico: The Forgotten Heritage, 1880–1954." In *Women's Participation in Mexican Political Life*, edited by Elizabeth Rodríguez. Boulder, CO: Westview Press, 1998.

Ramos Núñez, Carlos Augusto. *Historia del Derecho Civil Peruano Siglos XIX y XX*. Lima: PUCP-Fondo Editorial, 2011.

Recalde Héctor, ed. *Señoras, universitarias y mujeres (1910–2010). La cuestión femenina entre el centenario y el bicentenario de la Revolución de Mayo*. Granada: Grupo Editor Universitario, 2010.

Rendón, Zoila G. *Condición social y política de la mujer a la luz de la historia de la civilización humana*. Quito: Imprenta Nacional, 1925.

———. *La mujer en el hogar y en la Sociedad*, 1923, 1933. Quito: Editorial Universitaria, 1961.

República del Ecuador. *Anales de Diputados*. Quito: República del Ecuador, 1910.

———. *Código Civil de la República del Ecuador*. Quito: Imprenta de los Huérfanos de Valencia, 1860.

Ríos Cárdenas, María. *La mujer mexicana es ciudadana; historia, con fisonomía de una novela de costumbres, 1930-época-1940*. Mexico City: A. del Bosque, impresor, 1942.

Rivera Bustamante, Emilia Tirza. *Proyección de la mujer en las américas y desarrollo histórico de la Comisión Interamericana de Mujeres de la Organización de los Estados Americanos*. Washington, DC: OEA and CIM, 1981.

Rivera Lassén, Ana Irma, and Elizabeth Crespo Kebler. *Documentos del Feminismo en Puerto Rico: Facsímiles de la historia*, Vol. 1. San Juan: Editorial del Universidad de Puerto Rico, 2001.

Rivera-Giusti, I. "Gender, Labor, and Working-Class Activism in the Puerto Rican Tobacco Industry, 1898–1924." PhD dissertation, State University of New York, Binghamton, 2004.

Robalino Bolle, Isabel. *El sindicalismo en el Ecuador, 1976*. Quito: PUCE, 1992.

Roca de Salonen, Elsa. "La mujer obtuvo el voto." *Silvia* 1 (1981): 44.

Roces, Mina. "Orienting the Global Women's Suffrage Movement." In *Women's Suffrage in Asia: Gender, Nationalism and Democracy*, edited by Louise P. Edwards and Mina Roces. London: Routledge Curzon, 2004.

———. "Women in Philippine Politics and Society." In *Mixed Blessing: The Impact of the American Colonial Experience on Politics and Society in the Philippines*, edited by Hazel M. McFerson. Quezon City: University of the Philippines Press, 2011.

Rocha, Elaine P. "Introdução, notas e posfácio." In *O inicio do feminismo: subsidios para a historia Brasilia*, edited by L. F. Daltro. Brasília: Edicoes Camara, 2022.

———. "Vida de professora: ideias e aventuras de Leolinda de Figueiredo Daltro durante a Primeira Republica." *Mundos do Trabalho* 8, no. 15 (2016): 29–47.

Rodás Morales, Raquel. *Crónica de un sueño: Las escuelas indígenas de Dolores Cacuango*. Quito: Ministerio de Educación y Cultura, Sociedad Alemana de Cooperación Técnica, 1989.

Rodás Morales, Raquel, ed. *Historia del voto femenino en el Ecuador*. Quito: CONAMU, 2009.

Rodríguez, C. *Lencinas y Cantoni, el populismo cuyano en tiempos de Yrigoyen*. Buenos Aires: Editorial de Belgrano, 1979.

Rodríguez, Eugenia. "Anticomunismo, Género y Guerra Fría: Las Mujeres y el Partido Comunista de Costa Rica (1931–1948)." In *Queridas Camaradas. Historias Iberoamericanas de Mujeres Comunistas, 1935–1975*, edited by Adriana Valobra and Mercedes Yusta, pp. 133–52. Madrid: Editorial Miño y Dávila SRL, 2017.

———. "Del hogar al colegio y del colegio al hogar y a la calle. Acceso a la educación e identidades de género: el Colegio Superior de Señoritas. Costa Rica, 1888–1940." In *La educación de las mujeres en Iberoamérica*, edited by Teresa González Pérez, pp. 181–220. Valencia: Tirant Humanidades, Gobierno de Canarias, 2019.

———. "'Desde Hoy el Voto Queda Bajo Las Caprichosas Influencias del Sexo': Ciudadanía, Participación Política y Luchas por el Sufragio Femenino en América Central (1900–1965)." In *Historia Comparada de las Mujeres en las Américas*, edited by Patricia Galeana, pp. 397–444. Mexico City: Instituto Panamericano de Geografía e Historia, CIALC-UNAM, CIAN-UANM, Federación Mexicana de Universitarias, 2012.

———. "Historia de las Mujeres y de Género." In *Innovación y Diversidad. La Historiografía Costarricense en la Segunda Década del Siglo XXI*, edited by Iván Molina and David Díaz, pp. 189–211. San José: Editorial de la Universidad de Costa Rica, CIHAC.

———. "La lucha por el sufragio femenino en Costa Rica (1890–1949)." In *Un Siglo de Luchas Femeninas en América Latina Historia*, edited by Eugenia Rodríguez, pp. 87–110. San José: Editorial Universidad de Costa Rica, 2002.

———. "Las mujeres y el Partido Comunista de Costa Rica: feminismo y conquista del sufragio femenino (1931–1949)." *Historia Regional* 49, no. 2 (2023): 1–16.

———. "Madres, Reformas Sociales y Sufragismo: el Partido Comunista de Costa Rica y sus Discursos de Movilización Política de las Mujeres (1931–1948)," *Cuadernos Intercambio* 11, no 1 (2014): 49–84.

———. "Movimientos Feministas y Sufragistas en América Central (1890–1965)." In *Sufragio Femenino: Prácticas y Debates Políticos, Religiosos y Culturales en Argentina y América Latina*, edited by Carolina Barry, pp. 283–308. Buenos Aires: Editorial de la Universidad de Tres de Febrero, 2011.

———. "Mujeres, Elecciones, Democracia y Guerra Fría en Costa Rica (1948–1953)." In *El Verdadero Anticomunismo. Política, Género y Guerra Fría en Costa Rica (1948–1973)*, edited by Iván Molina and David Díaz, pp. 39–75. San José: Editorial Universidad Estatal a Distancia, 2017.

———. "Women in Central America since Independence." In *The Oxford Handbook of Central American History*, edited by Robert H. Holden, pp. 431–53. New York: Oxford University Press, 2022.

Rodríguez, Manuel Á., Oliva Solís Hernández, and Alfonso Serna Jiménez. *Las mujeres en la lucha por el voto*. Mexico City: Editorial Miguel Ángel Porrúa, 2015.

Rojas de Moreno, María Eugenia. *Rojas Pinilla mi padre*. Bogotá: Panamericana Formas e Impresos, 2000.

Rojina Villegas, Rafael. "Capacidad de la mujer en el derecho civil y condición jurídica de la esposa y de la concubine." In *La Situación Jurídica de la Mujer Mexicana*. Mexico City: Alianza de Mujeres de Mexico, Estudios Jurídicos, 1953.

Rolland, P. "Quel Libéral Laboulaye Était-Il?" *Revue Française d´Histoire des Idées Politiques* 47, no. 1 (2018): 33–58.

Romo Leroux G., Ketty. *El movimiento de mujeres en el Ecuador*. Guayaquil: Editorial de la Universidad de Guayaquil, 1997.

Rosanvallon, P. "Guizot et la question du suffrage universel au XIXe siècle." In *François Guizot et la culture politique de son temps*, edited by M. Valentise. Paris: Gallimard, 1991.

———. *Le sacre du citoyen. Histoire du suffrage universel en France*. Paris: Gallimard, 1992.

Roure, Agenor. *A Constituinte Republicana, 1918*. Brasília: Senado Federal, 1979.

Rowbotham, Sheila. *A Century of Women: The History of Women in Britain and the United States*. London: Viking, 1997.

Ruchwarger, Gary. *People in Power: Forging a Grassroots Democracy in Nicaragua*. South Hadley, MA: Bergin and Garvey, 1987.

Rupp, Leila J. *Worlds of Women: The Making of an International Women's Movement*. Princeton, NJ: Princeton University Press, 1997.

Sabato, Hilda, "Elecciones y prácticas electorales en Buenos Aires, 1860–1880. ¿Sufragio universal sin ciudadanía política?" In *Historia de las elecciones en Iberoamérica, siglo XIX*, edited by Antonio Annino, pp. 107–42. Buenos Aires: Fondo de Cultura Económica, 1995.

Sáenz Quesada, María. *La primera presidente*. Buenos Aires: Sudamericana, 2016.

Saffioti, Heleith. *A mulher na sociedade de classes: mito e realidade*. Petropolis: Vozes, 1976.

———. *Women in Class Society*. New York: Monthly Review Press, 1978.

Safford, Frank, and Marco Palacios. *Colombia: Fragmented Land, Divided Society*. Oxford: Oxford University Press, 2002.

Salerno, Beth A. *Sister Societies: Women's Antislavery Organizations in Antebellum America*. DeKalb: Northern Illinois University, 2008.

Saltalamacchia, H. "¿Para qué sirve el 'populismo'?" *América Latina en Movimiento*, February 10, 2017. https://www.alainet.org/es/articulo/183431.

Sanchez, George. "'Go After the Women': Americanization and the Mexican Immigrant Woman, 1915–1929." In *Mothers & Motherhood: Readings in American History*, edited by Rima D. Apple and Janet Lynne Golden. Columbus: Ohio State University Press, 1997.

Sandoval Sánchez, Yndira. "Sin despatriarcalización no habrá transformación." *Pluralidad y Consenso* 10, no. 43 (2020): 61–64. http://revista.ibd.senado.gob.mx/index.php/PluralidadyConsenso/article/view/652.

Sangster, Joan. *Demanding Equality: One Hundred Years of Canadian Feminism*. Vancouver: UBC Press, 2021.

———. *One Hundred Years of Struggle: The History of Women and the Vote in Canada*. Vancouver: UBC Press 2018.

Santangelo, Lauren. *Suffrage and the City: New York Women Battle for the Ballot*. New York: Oxford University Press, 2019.

Santos, Ana R. T. *Tratado sobre emancipação política da mulher e direito de votar, 1868*. Brasilia: Edições Câmara, 2022.

Santos, Carlos Maximiliano. *Comentários à Constituição Brasileira de 1891, 1918*. Brasilia: Senado Federal, 2005.

Santos, Enrique. "Danza de las Horas." *El Tiempo*, October 24, 1944.

Santos, W. G. "A práxis liberal no Brasil." In *Décadas de espanto e uma apologia*, edited by W. G. Santos. Rio de Janeiro: Rocco, 1998.

Sarraceno, Chiara. "La estructura de género de la ciudadanía." In *Congreso de mujer y realidad social*. Bilbao: Universidad del País Vasco y Gobierno Vasco, 1998.

Scott, Joan Wallach. *Only Paradoxes to Offer: French Feminists and the Rights of Man*. Cambridge, MA: Harvard University Press, 1996.

Segura, María Marta. "Trayectorias del sufragio femenino en Tucumán: los proyectos durante el Segundo Congreso de Municipalidades (1928)." *Descentrada. Revista interdisciplinaria de feminismos y género* 6, no. 1 (2022): e168. https://doi.org/10.24215/25457284e168.

Sharrat, Sara. "The Suffragist Movement in Costa Rica, 1889–1949. Centennial of Democracy?" In *The Costa Rican Women's Movement: A Reader*, edited by Ilse Abshagen Leitinger, pp. 61–83. Pittsburgh: University of Pittsburgh Press, 1997.

Silveira, M. M. "Escrever, ser útil à sociedade: Uma análise da produção intelectual de Myrthes de Campos." *Estudos Ibero-Americanos* 47, no. 3 (September–December 2021): 1–16.

Simon Collier, and William Sater. *Historia de Chile 1808–1994*. Cambridge: Cambridge University Press, 1998.

Sinha, Manisha. *The Slave's Cause: A History of Abolition*. New Haven, CT: Yale University Press, 2016.

Sneider, Allison L. *Suffragists in an Imperial Age: US Expansion and the Woman Question, 1870–1929.* Oxford: Oxford University Press, 2008.

Sobrado, Luis Antonio. "El régimen electoral en la Constitución de 1949." *Revista de Derecho Electoral* 9, no. 1 (2010): 1–29.

———. "Experiencia costarricense del voto de personas privadas de libertad," *Revista de Derecho Electoral* 7, no. 1 (2007): 1–22.

———. "La inscripción automática de electores en el ordenamiento electoral costarricense." *Revista de Derecho Electoral* 7, no. 2 (2007): 1–12.

Solano, Marta Eugenia. "La Liga Feminista Costarricense y el inicio del largo camino por el voto de las mujeres en Costa Rica." Master's thesis, University of Costa Rica, San José, 2005.

Solar, D. "La mujer sufragante en San Juan: reforma constitucional de 1878." *Revista Dos Puntas* 8, no. 14 (2016): 201–16. https://dialnet.unirioja.es/servlet/articulo?codigo=6079488.

Sosa-Bucholz, Ximena. "Changing Images of Male and Female in Ecuador: José María Velasco Ibarrra and Abdalá Bucarám." In *Gender and Populism in Latin America: Passionate Politics,* edited by Karen Kampwirth, pp. 47–66. University Park: Pennsylvania State University Press, 2010.

Soto, Shirlene Ann. *Emergence of the Modern Mexican Woman.* Denver: Arden Press, 1990.

Souza, F. Belizário Soares. *O sistema eleitoral no Império,* 1871. Brasilia: Senado Federal, 1979.

Spinetta, Marina. "Género y ciudadanía: una mirada desde el I Congreso Nacional Femenino Radical (Córdoba, 1949)." *Descentrada* 6, no. 2 (2002): e179. https://doi.org/10.24215/25457284e179.

———. "Participación política femenina: escenarios, prácticas e identidades en el radicalismo y el peronismo (Córdoba, 1945–1955)." PhD thesis, Universidad Nacional de Córdoba, 2020.

Spota Valencia, Alma. *La igualdad jurídica y social de los sexos.* Mexico City: Talleres de Unión Gráfica, 1967.

Stabili, María Rosaria. "El sexo de la ciudadanía: las mujeres y el sufragio en el Chile liberal 1875–1917." In *Mujeres y naciones en América Latina,* edited by Bárbara Potthast and Eugenia Scarzanella, pp. 135–59. Frankfurt: Vervuet-Iberoamericana, 2001.

———. "Las Res-Públicas de las mujeres." In *Historia política de Chile 1810–2010,* Vol. 1, *Practicas Políticas,* edited by Iván Jaksic and Juan Luis Ossa, pp. 243–70. Santiago: Fondo de Cultura Económica, 2017.

Stanton, Elizabeth Cady, Susan B. Anthony, and Matilda Joslyn Gage, eds. *History of Woman Suffrage,* Vol. 1. Rochester, NY: Charles Mann, 1881.

Stepan, N. L. "Race, Gender, Science and Citizenship." *Gender & History* 10, no. 1 (April 1998): 26–52.

Stevens, Doris. *Jailed for Freedom: A First-Person Account of the Militant Fight for Women's Rights.* New York: Black Dog & Leventhal, 2020.

Streitmatter, Rodger. *Raising Her Voice: African-American Women Journalists Who Changed History*. Lexington: University of Kentucky Press, 1994.

Strong-Boag, Veronica. *The Last Suffragist Standing: The Life and Times of Laura Marshall Jamieson*. Vancouver: UBC Press, 2018.

———. *A Liberal-Labour Lady: The Times and Life of Mary Ellen Spear Smith*. Vancouver: UBC Press, 2021.

Strong-Boag, Veronica, and Michelle Lynn Rosa, eds. *Nellie McClung: The Complete Autobiography*. Peterborough, ON: Broadview Press, 2003.

Sulmont, Denis. *El Movimiento Obrero Peruano, 1890: Reseña Histórica*. 3rd. ed. Lima: Tarea, 1982.

Swerdlow, Amy. "Abolition's Conservative Sisters." In *The Abolitionist Sisterhood: Women's Political Culture in Antebellum America*, edited by Jean Fagan Yellin and John C. Van Horne. Ithaca, NY: Cornell University Press.

Tarrow, Sidney. *El poder en movimiento. Los movimientos sociales, la acción colectiva y la política*. Madrid: Alianza Editorial, 2012.

Tauro del Pino, Alberto. *Enciclopedia ilustrada del Perú*, Vol. 3. Lima: PEISA, 2001.

Taylor, Christopher. *Empire of Neglect: The West Indies in the Wake of British Liberalism*. Durham, NC: Duke University Press, 2018.

Teele, Dawn Langan. *Forging the Franchise: The Political Origins of the Women's Vote*. Princeton, NJ: Princeton University Press, 2018.

Teitelbaum, Vanesa. "Protestas, derechos y violencias en enero de 1919 en Argentina. Una reflexión a partir del libro de viajes de Katherine Dreier y de la prensa." *Cuadernos del CIESAL* 14, no. 16 (December 2017): 186–207.

Tejerina, María E., and María Mercedes Quiñonez. "Mujeres y representación política en Salta." *Revista Escuela de historia* 1, no. 3 (2004). https://www. redalyc.org/pdf/638/63810310.pdf.

Terborg-Penn, Rosalyn. *African American Women in the Struggle for the Vote, 1850 to 1920*. Bloomington: Indiana University Press, 1998.

Terzaghi, María Teresa. "Tensiones sufragistas en los años fundacionales del Partido Socialista Argentino." In *Imperativos, desazones y promesas. Género y modernización en Argentina (1880–1970)*, edited by Guillermina Guillamón and Adriana Valobra, pp. 219–40. Temperley: Tren en Movimiento, 2022.

———. "Miradas de Alicia Moreau sobre ciudadanía, género y educación." National University of La Plata, 2017. http://sedici.unlp.edu.ar/handle/10915/65075.

Tetrault, Lisa. *The Myth of Seneca Falls: Memory and the Women's Suffrage Movement, 1848–1898*. Chapel Hill: University of North Carolina Press, 2014.

Thorp, Rosemary, and Geoffrey Bertram. *Perú: 1890–1977: Crecimiento y políticas en una economía abierta*. Lima: Mosca Azul, 2013.

Threlkeld, Megan. *Pan American Women: U.S. Internationalists and Revolutionary Mexico*. Philadelphia: University of Pennsylvania Press, 2014.

Ticas, Sonia. "Avances y retrocesos en el movimiento sufragista femenino salvadoreño en la década de 1920." *Identidades* 13 (2018): 162–63.

Teixeira Freitas, A. *Consolidação das leis civis. Publicação autorizada pelo Governo.* Rio de Janeiro: Garnier, 1876.

Teixeira Mendes, R. *A proeminência social e moral da mulher.* Rio de Janeiro: Igreja Positivista, 1931.

Tilly, Charles, and Sidney Tarrow. *Contentious Politics.* London: Paradigm Publishers, 2006.

Tiongson, Nicanor G. *The Women of Malolos.* Manila: Ateneo de Manila University Press, 2004.

Toledo de Aguerri, Josefa. *Educación y feminismo.* Managua: Talleres Nacionales de Imprenta y Encuadernación, 1940.

Torres, Isabel. "Paridad para el fortalecimiento de la democracia incluyente: el caso de Costa Rica." In *La apuesta por la paridad: democratizando el sistema político en América Latina. Los casos de Ecuador, Bolivia y Costa Rica*, pp. 179–235. Lima: IDEA, CIM, 2013.

Torres Martinez, Lizandra. "Procesos sociales, política, poder y género: Fuerza política y autonomía relativa: participación sindical, sufragismo y movimientos feministas de la década de los setenta" In *Género, Sociedad y Cultura*, edited by Loida M. Martinez Ramos and Maribel Tamargo Lóperz, pp. 136–59. Río Piedras: Publicaciones Gaviota, 2003.

Towner, Margaret. "Monopoly Capitalism and Women's Work during the Porfiriato." *Latin American Perspectives* 4, nos. 1–2 (1977).

Trimble, Linda, Jane Arscott, and Manon Tremblay, eds. *Stalled: The Representation of Women in Canadian Governments.* Vancouver: UBC Press, 2013.

Trindade, H., ed. *O Positivismo: teoria e prática.* Porto Alegre: UFRGS; Brasília, Unesco, 2007.

Tuñón Pablos, Enriqueta. "El otorgamiento del sufragio femenino en México." PhD thesis, Facultad de Filosofía y Letras, Universidad Nacional Autónoma de México.

———. *¡Por fin—ya podemos elegir y ser electas! el sufragio femenino en México, 1935–1953.* Mexico City: Plaza y Valdés, 2002.

Tuñon Pablos, Esperanza. *Mujeres que se organizan: El frente único pro-derechos de la mujer, 1935–1938.* Mexico City: Porrúa, 1992.

Tuñon Pablos, Julia. *Women in Mexico: A Past Unveiled.* Austin: University of Texas Press, 1999.

Undurraga Fernández, Pedro. "Los Derechos Políticos de la Mujer." PhD dissertation, Universidad Central de Quito, 1927.

Uribe de Acosta, Ofelia. *Una voz insurgente.* Bogotá: Editorial Guadalupe, 1963.

Valenzuela, Samuel J. "Orígenes y transformaciones del sistema de partidos en Chile." *Revista Estudios Públicos*, no. 58 (1995).

Valobra, Adriana. *Del Hogar a las Urnas. Recorridos de la Ciudadanía Política Femenina: Argentina, 1946–1955.* Rosario, Argentina: Prohistoria Ediciones, 2010.

———. "Derechos políticos femeninos en la Junta Consultiva Nacional." *Estudios*

Sociales, no. 45 (2013): 167–201. https://bibliotecavirtual.unl.edu.ar/publicaciones/index.php/EstudiosSociales/article/view/4456/6773.

————. "Elogio de la mujer que vota: El voto municipal femenino en Santa Fe, Argentina." *Meridional: Revista Chilena De Estudios Latinoamericanos* 17 (2021): 125–55. https://doi.org/10.5354/0719-4862.2021.64855.

————. "La ciudadanía política de las mujeres y las elecciones de 1951." *Anuario De Historia Argentina*, no. 8 (2008): 53–89. http://www.fuentesmemoria.fahce.unlp.edu.ar/art_revistas/pr.3211/pr.3211.pdf.

————. "La tradición femenina en el radicalismo y la lucha de Clotilde Sabattini por el reconocimiento de la equidad política, 1946–1955." *Clepsydra*, no. 6 (2007): 25–41. https://riull.ull.es/xmlui/bitstream/handle/915/14907/CL_06_%282007%29_02.pdf?sequence=1&isAllowed=y.

————. "Los derechos políticos en Argentina y los vaivenes internacionales y nacionales." *Travesía* 20, no. 2 (2018): 93–119.

————. "Los discursos de Eva Perón sobre los derechos políticos de las mujeres en el contexto de debate, promulgación y aplicación de la ley 13010/47." In *Historia y Metodología: aproximaciones al análisis del discurso*, edited by Nadia Ledesma Prietto, Guillermo de Martinelli, and Adriana Maria Valobra, pp. 102–35. Buenos Aires: LECPYS, CHAYA-EDULP, 2014. https://www.libros.fahce.unlp.edu.ar/index.php/libros/catalog/book/23.

————. *Mujeres en espacios bonaerenses* Buenos Aires: EDULP, 2009.

————. "Paradojas de la historia política. Aportes para la construcción de un debate." *POLHIS Boletín Bibliográfico Electrónico del Programa Buenos Aires de Historia Política* 4, no. 8 (2011): 300–306. http://historiapolitica.com/datos/boletin/PolHis_8.pdf.

————. "Participación de la mujer en la vida pública. Notas sobre el Seminario Nacional de 1960." *Cuadernos de H Ideas* 7, no. 7 (2013): 1–18. http://perio.unlp.edu.ar/ojs/index.php/cps/index.

————. "Representación política y derechos de las trabajadoras en Argentina. El caso de la Convención Constituyente de 1957." *Nuevo Mundo, Mundos Nuevos*, 2013. https://doi.org/10.4000/nuevomundo.66068.

————. "Una historia para el voto femenino municipal en San Juan: problemas, conceptos, metodología." *Revista Electrónica de Fuentes y Archivos* 11, no. 11 (2020). https://refa.org.ar/file.php?tipo=Contenido&id=263.

Valobra, Adriana, and Natalia Casola. "When My Life Goes Out: Biography of the Argentinian Communist Activist Fanny Edelman (1911–2011)." In *The Palgrave Handbook of Communist Women Activists around the World*, edited by F. de Haan, pp. 643–68. Camden: Palgrave Macmillan, 2023.

Valobra, Adriana, and Verónica Giordano. "Absolute Divorce in Argentina, 1954–1956. Debates and Practices Regarding a Short-Lived Law." *History of the Family* 18, no. 1 (2013): 3–25. http://www.tandfonline.com/doi/abs/10.1080/1081602X.2012.753848#.UglsYdI9-So.

———. "Formación de cuadros y frentes populares: las mujeres en el Partido Comunista de Argentina." *Izquierdas*, no. 23 (2015): 127–56. http://www.izquierdas.cl/images/pdf/2015/n23/art07.pdf.

———. "Las comunistas argentinas durante la política de frentes y la guerra fría, 1935–1967." In *Queridas Camaradas. Historias iberoamericanas de mujeres comunistas. 1935–1975*, edited by Adriana Valobra and Rodrigo Yusta, pp. 71–90. Buenos Aires: Editorial Miño y Dávila, 2017.

———. "Los discursos de Eva Perón sobre los derechos políticos de las mujeres en el contexto de debate, promulgación y aplicación de la ley 13010/47." In *Historia y Metodología: aproximaciones al análisis del discurso*, edited by Guillermo Martinelli, Nadia Ledesma Prietto, and Adriana Valobra, pp. 102–35. Buenos Aires: LECPYS, CHAYA-EDULP, 2014. http://www.memoria.fahce.unlp.edu.ar/libros/pm.362/pm.362.pdf.

———. "Las mujeres de los Partidos Comunistas de Argentina y de Chile entre los '30 y '60." *Anuario de la Escuela de Historia Virtual*, no. 11 (2017): 23–46. https://revistas.unc.edu.ar/index.php/anuariohistoria/article/view/17316.

———. "'Mujeres-sombra' y 'Barbudas' Género y política en el Primer Congreso Latinoamericano de Mujeres, Chile. 1959." *Anuario De Historia Argentina*, no. 14 (2014). http://www.anuarioiha.fahce.unlp.edu.ar/article/view/5558.

———. "No hablan, trabajan: Acercamiento a la trayectoria de una diputada intransigente." In *Historias de mujeres en la acción política. De la Revolución Rusa a nuestros días*, edited by Débora D'Antonio, Karin Grammático, and Adriana Valobra, pp. 83–94. Buenos Aires: Imago Mundi, 2020.

———. "Una santafesina en el Congreso Nacional: Palmira Grandi de Martín, legisladora desarrollista." In *La resistencia de las mujeres en gobiernos autoritarios: Argentina y Brasil (1955–1968)*, edited by Paula Lenguita, pp. 167–89. Buenos Aires: CEIL, 2020. http://cdi.mecon.gov.ar/bases/docelec/gro118.pdf.

Valobra, A. M., and Mercedes Yusta Rodrigo, eds. *Queridas Camaradas. Historias iberoamericanas de mujeres comunistas, 1935–1975*. Buenos Aires: Editorial Miño y Dávila, 2017.

Van Aken, Mark. "The Lingering Death of Indian Tribute in Ecuador." *Hispanic American Historical Review* 6, no. 3 (1981): 429–59.

Van Voris, Jacqueline. *Carrie Chapman Catt: A Public Life*. New York: Feminist Press at CUNY, 1996.

Vargas, Virginia. "Los nuevos derroteros a fin de milenio: derechos y autonomía." In *El siglo de las mujeres*, edited by Ana María Portugal and Carmen Torres. Santiago: Isis internacional, 1999.

Varley, Ann. "Women and the Home in Mexican Family Law." In *Hidden Histories of Gender and the State in Latin America*, edited by Elizabeth Dore and Maxine Molineux. Durham, NC: Duke University Press, 2000.

Vassallo, Alejandra. "Entre el conflicto y la negociación. Los feminismos argentinos en los inicios del Consejo Nacional de Mujeres, 1990–1910." In *Historia de las mujeres en la Argentina. Siglo XX*, Vol. 2, edited by Fernanda Gil Lozano, Valeria Pita, and María Gabriela Ini, pp. 177–95. Buenos Aires: Taurus, 2000.

Vaughan, Mary Kay. "Women, Class, and Education in Mexico, 1880–1928." *Latin American Perspectives* 4, nos. 1–2 (1977): 135–52.

Vega, Joaquina. "Exposición Del Comité Central Femenino Pro-Voto de la Mujer de Nicaragua." Presentation to the Nicaraguan congress, Managua, 1950.

Velázquez Toro, Magdala. "La República Liberal y la lucha por los derechos civiles y políticos de las mujeres." In *Las mujeres en la historia de Colombia*, Vol. 1, edited by Magdala Velázquez Toro. Bogotá: Grupo Editorial Norma, 1995.

Velázquez Toro, Magdala, and Catalina Reyes. "Proceso histórico y derechos de las mujeres, años 50 y 60." In *Las mujeres en la historia de Colombia*, Vol. 1, edited by Magdala Velázquez Toro. Bogotá: Grupo Editorial Norma, 1995.

Venet, Wendy Hamand. *Neither Ballots nor Bullets: Women Abolitionists and the Civil War*. Charlottesville: University Press of Virginia, 1991.

Ventura, Theresa. "Medicalizing Gutom: Hunger, Diet, and Beriberi during the American Period." *Philippine Studies: Historical and Ethnographic Viewpoints* 63, no. 1 (2015): 39–69. https://doi.org/10.1353/phs.2015.0000.

Verjus, A. *Le cens de la famille: les femmes et le vote, 1789–1848*. Paris: Belin, 2002.

Versiani, F., and L. P. Noguerol, eds. *Muitos escravos, muitos senhores: escravidão nordestina e gaúcha no século XIX*. Brasília: Editoria UnB, 2016.

Vicuña, Manuel. *La belle époque chilena*. Santiago: Sudamericana, 2001.

Videla, Horacio. *Historia de San Juan*. Buenos Aires: Academia del Plata, 1962.

Videla, O. R. "Elecciones, partidos y conflicto social a finales de los años veinte del siglo XX en Rosario (Argentina)." *Secuencia* 104 (2019). https://doi.org/10.18234/secuencia.v0i104.1392

Vignoli, Marcela. "Cecilia Grierson y las damas de la Beneficencia oficial en los orígenes del Consejo Nacional de la Mujer en Argentina, 1887–1906." *Boletín de Instituto de Historia Argentina y Americana Emilio Ravignani*, no. 55 (July–December 2021): 1–26. http://10.34096/bol.rav.n55.10348.

———. "El Consejo Nacional de la Mujer en Argentina y su dimensión internacional, 1900–1910." *Revista Travesía* 20, no. 2 (2018): 121–47.

———. "Elvira Rawson, la Asociación Pro-Derechos de la Mujer y el primer proyecto legislativo de derechos políticos femeninos en Argentina (1918–1923)." *Quinto Sol* 27, no. 1 (January–April 2023): 1–23. http://dx.doi.org/10.19137/qs.v27i1.6495.

Viguera, A. "'Populismo' y 'neopopulismo' en América Latina." *Revista Mexicana de Sociología* 55, no. 3 (1993): 49–66. https://doi.org/https://www.jstor.org/stable/3540921.

Vilas, Carlos. *The Sandinista Revolution: National Liberation and Social Transformation in Central America*. New York: Monthly Review Press, 1986.

Villanueva Kalaw, Pura. *How the Filipina Got the Vote*. Manila, 1952.

Villars, Rina. *Para la casa más que para el mundo: sufragismo y feminismo en la historia de Honduras*. Tegucigalpa: Editorial Guaymuras, 2001.

Villavicencio, Maritza. *Breve Historia de las Vertientes del Movimiento de Mujeres en El Perú*. Lima: Centro de la Mujer Peruana Flora Tristán, 1990.

Villavicencio, Maritza, and Margarita Zegarra. *Del Silencio a la Palabra: Mujeres peruanas en los siglos XIX y XX.* Lima: Centro de la Mujer Peruana Flora Tristán, 1992.

Wagner, Sally Roesch. *Sisters in Spirit: Haudenosaunee (Iroquois) Influence on Early American Feminists.* Summertown, TN: Native Voices, 2001.

———. *A Time of Protest: Suffragists Challenge the Republic: 1870–1887.* Aberdeen, SD: Sky Carrier Press, 1992.

Ware, Susan. "Carrie & Mollie & Anna & Lucy: Queering the Women's Suffrage Movement." Public Broadcasting Service, October 23, 2020. https://www.pbs.org/wgbh/americanexperience/features/vote-carrie-mollie-anna-lucy/.

Weaver, Kathleen. *Peruvian Rebel: The World of Magda Portal, with a Selection of Her Poems.* University Park: Pennsylvania State University Press, 2009.

Wellman, Judith. *The Road to Seneca Falls: Elizabeth Cady Stanton and the First Woman's Rights Convention.* Urbana: University of Illinois Press, 2004.

Williams, M. Todaro. "The Politicization of the Brazilian Catholic Church: The Catholic Electoral League." *Journal of Inter-American Studies and World Affairs* 16, no. 3 (August 1974).

Wills, Maria Emma. "Cincuenta años del sufragio femenino en Colombia. *Análisis Político* 18, no. 53 (2005): 39–57.

Wood, Leonard, and W. Cameron Forbes. *Report of the Special Mission on Investigations to the Philippine Islands.* Washington DC: Government Printing Office, 1921.

Yee, Shirley J. *Black Women Abolitionists: A Study in Activism, 1828–1860.* Knoxville: University of Tennessee Press, 1992.

Yellin, Jean Fagan. *Harriet Jacobs, a Life: The Remarkable Adventures of the Woman Who Wrote Incidents in the Life of a Slave Girl.* New York: Basic Civitas Books, 2004.

Zahniser, J. D. *Alice Paul: Claiming Power.* New York: Oxford University Press, 2014.

Zakaria, Fareed. *The Future of Freedom: Illiberal Democracy at Home and Abroad.* New York: W. W. Norton, 2003.

Zamora, Eugenia María. *Mujeres y derechos políticos electorales: Costa Rica 1988–2018.* San José: Tribunal Supremo de Elecciones, Instituto de Formación y Estudios en Democracia, 2018.

Zanca, José. "Dios y libertad. Católicas antifascistas en la Argentina de entreguerras." *Arenal* 22, no. 1 (January–June 2015): 67–87. https://doi.org/10.30827/arenal.v22i1.3152.

Zegarra Florez, Margarita. "María Jesús Alvarado y el rol de las mujeres peruanas en la construcción de la patria." In *Mujeres, Familia y Sociedad en la Historia de América Latina, Siglos XVIII–XXI.* Lima: CENDOC-Mujer, IRA-PUCP, IFEA, 2006.

———. "María Jesús Alvarado: la construcción de una intelectual feminista en Lima, 1878–1915." Master's thesis, Universidad Mayor de San Marcos, Lima, 2011.

Zink, Mirta. "De los dichos a los hechos. La experiencia política de una de las primeras legisladoras pampeanas." *Anuario de la Facultad de Ciencias Humanas* 3, no. 3 (2001): 165–78.

Contributors

Roisida Aguilar is a Peruvian historian who divides her time between the Pontificia Universidad Católica del Perú and the Universidad de Salamanca in Spain. Peru has an underdeveloped historiography in women's history generally. She is one of a handful of people in the world who has published on Peruvian women's suffrage.

Roxanna Domenech Cruz is an associate professor in the Liberal Arts Division of the Universidad Ana G. Méndez in San Juan, Puerto Rico, where she also directs and is the chief editor for *Cruce*, a journal on contemporary social-cultural criticism. She has published on women's history, women's suffrage, and anticolonialism as well as race, gender, and environmental movements in Puerto Rico.

Guiomar Dueñas is a professor of history at the University of Memphis. She normally focuses on the history of women and the family in the colonial period and the nineteenth century; however, Colombian women's history is also significantly underdeveloped, and she is one of very few scholars with authority of Colombian women's suffrage. She is also active feminist in Colombia, where she is a frequent contributor to the feminist journal *In Other Words*.

Victoria González-Rivera is an associate professor in the Department of Chicana and Chicano Studies at San Diego State University. She is the author of *Before the Revolution: Women's Rights and Right-Wing Politics in Nicaragua, 1821–1979*, the coeditor of *Radical Women in Latin America: Left and Right*, and the author of the forthcoming book *500 Years of LGBTQIA+ History in Western Nicaragua*.

Susan Goodier holds a fellowship at the Massachusetts Historical Society in Boston. She previously taught women's history at the State University of New York (SUNY) Oneonta. She has published several works on suffrage movements in the United States. She brings specific expertise on elements of the anti-suffrage movement and activism of Black and Native women within US suffrage movements.

Claudia Montero is a senior professor at the Humanities Faculty at the Universidad de Valparaiso in Chile. She has published widely on Chilean feminist history and directs the research project "Prensa de mujeres chilenas." She brings special expertise in women's use of the press.

Teresa Cristina de Novaes Marques is a historian at the Universidade de Brasilia in Brazil. She has authored three books on the campaign for women's suffrage in Brazil, including a highly accessible history of the struggle for the vote that is available online and in English, *Women's Vote in Brazil* (*O Voto Feminino no Brasil*). She has also published a number of academic articles on women's political activism, women's labor history, and the diplomacy of women's rights. She is currently finishing a book about the first national election in 1933 in which women could participate as electors.

Erin E. O'Connor is a professor of history at Bridgewater State University. She is currently chair of the History Department, and she has served as coordinator of the Women's and Gender Studies Program. Among her publications of gender and Latin American history is *Gender, Indian, Nation: The Contradictions of Making Ecuador, 1830–1945*. Her current research focuses on how notions of domesticity shaped politics and society in early twentieth-century Ecuador.

Christine Peralta is a tenure-track assistant professor in history and sexuality, women's, and gender studies at Amherst College. She received her doctorate in history at the University of Illinois at Urbana-Champaign. She writes on the US empire, gender, and race. Her work has been published in *Amerasia Journal* and in *Global Migration, Gender, and Professional Credentials*.

She is currently working on a book entitled *Insurgent Care: Reimagining Filipino Women's Health Work under U.S. Empire.*

Eugenia Rodríguez-Sáenz is a senior scholar and a professor of history at the University of Costa Rica, where she currently serves as the coordinator of the Research Program on Genders and Identities in Latin America. She is without doubt the foremost specialist alive today on Costa Rica women's history. Her many publications reflect work on other Central American countries as well.

Veronica Strong-Boag is a professor emerita at the University of British Colombia, former president of the Canadian Historical Association, and founding director of UBC's Centre for Women's and Gender Studies. She has authored many publications on the history of women and gender in Canada and received many scholarly prizes and awards, including appointment to the Royal Society of Canada and the Order of Canada.

Adriana Valobra is a full professor at the Universidad Nacional de la Plata in Argentina, where she also directs the Interdisciplinary Center on Gender Research. She founded the feminist academic journal *Descentrada*. She is a leading specialist on women's history in Argentina and has written or edited seven books and some fifty articles on the subject.

Index

Abadía, Mercedes, 153

Abella de Ramírez, María, 129

abolitionism, xi, xviin10, 89, 327, 362; in Brazil, 103–4, 108, 119n27; in the United States, 54, 68–70, 307. *See also* antislavery

Acosta de Samper, Soledad, 147, 163n3, 365

Acuña, Ángela, 24–26, 37

Agitación Femenina (Colombia), 152, 155, 164n16

Aguirre Cerda, Pedro, 206–8

Alessandri, Arturo, 204

Alianza Femenina de Colombia (Colombian Feminine Alliance, Colombia), 153. *See also* Federación Femenina Nacional

Alianza Popular Revolucionaria Americana (American Popular Revolutionary Alliance, Peru), 281–84, 286, 298, 290–92, 298n72, 299n84, 300n111

Alvarado, Salvador, 171

Alvarado Rivera, María Jesús, 274, 277–80, 289, 294, 296n22, 296n24, 296n27, 296n32, 300n101

American Anti-Slavery Society, 68

American Declaration of the Rights and Duties of Man, 288, 300n95

American Equal Rights Association, 70–72, 85n34–36, 375

American Woman Suffrage Association (USA), 72, 74

Amunategui Decree (Chile), 200

Andrada e Silva, Jose Bonifácio, 99, 100–101, 105

Andreu Almazán, Juan, 183

Andreu de Aguilar, Isabel, 335, 339

Anthony, Susan B., xiii, 70–72, 75

antislavery, 68–69, 106, 307; Anti-Slavery Convention of American Women, 68. *See also* abolition

Arboleda, Esmeralda, 160–63

Arenas de Lara, Mercedes, 152

Argelis, María Luisa de, 335, 354n35

Argentine Women's Union, 131

Aristocratic Republic (Peru), 227

Armiño, Franca de, 335

Asian Americans: in Canada, 43–45, 48–50, 54, 57; in the United States, 13n1, 78, 83; stereotypes of, 311, 318

Asociación de la Juventud Católica Femenina (Association of Feminine Catholic Youth, Chile), 202

Asociación Femenina Ecuatoriana (Ecuadorian Women's Association), 265, 272n81

Asociación Feminista Ilonga (Philippines), 313

Ávila Camacho, Manuel, 183

Azevedo, Josephina de, 103, 119n37